WITH MY HEAD IN THE CLOUDS

CLOUDS

Part 2

by Gwyn Mullett

Typeset in Gentium Book Basic and Philosopher

Editing, design and publishing by UK Book Publishing

www.ukbookpublishing.com

ISBN: 978-1-910223-35-2

Dedication

The year is 2015 and I have been retired from British
Airways for 14 years now. I now live in Berlin and
have just arrived at the tender age of 69.

Both of my kids are now grown up with Jenny, now 31 years
of age, living with her mother, Moya, in England and she has
a son Jamie who is six years of age and is in full-time school. I
am a proud granddad. Paul is 34 years of age and somewhere
out in the world making his living. My ex-wife Moya works
for a living. I wish them all the very best for the future.

My marriage to Jo has now settled down and finally I am
at peace in that department. It is Jo that I dedicate this
book to since it is Jo and Jo alone who will look after me
as I get older and who knows what that may bring.

I rest my case again.

Acknowledgements

Below is a list of people, organisations or web sites that helped me writing my book.

The pictures of the various aircraft were copied from the following web sites:

- *www.airliners.net*

Individual pictures were kindly approved by the following people or organisations:

- Jerry Hughes (Piper Aztec)
- Paul Thallon (B. 737-200 in original BA colours)
- Marc Hasenbein (B. 737-200,-300-400 in Landor colours)
- Vincent Edlinger (B. 747-400 in Chatham colours)

Various news items and quotations were courtesy of:

- The Wikipedia, the free encyclopaedia web site

Various family members and friends contributed towards jogging the brain cells into action

I would also like to give a huge thanks to my sponsors who had absolute faith in me allowing the book to be published. They are my very good friends:

Captain Bob Young	Ex-BCAL and BA who flew the DC-10 and 747-400
Captain Ian Davis	Ex-BEA and BA who flew the Trident and 747-400
Captain Tony Partridge	Ex-BEA and BA who flew the Trident and 747-400

Without them my story would still be a dream

To contact the author on email: *gwyn@withmyheadintheclouds.com*

or via Web site: *www.withmyheadintheclouds.com*

Preface

My name is Gwyn Mullett and I was born on 27th January 1946 in Montreal, Canada. We moved to Bristol, England in 1949. In 1953 we then moved again to the town of Wokingham being about 30 miles to the west of the new London airport named Heathrow. It was here that I grew up until I had completed my education and, in 1964, had qualified to go to the College of Air Training on the south coast at Hamble, near to Southampton.

I graduated in the summer of 1966 and joined BOAC in the August. I started my airline life flying the superb Vickers VC-10. On May 5th 1967 my lovely mother died and left a big void in my life. In 1968 I qualified as a Flight Navigator and ended up both flying and navigating up to 1971 when I converted onto the new 747 that had just been delivered from Mr Boeing. In late 1971 BOAC and BEA combined their talents to form British Airways, or BA for short. In 1976 I went back to the VC-10 and completed a command course that year and became the youngest Captain since 1949 in the airline. In 1981 I converted to the 737 and discovered Europe, and in particular Berlin. I stayed until 1992 when I then converted onto the newer 747 model and remained there until my retirement on 27th January 2001.

My private life remains pretty colourful throughout my career.

This is the continuation of my story of my life from the beginning of 1980 to my retirement in January 2001.

There were times when I was sad and there were times when I was happy. There were times when I could not believe what I had done. I was stupid on some occasions but the funny thing is that if I was asked to do it all over again I would do exactly the same.

Enjoy Part 2

I have now arrived at the start of 1980 with me and Moya as free as a bird since I am sitting at home on 'paid leave' having completed my last flight on the mighty VC-10 in 1979. My story continues.

CHAPTER 8

– MY FLYING OUTSIDE OF BA

So 1980 came along and there we were both of us as free as a bird with me being paid a full basic salary for just sitting around at home. It seems very strange to be in that position but there it was. The original plan for three months on paid leave had been extended until either I successfully bid for another aircraft type or BA wanted me back. Suited me! As I said before Moya stopped as well and everything was great between us so we just laid back and enjoyed it. What would happen in BA was that every autumn a bidding list would arrive on my doorstep giving me the opportunity to bid for another aircraft within the company and the fact that both BOAC and BEA were now totally merged I was free to cross the line into the short-haul scene if I wanted to. You could even bid to be a co-pilot on any aircraft. The only thing that governed it was my seniority number according to my date of joining. In the past BOAC had its own list and BEA had their own list. BALPA, our union, managed to get agreement to merge these lists into one grand one. There was a lot of local in-fighting when it was first published but by the summer of 1980 it was set in stone ready for the 80/81 training season.

In early April Moya and I flew to Toronto, Canada to stay with my stepsister Angela and her husband Roger. Whilst we were there our world changed dramatically when Moya revealed that something was up with her 'female make up' and, following a simple test, Moya revealed that she was pregnant.

Well, I wonder how that could have happened? I thought to myself. Stupid boy!

So I was going to be a dad. It took a little time for it to sink in for both of us but there you go.

I was pretty gobsmacked since Moya had had an operation some months before that put the chances of her having children as pretty remote. Once we got used to the idea there were two broad smiles on our faces. We told Angela the news. Angela had been told that she could never have children so the celebrations were a bit muted. Orange Juice for Moya!

In the April news was out about a US military operation from an aircraft carrier in the Gulf area to rescue the hostages held in the US embassy in Tehran. It all came to a grinding halt at a landing area south of Tehran called 'Desert 1' where a helicopter broke down and a few aircraft collided into each other. One of the root causes was the failure to install sand filters in the air intakes of the helicopters. Total chaos reigned and the attempt was abandoned with President Carter ending up with egg on his face. In the UK we had our own drama with a group of fanatics breaking into the Iranian Embassy in London and holding hostages. In the end negotiations broke down and it took a well prepared assault by the British Army Special Air Service (SAS) that saved the day and a lot of lives. The Prime Minister, Margaret Thatcher, basked in the limelight of success in the eyes of the world. Also in April a Dan-Air Boeing 727 smashed into a hillside in Tenerife killing over 150 people. It seems impossible to fly into a hill like that but it happened. This type of accident was becoming the main cause of air crashes and prompted the boffins to come up with some sort of warning device. Over the next few years a piece of kit was developed that sensed the height above the local terrain and did its sums and decided if you were on a collision course with the ground it would fire up and set off various warnings in the Flight Deck. The unit was very successful and is continually being developed to this present day under the name of the 'Ground Proximity Warning System' or GPWS for short. The world of electronics and computer power was coming in the Flight Deck door fast and you had to keep up with it or fall by the wayside.

At the end of May Moya and I flew with some friends, Keith and Clare, to Miami, Florida and drove north to Boca Rotan for a few days. Keith was an Air Traffic Controller but had a wish to build up his flying hours and then apply for a Commercial Flying Licence. Florida was a cheap place to fly compared with the UK and so we all went with him for a bit of a holiday and it was for me to fly with Keith as his safety pilot. The local airfield at Boca Raton was one of those deserted places save for a small flying club tucked away in one corner so was ideal for Keith. It had been quite a while since I had flown in a small single-engined aircraft so it was to become a bit of an adventure for us both. The aircraft we used was a Piper Cherokee and so off we went flying around Florida. The procedures were quite simple whereby if we fancied a flight out of the local area we just picked up the Federal Aviation Agency (FAA) phone at the departure airfield and gave them the details of the flight and that was that. On arrival we just picked up the local FAA phone again and let them know we had arrived OK. Simplicity itself! I think we did some six or so flights. One we did was to fly up to the space centre at Cape Kennedy in northern Florida. As we approached we called up the local US Air Force base and asked if we could fly over the launch pads of the new 'Shuttle' spacecraft. To our amazement they said that we were OK to fly over there but due to some altitude measurements we were not to fly above 500ft. Are they kidding or what! Lovely Jubbly!

So there we were circling the famous launch pad 39A where the first space shuttle 'Columbia' would be launched the following year to herald the start of the 'Space Transportation System' programme as it was officially called. The shuttle itself would be perched on the launch pad together with two external boosters and the huge external tank all strapped together like a big Airfix kit. Up to this point only the space shuttle 'Enterprise' had done some gliding tests and next year was to be the first launch into space. We were looking at history at 500ft. I got a bit carried away and asked if we could do a 'touch and go' on the huge runway at the Cape that was intended for the final landing site after the Shuttle returned to Earth. It was mind-blowing when they said that it would be OK for one 'touch and go'. There was not the slightest security implication in anything we did. What a wonderful world it was then! After our historic 'Touch and Go' we flew over to Naples on the West Coast of Florida and landed with all the big boys at 'John Wayne International' Airport. We refuelled and had a well-earned sandwich and coffee. We got back to Boca Raton in the late afternoon after quite an amazing day out.

Another flight took us well into the Florida Everglades and, as we cruised along at 1,500ft looking down at the wilderness, I spotted some very large birds flying close to us. In fact, some of them were above us and looked awfully close. If we had had hit one we would have done a beautiful pirouette downwards into the mouth of some hungry alligator. I got Keith to climb up above the birds and it was amazing since we had to get to 4,000ft to be clear of them. I never knew birds could fly so high. But this was America!

One interesting flight was to fly from Boca Raton to Nassau and Freeport in the Bahamas and then back via 'Fort Lauderdale'. The club gave us a rather dubious looking 2-man inflatable dinghy plus two equally vintage life jackets. Chances were slim if we splashed down in the water. We might have just been able to inflate everything and then become lunch for some 'Big White' who happened to be out for his lunchtime stroll. Anyway, we did the flight OK and survived to tell the tale.

After six days or so we headed back to Heathrow. The problem was that the small excursion into flying whetted my appetite to go flying again and soon. By the way Moya's small bump was becoming a wriggling lump by now with mid-November being 'Launch Day'.

By the time June came along I was getting really itchy feet to be flying again in some form or another. I drove up to the local airfield at Blackbush where I used to look at the aeroplanes many years before and bumped into Howard Rose, a fellow Hamster, who ran a small executive air taxi company called 'Topflight'. They had a Piper Aztec based at an airfield near Oxford and flew it out of there under the banner of 'Air Oxford'. The outfit was run by Howard and another BA Captain Noddy Nayland and they were looking for another 'Aztec' pilot so off Howard and I went to Oxford and climbed aboard G-ATFF or 'FF' and I got checked out on the Aztec. I was back in the flying world again.

Also in June a news channel was launched in the USA called the Cable News Network or CNN. OK, hands up who remembers Bobby Batista the cross-eyed presenter?

As to my flying with Topflight the Aztec was like an up-market Piper Apache that I had flown at Hamble and I did the first flight for them very shortly after being cleared taking some businessman to the Isle of Man TT Motorbike races and spent the day mixing with other air taxi pilots sitting on the grass enjoying the sunshine. There were a few familiar faces amongst the collection. My second flight was from Blackbush to Southend and would you believe it, I had a CAA inspector along for the ride. I thought that they only did the big boys but there I was doing the business with this chap watching my every move sitting alongside. When we got back to Blackbush he went over a few points which were fine since I was new at this air taxi scene but overall he was very happy and so were Howard and Noddy. I had survived again. I seemed to be in demand a fair bit since I was called every other day for some sort of excursion somewhere. One of these was to fly this rather arrogant, grumpy business chap to a small airfield near Paris called Rouen and then on to Geneva for the night eventually landing in Nice the following day. This did, in fact, become a bit of an epic flight for me. I met the chap at Oxford and the weather was pretty awful with heavy rain and low cloud. For me to go to Rouen I had to clear French customs at Le Havre on the way. As we flew across the Channel the weather got worse and I was down to about 1,000 ft to be able to see the ground. The secret with Air Taxi work was to not commit to flying in cloud and be unable to see the ground since the cost of employing the full facilities of the Air Traffic Control (ATC) more than likely wiped out the profit of the trip. There was a fine line between being 'brave' and 'giving in' which was what I was facing as I flew further south towards France. The Aztec I was flying had a full suite of radio aids that I could use to help the navigational part of the flight and as I approached the French coast I could just about make out the murky outline of it but just at that point I entered a thick layer of low cloud. I could not keep at 1,000 ft for long since I didn't fancy giving the cliffs on the coast a glancing blow so I climbed up to a sensible height and looked as to how the navigational radios could help me get down safely. I figured out that if I did this using one of the local beacons I could arrive at about 500ft just off the coast and all I then had to do was to execute a quick right turn and bingo there was the airfield at Le Havre. I had no Co-pilot to help me and it was all down to my brain and stopwatch. Anyway, I started this self-inspired approach and at about 600ft I spotted a pretty wild looking sea below me with the added attraction that I had arrived in the middle of a large fleet of fishing boats. They must have got a big shock when this aircraft suddenly appeared in their midst. I looked to the right and I could just make out some cliffs and I knew that on the other side of these was the airfield. I actually had to climb to get over the cliffs and suddenly there was the airfield looking pretty rain soaked and windswept. I sort of got the aircraft to the runway in use and landed OK, much to my relief.

"Bloody hell, this is only the start of the trip," I muttered as we splattered our way to the ramp.

I left Mr Grumpy in the aircraft and wandered over to the Customs point to pay my respects and then moved onto the flight report area to check on the weather at my next port of call. I need not have bothered since it was all the same over the whole of Northern France. This was going to be a real fun day out. We took off again into the clag and off we went to Rouen. The weather there was just as bad but there was a published precision approach that I could use; the problem, however, was that it was lunchtime and the bloody French controllers had gone off to lunch and left the tower deserted.

"Bugger them, I will do the approach and see what happens" was my reaction.

As it was the weather was a bit kinder to me and I landed off the approach and taxied to the ramp and dropped Mr Grumpy off for a couple of hours. I went to the airport restaurant for a well-earned sandwich and to plan the flight to Geneva. I was met by a couple of rather irate controllers who started ranting and raving about me doing an unauthorised approach. I pointed out to them that according to the notices the tower should be manned continuously during daylight hours and that I could not afford to hang around for them to finish their 'Jambons'. That shut them up.

England 1 France 0.

The flight to Geneva was going to be about three hours and so after I got the aircraft refuelled I settled down to sort out the flight plan and the dreaded weather. There seemed to be a clear area South of Paris and then it would be getting worse as we approached the Alps. Geneva was pretty grim and so I was in for a rough ride. The Alps are pretty high of course so I had to be well aware of my position in relation to the local ground or 'Cumulus Granite' as it was known to us airmen. After a couple of hours Mr Grumpy turned up and away we went to Geneva. The weather did improve south of Paris but as I approached the Lyon area it was not looking good with the cloud base getting lower and lower and eventually I ended up back in the cloud. I called the Lyon radar controller so as to establish a good solid fix before venturing over the Alps. I remember the safety height for my route was 6,300ft and so I felt not too bad at 8,500ft but then I encountered icing. The poor old Aztec has a thick wing and so catches every droplet of the icicles. The only protection the aircraft had was that the front edge or leading edge of the wing is constructed out of a reinforced rubber material than can pulsate if fed with air from the engine. The deal is that you wait for a good layer of ice to build up and then pump the leading edge so as to break off the offending stuff. If you do it too early then it is ineffective since all it does is pulsate away but leaving like a hollow tube with ice still firmly attached. I won't go into the case of being too late.

The total downside is that the ice creates a lot of drag and you lose a lot of engine power while you are operating the system or 'Booting' as it is called. I had to 'Boot' a few times and watched my airspeed fall away. I gradually put on more power to help the scene but I then felt that the throttles were at the full power stop and we were still slowing down. I had no choice but to descend to get the speed back and hopefully get out of the ice. I eventually got down about 6,500ft when things slowly got better. I was still in the cloud with some sort of workable airspeed and had a chance to bring the engines back from full power. They had been at full power for some 20 minutes and were getting hot. Memories of Hamble and my encounter with Membury mast on the M4 came flooding back. Mr Grumpy features in the back was totally oblivious to my dramas and all he did was to moan that it was cold in the back.

It's not bloody cold where I am sitting, mate, was my thought for today.

I managed after about 30 minutes of wallowing around at this dangerous height to climb a little so as to give myself some air space and to slow my heartbeat down. I was now emerging on the south side of the Alps but still totally clagged up. I decided to commit myself to flying under the control of the Air Traffic Control and accept the cost.

Howard would understand my dilemma. If I had landed at Geneva
they would have questioned me as to how it was possible for me to fly
visually when the weather was so bad that some of the airlines were
a bit dubious about even going to Geneva. I called up the controller at
Geneva and committed myself to Instrument Flight Rules (IFR) and
they found me on the radar pretty well where I expected to be and told
me to go to a local beacon off to the northeast of the airport and 'hold'
there for maybe 40 minutes whilst they tried to fit me into the landing
sequence with all the big boys. This was just what I needed after my
Alpine experience and what's more the rain was truly hammering
down on the windscreen to the point that I thought the screen might
shatter and we would all get bloody wet. The rain alternated with hail
and cracks of lightning all round. No radar on board! They ordered me
to 7,000ft for the holding and I was so punched up with adrenalin that I
did not move an inch either way for the height. No Autopilot on board!
We were having six bells knocked out of us but the only consolation
was that the rain and hail were warm so no icing. After about 20
minutes or so they sent me down to 6,500ft and would you believe it,
as I left 6,999ft I burst into blue sky and Lake Geneva. I laughed at my
predicament whereby I had been flying in the bottom foot of this cloud
and now all was blue and lovely. I know it sounds like a John Wayne
movie but believe me it was horribly scary. We finally landed after an
epic four-hour flight and I nearly did the 'Pope' thing and kissed the
ground.

Mr Grumpy said very little as he climbed out but I think even he was
a bit shook up.

"OK, I will stay the night here on business and then tomorrow you
can take me on to Nice," he said casually.

"Sorry Sir, but the aircraft is a bit of a mess and I have to fly her
back to Oxford soonest for attention," I replied as I surveyed a rather
battered wing leading edge with a lot of paint stripped back.

"That is very inconvenient for my schedule. Airfares cost money you
know!" he muttered as he stomped off to the terminal.

"Don't bloody care. Take a taxi!" I mouthed at him as I watched him
go.

Now, here's the rub. Having struggled to get to Geneva there was no fancy car laid on to take me to a nice 5-star hotel. I stood in my kit and looked around in the reception area of the airport wondering which way to go. Eventually I found the 'hotels desk' and got a bed at the downtown Ramada hotel for a reasonable rate so off I went on the local city bus and spent the night there. I called Howard and he asked me to get the aircraft back home soonest. So off I went back to the airport the next morning and had a good look at the wing and felt it was fine to get me home. I refuelled and took off in the bright sunshine back the way I had come to Southampton airport for customs, then onto Oxford and finally home. The flight back was very relaxing with good weather all the way. As I flew over the Alps going north I shuddered as I looked down at the mountains that I had flown over the day before. I got back to Oxford in the late afternoon and Howard met me and we checked the aircraft over carefully for damage. Apart from some peeling paint marks and the odd mark on the wing leading edge it seemed it good condition. A maintenance check was due soon and that would get the poor old girl back on top form.

In the news in August Poland was seen to be emerging from years under the Soviets with the Gdansk shipyards leading the way under the banner of the 'Solidarity Movement'. Things were starting to churn up in the Soviet Block behind the Iron Curtain. Prime Minister Maggie Thatcher was doing her utmost to hasten the possible breakup of the Eastern Block with some strong speeches. She was alone in her rhetoric but things would change in 1980.

The bad weather experienced going to Geneva seemed to follow me around since in August I was asked to fly a 'well-to-do' family from Oxford up to Perth for the start of the Grouse shooting season or 'The glorious 12th' as it was known. The rain was sheeting down as I loaded the party into the Aztec for the flight north. From the navigational point of view the route was set with traps all the way since I had to fly through the Birmingham and Manchester airport airspace and then avoid all the military zones up to Scotland. It was not an easy flight since apart from those problems I had the son of the family sitting next to me asking me all sorts of stupid questions. Anyway, as I approached Edinburgh Airport I asked the tower for the Perth weather. It was fricking horrible with low cloud, heavy rain and a vicious southerly wind blowing.

"Welcome to Scotland!" I thought to myself.

Anyway, Perth had no radar or real aids to help me land so it was down to me and my trusty map again. I got the radar people to descend me safely off the coast and I broke cloud at about 300ft about two miles off-shore heading north. I followed the coastline leaving it off to my left and flew until I spotted the entrance to the Firth of Tay. I then turned to follow the coastline again to the west and passed the RAF station of Leuchers. Courtesy call needed there in case they thought I was a Russian submarine. I felt like one! I passed the famous St Andrews golf course and reckoned that if I found the town of Scone which was right at the head of the Firth of Tay and then turned to the northeast for four miles, at this height then I might spot the airport at Perth. As I flew westwards towards Scone I looked at the map and spotted to my horror a bridge in the way and at this height I could well hit it. So I climbed up but still trying to see the ground and low and behold this huge bridge appeared out of the gloom and I climbed up over the top and then descended back down again to about 400ft to get a good fix over the town of Scone. It was all happening again to me just like Geneva. I had to rely on the 'Mark1 Eyeball' and the good old stopwatch. I turned over the centre of Scone towards the northeast and started the stopwatch which I reckoned would put me near the airfield after three and a half minutes. If nothing at that point I would climb back into the murk and go back to Dundee or Edinburgh. The other problem was it was getting dark so the ground was becoming a bit indistinguishable. I concentrated on the flying and timing and after about three minutes a set of bright red lights appeared just left of centre and I realised that these were the approach lights for the northerly runway at Perth. I homed in on them and then the runway lights appeared but I had to land pointing the other way. I then remembered the famous 'Runway reversal procedure' that I did on my VC-10 command course at Shannon and so I did just that and low and behold I landed on the right runway in a rather soggy mess. I taxied to the ramp and shut down. As we all climbed out it was into a very wet and windy early evening. The group trudged off to the small reception area. I got some help from the attending Engineer to tie the aircraft down for the night. As I was doing the 'Indian Rope Trick' a car pulled up and out popped one of my old VC-10 instructors who did some of my original base training at Shannon. He had left BA and was now the boss of the Air Service Training school here at Perth. He was a bit shocked that I had actually landed in the weather conditions but when I mentioned the 'Runway reversal procedure' straight out of the VC-10 flying manual he chuckled and shook my hand like a long lost brother.

I re-joined the party and there was a rather large station wagon sitting there into which they were all piling their stuff. One of them casually handed me the keys and ordained me as the driver since they all fancied a 'Snifter' once on the road. So off I went from Pilot to Chauffer and we drove to a town called Pitlochry and stopped outside a rather splendid house. These 'well-to-do' sorts seemed to live in a different world. We were all greeted at the door by a rather splendid Butler with a tray of drinks consisting mainly of various brands of whisky. When the tray was shoved under my nose I asked for a beer. I got the look of death and he flicked his fingers at another 'Sub-butler' who scurried off to get a beer. This house was only a pit stop for dinner and I was needed to drive again hence only one beer. I have to say that we had a rather splendid dinner with me supping gently on my lonely beer and watching the assembled party knocking back various hard drinks at an alarming rate. I remembered the old routine of 'outside-in' when it came to surveying the vast array of knives and forks in front of me. After dinner off we went back to the station wagon for about an hour's journey further north in the rain to a lodge where we would stay the night. We were greeted by the gamekeeper whom I could only describe as being one unit high and two units wide. Once again the whisky tray arrived and I did indulge this time since we were finally at the journey's end. By this time I was pretty burnt out and crashed into my bed at about 1 am. I still could hear the drinking session gaining momentum as I closed my eyes.

After what seemed about two minutes' sleep I was shaken awake by a 'Braveheart' type of Scotsman. You know – the one with the axe. He informed me that breakfast was being served in 20 minutes. I staggered to the table only to realise that the time was showing a little after 4 am. It was no wonder I was feeling totally crap. The assembled party seemed to be chatting as normal as if they had had about 12 hours' sleep. After breakfast we all climbed into a collection of 'four-wheel drives' and off we went to some isolated part of a Scottish Moor. Out came the sherry from the back of one of the vehicles and so the drinking scene started again. I had never been on a Grouse shoot before or, in fact, any sort of shooting expedition so it was all very strange to me. I linked up with the least harmless member of the group and walked with him across the moor. The weather was a slight improvement from the day before and I have to say the surroundings were quite stunning even at that ungodly hour. We had a dog along as company. We could see in the distance a line of chaps slowly walking towards us beating the ground with sticks. Suddenly there was a flurry of activity about 20 metres away and this rather pretty bird, a Grouse, flew up out of a bush. I was just about to remark how pretty it looked when 'Bang' this bloody gun that my partner was carrying went off and I nearly jumped into the next world. The pretty bird exploded in front of my eyes and crashed to the ground and lay there twitching. Within seconds the rather docile dog was transformed into a speed merchant and galloped across the moor and, with one swoop, plucked the twitching mass of feathers in its mouth and roared back and deposited it at our feet.

Poor bird, it was only having a look around and suddenly 'Zappo' it was dead, was my thought at that moment.

The ringing in my ears from the gun was still twanging around my head as the scene was repeated again when another luckless Grouse popped up for a look around.

"Stupid birds, don't they know about this date in the calendar?" I muttered to myself.

The whole moor reverberated to the sound of gunshots, dead Grouse hitting the ground and barking dogs flying all over the place. I really felt sorry for the Grouse. After about one and a half hours of this slaughter the party retired back to the vehicles and guess what - out came the sherry again. A cardboard box was produced and the catch of the day was thrown into it with the odd twitch here and there. More sherry was consumed. After a sort of boozy lunch for the party on the moor we made our way back to the airport and it was my job to load the cardboard box of dead Grouse into the front baggage compartment and then pile everybody on board for the flight home to Oxford. The weather was still pretty grim so I elected to go out the way I had come in and so off we went down the Firth of Tay at 300ft until well clear of the land and then I climbed up to some sort of normal height and set sail southwards. By the time we had been airborne for some 20 minutes the snoring chorus started and all of the party were in the land of nod. Suited me though since all I had to do was to get them back safely and then get home for a well-earned sleep. I finally landed at Oxford and offloaded a rather sleepy bunch of people. It was very strange when they gave me a large tip. That's a first one for me! I finally got home to Binfield and passed out for a few hours.

Another event happened in August which was pretty damn good: Moya and I got married at the Bracknell Registry Office and we had the reception at my dad's place at Wokingham. Moya's bump was not too prominent so as to not to cause attention but everybody knew that something was happening. We never did have a honeymoon since Moya's hospital check-ups got in the way. She did suffer from an incredible affliction of itching feet, together with a fetish for beetroot and jam sandwiches in the middle of the night which made for a pretty lively time. We still had our social scene over at Woodley but were slowly developing a social scene in Binfield, so all was very good apart from the itching scene that poor Moya had to endure. We moved out of the flat into a small three-bedroom house just up the road. It was then 'operation nursery' ready for the November.

In September another punch up had started in the Middle East with Iraq and Iran going to war with each other. Saddam Hussein, the leader of the Iraqis, was becoming the strong man of the area and a few diplomatic eyebrows were being raised worldwide. The war was a local affair you might say and, apart from the usual worldwide condemnations of the event, the two warring countries were left alone. The carnage was terrible and millions died in the eight years that it lasted.

The annual bidding process also arrived in early September and I had to decide my next flying move within BA. I had enough seniority to remain as a Captain and BA needed all of us back to work for the 1981 season. The question was which aircraft I fancied flying. I could have gone back onto the 747 Classic, Tri-Star or DC-10. The other thought was to do something totally different and move across to the Short-Haul arena on the newly acquired Boeing 737-200, Trident or BAC-111. I eventually opted to go to the 737-200. Brave move since to that date I had always been regarded as part of the Long-Haul institution.

In the October the bidding results came out and low and behold I was awarded a 737 course starting in the December. Well, I had made the leap across the great divide. Another VC-10 Captain, Ted Collis, also did the same and so we were the first two people to go from Long-Haul to Short-Haul. That month there was a dinner to mark the ending of the VC-10 fleet held at the Queen Elizabeth Hotel in west London. Moya and I went along and we found ourselves seated on the table full of my fellow Hamsters who had made the grade. As the evening progressed there were the usual speeches and the drinks were flowing well. At one point in the table conversation the bidding awards were talked about and everybody was talking about their next course ranging from 747 Classic to Tri-stars. Someone asked me casually when my course would be and I dumfounded them all by saying that I had a 737 course in December. You could have heard a pin drop. The thought of an ex-BOAC chap crossing the river to join the BEA side was too much for them to bear and the conversation sorted of drifted from that point on.

I did a few more trips for Howard during this period but as Moya was on the final countdown these slowly wound down since she needed quite a few hospital visits to St Peter's in Chertsey. Our social scene slowed up a lot which is quite understandable considering all.

On November 13th at about 1am in the morning after around 16 tense hours of Moya's labour Paul Lawrence Mullett was born and was pronounced a healthy boy. As long as I live I cannot describe the feeling I experienced when I watched the childbirth. All seems remote and suddenly out pops a baby which has two arms and two legs and screams the house down. It is totally magical and will forever be etched on my memory. Well done Moya!

Paul was kept under observation for a day as a result of the long labour and after about three days all three of us went home to Binfield. That was then the realisation of another member to the family hit home. Sleep – what was that?! Where had those leisurely times gone when the conversation ranged from

'What shall we do today?'

to

'Where's the next party?'

It was now:

'Must get some more nappies'

To

'Will he ever shut up?'

What's more, in a few weeks I would be starting a 737 course at Cranebank and get back into the BA flying mode.

In the news a new US President was voted in. His name was Ronald Reagan, once a two-bit Hollywood actor. He had one of those 'toothpaste' smiles and a soft west coast voice. So now the first two members of the western leaders to change the world order were in place with more to come.

CHAPTER 9

– FLYING THE 737

After about two weeks of total chaos interspersed with times of sheer drama things started to settle down in the Mullett household and some sort of routine began to emerge. I was off to Cranebank for the 737 course. Prior to this course eight weeks was generally the norm for a conversion, but not nowadays. The technical side was allocated ten working days plus three for bits and bobs. The Simulator course took about a further ten days, so within three weeks you were ready for the route training flying bit which was scheduled for a week or so in Short-Haul. The final outcome was to be on the line up and running within four weeks, give or take a couple of minutes. This is exactly what happened. I was lined up with an ex-Trident Co-pilot by the name of John Brassington and after introductions we sat in this cardboard mock-up of the 737 Flight Deck, pressed the button and sat back whilst a film presentation of each system played on a screen where the windows were. Having been away from BA for a while plus a lack of sleep at home my brain hurt with all these facts and figures being thrown at it. I made it through the technical course OK and then the following Monday did the Safety Equipment bit with no problem since the aircraft had no life rafts or the like as they did not intend to make them go transatlantic just as yet. The performance course was pretty simple since very little was needed. Europe was the domain of the 737 so no worries there.

At the start of the third week John and I started the simulator course. Now, here was a difference to my previous aircraft since there was no Flight Engineer or INS to get involved with. In fact, it was a backward step for me and reminded me of the original VC-10 operation where I had to use my brain to figure out exactly where I was at any time. I have to say I found the trainers a very nice bunch of guys and a total change from what I was used to. Of course, there was a lot of banter aimed at me since I had crossed the great divide. The 737 had another difference which is worthy of note. It had only two engines as opposed to the four I was weaned on. Consider that out of four engines one fails then you are left with three quarters of your available power but with two engines you get left with only half so when you have an engine failure on a 737 it is all 'eyes down looking'. When the trainer failed an engine at the rotation point on take-off the flight instrument that grabs your attention first is normally the Artificial Horizon but because the electrical system has to reset itself the display does a sort of half barrel role before settling down. This all takes about 1-2 seconds but when it is doing its gyrations it seems like an eternity. Whilst this is all happening the aircraft is wallowing around waiting for you to 'grab it by the horns' and try to get some sort of control. There is no Flight Engineer to help you and the only help is the Co-pilot who is busy doing his side of the scene. Tends to focus the mind, it does! Anyway, John and I survived the simulator course OK so off to Prestwick we went for a spot of base training. Back in the old days I could envisage maybe a week minimum with about six to seven flights to get cleared. This was not so on the 737! I had precisely one hour in the circuit with a really nice trainer and John had the same and by the end of day two we were on our way back to Heathrow on the shuttle Trident for an enforced break over Xmas before starting the route training. So ended 1980 in which I got married again, Paul arrived on the scene and I got to grips with a new aircraft. It was a good year by all accounts.

1981 came along and I was home for two days before they called me for my first line training trip to Stockholm, Sweden so within about three weeks of the start of the course I was on the route. I have to say it was all done very professionally and what was more important it was conducted in a very relaxed manner. I duly reported for my first trip in Short Haul and met up with the trainer Captain B who was an excellent guy. We did have a third pilot since this was my first outing but he soon disappeared down the back and was rarely seen. The departure was in the early evening getting back at about 10 pm. Stockholm in winter could be a bit challenging but someone up there must have liked me since the weather was very cold but very clear. It was quite a treat to see Europe unfold and the various cities brightly lit up as we flew up the North Sea towards Denmark and beyond. Navigation was pretty simple but you still needed to be a bit focused since the aircraft had a very basic navigation kit as I said before. The route into Stockholm was pretty standard and what made a change was to have the Controllers speaking in good English and be very good at their job. Landing aids in Europe were the top of the range with no rather crude approaches as to what I was used to in the middle of Africa. I had the feeling that I was going to enjoy this different lifestyle. I got back late night and the trainer seemed very happy with it all so it was onwards and upwards. I then did a trip to Rome, Italy and back, quickly followed by a Dublin, Ireland and then got my final clearance on a trip to Stavanger, Norway where the weather was less than kind with a lot of snow and ice around but I made it OK and by mid-January I was back in harness as a Captain on the 737 and loving it.

My first trip on my own was a simple night stop in Aberdeen, Scotland. On the flight north the weather reports at Aberdeen were getting worse and worse with snow, low cloud and a vicious wind from the east. The runway lay pretty well north to south so whichever way I attempted to land I would have a large crosswind to deal with plus a very slippery surface. We approached using the runway towards the South and boy was it rough on the approach. The 737 came into its own in these sorts of conditions and behaved like an agile little terrier being very responsive on the controls. At about 400ft I saw a blur of the runway in the right hand windscreen and I managed to steer us to a sort of landing at about the right point. Not the smoothest but workable. As we taxied to the ramp I remarked to the controller that it was a pretty bad night here in Aberdeen.

"Aye, it's not too bad at the moment. You wait until it really gets bad," he replied in a thick Scottish accent.

Very funny, I thought.

The next day all was lovely in the weather department and we had a gentle ride back to Heathrow. After about two hours on the ground off I went to Newcastle and back so here I was doing three, four or five sectors a day as opposed to one long one back in Long-Haul.

In the news in January, Ronald Reagan was inaugurated as the new US President and within minutes the hostages in the US embassy in

Tehran were released. Politics are strange!

As for my life on the 737 I was really enjoying it and BA in its wisdom decreed that early starts out of a European city was better for business so a lot of night stops within Europe became the scene of the day. I could have up to 15 night stops in any one month which varied from Lisbon to Rome to Frankfurt to Oslo. The crews were a great bunch of lads and also ready for a beer or two wherever we pulled up for the night. There was none of the time change problems and also the Cabin Crew were really very pleasant and generally ready to socialise. In Gatwick there was a small fleet of 737s that flew under the banner of Airtours which was the charter side of BA. On occasions we were called to do the odd charter for them. A classic example would be the flight on a Saturday night from Gatwick to Palma, Majorca and back. It was a bit tiring but all good fun with all the British tourists behaving as only tourists do. Also out of Gatwick we did flights to Madrid, Spain and other Mediterranean destinations. What would happen is that we would go down to Gatwick and stay in some fancy 5-star hotel for maybe five days in a row. The one advantage was that we usually ended up in Gatwick for the night so it was the 'Six Bells' in Horley for the social side of life meeting and chatting to the local aircrew and quite often we would end up at some party somewhere. What a life we were having.

Mr Boeing had, at that time, launched a new short range aircraft known as the 757 and BA ordered a serious number of them to replace the Trident aircraft that had been the mainstay of the European network up until then but were coming to the end of their useful life.

In March Ronald Reagan was shot at by some nutter so it seemed his period as president had got off to lively start. In the April the space shuttle 'Columbia' flew for the first time in space and marked the beginning of getting the Americans back in the space race since the Russians now totally dominated it after the moon landings. It was the same craft that broke up on re-entry in 2003 killing all on board.

I won't go through every trip with you on the 737 but just highlight some of them. Jersey was always an interesting destination because you just did not know what to expect, weather-wise. It could vary daily from clear skies to thick fog and a 20 knot wind blowing right across the runway in a phenomenon known as 'sea fog'. Bilbao, Spain was another airport that was interesting, being stuck in the middle of a valley surrounded by mountains. The timing of our flight usually coincided with arriving just as the airport was closing for the night and once you did a rather tricky approach and landed the airport lights would go as you got onto the ramp. Good night stop though. Turin, Italy was a strange one as we had a three day stop-over there since we mixed it with the BAC- 111 and so provided us with the chance to get out of the city and there was nothing nicer when the weather was right to go to the lakes north of Turin and chill out over a glass of Chianti or two. My position on the bidding list seemed to be getting better and better.

The bid line package came through every month. I have mentioned the bid line before but this might be a good time to explain its working a bit more. It consisted of, firstly, trip lines that by name contained a run of trips for the next month and varied in content from lots of night stops to very few according to your taste. Secondly, the next set of lines in the pecking order were known as blind lines and were blank but would have a series of trips on them once the bidding process was completed. The disadvantage of these lines was that the least favourable trips were put on these lines. Finally, there were the reserve lines and showed a series of standbys and days off that you could bid for in the next month. These lines were not too inspiring but could be built up into a reasonable working month with the days off that you wanted. As I said before, seniority ruled the waves with the senior boys getting the plum trips and everybody else scrambling for something workable. All the bids for work had to be sent in by a certain date and then they were sorted by a planning department and any trips left over were re-listed and sent out again for a second round of bidding. Finally when the basket had been well and truly shaken up we got our plan for the following month with about ten days to spare. After that point on, any trips spare were entered into what was known as the 'open time' book and you could bid for these according to certain ground rules that I never did understand. As I said, everything was based on seniority and in the lower ranks you spent your month bidding only to be zapped by some senior guy. It was a real bun-fight I can tell you. By the way, any trips that were promulgated after all the bidding had closed were known as 'draft' trips and were paid at a very generous overtime rate. The ultimate was a 'forced draft' when double the overtime rate was paid. On the 737 and in short haul in general there was good money to be made in the overtime scene. There were various scams going around on the various fleets with the Shuttle lot keeping the top spot always. The Shuttle was a simple 'turn up and go' service to Glasgow, Edinburgh, Manchester and Belfast from Heathrow such that if there was no seat available on the first flight a back-up aircraft would be called in and fly the route with maybe five passengers only. It was a brilliant concept but expensive. The back-up crews would frequent the coffee lounge at the crew report centre. So, apart from the being the hub of all the rumours, plans and union affairs, there was this bunch of pilots scouring the rule book so as to maximise their earnings. It was a right game!

On the home front things were settling down a bit with the odd drama thrown in. It is hard work when a new baby arrives and not as sometimes portrayed in the movies. A classic example was bedtime that was usually at about 7 pm. Would Paul go to sleep as ordered? Not a bloody chance! When we strapped him into his carrycot in the car he would sleep beautifully and so plan 'A' was to put him in his carrycot in the car and drive around until he fell asleep and then pick him up and put him in his cot when arriving back at the ranch. Master plan or what! OK he would fall asleep in the car but as soon as I pulled into the drive this little head would bob up all wide-eyed and bushy-tailed. So off I would go again for another circuit and the bobbing would happen again on arrival. Cost me a fortune in petrol. Plan 'B' then came into play. Put him in his cot and ignore the crying and yelling. There are experts around who advocate this form of attack but they had not met young Paul. Boy, could he let rip! Out of a small body he could issue a cry that could wake the dead. So there was Moya and me sitting downstairs trying to be all calm and collected with this chorus of verbal abuse echoing throughout the house and maybe the street. After about ten minutes of this one of us would give in and climb the stairs on the assumption that Paul was in the midst of dying of over-active lungs. The moment you picked him up the vocal tap switched off and he was all smiles. Cunning sod he was!

There was an occasion when I was doing a bit of DIY work whereby I was hammering down the upstairs floorboards to stop the creaking sound while we were moving around trying to be silent. So there I was with hammer in hand casually tapping in tacks when suddenly a small fountain of water erupted where I had put the final blow. Yes, you've guessed it – I had gone right into a water pipe which was embedded just below the floorboard. A water pipe is so small compared with the floor area that it took real skill to find it, but I did. Moya was downstairs with Paul and by fluke he was asleep in his cot. I sort of came downstairs casually at the gallop and shut down the water at the main cock suggesting that we call the plumber soonest. As it was we knew our local man Ray and by chance he was in so 'no problem' and that he was on his way. He suggested that to save him time I get a saw out and cut around the leak area so all he had to do was to seal up the leak and hey presto all would be good. So out comes the Mark 1 jigsaw freshly purchased some days before and off I went back upstairs and fired it up and using the appliance of science cut a perfectly round hole. As I completed the hole there was the sound of not one but three 'clonks' and as the hole was revealed there was the original pipe neatly severed plus two central heating pipes, also neatly severed, lying there plus a torrent of about 2,000 gallons, or so it seemed, of mucky central heating water cascading everywhere on the ceiling of downstairs. There was a shout from downstairs that water was pouring out of the ceiling light socket and a biblical flood has started on the carpet. I hit the stairs in one leap and killed the house electricity and then stormed around the house like a demented wreck trying to find the tap to shut off the central heating water. I covered every square foot in about 20 seconds and found nothing. At this point Ray turned up at the door and waded in and stood in amazement at this so-called professional guy grovelling around on the floor. What I did not notice is that the waterfall had stopped on its own since there was no water left in the system. The house had gone from a normal operating scene to a shell within a few minutes due to my superb bit of DIY. To this day I never touch anything to do with plumbing and if the floorboards creak then so be it. Ray had a fit of the giggles as he set about rebuilding the house and kept repeating his admiration of the clean precision cuts that I had made. I just nodded and mumbled as he did his work and finally after about three hours some sort of order returned to the household. Paul in the meantime slept through the whole escapade. Typical!

Stick to your day job, Gwyn, was my thought for the day.

In the May Pope John Paul II was shot in St Peter's Square at the Vatican in Rome by a deranged Turkish guy. He did recover and proved to be one of the most popular Popes of modern times. I did hear a story that when he was first installed he was asked to address a huge gathering of Italian youth in Rome. Instead of arriving in the 'Pope mobile' as was expected he arrived sitting in the back of a bright red Ferrari and the young crowd cheered and cheered him for the gesture.

As for me I continued my flying on the 737 and what I did find was that with sector lengths of generally under two hours, I, together with the rest of the fleet, became pretty good at flying the aircraft in all sorts of conditions. The aircraft itself was becoming groomed for approach and landings in very low visibilities and this was all done on the back of the work done on the Trident but with more modern equipment. It was not long before we could land in 200 metres of fog on the runway and we were all gradually being cleared on the simulator for this. I remember they had tried it on the VC-10 but failed miserably. The beauty of the 737 was that we had a wonderful and very capable autopilot and we could rely on it at all times, except, that is, when we did our Simulator checks every six months when we spent most of the time manually flying it around. This was to be expected since we were still not in the 'Autopilot dependent' world yet.

We picked up a route off the Trident 2 aircraft that had the code of 'SVO'.

Never heard of it! I thought when rostered it in early June. When I looked closer I saw that it had a flying time of about four hours.

"What's this bloody Long-Haul stuff?" I remarked to the co-pilot when we met up for the flight.

"Moscow, Captain," was his reply.

So there I was on my way to Moscow which was about the limit of the range of the aircraft. As we flew up the Baltic with Latvia off to the right and Finland off to the left I realised that the navigation in

Russia was very primitive and relied on beacons that had been put there many years before. When they were selected for use on our instrument displays they seemed to dance all over the place around some sort of mean point which one hoped was in the middle of the airway. The Russians were very sensitive in those days to anyone who drifted out of the airway and would think nothing about putting a MIG fighter up to have a look at any wanderers. Flying in Russia was once described as keeping one eye on the script with your finger on the line and the other on the average direction of the dancing needles. The other problem was that the Russians flew using metres for height as opposed to feet. The 737 altimeter only worked in feet. For example 10,300 metres was 33,100ft and so you were provided with a large sheet of paper with all the conversions on it. It was OK in the cruise but once the descent had started you had to be a member of the 'Brain's Trust' to work out what the controller said in his very basic English and then change the metres to feet, at the same time keeping the eyes on the script as described earlier. The brain was working overtime and getting hotter and hotter! When we finally got on the ground and parked then more fun would start. As I looked out of the window a rickety old truck would turn up. It was bristling with aerials and it turned out to be a listening post eavesdropping on the conversation between us and our Russian Airline staff. Don't forget this was 1981 and there was still a lot of confrontation between east and west still going on. On the return sector it was so nice to pick up Finnish radar as we entered the Baltic. The Russians claimed not to have radar as we would dance our way down the airways but once we got near one of the boundaries they were very quick to call us and ask us in no uncertain terms to change our heading to get back in the middle of the airway, wherever that was.

In the June the Middle East bubbled up again when the Israeli Air Force managed to bomb a suspected nuclear site in Iraq. Work of art I would like to add, since the operation must have crossed many boundaries of unfriendly nations. The effect was the usual hiatus of outgoings against Israel. Nothing had changed since 1967 when the first punch-ups started. It was in the same month that the Queen was riding down the Mall in London whilst doing her 'Trooping the Colour' bit when some moron fired a starting gun in the crowd and the procession upped sticks and increased tempo to a steady gallop. This was becoming the year of prominent people being shot at.

In the July, Moya, Paul and I went to Portugal with Moya's parents for a holiday. The place was on the southern coast, being a holiday complex of some sort. Paul was by now just starting to get his legs and was becoming a right handful. Moya's dad, Paddy, was a true Irishman at heart and a lovely, lovely chap. He came from the Wicklow hills south of Dublin and came to England in the late forties to seek his fortune. He married Mary who can only be described as a classic English rose. Moya had an elder brother, Patrick and a younger one, Paul. There were a lot of Marys in the family since both Patrick and Paul married a Mary and Moya is the Irish name for Mary. At a family get-together all you had to say was 'Mary' then a number of heads would bob up. Anyway off we all went on holiday. In our bedroom a cot had been installed for Paul.

"OK, so what!" I hear you say.

What we would do is to put him down in it at night trying to ignore the verbal protests and maybe have a drink or two downstairs. I remember one night hearing a bang and a crash from upstairs. Moya and I bolted upstairs fearing that some drama had occurred and there was Paul with a big cheesy grin standing proud as punch outside his cot on the floor. That was our night ruined!

As I said Paul was finding his legs which was a bit surprising since he was still only eight months old and on one occasion we were all camped out by the 'Kiddie' pool and watched Paul wobbling along with an ice cream firmly held in his hand when suddenly 'splosh' and in he went headlong into the water. I leapt up like 'Hercules Unchained' and roared through the water and pulled him out. It was only about 20cm deep but to Paul it must have felt like the Atlantic. I lifted up this dripping mass of body and there he was still clutching the rather wet remains of the ice cream. Good boy! Never leave your food!

When we got back to the UK we were greeted by the fact that in Toxteth, near Liverpool there had been race riots and further south in Brixton, south London. I was led to believe they were racially motivated but a bit of a shock to the English way.

I went back to work and the next event that took place was the wedding of Prince Charles and Diana which gave the nation a day off.

In the cul-de-sac where we lived a street party was organised and good fun was had by one and all. Little did we know the final outcome of the marriage but at the time it filled the nation with pride.

The number of 737 aircraft that the company was getting from Mr Boeing was increasing at a steady rate since I had joined the fleet so the crew numbers were building as well and more and more of my fellow Long-Haulers came across and joined me so that every now and again I would spot an ex VC-10 or 707 chap. The conversations would be based maybe around a particular German night stop as opposed to some far flung outpost in the Far East. Most of us who had come over, including me, seemed to settle in well and even perfected the art of a ten minute 'catnap' in the cruise. The modern equivalent is known as a 'power nap'. It actually worked very well to switch off for say 10 to 15 minutes and then wake up fully alert or rather as alert as one could be. The other by-product of the short haul fleet, as I said before, is that you would never be too affected by time zone changes so that when you worked all day and ended up in, say, Brussels, for the night with a late start the following day then a social eating and drinking evening was usually on the cards. The fleet was becoming a little gem in the BA collection and I had chosen well to join it. We pretty well covered most of Europe from Scandinavia in the north, Italy in the south, Madrid in the west and Greece in the east.

The summer of '81 drifted on in much the same vein of night stops and a good home social scene with Paul finally getting into a good routine and starting to talk a little and even going through the night without a panic attack from Moya or me. In fact, the first few times that he slept through the night one of us would assume that he was dead and go upstairs to check his breathing. Within the cul-de-sac where we lived there were a number of young families and so the conversations had a common theme. That was, until the second glass of wine had been consumed, when the usual silly chit chat ensued.

The world of the home PC descended on us in August when IBM launched a new range of computers designed for the family. How did we survive without them! Now I have two PCs and two laptops to my name. Not to mention iPhones, iPod, iPad etc, etc. There was also a young entrepreneur by the name of Alan Sugar who announced a new range of PCs under the banner of 'Amstrad'.

In the September Boeing launched the 767 as the dig daddy of the 757 and BA ordered a batch of them but specified Rolls Royce engines which in the end was a good move since the 747 was in the middle of a remake and the proposed new model would use the same engine and the 767. In the end only BA had this variant which delayed the arrival of the new fleet. BA also decreed that crews could fly both the 757 and the 767 on the same ticket so there was flexibility all round. The world of training was changing fast from the old days. Our own 737 simulator was a pretty realistic piece of kit. Mind you, the excuse of:

"It does not fly like the real thing so it must be a simulator fault" was wearing a bit thin.

Once again, the Middle East hit the headlines in the October when the president of Egypt, Anwar Sadat, was assassinated during a military rally. This was the fourth shooting of a prominent figure this year. With problems in the Middle East never far from the headlines I felt quite safe from any airline involvement on my little 737. The cabin crew, as I mentioned before, were generally a good bunch of people and quite similar to the old crowd off the VC-10. Quite often on a night stop most of them would come out with us and socialise. There certainly was no bridge between us as there was on the 747. Nice!

As the winter approached the usual delays would build up with fog and snow. We had a simple system of standbys whereby you could stay at home with the proviso that you could get to the airport within one and a half hours. This was easy for me living in Binfield. The mobile phone was in its embryonic stage in 1981 and was deemed to be beyond the cost of anyone who was not rich. So all I did was to stay at home and wait for the phone call. It was strange but it felt that whenever BA rang to get your attention the phone seemed to have a different tone to it.

"That'll be BA calling," I would say reaching for the phone.

Don't ask me how I knew but most of the time I was right.

The other standby was at the airport where I usually adjourned to the infamous coffee lounge to catch up with the latest gossip. Suddenly the speaker would blare out your name and you were on your way. What quite often happened is that a particular service would have a

757 assigned to it but on the day the passenger load would be a bit low and they would substitute a 737 for the service to save some operating costs. So there you were slumming it in the lounge with a 'jaw dropping' bit of scandal when within minutes you were on your way to Paris and back.

It was in the December on a day when I was doing my standby at the airport with the snow crashing down that I got called to the Operations and asked to fly up on British Midland to Birmingham and bring back a 737 that had been parked there for some time. It sounded straightforward so me and my trusty Co-pilot went over to the terminal and clambered aboard this rather old Fokker F-27 and then waited for some three hours for our turn to get de-iced. We eventually got airborne and arrived in Birmingham after a short while. As we taxied into the ramp I peered out of the window expecting to see a shiny fully de-iced 737 sitting there. There was nothing out there expect for a mountain of snow shaped like an aeroplane which I ignored. Silly me! Underneath this snow sculpture was my 737 that had actually been there for three days and had taken the full brunt of the blizzard the night before. I was not exactly dressed for the Arctic and it was becoming a bit of an adventure. We went to operations and enquired when we would be de-iced and ready to go.

"Captain, the airport has run out of de-icing fluid and the tanker with a fresh supply is on its way from Cleveland but has got stuck in the ice on some motorway," I was told.

Cleveland is in the far north of England and a good six hours' drive on a normal day.

"What time do you expect it then?" I asked gingerly.

"About 3 am, Captain," was his reply with a sort of shrug of his shoulders.

It was now about 2 in the afternoon so we abandoned any hope of going anywhere and retired to a local hotel to take a ten hour break to make us legal. While we were waiting for the taxi to the hotel we spotted a Kenya Airways 707 taking off shedding buckets of snow off its wing as it rolled down the runway. Our comments were not for publication. We heard later that it had actually landed at Heathrow and gracefully slid off the side of the runway thus closing Heathrow to any landings for at least six hours. Nobody was going anywhere! Not even the tanker driver up north was going anywhere. The hotel had become a refuge for all the stranded passengers in various degrees of temperament ranging from screaming and yelling to breaking down and crying. We slinked off to our rooms and awaited developments. In the early hours of the next day I got a call that the tanker had finally arrived and they would start de-icing our aircraft soon. So off we go back to the airport and go out onto the ramp to survey the scene. The 737 was engulfed in a mountain of snow and the shape of it could only just be made out. A team of men started to sweep the area so that at least we might get near the front door. A blower was brought in to blow some of the powdery snow off the wings. It felt like we were in the middle of the Arctic and, of course, we were both bloody cold since we had not anticipated standing on a frozen ramp in the early hours. We must have looked like a right pair of frozen lemons. After about an hour we were able to climb aboard and get the auxiliary power unit started, to get our home for the next few hours warmish. Slowly but surely the 737 came to life and a bit more user-friendly. After about two hours we were finally in the position to get the engines started. Heathrow had the night ban lifted so we were ready and able to go. We started the engines and it took about ten minutes for all the systems to settle down and work. We eventually departed and landed in Heathrow at about 6 am which was about 24 hours after we had started our airport standby stint and all we did was to go to Birmingham and back. That was the last flight I did in 1981 and so I was at home for the Xmas festivities.

1982 arrived and it transpired that it was one of the coldest winters on record. Heathrow managed as best it could with temperatures down to -15C on some nights. The flying schedules became totally disrupted and involved the crews doing some long and arduous duties. In Washington, USA a 737 of Air Florida similar to ours crashed after take-off into the Potomac river with many deaths. Of course, we were all curious as to the cause but it transpired that it was pilot error and nothing to do with the aircraft systems. They had simply forgotten to put on the engine anti-icing before take-off. Amazing to miss something so simple!

In early February whilst I was doing a stint of standby at the airport I was called into Operations and told that an Air Tanzanian 737 had been hijacked in Africa and had managed to find its way to Stansted airport, north of London.

"Gwyn, the aircraft at Stansted is a 737 like ours and we have been asked by the powers-that-be to get one of our aircraft to fly to a RAF military airfield close to Stansted so that the British Army SAS can practise on the aircraft just in case they need to do an operation to rescue the passengers in Stansted if the hijackers get nasty," I was told.

"Well, this is different!" I remarked.

At that particular time there was a catering dispute within BA and the only catering offered for most flights was a lunchbox of some sort filled with all sorts of goodies. My co-pilot Ian Osborne and I made our way out to a 737 parked slightly away from the usual gates. As we arrived at the steps we were met by a police officer who said, "Is it all right to put the dogs on board in the cabin, Captain?"

This is certainly different! I thought to myself.

Having said that it would be OK I watched as about six of the meanest looking dogs I had ever seen complete with even meaner looking handlers all piled out of the back of this van and sort of stormed aboard. Who was running the show between the dogs and the handlers I was not sure. The dispatcher rolled up and his jaw dropped at the sight of the dogs.

"Captain, I have to complete the load sheet and I am not sure of the weight of these dogs," he spluttered out.

"About the weight of a man I would think," was my reply.

I knew the dispatcher carried a supply of the famous lunch boxes in the back of his van so asked him to offload the lot for the flight.

"What's the destination?" he asked.

"RAF Wethersfield in Essex," I replied with a grin.

"I didn't know we went there in British Airways. Mind you, they never tell us anything in the office about new destinations," he said with a quizzical look on his face.

We finally got airborne in the late afternoon and made our way up to this RAF airfield in Essex. The weather was not particularly good and the RAF offered us a radar assisted approach which was something very new to me but, since we were needed on the ground, I accepted it and we finally landed OK and were directed to a remote part of the airfield and shut down the engines and made ourselves a cup of tea and waited for things to happen. The dogs and their handlers offloaded themselves and disappeared into the night. At about 10 pm a Range Rover turned up at the aircraft steps and out stepped a military looking guy dressed in a one-piece olive green garb who bounded up the steps three at a time. He introduced himself as a Major from Hereford. Hereford is the home of the SAS. After the niceties he explained that his 'boys' would be here soon and they would need to practise an assault on our aircraft. This was going to be an interesting night to say the least.

Soon after that a bus turned up and a bunch of the meanest looking guys fell out and stood around listening to the Major. They looked like a group of total scruffs out for a Saturday night fight at the local pub. They all piled aboard and spread themselves out in the cabin.

"Any chance of a cup of tea for us please?" the Major asked.

So there I was in the galley doing my cabin crew bit brewing up the small pot about eight times with Ian mincing through the cabin dishing it out. One thing that struck me was that the manners of these 'boys' were pretty good even if they were a bit rough and tumble. Once the tea service was over then the Major set about briefing his guys about the 737 with some input from me as to what and where everything was. The object was to clamber on the wing and carefully open the emergency hatches together with another group placing a ladder against the main doors. At a signal then they would hit the hatches at the same time and leap into the cabin. All this was done in total darkness with only the infrared illuminators of the weapons showing the way. They looked pretty scary in their famous black balaclavas all screaming and yelling. The Major sat with us on the flight deck to watch the door lights lighting up to check that they all were opening at the same time. Within five to six seconds there were about ten of them on board all poised with their weapons raised and their hands on the trigger. Wow, it was very impressive. The Major was less than impressed since the doors did not open at exactly the same time and they were about one second late. Did he give them a bollocking or what!

The practising went on for most of the night until the Major seemed

happy with it. At about 4 am Ian and I did our cabin service bit again
dishing out the famous lunch boxes. The 'boys' were all still very
courteous to us. I remember one guy casually pulling a knife from
the back of his neck collar and trimming his nails. I have to say I was
incredibly impressed with them as a unit. After dinner was served they
all clambered down the steps and appeared to move out. Ian and I then
made a cup of tea after closing all the doors and sat on the flight deck.
Unbeknown to us, this was what they wanted us to do since after a
short while there was a crash and a bang and suddenly the flight deck
door left its hinges and there was a barrel of a gun stuck up my nose.
Ian had the same treatment. The guy looked incredibly menacing just
staring at me as if I was next on the list for extermination. The Major
climbed on board and barked an order that the exercise was complete.
At this point my would-be assassin's face broke out into a large cheesy
grin and said in a very broad Scottish accent:

"I would love a cup of tea please, Sir!"

Blimey the British Army seems to march on cups of tea. No tea = no
war!

So, once again, it was tea all round. The Major explained that he
had spotted us sitting quietly on the flight deck and decided to do one
more assault practice. We eventually finished at about 6 am and Ian
and I managed a couple of hours' sleep in the cabin. We were woken
at about 9 am to the news that the 737 at Stansted was on the move.
In Wethersfield the Major introduced us to a guy who was a dedicated
pilot and asked if he could be briefed on the procedures of the aircraft.
He was very quick to pick up the basics of how it all operated and
remarked to me that in his line of profession he did conversion courses
at BA for all the aircraft in the various fleets. Clever guy!

His mobile phone suddenly went off and he then turned to me and
said:

"What we are worried about is that he might fly off and we would
miss the chance to grab the hijackers."

"We have agreements with many countries who consider us amongst
the best when dealing with hijacks. Remember Mogadishu where we
helped the Germans to attack the aircraft after the Captain was shot?"
he continued.

"So, what we will do is to get you fuelled up now and get airborne and follow him wherever he goes. You will have to tuck in close underneath him to avoid the radar picture looking like two aircraft. Is that OK, Captain?" he concluded.

At this point I gulped and said that I needed some sort of authority to do this and asked him if he could get me that. I must admit I did not relish the idea of being tucked up close to another aircraft for however long it might take.

"No problem, I will get you the lady on the phone," he replied.

He was referring to the Prime Minister, Maggie Thatcher, and so there I was talking to her about what they asking me to do. She said that it was fine with her to do as they asked and that she would talk to BA to confirm this fact. I was a bit shell-shocked by the phone call but what could I do? The next problem was getting out of the rather tight spot that I been parked in since this was an old fighter station and not designed for the likes of a 737. I explained that the easiest way to get out of this spot was to be pushed back onto the main taxiway behind me but I doubted if the station had a push-back tug. To go forward and get back onto the taxiway would be fine except for a large sign-post on the edge of the tarmac that may be in the way.

"No problem with that sign. I will get John to get rid of it for you," the Major said casually as he wandered off to the Range Rover.

"Bloody hell, this is getting more like a John Wayne movie," I said to Ian.

As John approached the sign and was selecting a suitable bit of kit to blow the offending signpost into outer space the phone suddenly rang in the Range Rover and the Major conversed for a few minutes and then he announced:

"It's all over, folks. The hijackers have given themselves up. Bloody shame, I was looking forward to a few fireworks. Let's pack up and go home."

I must admit I did breathe a sigh of relief at this point that my bit was done and celebrated with yet another cup of tea. Pity there was nothing stronger available. It was by this time approaching midday and so the Major suggested that in repayment for our help he would buy us lunch and then they would depart. We all went to the station restaurant and enjoyed the lunch which made a change from the cardboard box. In the restaurant there was the RAF aircrew from the Hercules that had flown in from RAF Lyneham with all the bits and pieces for the SAS and also the RAF Chinook helicopter that would take the 'boys' back to Hereford. Ian and I chatted to both crews. What I found amazing is that the Hercules crew sat on their table well away from the Chinook crew.

"We don't talk to that lot off the Chinook and they don't talk to us," the Hercules pilot explained as if the other lot were infected by a weird disease.

Amazing, I thought we were all fighting for the same lot as one big happy family, I thought to myself.

Anyway, after lunch Ian and I went back to our aircraft after a short courteous farewell and surveyed the possible damage done to the 737. On the wing their great big hobnail boots had made some dents but fortunately on the pre-designated walkway areas. There were no cracks that I could see so that was OK. We struggled to replace the emergency exits and looked in the cabin at the carnage of debris of leftover teacups and lunch boxes. I managed to talk to a BA aircraft flying overhead and they relayed back to me that if I was happy they would get me clearance back to Heathrow and to taxi the aircraft to the hangers after landing. After avoiding the famous sign we finally departed back to Heathrow late in the afternoon and I got back home in the early evening. Boy, did I have a tale to tell. I could have dined out for months on my adventures. I was soon brought down to earth with the news that Paul had given Moya a sleepless night since his big back teeth were coming through. What a comedown from the John Wayne film set! Never mind!

After my escapade with the SAS I was given a week off. When I went back to work a lot of people asked me about the episode. I felt like a bit of a celebrity at the time but it could have happened to anyone. My Flight Manager informed me that the damage to the aircraft amounted to about half a million pounds and that the Ministry of Defence were quite happy to stomp up the cash.

News was out in the middle of February that Laker Airways had gone bust. The airline started its famous 'Skytrain' service to JFK back in 1977 and finally ground to a halt in 1982. It transpired many years later that BA had a hand in its demise and paid a hefty fine for its involvement but the deed was done.

In the March there was an interesting news item that caught the eye. Way down in the South Atlantic there were a bunch of islands known as the Falklands. I had never heard of them to that date but this news item referred to a smaller island further south towards the Antarctic known as South Georgia. The story was that we nicked them off the Spanish many years ago when all along Argentina claimed them as their own. They seemed so far away as not to be of interest but what had happened was that an Argentinean trader of some sorts had raised his country's flag on South Georgia. Maggie Thatcher and her cronies took great exception to this and demanded it be removed or else!

Things then escalated in Argentina under the leadership of Leopoldo Galtieri, the dictator who ran the country at that time. About two weeks later the Falkland Islands were invaded. After a fight with a small contingent of Royal Marines, who were totally outnumbered, he claimed the islands for Argentina. Well, back in London Maggie was not impressed and ordered a task force to be assembled and to sail some 8,000 miles and get the islands back into British hands. No mean feat considering the distances involved and the logistics needed to do it.

At work the only thing talked about was the possibility of a punch-up in the South Atlantic. Trade unionism was rife at the time but it was amazing to see how these same people picked up their tools and got to work to get the country ready to possibly go to war with Argentina. The passenger liners Queen Elizabeth 2 and the Canberra were hastily converted into troopships complete with a helicopter landing platform. In those days we had an Army, Navy and Air force that were large enough to cope. Not a chance nowadays!

Some of our flights out of Gatwick took us out over the naval base at Portsmouth on the south coast and we could see smoke plumes all over the docks as ships were readied for action. Every evening we were glued to the TV to catch the latest action. In early April the task force set sail with great aplomb to go and get the islands back. We felt very patriotic seeing all the action as it was happening. It was the talk of the town. As for us we ended up flying quite a few military types around the country as they scurried around doing their bit.

It took about six weeks to get the 'task force' into position to the north of the Falklands and we then heard the news that South Georgia had been retaken with little trouble so it was now on to the Falklands and 'let's get the job done' as they say. In the meantime, one of our Royal Navy submarines had sunk an Argentine Cruiser the Belgrano that was just on the fringe of the exclusion zone that had been promulgated by the British Commander Sandy Woodwood. I could relate every day of action of the war but, since this is not an historic book, all I can say is that the war was eventually won in the late June. We lost four ships and over 200 men in the process. The RAF even managed to mount a Vulcan mission to bomb the airfield at Stanley, the capital of the Falklands. It involved a round trip of over 15 or so hours using about 16 Victor airborne tankers to do the job. This was where the old INS units in the stored VC-10s came in useful as I mentioned in Part 1. As a Brit I felt very proud of our nation and it put a spring back in my step. I can remember flying to Moscow just after the final blow had been struck and the Russian dispatcher congratulating us on the victory.

"You had better watch out or you lot could be next on the list," I laughingly said to him.

On one occasion I was flying out of Gatwick and over the Southampton water when we spotted the QE2 and the Canberra sailing home towards their berths surrounded by an armada of small ships. We were not very high at the time and the controller allowed us to do a majestic circuit around the ships as if in salute of their achievements. Dad had made his way down to Portsmouth and even got on board a small ship to record the arrival of HMS Invincible after some four months away. At some point a flight of seven Fleet Air Arm Harriers flew overhead in salute. The Harrier was the famous jump jet built by a bygone company called Hawker and was instrumental in winning the air war down South. He took a photograph of the ship and from that painted a superb picture which hangs with pride in my study now.

Also, at the end of June a 747 which was flying from Kuala Lumpur to Perth flew into an area of volcanic ash and all four engines failed. The aircraft then became a lumbering glider and Captain Eric Moody, a friend of mine, and the rest of the flight crew managed to get three engines going again at about 13,000ft and made an emergency landing in Djakarta, Indonesia. Heroes all round!

In the July it was time to take the family on holiday. By chance, Moya had spotted an advert in the local paper about an apartment in Cala Vinyas, Majorca and she made enquiries and found the deal pretty good and, by chance, Moya's brother Paul and his wife Mary plus their boy Kevin were also on holiday in the area and so we could all meet up out there. So I got a flight deal and away we went. When we arrived we picked up a hire car locally and made our way to the apartment. It was in a small terrace of about eight similar units and was in an ideal spot away from all the noise and lights. It was on two floors with two bedrooms, lounge, kitchen and a small balcony. I have to say it suited us very well and we even found a local 'Supermercado' up the road and so the stocks were soon in, together with a suitcase full of 'Pampers'. We were set to rock and roll. We soon met up with Paul's lot and found that there was a small beach complete with café for us to lounge around on. Total bliss! We found a small restaurant in the evenings known as 'San Francisco 2' and really enjoyed our own company. It was a very social spot and the inter table conversations drifted on as the evening went on as they do with the flow of wine to help with the pronunciations. When the holiday came to an end it was with the promise that we would come back next year. The place was lovely.

On our return from Majorca I continued to ply my trade within Europe and even managed to take Moya away for a night in Brussels followed by one in Dublin, Ireland. It transpired that one of her dad's cousins was an Air Traffic Controller at Dublin airport so he joined us in the hotel for a bit of a party that night. Moya's mum had come down to look after Paul and it was at his point that both of us noticed that she was getting very forgetful over and above the normal ageing process. It was only small little things but we did not have a good feeling about it. Moya's dad was also not in the best of health and had been in hospital for a routine operation when it transpired that he had stomach cancer.

Why does it always happen to the nice people and not the nasty ones? I have often thought to myself.

Within BA I joined the Flying Staff Recreation Club (FSRC), of which I spoke about before, as a committee member in about 1982 and set about getting some things for the European scene. For example, in Stockholm we had a day off on some schedules and adjacent to the hotel was a very respectable golf course so 'sticks' were duly delivered. The FSRC committee met about once a month somewhere within the BA offices. The secretary was Sue Mason who was a larger than life girl and, with her mate Debbie Saville, could cause total chaos at the drop of a hat. The chairman then was Chris Baxter who was a Flight Engineer and so there was always a bit of tension when I requested a bicycle for Copenhagen for example. What I endeavoured to do was to do a promotion within the short haul arena to increase the membership. The campaign to recruit members became quite successful and we did get our bikes in Copenhagen. The membership swelled to about 8,000 and I got the job as vice-chairman. The link man within BA was Andy Homewood whose real role was to deal with all of the hotel bookings for the crews and everybody else within BA who needed a room for the night anywhere in the world when on company business. The best bit about Andy was he knew everybody within BA when a favour needed to be done. We actually had a store room allocated by BA in the crew report area which was like a treasure trove. The FSRC grew over the years to what it is today and is a credit to the volunteers who would take time out to keep it running.

Another one of the interesting airports we went to was Cork, which was situated in the south west corner of Ireland. Moya's dad, being a Dubliner, would refer to the Cork people as the 'Shopkeepers of Ireland'. The airport was plonked right on top of a hill and was always a challenge when the weather turned nasty, albeit fog or rain. The ramp would hold about two 737s at the most. The runways were at right angles to each other heading north to south and east to west. Being on the western side of Ireland it faced the onslaught of what the Atlantic decided to drop onto it. The east to west runway was quite short with no aids to help you and when it rained it flooded quickly. This made the approach and landing on the north to south runway a bit character forming when trying to fight off an Atlantic gale blowing right across it. Fog was the other danger and I remember arriving once with thick fog at the airport. We made an approach on the southerly runway that had a precision approach aid of a rather basic standard and the ATC controller kept reading out the visibility to us as we descended. Right on the limits I spotted just about enough of the approach lights and landed. As we rolled down the runway I spotted an airport vehicle off to the left and asked the tower what he was doing.

"Captain, Sir, he was reading out the visibility for us by counting the number of runway lights he could see from his cab and we could then change them into metres for your approach," he replied.

So there I was with a modern aircraft making an approach in very foggy conditions based on what a driver saw out of his window. The mind boggled!

"By the way, sir, you are our first arrival into Cork for three days so please have a coffee on us," the controller added.

It could only be the Irish that would say that!

Now, here is a question: When did the first commercial CD enter mass production and officially render the old 45 record to the history books? August 1982.

The workload on the 737 was now pretty steady and we added some extra charter flights for Airtours and I would again find myself at Gatwick on a Saturday night taking a bunch of English party animals to Palma, Majorca and bringing back a bunch of burnt-out ones. We would depart Gatwick at maybe 10 pm and not get back home until 8 am the next day. It was not really my scene but these trips happened with little notice due to an aircraft of Airtours going unserviceable at the last moment and so invariably these trips were paid overtime and were financially worth the pain.

The chairman of BA at the time was Lord King who was dubbed 'Maggie Thatcher's favourite businessman'. He had arrived in 1981, soon followed by Sir Colin Marshall and these two formed a formidable team. The government of the day felt that BA would be an excellent company to de-nationalise and so King and Marshall were put there to prepare the way for BA to go private. The time-scale was not too important but what BA needed was a total re-organisation in view of the privatisation plans. Being a nationalised company the finances were based around a bottomless pit of some government department so there were managers and sub-managers and staff numbers were up to over 55,000 people to run about 120 aircraft which equates to over 400 staff per aircraft. Every overseas station had it full complement of managers and secretaries and so on. At the time the big American airlines were running with barely 200 staff per aircraft so there was a lot to be done. A redundancy package was put together for certain sections within BA including engineering which was, at the time, a large consumer of funds. The Flight Crew were pretty well established but even the older pilots amongst us got the offer. It was very generous and well oversubscribed within BA so very soon the numbers fell to more manageable proportions. So, by the time late 1982 came, the world of BA was changing daily. The other thing that was needed was to get a workforce that felt motivated in their work. We had all had fallen into the trap that the operation was fine and if we kept the engines running longer than necessary then that was fine being ignorant of the cost involved. Sir Colin Marshall was the man to get that task done and instigated a series of pro-active presentations starting with the one entitled 'To be the best'. Being cynical people we were at a loss as to why the company would spend a tiny fortune to try to educate us. I might add that Pilots are amongst the most cynical group of people based on the theory that:

'Why try to fix something that seems to be running OK?'

So, on a wet October morning I made why way to the BA Concorde Centre and joined about 200 other BA employees to attend the 'To be the best' forum. It all started with us being issued with name badges so that we could advertise who we were. OK, I went along with that. We then all assembled in the main hall and sat in our assigned seats on tables of about eight of us. My companions for the day came from all sorts of areas within BA. The introductions were done by all reading each other's name badge. There then followed a series of presentations by a company based in Denmark contracted to BA. I have to say that after the first 20 minutes or so I was struggling to keep awake but as the morning went on it became quite interesting. One of the topics was the science of body language and I was not aware of what a science it was. For example, if you are at an interview and you lean forward with your arms going forward as well this is interpreted as aggression. Likewise, if you lie back in your chair it infers a total lack of interest and over-confidence. So what was I doing to start with? Yes you guessed it: I was sprawled against the back of the chair with my arms folded. The interaction between the presenters and the audience was quite startling since at one point he asked us to survey the people on our assigned tables and low and behold most of us were slumped back in our chairs and suddenly, as one, we all sat bolt upright so as not to be the one caught out. As lunchtime came it seemed that the presenters had us all quite mesmerised with their outpourings. Lunch was good as well as being free! I have not referred to my waistline lately since it seemed to have reached a sort of plateau being not too large and not too small. You might say 'in-between' if you know what I mean!

The afternoon session was along similar lines but we were compelled to work as a team solving some nebulous problem. Of course, we had to have a spokesperson and since I did the cabin address to passengers I was chosen. What they did not understand was that I never saw my audience and always had my back to them. When it was our turn to present our findings there I was on stage facing the multitude. It was a bit daunting but I had the solution. I simply turned my back on the audience and explained that since I never see the people I talk to from the Flight deck I might survive better this way. I must have hit a chord since a few jeers and cheers erupted and so I turned around and then found my confidence and could not stop talking for the allocated time. Perhaps I missed my vocation! Anyway at about 4 pm Sir Colin Marshall arrived and made a speech. I have heard a few top people talk but he was quite excellent. He never used a cue card and there was not a single 'Um' or 'Ah' in his speech. He really did impress all of us. I refer to him as 'Sir Colin' when, in fact, in those days he was just plain 'Colin' since he was not knighted at that time. On the drive home I reflected on the day and to my surprise I confess that I enjoyed it, especially the 'body language' bit.

I will try this out on Moya when I get home and maybe I might understand women more, I thought to myself.

The occasion arose when I spotted Moya doing a pose that I had been told about on the day. I told her of my interpretation of the event and lasted about two more minutes and then I got shot down in flames. So much for the body language theory! Doesn't work in this house, I concluded and that was that.

Lost again!

In the October Helmut Kohl was elected as the new German Chancellor and so the third member of the big four had been slotted into place. You might wonder where all this is leading up to but wait for it! October drifted into November and with Paul celebrating his second birthday and time seemed to be flying by – and would you believe that in the same month Michael Jackson turned the musical world on its back with the 'Thriller' album complete with an incredible video. The world of music presentation changed at that moment forever. Moya's birthday was at the end of November and that tended to mark the beginning of the Xmas social scene which by now was centred round Binfield. I had some leave over Xmas which stretched from the middle of December until early January. And so 1982 ended within another interesting year done and dusted.

1983 arrived and with it came the news that the 737 had achieved a milestone within BA such that it was now certified to land in the lowest visibility conditions of any airline. It might seem unimportant to anyone but the crews, but what it meant was we could generally land anywhere within the network, provided that the airport was equipped correctly, with pretty well any sort of fog or low cloud. For the guys who were off the Trident this ability was old hat but to me it was a whole new ball game and enabled us to see off the competition and run a pretty good schedule in any weather. It was quite amazing to fly the approach with the autopilot doing all the work including an auto-throttle controlling the speed with amazing skill and be in cloud all the way down excepting for maybe the final ten seconds. Nowadays, all new aircraft have this facility built-in from day one and it is taken as read but in 1983 BA was the leader in this field and I was amongst it. The big problem was finding your way around the taxiways once you had landed or you were on your way out to the take-off point. There was something very satisfying about doing maybe four of these type of approaches in a day pretty well on schedule when most of the other airlines were diverting all over the place. The downside was crawling back down the M4 at the end of the day at about 10 mph along with all the other cars. In 1983 the first mobile phones hit the market but were still very expensive – would have been useful going home to Binfield in the fog whereby I could have ordered my dinner 'en route' and have a nice glass of wine waiting for me as I pulled in the drive.

How did we ever survive without the mobile phone or home PC in those days? I often asked myself the same question over and over again.

You know what! We did very nicely without them amazingly enough and seemed to run an orderly life based around the telephone and the post box. TV was one of the main sources of entertainment during the week. For Paul there was a good amount of programmes designed for his age group and it was like an oasis for Moya and me to plonk him in front of the screen for maybe 30 minutes so as to get some peace and a cup of coffee that did not ice up before you got to it. If I look back there were some really tacky programmes with constant streams of American rubbish where at least ten people were shot before the first advert appeared. Having said that, one of the favourites was 'M*A*S*H' that was based on a field hospital in South Korea during the Korean War. It had a cross section of characters that made it what it was but in the February is showed the last episode. Real shame! I always chuckle when I hear the expression:

'She has the lips just like hot-lips Houlihan'.

In the world of politics President Reagan was squaring off against the Russians with his proclamation that he would develop a 'Strategic Defence Initiative' to totally protect the USA from any aggressor irrespective of direction. The nickname for this became 'Star Wars' and amongst the plans was to forward base all sorts of bits of gadgetry right up the border of Russia. I think, looking back, that it was the absolute astronomical cost of Star Wars that scared the Russians into talking to the Americans about all things worldly. The beginning of the end of the world order as we knew it then was slowly being mapped out. Both Maggie Thatcher and Helmut Kohl put their weight behind the USA and so the virtual war of Europe began. This was in the March.

CHAPTER 10

– WELCOME TO BERLIN

Also in the March I did a trip that would change my flying world forever when I flew from Heathrow to Hanover and then onto Berlin, Germany for a night stop.

Let me pause to give you a potted history of airline activity in Berlin after 1945. This is not a history lesson but an explanation as to why Berlin was so special for the aviator. After the war Germany was split into regions amongst Britain, France, Russia and the USA with Russia getting the lion's share. East Germany was controlled by the Russians and become known as the German Democratic Republic (GDR). The remainder became West Germany under the control of Britain, France and the USA. Geographically, Berlin was about 120 miles inside East Germany and the city was itself divided up into four sectors, again with Russia controlling East Berlin. There were four airports in the Berlin area with each zone having its own. In the Russian East Berlin sector there was Schönefeld, which was a large sprawling airport to the south-east of Berlin. In the British sector to the south-west there was Gatow which was the main airport from 1945 until 1951. It remained after that time as an exclusive British military base or RAF Gatow. In the American sector of West Berlin to the south of the city there was Tempelhof which was the main West Berlin airport from 1951 to 1975. It was known as the 'City airport' since it was literally enclosed by apartment blocks and would give an interesting view to all on board during the final stages of the approach. In the French sector to the west and northwest there was the French airport of Tegel which came on line as the main West Berlin airport from 1975 onwards. So when I first arrived in Berlin Tegel was the main airport for West Berlin and Schönefeld was the main one for East Berlin with Tempelhof being a small subsidiary airport for the west. Tegel was very well equipped with two parallel runways running east to west with full precision approach aids which suited BA 737s for landing in foggy conditions. To actually land on the westerly runway involved flying over East Berlin but I will give you the full low-down on that later. To fly into Berlin which, as I said, was deep inside East Germany, the Russians had set up three distinctive routes or 'air corridors' in which we had to fly. If we strayed outside of these air corridors it was at our peril and within minutes you could be staring down the barrel of a MIG's guns. The air corridors, each of which was only 25 miles wide and compelled aircraft to fly at a maximum height of 10,000 feet, connected the three West Berlin airports of Tempelhof, Tegel and Gatow with other airfields/ airports in the following directions:

- Northern air corridor: to Hamburg, Bremen and Northern Europe.
- Centre air corridor: to Hanover, Düsseldorf, Cologne/Bonn and Western Europe.
- Southern air corridor: to Frankfurt, Stuttgart, Munich, Nuremburg and Southern Europe.

In June 1948 the Russians closed all surface links to Berlin that crossed its territory and Berlin became totally isolated, so the famous 'Berlin Airlift' started with all sort of aircraft streaming down the corridors to keep the Berlin people alive especially during the cold winter looming. There were even RAF flying boats landing on the Havel Lake near the city centre delivering coal. The airlift continued until May 1949 when the Russians opened the surface routes again. The effect of this gave Berlin the symbol of the Cold War and earned the city the expression of 'The last piece of Western decadence in the East'.

The one amazing fact was that Lufthansa, or any other German airline, were prohibited to operate into or out of Berlin. It was left to the British, American and French airlines to do the job on behalf of the fledgling German government. The French did not seem to be interested in operating any flights using Air France but kept up a military presence using Tegel as its base. For the Americans, Panam was the designated airline using Tempelhof, which also doubled as their military base. The forerunner of British Airways, BEA, operated a variety of old aircraft into and out of Berlin after the war based at their military airfield at Gatow and then, with the move to Tempelhof in 1951, they acquired a fleet of Vickers Viscounts and ran them very successfully until Panam introduced the Boeing 727-100 and went all-jet. BEA responded with an upgraded cabin and used the De Havilland Comet 4B on some routes which proved very uneconomical. They eventually went all-jet with the BAC Super 1-11 which was ideally suited for the short hops around Germany. In 1961 the Russians really complicated everything by building a wall to literally divide the city. In some parts a road would be dissected crossways. This act alone added an air of tension within the world powers. The Internal German Services (IGS) became the lifeline to the city. Eventually, BEA and Panam settled for a destination split which made sense at the time. BEA ended up serving most of the Central and Northern German airports whereas Panam the Central and Southern airports. In 1975 all operations moved to Tegel and in 1983 it was decided by BA that the 737 would replace the BAC 1-11 on the IGS. At one time more profit was made on the IGS than the whole of the European network so to put a higher capacity aircraft into Berlin seemed good logic. Besides, we were much quieter. This is where I came into the scene arriving in Tegel that March.

"Welcome to Berlin, Captain," were the words that greeted me when I walked into operations.

At that time there was still some of the BAC 1-11s still flying the IGS. If I thought there was a rivalry between the VC-10 and the 707 I had not seen anything yet. This was war! These 1-11 guys had been flying in Germany since Pontius was a pilot and suddenly this bunch of 737 pilots arrived to take their crown. Of course it was a red rag to a bull but we gave as good as we got. When the opposition found out that I was ex-Long haul the battle really hotted up. It never got to fisticuffs but it was a bit of a game at the time. What actually happened in the end is that most of the 1-11 pilots converted to the 737 and got their crown back.

The approach and landing to Tegel when using the westerly runway was very interesting since the airport was about three miles west of the Berlin wall. You only flew on the south side of Tegel and started

the downwind leg over RAF Gatow and then heading east along
the Bismacker Street or Straße heading directly towards the huge
television tower on Alexander Platz in the east of the city. It was
actually a huge listening post for the East Berlin authorities. It was
locally know to the pilots as the 'onion'. The track towards it was helped
by a large square building with a sharp distinctive outline that became
known as the 'goal post'. As you neared the 'onion' and flying over East
Berlin you then did a sharp left turn and picked up the Berlin wall
descending all of the time. You then followed the wall until you spotted
a house that had a distinctive blue roof. You then turned to the left
again and hey presto! There were the two parallel westerly runways
dead ahead. You aimed to cross the house at 1,000ft with everything
hanging down and out and just shifted left or right for your designated
arrival runway. The beauty of all of this was that you could do visual
circuits every time, weather permitting, and thus save a lot of time
and fuel. It became an art to arrive and depart dead on schedule. You
could actually use the visual approach even when the weather was not
so good. There were very few places in Europe at the time that allowed
these visual approaches and so you became quite proficient in doing
them. With generally only BA and Panam in the circuit flying became
real fun with friendly rivalry to the fore. As I said the BAC 1-11 had the
reputation of being a noisy beast and that was one of the main reasons
for the 737 replacing it but the version that we flew was itself pretty
noisy.

As for accommodation, we were put in the Intercontinental Hotel
which was pretty well in the centre of the action with plenty of good
restaurants and bars in the area plus an abundance of shady clubs.
On the flying side BA had about eight 737s based in Berlin and a
pretty hectic route network to go with it. At that time we operated
to Munich, Düsseldorf, Cologne, Hanover, Stuttgart and Bremen. The
flights to these destinations usually operated hourly during the day
so as to accommodate the ever flowing amount of businessmen who
would do their work in Berlin from around Germany. As far as our
rosters within the IGS were concerned the crew were generally split
between the early starts or the 'early crew' as they were known as, or
the afternoon shift or 'late crew'. You invariably did up to four sectors

per shift and so the early crew would finish about lunchtime and the late crew would get back in the late evening. Whether you were the late or early crew had its advantages socially since the early lot could meet up in the evening at a normal time and get stuck in until the time restraints dictated bedtime. The late crew lot would high-tail it back to the hotel and do a thirty-second change of kit and out on the town until the early hours with a lie-in to look forward to. West Berlin, as it was then, was an amazingly social place with our regular haunts being invaded by us at some time in the evening hours. The hotel staff were used to our shenanigans and looked after us extremely well. They even gave us a 'party room' known as 1222 which became the meeting place for anyone who was in town on a night stop and the appointed hour was 7 pm precisely. From there the latest gossip would be digested and opinions made followed by a heated discussion as to where to eat. Once the eating was done and dusted then the refugees left over would drift over to, maybe, 'Georges Bar' which was right next to a small shopping arcade known as the Europa centre. Other bars that were popular included the Irish bars in the area plus many other equally shady joints. If you look in the cold light of day you might think 'What a waste of time just eating and drinking' but Berlin was what it was in that respect. Something to do with the location within East Germany methinks! The guys on the 737 were top class and lots of fun. The old days of the Captain being god almighty were definitely over. You worked as a team in the Flight Deck and then socialised as a team. Perfect!

So, Berlin became a firm favourite of mine from my first arrival and totally altered my bidding pattern. In addition to the schedules on the IGS there was a rather relaxed trip where you flew out to Berlin and sat around for five days on a sort of standby to cover any cock-ups that occurred to the normal schedule. Absolute piece of doddle it was. In the hotel there was a large indoor swimming pool so many days were spent lounging around the pool when the weather was not too good waiting for a phone call. I would bid as often as I could to get to Berlin. The 737 route network was really starting to get a buzz to it with even Istanbul and Ankara, Turkey on the agenda.

In the April once again the Middle East roused its ugly head with the bombing of the American Embassy in Beirut, Lebanon leaving 63 people dead. This galvanised the Americans into entering the affray in Lebanon following the invasion by the Israelis from the south. The Americans went in big time with a carrier off the coast and hundreds of Marines landing on the beaches. It transpired that the invasion of Lebanon by the Americans supported by the Israelis was a pretty disastrous affair as time would show.

It was also in April that Moya announced that No.2 was on the way. St Valentine's Day has a lot to answer for. So there we have it with the second one due in the November. I was hoping for a girl.

Easy! I thought to myself. Well, read on folks.

The spring turned into summer and with my position on the infamous seniority list getting better by the day, I became a regular visitor to Berlin. I took advantage of some free time there to explore the city. The excursion coaches were an ideal way of seeing all the sights of West Berlin and I found the history of the city most fascinating. I even stood on the famous Glienicke Bridge in the south of the city where all the spies were exchanged. It was the only point where the west could face the east directly and it became known as the 'Bridge of the Spies'. I also did a tour into East Berlin complete with passport and found the contrast quite something. Everywhere was drab and, seemingly unwashed or uncared for, but on the other hand, the cemetery holding some two million Russian soldiers was very moving. We entered East Berlin near the spot where Hitler's bunker was situated but was now right in the middle of 'no man's land' with the wall towering over the scene. We exited via the famous 'Checkpoint Charlie' manned by the Americans in full battle order, such was the distrust by the various authorities. There was also a Russian cemetery in West Berlin just to the west of the wall in the British sector by the famous Brandenburg Gate. It was quite amusing to see the Russian military guard marching through the gate with the equivalent British guard escorting them to their cemetery and ending up with the Russians marching clockwise and the British marching anti-clockwise around the cemetery watching each other for any false moves. The British Military had a strong presence in the city with the RAF established at Gatow and the British Army based a short distance south of Gatow at the 'Montgomery Barracks' which, amazingly enough, was just across from an East German Russian barracks with about five metres separating them. In Spandau, to the west of the city, there was a large British Army barracks based in the old Spandau prison which housed all of the old ex-Nazi members convicted to do a prison term after the famous 'Nuremburg Trials'. When I arrived there was only one left in there: Rudolph Hess, who was Hitler's deputy, guarded by a large number of British Army personnel. It was amazing to see the remnants of modern history for real. I happened to be in Berlin on the 17th June that year and was fussing around my room when I heard the sounds of heavy vehicles outside and when I looked out of my window I was staggered to see a military procession moving along the road. It involved all the three main military factions based in West Berlin and included a large number of tanks, armoured cars etc. There were also great blocks of soldiers marching along plus, of course, the famous band of the Royal Marines who looked splendid as they always did. I made my way down to the street to get a better view and picked up a leaflet as to the reason for the parade. On 17th June 1953 the East German people rose up against their Russian bosses demanding democracy amongst other things. The Russians and the East German authorities responded with tanks and large numbers of Russian troops who totally and brutally crushed the rebellion leaving many dead in its wake. As the day that I watched the parade moved into the evening there was the sound of heavy gunfire which was a bit alarming. It was explained to me that the tanks in the parade had all assembled at the wall and fired blanks so that the East German people knew that they had friends in the west. The day was known as the 'Day of German Unity' and, once again, I was witnessing history as it was unfolding. They even renamed a Straße after that infamous day.

A further word about the set-up in Berlin and how the IGS worked. As I said before BA had, on average, about eight 737s based in Berlin to do the work. We had a fully operational hangar to complete maintenance issues so that a lot of what they called 'inter checks' could be done on site. Amazingly enough, the catering side was done by Lufthansa. Strange to see their logo plastered all over the catering trucks. There was also a large contingent of local Berlin Cabin Crew which I believe numbered over 200. The majority of these were stewardesses and they all seemed to like our English quirky sense of humour so there was a lot of fun to be had with them in Berlin and on the IGS. There was Ingrid, Gabi, Manuela, Heidi, Christa, Christina, Andrea, Annette, Babsi, Monika, Ramona, Amanda and Silke to name but a few. There was also a small bunch of Stewards who were great lads. There was Ian, Albert, Martin, Peter and Stuart amongst this group of lads. All in all they were a very good bunch of people. As for the social side therein lies another tale. At that particular time I was really chuffed that I had found a girl like Moya and to stray 'outside of my contract' was not now in my make-up.

Wow, what a change of character I am, considering my past escapades! I thought to myself.

I was quoted once about the social pitfalls of Berlin by the saying:

"Don't do it, laddie! You will end up painting the ceiling you enjoy looking at."

Not sure that I fully understood it at the time until one of our pilots who frequented the company of one of the 'Berlin Girls' said casually in the crew bus one day:

"Sorry Gwyn, I can't come out to play tonight. I am doing a paint job on my friend's apartment tonight as I promised her."

"Gordon Bennett! I do the painting at home and that nearly kills me so to do it when I am away is sheer suicide," I chuckled to myself.

On some occasions we would be on our way to the hotel from the airport with maybe six of us on board when quite often a detour would be made to drop one of the philanderers off at some apartment block. He would jump out, complete with suitcase, briefcase and maybe a pot of paint and disappear into thin air. By the time I got to the hotel I was, maybe, the only one left in it with a very patient driver mumbling some choice German words under his breath. The reverse might happen in the morning when maybe only a couple of us would get on board, and then we would meander around the streets and back alleys picking up the refugees. What a complicated life these two-timers must have led.

In addition to the cabin crew there were the Operations people who kept the show running against all odds. They were led by Mel Sawnden and included Joachim, Jack, Martin, Steve, Rainer and Helmut who made up the team. The most important person was, of course, the one who dished out the allowances. I cannot pass this point without referring to 'Mini' as she became known to us with affection. I would stand there and watch her patiently counting out the money for me to cover, maybe, five days in Berlin. She felt like it was her own personal money and seemed to begrudge this sordid act as I swept up the ill-gotten gains, stuffed it in my pocket casually and strolled out of the door to the waiting transport. There was a small deduction taken for every day that you were in Germany flying out of Berlin which went into the 'Pilots' Fund' but more about that later. I can actually understand 'Mini' and her reluctance on the money issue since the allowance that I collected could well have equated to a large percentage of her monthly 'take-home' pay.

I am sure that I have missed out a lot of people who contributed to the safe running of the IGS since I have only scratched the surface. As I said, I did not fall into the trap of establishing a second family for want of a better name, so my social life in Berlin was based around the other pilots who were in town at the time. Made life simple!

In parallel to the Berlin scene I was still doing night stops around the rest of Europe and all in all I was out of my home bed maybe 20 days a month. Not bad if I compared it with the old long haul days.

In the July the family went off to Majorca again for another lovely two weeks in the sun. Always on the first evening out we would sit at 'San Francisco 2' and light up a local weed or 'Ducados' cigarette and drink a local cocktail called 'Cuarenta Y Tres' or '43' for short.

"Spain, we have arrived," I would announce whilst pouring another one.

In the news the Space Shuttle was becoming old news with each trip successfully completed but in the June you would never have guessed it but a woman by the name of Sally Ride was amongst the crew of 'Challenger'. Whatever next – Lady Pilots! In the July a Japanese computer company launched the 'Nintendo' computer game and all kids everywhere hung up their brains. There was a very bad helicopter crash just off the south-west coast of Cornwall whereby a commercial S-61 just seemed to hit the sea whilst descending off the Scilly's coast. Twenty people died as a result and the final conclusion reached was that the sea was so calm that it became indistinguishable from the sky. Strange but true!

Back in Binfield the scene was being organised for the arrival in the November of No.2 child with a complete make-over of the house and allocation of rooms. On our many visits to see Moya's mum and dad it became obvious that Mary was suffering from memory loss more and more. Paddy was slowly recovering from his various health problems and so the visits were often tinged with a lot of sadness since his retirement had not quite worked out as he had planned. Paddy had spent his working life as a salesman in a local hardware store called 'Pipers' and instead of getting a well-deserved Xmas bonus each year he would ask the owner to put the money aside for his retirement. On top of his health problems and poor Mary the shop went bankrupt so Paddy lost all of his retirement nest egg. Bloody shame!

Back in the flying world I was now in my third year on the 737 and, by now, a well-established member of the Short-Haul fraternity. Berlin featured most days in the monthly cycle of trips. It came to the point that I knew the city of Berlin better than my own capital city, London. Just to refer back to the nightly contribution to the Pilots' fund I met up with another Captain, Joe Hall, on one of my IGS night stops and we formed a friendship that has stood the test of time to the present day. He made the suggestion that we both combined our brains and run the Pilots' fund since the original people had long departed.

"Let's go for it!" I responded.

So, Joe and I approached Mel Sawnden and we set in motion the running of the fund. We were pleasantly surprised to find that the account had a large amount of 'dosh' in it so we set about trying to organise things better for the 'workers'. For example, we had two Opel Cadet cars at the hotel that were available for crews to get about in. Joe and I set about getting them serviced and tidied up. What was good about these cars was that they had British Military number plates and so enjoyed all the trappings that came with it. One advantage, for example, was that we could virtually park anywhere we wanted without fear of being towed away. I wrote a small write-up about all the facilities we had in Berlin entitled 'The Hitch-hikers Guide to the Berlin Galaxy' and that went down well with newcomers. Over the years the

Pilots had held an annual 'Pilots' Party' and so Joe and I decided that the time was right to revive that tradition. We looked around for a venue and decided on the British Officers' Club in the city. It was a wonderful establishment designed, as the name implies, for the officers of all the British military establishments in Berlin to relax in. What we did was to agree on a date between ourselves but not to release it until all trip bidding had been completed. This way it was just pot luck if you were around on the night. Joe and I would be there always since we had organised it. Perks of the job! We invited all the German staff irrespective of their role in the company and base, Panam pilots, The British Army and Royal Air Force officers in Berlin and the Air Traffic Controllers. We would all dress up for the night in our dinner suits complete with bow-ties. The Berlin girls all came along and really pushed the boat out to look good. There were some real stunners out there. We had a buffet and drinks laid on plus, of course, music to suit all tastes. Those evenings were brilliant and the subsequent hangovers were well deserved. Wonderful memories! In addition to the party scene we had bikes, tennis racquets, golf clubs and even German lessons organised. Joe and I worked well together to try to get it right. I think we did all right!

In September an air tragedy occurred when a Korean Airlines (KAL) 747 was shot down by the Russians north of Japan being mistaken for a US Air force military reconnaissance aircraft. The plane was in a very remote area disputed by the Japanese and the Russians. It was established after the event that the KAL 747 had, in fact, made a navigational error that put him in the middle of the disputed area. Absolute tragedy it was. The Americans and the Russians, being the main players, were still embroiled in the cold war and spent a lot of the time testing each other's defences and this sort of accident was tragic but inevitable. I am amazed looking back that there was no third world war. For example, in the same month there was a computer glitch at the Russian end whereby they thought that they were being attacked by the Americans and the glitch was only discovered at the very last minute.

So, as the summer slowly started to come to an end Moya began the final countdown toward the November arrival. Moya did suffer badly this time around with the affliction again whereby she could not stop scratching her feet to the point of even drawing blood. It made conversation a bit tricky when every other minute Moya would be bent double ripping her feet apart. I did feel very sorry for her but there was nothing either of us could do about it except to keep on scratching. And don't forget the beetroot and jam sandwiches in the middle of the night! Life was busy!

As for the flying it was very much routine with about 16 or 17 days in Berlin plus about five other night stops around Europe. The 737 version that we flew was an excellent aircraft as far as flexibility was concerned being very happy operationally on a 40 minute flight from Berlin to Hanover or a four hour flight from Heathrow to Moscow. As Flight Crew we became very skilful in eating whilst flying. Imagine the famous Berlin to Hanover sector leaving at about 6 am with a breakfast service to complete for maybe 100 passengers plus, of course, us two up front. It was the highlight of the day for a couple of starving hungry pilots who had struggled up at some dreadful hour. This is where the Berlin Cabin Crew came into their own. If we took off towards the west and landed in the same direction in Hanover then the airborne time could be as little as 35 minutes. How they did it was one of the Seven Wonders of the World! We would get a tray complete with a hot bit after about 15 minutes and with about five minutes to landing the tray would be whipped away together with the 'Cabin Secure' call. Work of art! We could then survive just about until lunchtime. The thing was that I never actually put on any weight whilst on the 737 which was amazing since I indulged on every meal and was very social when the need arose. I did, however, play plenty of golf and also did a lot of walking, mainly in Berlin.

The other joy about the European scene was that we knew all the good places to go for a meal or have fun at most of the night stops places. For example the fleet did revert to a simple night stop in Turin and some of us would assemble in double quick time after arrival and nip round the back of the hotel to a scruffy looking joint that had the most wonderful Italian food together with an old Italian 'Mamma' who seemed to treat us like royalty. None of us spoke Italian but she would give us a great gestured welcome and before we sat down the red wine would be on the table. Maybe she liked the colour of our money! In Munich there was another ritual which unfolded every time we stayed overnight. We would make our way in double quick time again to the local square and arrive at this particular establishment. The waitress there was of Russian origin called 'Sonya' and she would march us to our designated table and if someone was occupying it she would move them on. We would sit down and study the menu and make our choice. We would then call Sonya over and she would take over the menu and we would eat what she decided. It was the same with the drinks but, what the heck, we ate and drank her choice and it was usually bloody good. Her husband was Italian and worked as a test pilot for the Italian military so obviously she knew that maybe we could fly an aircraft, but anything else needed her guidance.

Once again, in the October the Middle East blew up when 305 US and French Marines were killed by a suicide bomber in Beirut. Total carnage! It seemed that on the world stage these acts of terrorism were getting more and more spectacular and it was only a matter of time before these spectaculars would spread to the air. In one of our many forums held within BA the 'on-board martyr' syndrome was coming more and more to the fore. Under the heading of 'Security' a human mushroom developed and it became an industry all of its own. Suddenly we were all issued with the infamous 'Identification Badge' (ID) and were required to have it on display at all times. If not shown, it could be 30 years hard labour without parole. Security guards sprung up everywhere and took great delight in confronting a Flight Crew over some minor infringement. The fact of the matter is that if a 'baddie' wanted to do his business there was nothing on this planet that could stop him. The other annoying thing that also started was a 'Health and Safety' phenomena that became paranoid about anything and everything. For example, if we ever ventured onto the tarmac in the ramp area then we were supposed to wear a yellow coloured waistcoat that made us very visible to all. I cannot seem to remember any accident or incident on the tarmac up to that time solely due to being invisible by one and all. I can compare it to being sent an email recently showing how we got away with murder when growing up and now it was thanks to all the modern restrictions that we should be thankful to have survived those times. My personal opinion on all of these so called life-threatening safeguards in the industry today is unprintable. Unfortunately you become hardened to this new way of life and just 'went with the flow'.

November arrived and so did Jennifer Mary Mullett in the Heatherwood Maternity Ward, Ascot at about 10 pm on the 12th November. This time Moya's labour was not so long and in the Maternity Suite she was the only one at it so all the staff gathered around her bed and we all pulled and pushed together. Jenny was a bit of a whopper turning in at about eight pounds or so. This time I did not have too far to travel home as opposed to Paul's arrival. Within about three days Moya and Jenny came home so once again we were all united under one roof and Paul seemed to like the idea of a sister. Well, that was then! Anyway in my mind the family was now complete with one of each. My troubles were only just beginning. Read on!

At the time it must have seemed a quite relaxing affair since I went back to work within a couple of days. Had to be a Moscow 'away day' though!

Back home, however, within a few days things changed. There are babies and there is Jenny! First thing was that she refused milk, screamed her lungs out non-stop and made Paul's initial upbringing seem like a walk in the park. Have you ever known a baby not like milk? So, the task was set in motion as to how to handle the scene. Various opinions were sought and all came to the conclusion that life was going to be fun with Jenny as she developed. Even Paddy, Moya's dad, was at a loss. Having said that, he did have a wonderful knack of lulling both Paul and Jenny off to sleep with a lovely Irish tune that even I found quite mesmerising. So the remainder of the year was a bit of a workout with Jenny and not forgetting Paul who was by now exerting his character on the world at the grand age of three.

There were not too many dramas in the world worthy of note and so 1983 closed on a quiet note with the exception of the Mullett household. Within the neighbourhood there seemed to be a routine of questions asked on a daily basis like:

"How's Jenny today?"

"How's it going?"

"Any good news yet about Jenny?"

1984 arrived with the thoughts of George Orwell's book 'Nineteen Eighty-Four' which depicted that we would all be ruled by an authoritarian master with words like 'Big Brother' is watching you. I feel that he was about 20 years too soon in his predictions. The world of gadgetry was arriving fast with the launch of the 'Apple Mac' computer that seemed to revolutionise the home PC scene. Mobile phones were coming down in price and even I, not wanting to be left behind, began to think seriously about these new-fangled things.

As for my flying I was moving up the famous list quite fast and spent most of the month in Berlin. The powers that be there decided to open up the Berlin route structure and we now had Frankfurt as a new destination. The other new route was to Munster, Osnabruck using an 'Avro 748' aircraft that up to this point had been the domain of the Scottish 'Highlands and Islands' network. This aircraft had about 50 seats and in its day was a great workhorse of British heritage but by the time it arrived in Berlin it was getting a bit long in the tooth. The Flight Crews were all very young and enthusiastic and added a new dimension to our life in Berlin. The only downside was that it had a habit of breaking down quite often and so the five-day standby that was considered up to this point a very leisurely affair took on new meaning. The Pilots' Fund had bought four telephone bleepers to make life even more relaxing for the standby crews but they were forever sounding off once the '748' arrived.

"Sorry to bother you, Gwyn, but one of the 748 aircraft has broken down and we would like to fly within the hour to Bremen, Munster, Hanover and back to Berlin to collect the stranded passengers. Have a great day!" was a common call.

Just what I needed since I was just planning the evening's festivities.

Within BA things were changing fast with the Trident fleet slowly running down and being replaced by the Boeing 757 aircraft. The last Concorde had been delivered and a deal was struck with the government so that the aircraft could actually start to make a profit. Miami was added to the Washington service three times a week and a small travel company, Goodwood Travel, found a niche in the market by selling charters on the Concorde like an afternoon trip around the

Bay of Biscay for an exorbitant fee. One of the strangest retirements occurred when the last 707 went to the knackers' yard in the January. It had outlived the VC-10 which I find hard to believe. What had happened was that seven of them had been sold to the charter arm, British Airtours, some years before and had soldiered on until now. Amazing!

The other thing that occurred was that the 'To be the best' forum that I spoke about earlier was deemed a wonderful success and it spurred the company on to organise more forums so off I would go to the Concorde Centre for another nail-biting session. The original concept worked well with an outside company providing the presenters, etc, but BA recruited within the company to continue the theme and, in my opinion, this move rather degraded the idea. The in-house presenters were all very good and I give them total respect but I found these new forums a total waste of time. I spent most of the time struggling to keep awake. I think this was the general feeling that I found amongst a lot of people.

Back in Binfield the house that we were in was becoming a bit cramped for the four of us so we moved into No.41 Emmets Park, Binfield. It was expensive at the time to buy but we got a good price for our present house and I felt that we could afford it. I will let you know that me and money never saw eye to eye and as time goes on it will raise its ugly head again.

In February came the news from the Middle East that the Americans had pulled out of the Lebanon and that the Israelis had withdrawn southwards to end a disastrous campaign for both parties after some two years. In the March the miners under the leadership, as I said before, of Arthur Scargill, went on strike again. This time they were up against Maggie Thatcher, our Prime Minister, and so the battle of the workers v the bosses started. It was a very grubby affair with family pitted against family in the coal fields of Northern England with a constant stream of police intervention. Depending on your politics you formed your own opinion as to the what, why and when questions. It actually lasted a year with the apparent victor being Maggie but it created total turmoil in the mining communities which to this day still exists. The knock-on effect was to curb other unions from action and, in the end, legislation was put into place to streamline industrial action. In my opinion I feel that unions are needed in every profession, but what are not needed are the far-left politically motivated groups of workers that had brought many great companies to their knees. Now, I am off my soapbox and back into the land of the living and Jenny!

On April 1st BA became British Airways PLC. Nothing really significant but it marked the step towards making BA a total private company and not dependent on the government for any major financial decisions and put us, as employees, in the limelight as far as performance was concerned. The process was being overseen by Lord King and Sir Colin Marshall whom, as I said before, were proving to be a formidable pair. The 737 version that we flew was starting to be a bit outdated and noisy. The environmental lobby was getting very restless when it came to the question of airport noise. The UK was rapidly following Europe in this field and BA took it upon themselves to order a new fleet of 737s which were very noise compliant and known as the 737-400. There was to be a time lapse of some two years before the first one would arrive so the present version plodded on regardless. In Berlin where the noise lobby was very strong BA leased four of the new quieter versions, the 737-300, from Maersk, an airline based in Denmark, exclusively for the IGS operation. The 737-300 was a slightly smaller version of the 737-400 that BA had ordered. Apart from the newer, quieter engines the systems were now upgraded to a new concept of having all the flight instruments displayed on a single large cathode ray tube (CRT) in front of the pilot instead of the older 'steam driven' instrument array. If I could describe the new flight deck displays as simply having in front of you two CRT displays, one above the other. The upper display would have the old type of flight instruments electronically displayed so that anything that the aircraft did in the vertical axis like attitude, height, speed and climb rate would be shown electronically. On the lower display would be shown anything done in the horizontal axis like direction, route and turn rate. The main source was a fancy unit located in the equipment hold that was based on the old inertial system that I had used on the 747 and Super VC-10 but with many additives that would feed directly to the displays on the Flight Deck. We even had readout to show how fast we were taxiing. The other additive to the lower display was to show the various points that we were going to or coming from and the track between the two as a magenta line. Everything that you had to chew over in your brain was there. No longer did we have to mentally work out the distance to go to the runway or how far off track we were since it was all shown in front of us on the screens. So, in summary, each pilot had these two displays in front of him and the expression of 'Follow the magenta line' became folk law. The engines were made by General Electric as opposed to Pratt and Witney and they had a different way of operating whereby the end result was the same but how you got there was totally different. BA proposed that both versions plus, in fact, the new fleet on the horizon, could all be flown by any of us using the single 737 licence that we had once we had qualified to fly the new type. It sounded a bit excessive but we agreed since it offered a tremendous flexibility for the company. Blimey, we moaned about the Standard and Super VC-10 differences! Times were changing fast. The only problem about the 737-300 recently acquired for the Berlin scene was that you had to do a three-day qualification course at Gatwick to actually fly them. The spectre of seniority came into play at this point and with still quite a few people above me on the famous list all anxious not to lose out on the Berlin scene they steamed in and got sorted out pretty soon, leaving me to consider Berlin temporarily a lost cause. On the very odd occasion I would get to Berlin, since with only four of these quieter models on the books, some services were flown by the older version. I had to wait my turn and it was as simple as that!

Back in Binfield, Moya and I were just about coping with Jenny and found that the new house was very airy and spacious with a large garden. It was definitely a step-up from the old one. The neighbours were very nice and soon a social network was forming around us. There were also plenty of young children around so time could be spent commiserating about our woes over a few glasses of wine with the neighbours. It was on one occasion in the April when we were watching TV on a Sunday night and, in particular, my favourite comic, Tommy Cooper, when all of a sudden he collapsed on stage and we learned very soon after that he had in fact died of a massive heart attack. He was a British institution and his untimely death was very sad. It was also in that month that there was a demonstration in front of the Libyan embassy in the middle of London and a Policewoman, Yvonne Fletcher, was killed by a single shot fired from within the embassy. The amazing thing was that a few days later the embassy staff were escorted by the police to Heathrow and flown to Libya with no charges being brought. How did the government allow this crime to go unpunished? Such is the power of diplomacy.

In the June BA got the shock of its life when the entrepreneur Richard Branson formed his own airline and named it Virgin Atlantic Airways. He attacked the cosy arrangement that BA had at Heathrow and decided to set up shop in the very heartland of BA. Laker Airways had come and gone thanks to the ruthlessness of BA but it was based in Gatwick and was not a real threat to Heathrow which was still the prime London airport. So there was this young businessman who had built his fortune in the record industry arriving on our doorstep. I am sure the BA top brass at the time dismissed him as a 'fly-by-night' out of the same stable as Freddie Laker, but suddenly a small fleet of 747 aircraft started to arrive at Heathrow. The colour scheme was very modern being overall white with a red cheat line and a wonderful figure of a lady on the nose just underneath the Flight Deck. The Cabin Crew was equally bedecked in red and mainly blondes looking pretty stunning. He found favour with the regulators both in the UK and the USA and picked the routes that he knew would hurt BA the most, being the most profitable. JFK was top of his list, as you could imagine, and suddenly the 'Virgin Lady' was not only up and running but creaming off BA passengers with their new modern, stylish airline. There must have been a lot of coffee and polite coughing going on in the BA boardroom at the time. One result of Virgin was to galvanise the company to try to emulate the competition by seeking a new colour scheme and a company called Landor were called in to do just this. The Cabin Crew uniform also came into the treatment room and yet another new design hit the drawing boards. Flight Crew did not escape the revamp either with a new uniform being designed.

I might look pretty in pink! was one of my more cynical thoughts.

All these changes were destined to be completed by the end of the year so it was all systems go in the paint shops and sewing rooms.

Also, in July, the Civil Aviation Authority (CAA), in its wisdom, following a government publication, decreed that the airline British Caledonian Airways (BCAL) should get some routes from BA on a 'swap' basis. It was finally decided that BA could fly to South America instead of BCal and that they could fly to Saudi Arabia instead of BA. In the event it was a very good move for BA since the routes to Saudi Arabia were not as lucrative as they once were and South America was emerging from dictatorship rule to democracy and international travel was in great demand. Even Argentina had got rid of the old style dictators and the Falklands war with the UK was consigned to the history books. BCAL was one of the main operators out of Gatwick and started the routes to Saudi Arabia but soon hit a mental wall since the Saudis wanted to land at Heathrow and considered Gatwick a small country airport. BA leased in a couple of long-range Lockheed Tri-Stars from Air Lanka and started direct flights to Rio de Janeiro, Brazil and even stretched the aircraft to Buenos Aires, Argentina with onward flights to Sao Paulo, Brazil and Santiago, Chile. The world of BA was expanding fast.

Coming back to Binfield and babies, have you ever noticed that all parents that have a baby that is maybe under two, all have a lean to the left or to the right? This is derived from picking up their little charges and hanging them on the left or right hip and leaning the other way so as to balance out their centre of gravity. The reason why I mention that is I have been looking at parents whilst on the bus or in the street and they all have this leaning syndrome. Even when the little one is released the lean remains there for some time. Funny that! Moya and I certainly developed the 'lean' from carrying Jenny or Paul around.

"Why not put them in the pushchair and be done with it?" I hear you say.

Well, out of those tiny pair of lungs can issue a sound that could be heard 20 miles away and could wake the dead. Talk about 8.0 on the Richter scale. Cunning little buggers they are!

Back at work I did some flights, as I said before, for Airtours, and there were, again, the weekend Saturday night flights to Spain. We became quite skilful with various tricks that we would employ to avoid the lengthy Air traffic Control (ATC) delays that were now becoming commonplace within Europe in the summer. Spain was a particular pain when it came to ATC delays. It was not uncommon to have a two-hour delay for start-up on the return flight to Gatwick. The secret was to judge when the aircraft would be ready to go and try to anticipate asking for start clearance. It even occurred that when you knew the delay would be really long then one of us would use the other radio whilst we were in the early stages of the approach to landing and contact the ground frequency and ask for start-up assuming that we would have say, an hour and a half on the ground, to unload and load and leave pretty well on time. Our Spanish comrades in the tower soon cottoned on to this and would ask us where we were on the ground and so on and so on. Back to the drawing board!

On another occasion I was in Oporto, Portugal and we were faced with a good three-hour delay going back to Heathrow. We were, in fact, due to go on to Oslo, Norway that evening for a day off which was always very pleasant. My Co-pilot on the day was more interested in the fact that a lady friend of his was coming to Oslo with us for some fun and frolics and if we had sat in Oporto with the delay another crew would have done the Oslo bit and all would be lost for the poor old Co-pilot. So what we did was to visit the operations office in the airport and I worked out that if we flew to the Spanish northwest coast and then turned a bit to the left we could circumvent the French airspace, which was where the lengthy delay was, and gently fly north about 100 miles offshore but just outside the so-called Atlantic region where I felt we could be totally legal. It meant finally arriving in the UK airspace over Land's End in Cornwall. We had a new navigation system on the Flight Deck and so it was time to put it to the test. All very good in theory at the time! We got the clearance to go that way and so off we went on schedule with the Co-pilot grinning from ear to ear and expressing his utmost adoration as to my skill at negotiation. I think it was the Oslo bit that really got him going methinks! We got to the Spanish coast and off we went into the Atlantic wilderness following the directions shown on our new fancy bit of kit. After about 30 minutes the first calamity occurred when we ran out of any communications with our short range VHF radio. We had no long range HF radio on the 737 so we sat in silence looking out to sea for, maybe, 30 minutes, until I heard another BA aircraft and remembered it was the flight number of the mid-morning departure to JFK and so I called him and asked him to let someone in Europe know where I thought we were. There seemed to be fits of giggles from the other aircraft since they seemed to recognise my rather distinctive voice and proceeded to analyse me as to why I was out in the middle of the ocean on a 737 when I should be in the middle of Europe.

"That is one way of getting back to Long-Haul," was one of the comments.

"No problems, I am clear of the Atlantic region according to my navigational system so I am doing no wrong," was my rather meek reply.

After a while I felt it was time the beacon at Land's End should start to flicker into life. Nothing! Shades of Barbados and my infamous navigational nightmare started to drift into my mind. I did remember a very strong long range beacon in the Shannon area and it showed I was miles to the west of where I thought I was. So much for this fancy new piece of kit!

Must have been made by Lego, I thought as I turned the aircraft a full 60 degrees to head east to, hopefully, dry land.

We must have been flying for a good 20 minutes before the needle started to swing on the Land's End beacon and calm returned to the Flight Deck. I did a rough calculation in my head and reckoned that we must have been at least 100 miles on the wrong side of the Atlantic region boundary and possibly in a lot of trouble. The radar boys picked us up some 150 miles west of Land's End and made gentle inquires as to the fact we were some 25 minutes late according to them. I must've bluffed my way from then on in and finally arrived in Heathrow albeit 20 minutes late with the new shiny navigational system showing me somewhere over the Sahara in North Africa.

"Bloody useful that!" I muttered to the Co-pilot.

Not that he took any notice since he was in 'Oslo night stop mode'. Not a word was said about my adventure into the Atlantic and it was only a few weeks later when I was talking to a good friend of mine in ATC that he mentioned that a Military Airborne Surveillance aircraft was following me all the time thinking I was a Russian spy plane and that the RAF was only just stopped in time launching a fighter to have a look. When it was revealed that it was a BA aircraft a little bit off course it confirmed their theory that civilian pilots were a waste of space compared with the military ones. Shades of 'Upside down in Hunter' sprang to mind.

In August off we went as a foursome to Majorca again. Jenny was about seven or eight months old so it was the full team plus pushchair, a suitcase full of disposable nappies and various other items to ensure that Jenny would survive the ordeal. The loveliest bit was when Jenny would doze off in her pushchair and allow Moya and me to relax. But where was Paul? One day he went missing on the beach and Moya, me and the pushchair, complete with a sleeping Jenny on board, went walkabout in a sort of controlled panic. After about 30 minutes another holidaymaker pointed him out up in the pine trees with a Spanish family and, in particular, a boy of his own age. The language barrier did not seem to be relevant to these two. Life was full of dramas where kids are concerned!

Also in the August an American airline, People's Express, announced that they had a lady Captain on one of their 747 aircraft and she was the first one of her kind. What can I say! What's more BA had got in on the act as well and now we had a breed of lady co-pilots to contend with. Forgive my cynicism but, at the time, I felt that the world of flying belonged to the male species. It was on a Jersey night stop that I first encountered my first female Co-pilot. Her name was Julie and we met in the Crew Report Centre as normal. As I casually strolled into the Flight Planning area looking for a lively partner for the Saturday night in Jersey this bubbly mousey blonde trotted up to me and announced with a lovely smile that we were together for the night in Jersey. Well, I just fell apart and blustered my way through the paperwork trying to be cool. The problem was I kept dropping my pen and saying things that did not make sense.

"Captain, I used to work in Jersey and know some pretty wild night spots if you are interested since it is a Saturday night," Julie said with a certain calming in her voice.

"Right, you're on then," was my muttered reply.

I have to say that once we got on the aircraft she was bloody good at her job but she did make me nervous. I think my nerves shone through since, at one point, Julie leaned across and touched me on the knee and said that she had been looking forward to flying with me. No idea why! Anyway we made it to Jersey and boy oh boy was I impressed! I remember thinking to myself at the time that why should the female pilot be any different to a male one. In fact, in the cold light of day, they had to be bloody good since they were entering a man's domain and had to overcome all the masculine suspicions that must have lain in their path. We got to the hotel in the early afternoon and agreed to meet up in bar at about 7 pm. At the appointed hour I spruced myself up and went on parade in the bar. I was enjoying the first drink and must have forgotten, for an instant, that my playmate for the night was female. I was looking around the bar at the other drinkers when this cracking looking female comes in and gives me a melting smile and strolls up and orders a Gin and Tonic and sits next to me. Gobsmacked I was since I did not even recognise her straightaway! Total dirk or what! So once I had recovered my composure we had a drink and off we went on the town. What a great night it turned out to be. Julie was right since she did know all the hotspots in Jersey. We were not due to fly until the following afternoon so we struggled back to the hotel in the early hours. We finally got back to Heathrow on the Sunday evening and from that point on I was a reformed man with regards to female pilots and, in particular, Julie. There was nothing sinister about our relationship but you know how people gossip. I simply found flying with Julie great fun and we did quite a few trips together from that point on. Julie came from a family of four girls and her father was a Training Captain with Britannia Airways so she was bred into the airline world at a very early age. Enough of that!

As the summer drifted into the autumn came the news in the October that the IRA had planted a bomb in the Grand Hotel in Brighton that very nearly killed Maggie Thatcher and her cabinet. None of her Cabinet colleagues died as a result but five other people died that night. The IRA issued a statement the following day claiming that their target was the complete UK cabinet. It was singularly one of the worst outrages the IRA had committed to date and brought home the fact to us just how vulnerable we all were.

In the November a 737 was ushered in total secrecy into a hangar

and was unveiled some days later to the press resplendent in the
new 'Landor' inspired colour scheme. Gone was the white fuselage
top with the familiar blue cheat line, replaced by a rather scruffy
looking grey colour stretching all the way down below the window
line with a dull red cheat line and an effigy on the tail which was
supposed to represent a modern version of the union jack. To think
they paid money for this new colour scheme was beyond me. A bunch
of kids could have come up with something brighter than this. In the
meantime Virgin was becoming very established at Heathrow with its
bright red and white colours and looked so distinctive as opposed to
the rather drab BA garb. Could you imagine on a grey winter's morning
who would stand out more the most between us and them!

In the November an ex-rat packer called Bob Geldof took it upon
himself to highlight to the world the plight of many Ethiopians who
were suffering the worst drought ever experienced and one of his
ventures was to create a record with a host of pop singers taking part.
The song was:

'Do they know it's Christmas'.

It was a worldwide success and still is a classic song. In addition to
that he organised a concert at Wembley Stadium known as 'Live Aid'.
Bob Young, a very good friend of mine, went to it. One of the acts was
the famous group Queen with Freddie Mercury at the helm. When he
told me about the concert he remarked that, in general, the weather
was cloudy with rain and not good for an outdoor event but as Freddie
stepped out on stage the sky suddenly cleared and out came the sun
right on cue as if God had arrived. Freddie Mercury was, in my mind,
one of the most outstanding performers of the day and it was a terrible
shame that he succumbed to Aids in later life.

In November it was also Jenny's first birthday, Paul's fourth and at
the end of the month it was Moya's, so it was a pretty hectic round of
social events. I think the first year with Jenny was pretty heavy going
and it seemed a relief that the year was over. The only problem with
kids is that at each stage of life there are different problems to solve.
Paul was, by then, enrolled in a small church school up the road and
it was there that he mixed with other kids of his own age who had
different backgrounds and home life. The result was that he picked up

other ideas, good and bad, and brought them home with him to try to inflict them on Moya and me. I do have a certain amount of patience but, on occasions, it was tested to the full. Take a simple case of a birthday party to organise. In my day Mum would bake a cake and make plates of sandwiches.

"Egg mayonnaise please, Mum," used to be my statement on the day.

I would then invite my friends around for my birthday tea and we would all sit around eating and playing games with my poor demented mum topping up the food as we went along. The great ceremony of the day was the blowing out of the candles and then ensuring that everybody got a piece of the cake. It was all home produced whereby we made our own entertainment. With Paul and Jenny along came McDonald's, Burger King, Pizza Hut or Kentucky Fried Chicken to name but a few, who would organise the birthday do for whoever in exchange for a lump sum of money from the hapless parents. OK, so why did we not do a home-made special? I think, maybe, the kids felt more grown up going out or it was the easy option. My mistake on that one I am afraid. Who said that bringing up children would be easy!

Anyway, back to the flying world and in early December I was senior enough to do the three-day conversion course at Gatwick to get on board the 737-300 aircraft complete with its new fancy kit. So off I trot to Gatwick and got stuck into the new concept of instrumentation. It was totally different to what I was used to but after keeping my head down for those three days I emerged ready to get the route training done and get back to Berlin. Within a day or so I travelled out to Düsseldorf and joined up with a trainer and off we went to Berlin that evening with me grappling with this new technology all the way. I think I must have flown about five sectors in all before I was let loose on my own. So now I was back on the Berlin circuit and felt really good about it all. By the time all of the training had been done it was well into the Xmas period which, as usual, was spent at home with the family. So ended 1984 with the year marked by the trials and tribulations of having two 'ankle-biters' around Moya and me with very little time for one-to-one stuff between us.

So, in comes 1985 and in late January I reach the tender age of 39 with 19 years in BA, 10,000 flying hours, one failed marriage, two kids and altogether a really nice life. There seemed to be a little bit of tension creeping into my relationship with Moya but nothing I could put my finger on. Maybe it was me? Was I a normal male or an abnormal one in the department of relationships? I think if my emotional history had been written by an expert in relationships (probably a woman) it might be said that I was a typical husband and happy with my lot and oblivious to things happening around me in respect to the opposite sex. Don't forget women are from Venus, men are from Mars and this spaceship picked up a selection from each planet and dumped them in a pile on planet Earth expecting them to get on. I think that if I look back I should have spotted the early signs of any tension between Moya and me and attempted to do something about it at the time.

"What could I have done?" I asked myself looking back.

But then I look at the other side of the equation and there we were in a nice house, two workable kids and a pretty good social life. My flying world was at its peak with Berlin back on the circuit. I was not a wanderer and never played outside of marriage. Perhaps I assumed that these points made a marriage. Pilots are strange creatures whereby it was rare for a marriage to survive throughout a career of flying. Tony and Ian were the exception to this rule and have to be admired for it. As I said on many occasions I was at my happiest with my head in the clouds. Philosophical Gwyn talking here!

As for the winter of 1984/5 it was a pretty harsh affair throughout Europe and the flying side was a bit fraught with delays and diversions. Europe was pretty well up to speed in the de-icing world and kept the operation going as best it could. Dublin, being not known for really cold winter weather, actually got snow for the first time in many years and really struggled to cope. At the other end of Europe, Helsinki was quite excellent in the de-icing of aircraft. What they did was to have the de-icing area right next to the runway in use and as you taxied out you simply joined the queue to get 'done'. Each aircraft, as it emerged from the 'doing area' had a distinctive colour or dye added to the fluid so as to distinguish it from other aircraft. I remember seeing an Air France 737 emerging completely transformed into a purple apparition.

Berlin coped very well. You might have been doing the early shift and got fully involved in the 'first flight of the day' scene and get totally involved in the de-icing. Overnight the temperature could well have got down to -25°C so it was a major job getting the aircraft warm and fully ready to go by the time the first schedule was due out at maybe 6 am. Invariably the job was done with the usual German efficiency and you would then complete, maybe, four sectors all pretty well on schedule. It was rather strange flying around the network with a harmless lump of ice sitting on the nose just in front of the windscreen. In those days the galley water waste would vent overboard and on occasions would form a solid lump of ice on the fuselage skin. When the aircraft descended and the skin warmed up just before the landing this lump would fly off and land in some back garden or at worse, on the roof of some poor resident's house below. Not a safe place to live in the winter. This practice was curtailed within a few years since the odd lump would fly into an engine and it would then spit it out followed by the innards of the engine very shortly afterwards.

So there I was sitting in the aircraft at Heathrow enduring a two-hour delay with a full load of passengers all getting restless. The Co-pilot was Phill 'Rocky' Reynolds and we were enjoying a cup of tea when a stewardess from the aircraft next door, which was enduring a similar delay, came over and into the Flight Deck to say hello. It was Rocky's wife Lisa whom he had married some years before. It was the same Lisa I had met 13 years before in Mumbai when I was a young Co-pilot on the 747. She was only popping in to say hello to Rocky and when she saw me there was a mutual gulping exercise. I think Lisa seemed to have got the shock of her life since there was her husband and then there was me. Small world you might say! Lisa retreated gracefully leaving me with a smirk on my face. Eventually, Rocky and I departed for a night stop in Jersey.

In the March Mikhail Gorbachev became the leader of the Russian Communist Party and so joined Ronald Reagan, Maggie Thatcher and Helmut Kohl as the fourth member of the quartet of political leaders who would change the world order for ever.

The springtime came like a breath of fresh air and the schedules returned to some sort of normality. Berlin in the spring was fantastic with all the local people emerging from their winter hibernation and the outside cafés and bars opened up and life was bloody good. We had a well-known expression that suited the 737 operation that was 'working hard and playing hard' and seemed to fit the bill very nicely.

Among our friends was a Stewardess called Beverly Owen who originated from Southern Rhodesia, now called Zimbabwe. It was now some six years since the end of the 'Rhodesian Bush War' (RBW) which had lasted some 14 years and began when the then Prime Minister, Ian Smith, declared that white rule was there to stay and declared a Unilateral Declaration of Independence (UDI). In the end all was settled in talks at Lancaster House, London and in 1979 one of the opposition guerrilla leaders Robert Mugabe was elected president. As an aside, during the ceasefire that followed the Lancaster House agreement, the UK supplied 50 English 'Bobbies' complete with their characteristic hat and teapot to be sent into the jungles to supervise the arrival of the Guerillas from their lairs. I think the sight of an English Bobby drinking a cup of tea complete with hat, notepad and pencil must have made them drop their arms and give themselves up and sit under the shade of a Baobab tree. There was an old Airline operating in the country called Central African Airways which was established at the time of UDI and Beverley's dad was one of the pilots. He died tragically shortly after UDI in a take-off accident of a DC-3 aircraft.

I am sorry about the short history lesson but I needed to set the scene when Beverley suggested that we fly to Harare, as it was now known (after previously being Salisbury), in the June and stay with her sister Minyon and sample Zimbabwe. We felt the politics were not the best but we could live with that. Moya had a certain fear of spiders and to be honest I was not far behind, or even in front of her, but we swallowed deeply and in early June we all flew in the 747 direct to Harare. We landed in the early morning on a beautiful warm African day and all our negative thoughts were soon washed away by the wonderful reception from Bev's sister Minyon. She and her husband Dave lived in the southern suburb of Borrowdale and on the way there we passed Government House where Mugabe resided. There was a ring of soldiers guarding the place. They had been trained in North Korea and were known as the third Brigade and were a pretty evil bunch and if anyone strayed too close to the perimeter of Government House then they would be dealt with in no uncertain terms. Dave and Minyon had three children, Gary, Jo and Matt, ranging from five to one years of age and so it all fitted in well with Paul and Jenny. They lived in a bungalow complete with a large garden and a small swimming pool. They had two local servants, Langton and Mary, who both seemed like part of the family. I seem to remember a gardener who came sometimes as well. It was a fantastic introduction for Paul and Jenny to see the world starting with Africa. After a well-earned sleep we woke up in the late afternoon to drinks by the pool and an early evening swim followed by a wonderful dinner cooked by Langton. All the meat and vegetables were as fresh as you can get them since nothing in the food world needed to be imported. The country was self-sufficient having developed the mentality of making do and cultivating their own small industries some years before when it was of necessity due to the harsh sanctions inflicted when Ian Smith proclaimed UDI. We talked and drank well into the evening and Moya and Minyon seemed to hit it off very well. Dave and I established a great rapport between us and the kids all seemed totally relaxed in their new surroundings. Even Jenny was not whining. Idyllic it was!

As each day went by we found that the world of Zimbabwe was like an oasis of fun. The area where we were was very safe to walk around and so we would wander off to the local shops and indulge in an ice-cream cone which was basically a standard issue cone but covered in a broken up 'crunchy bar'. Waist line dramas again! What the heck – it was wonderful. During our stay we flew on Air Zimbabwe up to Victoria Falls in the north-west part of the country on the border with Zambia, which incidentally was originally called Northern Rhodesia. It was a day trip and once we had arrived a guide met us and we had coffee at the famous Victoria Falls Hotel and then took the trail by the famous falls and just wondered at the enormous beauty and power of it all. In history the falls were discovered by that great English explorer Dr David Livingstone in 1841 and named after Queen Victoria. It is ironic that in Zambia they are called the Livingstone Falls. Dr Livingstone was eventually found by Henry Stanley after many years of being posted missing on the banks of Lake Tanganyika in Tanzania. He was greeted by the famous words:

"Dr Livingstone, I presume?"

After a soaking from the incessant spray off the falls we arrived at the famous bridge linking Zimbabwe and Zambia where the British Government had once attempted to negotiate with Ian Smith to bring an end to UDI. The talks took place in a railway carriage in the middle of the bridge so that neither party was seen to be invading another country. The talks failed!

After lunch we all climbed aboard a boat and sailed up the Zambezi river and enjoyed the short cruise with elephants roaming on the water's edge and crocodiles surveying the scene looking out for a late lunch. We ended up moored up to a jetty on a small island and wandered ashore to the be greeted by the clatter of many monkeys doing what they most probably did every time a bunch of tourists invaded their patch – nicked anything in sight. Cameras, sunglasses and handbags were amongst their haul. Right little business people they were. As we floated down the river the sound of a twin-engined aircraft was heard. It was the famous 'Flight of Angels' that offered a 20 minute flight over the falls and actually flew in the gorge with the head of the falls above the aircraft. Some flying skill needed there. For some unknown reason I did not fancy taking the flight and would rather stay messing about in boats. As it was, a few years later it actually crashed due to one of the engines failing as it was just emerging from the gorge. Not sure if anyone survived at all but it was discovered that corrosion was deeply embedded in the structure due to the constant exposure to the water spray off the falls. Perhaps I had a sixth sense. We finished our cruise with afternoon tea on the water complete with small dainty sandwiches. By the time we got back to Borrowdale it was early evening and happy hour. By the time we 'hit the hay' all that could be heard was a chorus of snoring from the various bedrooms. Well worth the day out I have to say!

We met up with Minyon's mum, Helen who, as I mentioned before had been widowed following her husband's air crash years before. She was a lovely lady. It was at about this time that I started to suffer from a cramp-like pain in the calf muscle of my left leg which seemed to just keep niggling away at me on and off. I can remember Helen sitting me down and stroking the area with what I can only describe as a total soothing pair of hands and seemed to have the effect of calming the pain down. It was difficult to describe the pain but it did start to slow me up. I was called 'Hop along' on many occasions and suffered in silence since I was unable to actually pin down the problem. It took many years to finally sort out the problem. Dave and Minyon also had a very good social circle of friends with the closest being Leslie and Charles. Dave and Charles met whilst fighting in the RBW and since then the families had become very close friends. So, apart from the wonderful country the social side was pretty good as well. I think it was a case of needing another holiday to get over this one. In those days I was a bit sporty so tennis was very much on the agenda followed by a swim and a very welcome beer. It was strange but once the feet moved around on the tennis court the pain seemed to abate. It was only when I stood still that it started again.

As with all good things the holiday came to an end and it was then that the drama began over 'would we' or 'wouldn't we' get on the aircraft back to Heathrow. The route was flown three times a week and the aircraft seats were generally totally sold out. So the routine started whereby we all trooped out to the airport on the appointed evening and gingerly handed in our staff tickets. It was a bit reminiscent of the scene with my dad many years before when I first sampled the delights of 'staff travel' excepting for the fact that I was the dad this time. We would then be told to come back in, maybe, one hour and get the final assessment. It had to be the longest hour imaginable but finally I would approach the desk with maybe my head bowed like my dad, and stand to attention awaiting the verdict. The lady would shuffle about the staff tickets and then pronounce that we had all got on but were stuffed down the back somewhere in Economy and a bit spread out. With Jenny being very young she went with Moya OK and Paul and I sorted ourselves out OK. It was amazing, but once on the aircraft we did a bit of diplomatic manoeuvring and all ended up together in the middle seats somewhere. The 747 used on this route was a newer version of the one I had flown with more powerful Rolls Royce engines and was able to cope with a higher passenger load hence was able to take off from Harare and get to Heathrow in one hit. This was the 747-200. When I was on the original 747-100 aircraft we would have had to land in Europe en-route for fuel which would make the flight a long one. As it was, the flight that night would have been all of ten hours or so and boy, did I get bored in the middle of the night being unable to sleep and trying to stretch my gammy leg out which was giving me a lot of grief. Finally, we landed at Heathrow in the early hours and made our way home to Binfield. I felt that I had been dragged through a hedge backwards and thanked my lucky stars that I had crossed the great divide into Short-Haul away from those long night flights. Little did I know what was in store for me!

And so it was back to work for me to the news that an Air India 747 had crashed off the West coast of Ireland and it was later revealed that it was a bomb planted by some Indian extremists while the aircraft was on the ground in Toronto, Canada that had brought the aircraft down; 329 people died in an instant. The world of terror had been brought into our living rooms by these extremists.

In the August I was sitting at home watching breakfast TV when a newsflash cut in that an aircraft had crashed during Take-off at Manchester. Obviously my curiosity was sharpened as to which airline and what sort of aircraft. After about 20 minutes it was revealed that it was a BA Airtours 737 that had crashed. I had flown that particular aircraft a few times so everything went by the board while I stayed glued to the TV to find out more. What had happened was that an engine had exploded on Take-off and by an amazing fluke a piece of shrapnel had penetrated a small 4-inch circular inspection plate in the lower surface of the wing and fuel simply poured out and ignited in a fiery mass. Since it was not the engine that had caught fire the Flight crew were unaware of what was actually happening. They abandoned the Take-off at quite a high speed and turned off the runway as one would do after an engine failure indication. What they did not know was that the left wing was on fire and the wind was blowing it over the fuselage. Once the tower and cabin crew alerted them as to what was going on then all hell broke loose and in the ensuing evacuation 55 people lost their lives. The TV images were dramatic to say the least since, with modern technology, you can get an up-to-date scene within minutes. The fire had totally gutted the aircraft and was still smouldering as I watched. The fact it was one of the aircraft I had flown and was part of the BA 737 fleet made it all the more tragic. My mind was actually focused, once the carnage was all over, as to what had happened with the engine to cause it to explode.

In any jet engine the air is drawn in and compressed through a series of blades known as the 'compressor' section. It then enters a combustion chamber or 'can' and fuel is added and the resultant expansion of, what is now, very hot fiery air is directed onto another set of blades or 'turbines' and is then blasted out of the back at breakneck speed so as to produce thrust and get the aircraft going forward. The turbine blades in fact rotate under the pressure of the air coming out of the can and are connected to the compressor blades which, in turn, draw in more air and so the cycle is complete. Simple, you might say!

What had actually happened with the Manchester aircraft was that one of these cans had fractured and it simply disintegrated. On the 737 engine there are nine of these cans and the one that blew was on the top of the engine and a small fragment of very hot metal escaped through the engine casing and, by another stroke of incredible bad luck, shot through this small inspection hatch on the lower surface of the wing. This inspection hatch was constructed of a thinner metal than the surrounding fuel tank and so it gave way very quickly when hit by the very hot piece of engine and the fuel in the wing tank was free to flow out. Where did it flow to? Right into the innards of the hottest part of the destroyed engine and caught fire. The resultant fire spread quickly and before long the complete wing was on fire. The engine instruments would not have shown the fact that the wing was on fire. The cabin filled with smoke from the fire and I can only imagine total chaos and panic was happening in the cabin compounded with the fact that you could have only seen about a foot in front of your face. It was a miracle that more people did not die on that day in August. The Cabin Crew did what they could and were highly and deservedly commended for their actions.

Once the initial drama was played out the big question was what had happened to the engine can to make it explode like that? It transpired that the particular can in question had a repair weld done to it recently which, although fully certified by the engine manufacturer could, under certain conditions, fail and that was the cause of the Airtours aircraft engine failure, remembering the fact that most of their flights involved take-offs at the higher weights than we had which, in turn, involved higher power settings thus adding to the problem. BA instigated a fleet-wide check and found that, in a lot of instances, the same conditions existed on a number of engines and a good part of the fleet was grounded. They leased in about four engines from South African Airways so that no serious disruption to the schedules occurred. About a week after the Manchester accident I did a flight from Heathrow to Athens for which I needed full power to carry the load plus the fuel. It was with a certain amount of trepidation when I set the engines to full power on the runway since at that stage nobody knew what the problem was exactly. Unfortunately the Cabin Crew had left a tray full of bits and pieces loosely on the galley top and as we rotated it fell off onto the floor with an almighty crash. The both of us leapt out of our skin and thought of our mothers. We stared at the engine instruments looking for the first clue of an engine failure. There was none! A few minutes later a very apologetic Cabin Crew member came onto the Flight deck and grovelled an apology. I was at the time in the process of putting my heart back into its correct place in my body and all he got was a grunt or two out of me.

I needed that like a hole in the head, was my thought for the day.

Drinks were on the Cabin Crew that night in Athens.

Once the root cause of the problem was sorted and a programme was put in place to replace any repaired cans then slowly things got back to normal but the whole episode left a bad taste in the mouth.

Back home things were getting into some sort of routine with Paul attending his local church school on a daily basis and Jenny finally getting her act together (maybe!). My relationship with Moya seemed fine on the surface but, as I said before, cracks were starting to appear below the surface. The house that we had bought appeared to be large enough for the family but the way it was constructed lent itself to be extended. There I was thinking money grew on trees! Anyway by that stage we were very friendly with a local builder and so it seemed natural to ask him for various quotes. In they came and without really thinking about the financial side I gave him the go ahead to start work.

Having said that, I was earning well with a good monthly figure to play with, considering the Berlin allowance scene so it all seemed to be within my capabilities. Silly man!

The autumn rolled on with a good mix of flying based around the older -200 and the newer -300 version. There was one exception to the route structure of the -300 whereby it flew the route from Heathrow to Malmo, Sweden via Copenhagen, Denmark. I consider Malmo to be one of the most boring cities on the planet. On occasions we would be rostered for a whole weekend there. With my seniority climbing quite well you would think that I could avoid these trips but I was qualified on the -300 and so I was in a small select group of pilots who could fly both types and had to settle for the rough as well as the smooth. The only mildly amusing bit of the weekend away was in the hotel bar early evening on the Saturday when the TV would show a weekly episode of Rowan Atkinson's 'Blackadder' which the Swedes found hilarious. It was to my taste as well but what happened was that the language spoken was English with Swedish sub-titles. There then would follow a ritual whereby I would laugh at the spoken word with the Swedes following up with an echo laugh about two seconds later having read the sub-titles. Sounds pathetic, but it shows how the 'little things pleased little minds' syndrome took me over whilst coping with the wonderful weekend break in Malmo.

Back in Berlin the friendship amongst the crews based there or passing through became quite strong with many characters emerging. A few of them shone out above the rest. One of these was Ernie Sailor who hailed from the London area and could only be described as a 'loveable rogue'. He had the habit of just turning up out of the blue from the middle of nowhere and then disappearing again just as fast. He was a great debater and was the sort of guy who could fall into a vat of pretty awful smelling liquid and come up smelling of roses. He lived in Edgware, North London with his wife, the ever suffering Valerie, and they had two children, Gavin and Diana. The reason why I mention Ernie at this stage is to set the scene for things that would happen in my future where he became a really close friend. Amongst the Scottish lot on the 748 there were some real characters with most of them coming from that part of the UK which I could refer to as 'North of

Watford'. They were a right collection and to be valued highly in the world of flying.

In the September the UK was subjected to more race riots. The country had built up over the years a large immigrant community with the majority of them from the old colonial countries. They seemed to congregate in particular areas. It was way back in 1968 when the famous Member of Parliament, Enoch Powell, made his famous speech in Birmingham heavily criticising the immigration policy of the government of the day. The speech got the ominous title of the 'Rivers of Blood' speech. Whether he was right or wrong was down to personal taste but he talked about race riots in the future and now the future was the present. The riots were mainly centred round the Brixton area, south of the river, in London and were pretty ugly. There were many repercussions in the government and total disbelief that this was happening in England. The riots went on for, maybe, three weeks before some sort of order was restored but not before an enormous amount of damage had been done. Not a pretty time at all.

Back in BA as the winter approached there was the usual flurry of activity within BA of checking that all the de-icing rigs were in perfect order. It happened every year at about this time with the same result every time. When the snow and freezing conditions arrived BA was taken totally by surprise and nothing worked. To be fair I think this is standard across the airline and airport world. As the famous British Rail spokesman would say:

"It's the wrong type of snow".

Back in Berlin, life was rolling along like one big party. It was quite amazing, that although we did let our hair down quite often, when it came to the actual job we were intended for we did it with great enthusiasm and took pride in keeping the schedules as close to the timetable as we could. We had one of those pilot-management meetings at about this time and the main point of discussion was the Manchester Airtours crash. It was very sobering to be shown the actual can that had ruptured on the aircraft. It had a perfect split where the weld was. On a lighter note we were told that the Berlin operation was the most punctual network in the BA European scene. This was amazing considering that the '748' was still up to its old tricks of breaking down regularly. The IGS was still making very good profits for BA and that made me feel really proud to be part of it.

Back home Paul had been enrolled in the local primary school and his real education started. Jenny was just being her usual self. November was the month of birthdays as I said before and with all the choices around of venues diplomacy was required so as to not upset either of them since they were a day apart. Moya was the better one to sort it all out and all I had to do was to turn up. It was at about this time that I became the chairman of the FSRC and so reigned supreme. The meetings were still being organised within BA by one of the secretaries and they all went like clockwork, or so it seemed. I acquired a bicycle from the club with the aim of, maybe, getting fit, having accumulated years of neglect in that department. Now Binfield is situated on the top of a hill with all roads gently sloping downwards. Therein lay the first clue which I missed. So off I go with a great ceremonial send-off with the words:

"Don't worry I will be back in an hour. I am just popping over to Wokingham to see Dad and Thirza".

Moya must have known something that I didn't know since she went to say something but stopped short and a sly smirk drifted across her face.

Bloody woman, what is that smirk for? I spent my childhood on a bike and one with no gears either so what is the problem? I thought.

I cantered off at an easy pace downwards from Binfield and then a bit of level road and finally downhill into Wokingham. I arrived at Dad and Thirza's and had a cup of tea and then set sail back home. All roads home now seemed to be like the North face of the Eiger and growing in length as I slipped the gears down through the complete range of 16. My legs whizzed around like a very old diesel engine and I covered about one metre per 20 revolutions of these human pistons.

One hour did I say? I will be lucky if I get home this week, was my muttered thought.

After about ten minutes the legs went into 'Overheat' mode, the voice went and the lungs were fast approaching meltdown. No longer was there this suave guy freewheeling his way outbound from Binfield. It was replaced by this total wreckage with distorted facial features and legs that were rapidly becoming independent units. You know when you watch the extreme athletes on the TV and they appear to be grimacing with pain as they push the limits. There was I with all the expressions of these people but my limit trailing about ten metres behind them. After about 30 minutes and what seemed to be about 300 piston revolutions completed I reached a level strength of road and the pace increased dramatically to about two metres per 20 revolutions as I gingerly moved the gears up a few cogs. The lungs returned from the edge of destruction and a few expletives were uttered to get my voice back into some kind of order. My legs were still in a world of their own but what the heck, two out of three isn't too bad. The level part of the journey seemed to come to an end all too quickly and the mountains of Binfield loomed up on the horizon. The gears went down again, the voice drifted off into the abyss, the lungs reverted to meltdown again and to cap it all it started raining. For any onlooker I must have looked a right sight and not a BA Captain out for an evening ride around his estate. The North face of the Eiger seemed to get steeper, the road longer and the rain heavier. I was now down to walking pace with the rain streaming down my face and me counting every dent and stone in my path. I was cold, totally miserable and cursing the day I ever suggested getting this stupid bike.

Suddenly, there was a bang and my legs totally left the planet like a runaway propeller and I was going nowhere. The chain had broken and was shredded, together with the fancy set of gears, into a million pieces leaving this snake-like trail of molten metal in my wake. Me and my infernal bike gracefully parted company at that point with me ending up in a crumpled heap on the grass verge. Now I was really, really miserable and just sat there surveying the wreckage of what was three hours before all bright and shiny. I eventually struggled to my feet and grabbed the remains of the bike and off I plodded towards home with the bike now become like one of those supermarket trolleys that wandered everywhere except where you wanted it to go. I was now super miserable and woe betide anyone who came within ten metres of me since I was not in the mood for small talk. Then it got dark!

The original hour planned for the famous bike ride had now stretched to four when I eventually struggled down the drive in the middle of an Indian Monsoon and, without ceremony, threw the metal beast somewhere. Moya must have heard the commotion and opened the front door and ushered me in. No words were exchanged. Pointless exercise anyway with my voice reduced to a wet whimper and being only just about able to walk properly. Recovery time was unknown but eventually I managed to utter a few words generally related to the need of a drink or two. The bike was never mentioned again which was just as well.

Now, how can I stop my legs moving up and down as if they are on some sort of mission? was my only thought.

I slept well that night. The pistons finally returned to normal in the early hours.

In the news in November Ronald Reagan met up with Mikhail Gorbachev for the first time and, by all accounts, all went well. Helmut Kohl got involved as well as Maggie Thatcher. When you look back over that time you realise that the four most powerful people in the civilized world were actually sitting down and talking to each other which has to an achievement in its own right. It transpired many years later that Helmut Kohl and Mikhail Gorbachev became very good friends as time went by.

Flying wise all was going well with the approaching winter looming. In the December I flew to Vienna and back which was quite normal. Twenty four hours later terrorists attacked Vienna and Rome airports with many casualties. I flew to Rome the following day and taxied in with half the Italian Army alongside. All a bit late as life never changes in the world or terrorism!

Xmas duly arrived with the usual family scene. Jenny was now well up to speed as to what it was all about and at about 4 am there they both were standing at the bottom of our bed demanding attention.

I was never like that surely? was my thought at the time.

"Shove off the pair of you and leave us alone!" I would say with a commanding tone.

It had no effect at all on these two. Xmas Day that year started early.

So, into 1986 we go with me approaching 40 years of age.

Bloody hell, I'm getting old, I thought as I struggled out of bed to get to the airport to operate the 6 am Newcastle flight.

In early January we all flew out to Zimbabwe for two weeks. This was our second visit and, as usual, the reception we received was wonderful and the African party truly started. As you can imagine the weather was superb with blue skies every day and the temperatures in the upper twenties all the time. The thought of England in January never seemed to enter my mind. I can remember sitting down with David, Minyon's husband, in the lounge casually devouring a well-earned beer after a session of gentle tennis. The TV was on in the background and suddenly there was a news flash about a disaster that had happened in Florida whereby the NASA 'Challenger' space shuttle had exploded just after lift-off from Cape Canaveral. The film footage was extraordinary in that it actually showed the whole sequence of events from lift-off to bits and pieces of hardware splashing down in the Atlantic. With me being an avid follower of space travel, and in particular the American efforts, I found the whole thing quite daunting to watch. It was revealed many months later that the cause of the catastrophe was a faulty seal between one of the supporting rocket boosters and the shuttle itself. The actual enquiry also pointed the finger at NASA for being very casual in its approach to the whole shuttle operation.

As for Zimbabwe the party eventually came to an end and we then faced the usual lottery of the seats for the flight home. Not wishing to say anything but with the four of us crammed in the centre section down the back and my leg cramp still playing up it was not a nice experience but, what the heck, I paid a small fraction of the real price so stop moaning and just sit there and enjoy the minutes ticking by. Why is it when you want time to speed up it slows down and vice versa?

Once reacquainted with a cold and miserable UK winter off I went back to work. At the end of January came my infamous fortieth birthday. I seem to remember we had a party and disco in the village hall with the usual gaggle of party animals. I was no longer a teenager and I knew that but, on the other hand, I didn't feel that old either. I was in the middle somewhere.

I remember well that the weather in late January and early February was dominated by fog all over the UK and Europe. I turned up for the flight to Moscow on such a day. The Co-pilot was Pete Larrett and, at the briefing, it transpired that we were completely full which was quite amazing for that time of year. The only downside was that fog was in the forecast for our arrival at Moscow.

"They must have been storing the passengers up for this flight," I remarked casually.

The 737-200 is a brilliant aircraft but it does have its limits. Normally a four-hour flight with an average load would be well within its capability but with a full load and a fog forecast at Moscow it was a little bit testing so we elected to 'drop' into Stockholm on the way for fuel. BA was very slick in this sort of one-off operation and our stop on the ground there was less than 30 minutes. So off we go into the Russian world with our finger on the script and following the ever wandering needles as I described earlier. To get the latest weather for Moscow was a bit of an art in its own right with the usual language problems with the controllers. Even when we got into the Moscow area we still did not have too much of an idea exactly what the landing conditions were. The air was full of Russian aircraft all going this way and that so it was obvious that some of the local airports were shut due to the fog. In Stockholm we had the sense to really load up with lots of extra fuel so that we would have lots to spare if needed. It was needed!

Pete and I worked like 'one-armed paperhangers' since we were being directed this way and that. Don't forget we were working in metres with no fancy television screen in front of us as to what to follow. Eventually we were directed to start the approach and from what we could deduce the fog was pretty thick and just about on our limits. So, down we go towards the runway with the air getting thicker and thicker as we descend. How we would do this sort of approach was pretty simple. I would set the auto-pilot up to fly the precision ILS and we would both keep our heads down staring at the instruments checking that the systems were running smoothly. At a pre-determined point I, as Captain, would look out of the window and try to look for the runway and ascertain that all was in order outside for us to land. The Co-pilot would simply keep monitoring the display and call out various heights relating to where we were with the main call being 'Decision Height'. At this point I would answer his call as to whether I had the requirements outside the window by saying 'Land' or, if not, I would say 'Go-around'. If the Co-pilot heard nothing he would press the buttons and off we would sail back upwards into the sky and abort the landing. It all sounds a bit melodramatic but it worked superbly and was gospel to all of us. When Pete called 'Decision Height' I saw nothing out of the window and 'Go-around' was the order of the day. The 737 is well overpowered as it leapt skywards. The problem in Moscow was the route to follow after the 'Go-around' was pretty complicated and took both of us to get it right by continually backing each other up. Pete was a very experienced Co-Pilot so we worked well.

When we settled down having weaved our way all over the Moscow area we elected to high-tail out of it and go to Helsinki, Finland which was about one and a half hours away. The route there was back the way we had come and then turn right at some point along it and go north over the Kola Peninsula and on to Helsinki. So there we were reading the script backwards with the familiar radio needles going all over the place as usual. As we turned north at a place called 'Gagarin' named after the first man in space we realised we were to fly through a very sensitive military area which covered pretty well the whole of the Kola Peninsula and it was not long before the Russian Radar people sent us this way and that way under the title of 'Radar assistance'. Finally we crossed the Russian/Finnish border and arrived after about 30 minutes into the calm of Helsinki. Bit of an epic day I would say with about ten hours of duty behind us.

We decided to stay with the passengers in Helsinki overnight and have another prod at Moscow in the morning. BA had a good team on the ground and within about an hour or so we were enjoying the delights of a beer. It was pretty expensive but well deserved.

In the morning we assembled our faithful band of passengers and loaded up with a lot of extra fuel again since the fog was still hanging around Moscow. I felt that maybe this time we would be a bit more fortunate and get everybody to where they wanted to go yesterday. So off we go back over the Kola Peninsula again heading south and entered the main east/west airway at Gagarin again. On this occasion the Russians were more on the ball and at about 100 miles to go to Moscow they told us that the fog was worse than yesterday and that the main Moscow airport was closed.

Snookered again! I thought to myself.

I pondered for a few minutes and then announced to Pete that I thought the best place to divert to would be Heathrow since it was pointless going to Helsinki again and sitting there all day only to repeat the exercise.

"We could end up spending our lives going up and down between Helsinki and Moscow and just wasting money and effort," I said to Pete as to my explanation for choosing Heathrow.

So off to Heathrow it was with the customary reading of the script backwards which was becoming a bit of an art. We looked at the fuel scene and it looked pretty good for the rest of the flight westwards and then I had the pleasure of telling the passengers and the Cabin Crew what was going on. Surprisingly enough there were very few grumbles amongst the passengers and the Cabin Crew were very happy since they were all on extended overtime and 'in the money'.

After five hours and 36 minutes of being cramped up in that small flight deck we eventually landed at Heathrow. That is a long time to be airborne in a 737 I have to say. On the way westwards we heard the next day's 737 on its way to Moscow and had a chat to them about the scene further east and they promptly turned around as well and followed us back home. It was by an amazing coincidence that we actually arrived at the very gate that we had departed from some two days before. So all we had achieved was a European tour for everybody without actually getting anywhere. That has to be a record!

On the home front things were seemingly ticking over quite well with our friendly builder doing a small extension for us which would slightly extend the lounge into the garden and give us a dining area. So off I went to the bank to get an extension to the mortgage to cover the work. In those days it was extremely easy to get money off your friendly bank manager. The seeds of a financial crisis had been sown. I have to say again that when it came to money matters I was on a different planet and kept things within myself which in a marriage was not a good idea. In hindsight I should have been totally transparent about everything but no, I fell at the first fence. On a more lighter note it was decided that Binfield needed livening up a bit and between Moya, me and a few other friends we decided to rent the village hall and get some discos organised. We called ourselves the 'Binfield over-30s Disco Club' and we had plenty of takers and for a while the 'club' seemed to flourish. We maybe got about 60 middle-aged ravers in the hall on a Saturday night. A good friend of ours, Dave Brown and I took it upon ourselves to run the bar. Not a good idea since Dave and I felt that we were the official tasters for all things alcoholic. We had a price list to follow but after an hour or so our thought boxes went a bit astray. On the whole the club was a great success but after a few months a few moans emerged from the participants and the venture faded into the 'out tray'. It is ironic that our good friend Dave Brown died many years later after becoming an alcoholic. Great guy! Great shame!

In the February there was agreement between France and England to construct a tunnel connecting the two countries. 'Sacre Bleu' as they say in France. Whatever next? We fought for many years against the French and now they want to join us together. Maybe it will be croissants for breakfast courtesy of British Rail. Also in the same month the Russians put into orbit a space station called 'Mir' that could accommodate up to five astronauts or cosmonauts for up to six months at a time. Coming shortly after the Challenger disaster it was a bitter pill the Americans had to swallow. The Swedish Prime Minister Olof Palme was shot down on the streets of Stockholm. Sweden was considered a non-aggressive European country which made the crime more startling.

My life on the 737 drifted on peacefully, having been on the aircraft for some seven years now and spending most of my time in Berlin. In total contrast to the usual fog of late January and early February strong winds become the flavour of the month from mid-February onwards and being on the Berlin IGS our flying ability was being continually tested maybe up to four times daily. The 737 had a landing cross-wind limit of over forty knots and for most of that time we were flying to these limits. I remember taxiing out one blustery morning in Düsseldorf and parked up waiting for my turn for take-off. I watched an Alitalia DC-9 bucking and weaving on the final approach to landing. From our angle it looked like he was pointing straight at us but what he was actually trying to do was to keep in line with the runway. At about 100ft there must have been a lull in the gale since he seemed to physically head straight at us. We were well back from the runway so it was all the more startling. At that point he opened up the power and climbed right over us missing us by, what seemed, about 20 metres. All I saw as I followed his trail was a good view looking up his rear end at two black dirty barrels of smoke coming out of his engines as he climbed away. The noise was pretty deafening. Put it another way: it certainly woke us up that morning. We took off shortly after that and the moment you got in the air you really earned you salary keeping things going the right way and, of course, trying to avoid the noisy areas around the airport by following quite a complicated route.

It was at about this time that the British Broadcasting Corporation (BBC) decided to do a documentary about a 747 flying from Heathrow direct overnight to Bangkok. The 747-200, as I mentioned before, had the range to do these ultra-long non-stop flights to Thailand and the Far East. Our trips to Zimbabwe that were considered long flights were nothing compared with going non-stop from Heathrow to Hong Kong or Bangkok. When I left the 747-100 fleet we did a schedule direct to Delhi which was considered the ultimate in its day. How the world has changed! Anyway, back to the BBC and its filming of this flight. Pilots generally have a certain mistrust of the press which I feel stems from the latter not understanding the world of flying and the various pressures put on it. I am not preaching here but just trying to explain the differences between the two professions. Anyway on this particular flight there was a change of Captain at the last minute since BA felt that the original one was a bit too outspoken and so the filming started at the briefing and went through the night to the arrival in Bangkok. The crewing for these flights consisted of, in fact, two complete crews of a Captain, Co-pilot and a Flight Engineer. The duties were split between these two crews with one crew designated as the 'operating crew' and the other crew were to act as relief during the cruise and were known as the 'heavy crew'. The timings of the various change-over points were such that both crews just about split the flight time equally. Considering that most of these flights left late at night and were up to 12 hours flight time the sleep factor was very important. Bunks were provided for the off-duty part of the flight. The Flight deck could get a bit full during change-over with four people in various states of dress all trying to clean their teeth at the same time. Add to this a BBC film crew who seemed to take delight in filming the whole thing with two Captains discussing the route, etc in their Y-fronts. And on top of this the Co-pilot of the heavy crew was a female. Right, she had seen it all before you might assume, but to the film crew this was wild stuff. There was this woman strutting about in her 'undies' with three men equally robed in their boxer shorts.

'Jane meets her Tarzans in the dark over India!' I could envisage as a headline.

In Bangkok the film crew seemed to take great delight in focusing on the leisure side of the stopover with no mention being made of the downside with respect to time change, sleepless nights etc. I am a supporter of a good social scene down route but these long range flights did create new problems for us to take on board. The TV film shown later on TV gave the impression that the modern pilot just flits from country to country with the flying side being purely incidental.

"Let the film crew sit come along with us across Europe and enjoy four sectors of being thrown around by Mother Nature," I said sarcastically on one occasion.

Incidentally, the reason why I knew so much about this flight was because the other Co-pilot was a very good friend of the family. Tim Inge lived in Binfield with Trudy and had two children. He tragically died some years later of cancer. What a tragedy life can be when you see good people going that way.

Another destination out of Berlin was the island of Sylt, part of the North Frisian Islands, which was just off the German north coast. It was famous within West Germany as the ultimate holiday isle where the wearing of clothes was optional. Considering that for most of my flights there the weather was generally quite atrocious and the thought of ripping one's kit off and dancing on the beach did not spring to mind, "Strange people!" I thought as I approached the island with a monsoon hammering down and hurricane Hugo giving its all.

The airfield was very limited in its landing aids so it was back to basics and was a bit challenging getting the landing at the right point. On more than one occasion we had to disembark the passengers through the small galley door at the front right hand side since we could not open the main door due to the strong wind. The funny side was that the passengers we took there and brought back were all very happy souls since this was a break for them.

The winter gradually faded away and the weather moved on towards the spring. One of our neighbours, Chris and Elaine and their two kids Clare and Martin had a caravan and they often disappeared during the school breaks to Cornwall and set up shop at one of the many sites. We decided to venture that way ourselves and drove down to Mevagissey in Cornwall to meet up with them at their site. The whole idea of jamming all our belongings into a caravan and then dragging it half way across the UK did not appeal. Besides, in life there is nothing that gives you more murderous thoughts than being stuck in a traffic queue following this modern 'horse and buggy' which had been waiting at the top of your road before pulling out just ahead of you and guess where he was going? Yes, you've got it. He was going to the same place as you and no way was he going to let you pass. These drivers seemed to have a sadistic streak.

However, once in Cornwall we linked up with Chris and Elaine and found the social benefits quite excellent, mainly based around the cost and the fact that you could load up with all sorts of things from home that would be normally be denied. So what did I do? I joined the 'Sadistic Streak' society and bought a caravan ready for the school half term break in the May. The car I had at the time was a standard issue English Austin Montego which basically had a wheel at each corner and not much in the middle. It was not the most powerful of cars and when you hitched a half-ton caravan on the back it positively wallowed and seemed to scream in protest at having to do anything strenuous. The drive at home had a marked slope to it and once the caravan was gently manoeuvred down the slope all seemed well. Then the loading commenced with all of us taking part. What is that expression?

'Everything, except the kitchen sink.' It must have originated on our drive.

Anyway, time to move out and I would duly hitch up the caravan and gently try to move forward. Howls of protest would erupt from under the bonnet and, being a manual gearbox, the clutch would take the most beating and issue a rather acrid smell. In the end it would take all of the family plus anybody silly enough to be standing around watching to throw their weight behind the immovable caravan and on the count of three all shove together with me and my faithful clutch doing the rest. Suddenly we would all move up the drive together and straddle the pavement on the level with a hot steaming engine panting as if it had just climbed Mount Everest. A long cooling time then followed in which we realised that all the heavy items were at the back of the 'van' and, being balanced on only two wheels, was lifting the rear end of the car up. So, everything was dragged out and strewn over the pavement whilst Chris and I would discuss the correct loading sequence. Chris had been at the game much longer than me so his word was generally accepted as final which would annoy me a bit. Of course, the main culprit of the 'weight and balance' issue was the seemingly enormous number of wine bottles being stowed.

"Surely we won't drink all that lot?" I would say rather meekly.

We did and some!

So, finally we were all balanced up and the two families ready to move out. We usually left in the evening and, if the destination was Cornwall, we aimed to get as far as the M6 south of Bristol and then lay up in a motorway service station for the night and then get going early the next day. Chris had pulled a caravan many times before so he was 'street wise' but there was me as a complete novice trying to coax the Montego out of third gear so that the engine might calm down and the journey be a bit quieter. Once on the M4 heading west things seemed to settle down except for the usual whining from the back seats.

"Are we there yet, Dad?" was the usual chorus.

Now, where have I heard that before?

One thing that is peculiar with towing something that is about 15 feet long and weighing about three quarters of a ton when fully loaded is that it sways around in its own world and tries to take the car with it. You became used to the swaying after a while but occasionally it would go the other way and off you went again wrestling with the wheel to keep in the lane. Because of the lack of urge from the engine the slow lane was the general option and if you got to 50mph you were considered going supersonic. The motorway was generally quiet at that time of night and in the rear view mirror you spot a large HGV lorry passing you. As he comes abeam the caravan springs into life and moves to the right as if a magnet had been put on the lorry designed to attract all caravans and pull them in. The first time it happened I leapt out of my skin and fought the wheel to stop the mutual attraction going any farther. The net result was that you, the car and the caravan snaked around the slow lane with all sorts of advice being issued by the passengers. Definitely time for a cigarette! The actual reason for the magnetic effect was a natural suction that happened when two tall vehicles pass close together going the same way.

"Right, I'll be ready for the next magnetic attack," was my statement for evening.

We eventually made it to the service station on the M6 south of Bristol and I am not sure who was more exhausted – me, Moya, the kids or the engine.

Now we came to the next task and that was parking the car plus caravan into one of the bays. Chris was the veteran and simply reversed into his bay and stood waiting for me to do likewise. Now to reverse with any sort of trailer on the back you simply reverse the steering wheel direction that you would normally use and 'Bingo'. When you have an audience of about four so-called helpers, it's raining and dark you are up against it. There you are in the middle of the slip lane with a queue of cars starting to build up and being directed backwards by maybe Chris on one side and Moya on the other, being helped by the kids. The rear-view mirrors were covered in rain and I was only able to look into one at a time and so you tend to become a bit fractious and wished that you had booked the local hotel instead of this self-inflicted torture.

"Swing it to the left!" Chris would shout.

"Swing what?" I would shout back. "The bloody wheel or the bloody caravan?"

There then would follow a chorus of "STOP!"

Eventually after much huffing and puffing I was parked in the bay. Not straight but sort of within the boundaries.

"I need a drink please and pretty quick!" I said as I switched off much to the engine's relief.

After a somewhat disturbed night with all the comings and goings of a service station we set sail to Cornwall and entered the world of narrow lanes and hedgerows that seem to spread themselves across the road with gay abandon. I was now a fully paid up member of the 'Sadistic Society' with passing drivers giving me the look of death. As for the narrow lanes I worked on the principle that if the car gets through the gap then all else will follow. I tended to follow Chris so I had an insight as to what was heading my way. Eventually we arrived at the caravan site and after the drama with the parking I could eventually breathe a sigh of relief that we had got here reasonably intact. In the end the stay was very good and life rotated about the caravan with the daily stroll to the washrooms which, in reality, never boasted a 5-star rating but did the job. The return journey was not quite so dramatic since the booze had been offloaded by then which helped lighten the load considerably and we did not stop off en-route so it was a simple matter of keeping my head down and going for it.

With the half-term break out of the way and Paul enrolled in the local primary school in Binfield plus Jenny doing pre-school life became a lot easier in the home. The only thing that niggled me was that the pain in my left leg calf muscle was now pretty consistent and really starting to restrict me somewhat. In Berlin I saw a specialist and he seemed to think the problem lay in the spine where, maybe, a disc had moved and was pressing against a nerve. The other end of this nerve was in the calf muscle and hence the feeling of cramp in the leg on quite a few occasions. Why I did not pursue it was that, other than the pain, I felt OK and I did not want anyone prodding about with my back. What I did do at home was to go to a Chiropractic centre in nearby Reading. Now that was fun! I got ushered into the consulting room and invited to lie face down on a contraption that was designed to hold you still while the consultant lady did her work. My eyes popped out of my head at her first attack.

"Think of something nice and it will help," she said calmly as she prepared for the follow-up attack.

Could I think of anything remotely nice? Not a chance! Not even the thought of my Mum's Welsh cakes helped. She assured me that once done I would feel better after a couple of days but at the time a couple of days felt like an eternity. I hobbled back home and silently waited for the 'couple of days' to come. She was right because on the third day there was no pain in the leg and walking more than 20 metres was no longer an endurance test. What a wonderful lady that Chiropractic doctor was!

April came along with spring in the air and the world of flying emerged from the winter in good shape. It turned out to be quite a month in the world and started with a bomb attack on a TWA 727 flying from Rome to Athens. Four passengers were killed but the aircraft managed to struggle on to the ground thanks to the skill of the pilots. The photographs showed a massive hole on one side of the fuselage just before the wing and it was amazing that the aircraft stayed in the air. Terrorism was at the fore again!

Berlin itself came in for a terrorist act when a disco was bombed leaving three dead. The disco was in the Tempelhof area and frequented by US servicemen. The finger was pointed at Libya and Ronald Reagan was not amused. Read on!

It was on a Sunday morning shortly after the Berlin bombing that I flew very early in the morning to Newcastle. On the weekend military activity over the UK was generally non-existent and we would fly just off the East Coast through the military zones on our way north. As we flew over East Anglia we were assigned a different radio frequency from the normal one and at the same time we were directed to change course left and right. There were a lot of other aircraft on the same frequency which were obviously military aircraft. The accents were unmistakably American and we were quite intrigued to know what was going on. Of course, no-one told us and after weaving our way to Newcastle the ground staff told us that Ronald Reagan had ordered a bombing raid on Libya on that Saturday night using fighter-bombers based in the UK. What we had flown through were these guys returning home after that raid. Incidentally the raid was successful and Colonel Gaddafi, the self-appointed president of Libya, got one heck of a shock when someone actually hit back at him. This President was showing his true colours and the rest of the world was starting to stir. Nobody more so than the Russian leader, Mikhail Gorbachev, who at that time was a staunch supporter of Libya. Reagan was, up to that point, maybe considered as an ex-Hollywood cowboy masquerading as a US

President. The fact that in his first tenure as President he had ordered the 'Star Wars' programme and now after some years was seeing results with the testing well advanced and the costs rising dramatically, this fact was putting the Soviet bloc under enormous pressure to negotiate their way out of this latest rat race at little cost. Together with the 'Iron Lady' Maggie Thatcher who had been re-elected for a second term in 1983 the balance of political power was firmly in Western hands.

In Berlin this effect was slowly being felt in East Berlin with snippets of information reaching the West that there was some unrest and demonstrations against their draconian rulers. Escapes to the West are well documented but one of the most spectacular ones was the hijacking of a Polish Tupolev TU-134 back in 1978 when an East German citizen managed to force the pilot to land in Tempelhof in West Berlin using an imitation starting pistol. The West Berlin authorities detained the hijacker but eventually granted him asylum after a protracted period of time. People escaped in balloons, light aircraft or by simply tunnelling their way across no-man's land. I had the privilege to be in a bar on one occasion where an escapee and his wife were celebrating their escape triumph. What he had done was to steal an East German military staff car that regularly drove to the West and secreted his wife under the floorboards and, dressed as a Russian officer, bluffed his way through Checkpoint Charlie. Amazing!

On one of my stays my Co-pilot and I drove up to the north-west area of Berlin which was under the control of the French military and we walked across a field right up to the wall. We stumbled across the original barbed wire that had preceded the wall. I climbed a tree that was leaning against the wall and peeped over. Not a good move since within about ten seconds a pair of binoculars were trained on me emulating from an East Berlin observation tower about 50 metres away. I retreated rather hastily like a scolded cat. It was late afternoon and we decided it was time for a beer. We spotted a likely bar, albeit a bit isolated, and wandered in casually. We were greeted by a large crowd of men all swigging beer and singing what appeared to be patriotic German songs. Looking at their ages and dress we twigged that this was some sort of reunion of wartime soldiers so we beat a hasty retreat back to the hotel. Interesting sort of day!

I am sorry to deviate from my flying world a bit but what happened in the news generally affected my profession in some way or other. In April again, for example, there was another major news item that may or may not have affected my world. Deep in Russia a nuclear power station at Chernobyl literally blew its top after the controllers screwed up. 'Pilot error' you might say. It was a research station in Sweden that first picked up a dramatic increase in atmospheric radiation and alerted the world. The Russians played down the whole affair until they came clean and admitted that a nuclear accident had occurred. Up to that time we all knew of the existence of nuclear power stations around the world but took little notice of the safety issues surrounding them since we expected the infrastructure of these places to be the best. With regards to Chernobyl a cloud of radiation covered most of Central and Western Europe and being in the air for a good part of the time I obviously got caught up in the health side of it as did hundreds of other pilots in Europe. Berlin took a large dose of this airborne killer but what can I say? I understand that if you stay one day in Aberdeen you are subjected to the equivalent of a chest X-ray daily due to the amount of granite in the local soil. I don't know enough about the subject to comment professionally but over the weeks that followed the media hype took over and it seemed that we would all die within months due to the Russians. The media world was becoming more and more outrageous in its headlines and seemed to excel in sensational headlines for the sole purpose of increasing circulation numbers as opposed to actually checking the facts before writing some amazing rubbish. I remember the Daily Telegraph had an air correspondent, one Air Vice-Marshall Donaldson, who obviously earned his title in the RAF but when it came to reporting on all things aviation he was as far from reality as one could get.

Back in my flying world the on-going threat from terrorism raised its ugly head when I was sat in the cockpit one day with the Co-pilot in April at Heathrow waiting for things to happen. I was parked alongside a 747 of El Al and was busy going through the checks when I casually looked out of the window to find the complete area totally deserted.

Where is everybody? I thought to myself.

I got out of my seat and opened the cockpit door and found that my aircraft was deserted as well. At that moment a British Army light tank comes roaring around the corner complete with soldiers all kitted out as if going to war. The co-pilot and I leapt down the aircraft steps and the tank swung round and came at us as if we were the enemy. It shuddered to a halt and a couple of the soldiers jumped down and demanded to see our IDs and did we know that there could well be a bomb on the El Al 747 and what were we doing still with our aircraft?

"Because nobody told us and we did not have our headsets on," I said diplomatically.

As if I would hang around and play the martyr bit knowing the whole area could go 'puff' at any moment. What did Captain Mainwaring say in 'Dad's Army'?

"Stupid boy!"

The army guys fussed about on their radios for a while and in the end offered both of us a ride on the tank back to the crew report area. So, I went to the aircraft on a bus and returned on a tank.

"All in a day's work," I muttered as we climbed down and went indoors.

So, all in all, April was quite a lively month for both me and the world. It was in the beginning of May that BA moved all its long haul operations to a newly built terminal on the South side known as Terminal 4. It was completed overnight which was a notable achievement, considering the amount of equipment involved. Some short haul services moved as well. The only downside was that the distance between the terminals by road was now some five miles which made switching from a Long-Haul flight to a Short-Haul one was a long drawn out affair. Beneath Heathrow an underground system was slowly coming together. It could actually link all the terminals with central London. The underground seemed the best solution but passenger bags had to go via road so once again switching flights was beset with problems. Of course with the Air Traffic delays that seemed to be commonplace across Europe we would bring in passengers that needed to transfer to Terminal 4 and so the drama would unfold. Quite often we would be met by a transfer bus on the tarmac and whisk Mr and Mrs X off to their Barbados flight but where did the bags go?

In the July Prince Andrew and Sarah Ferguson got married at

Westminster Abbey. Unfortunately the marriage went the same way as his elder brother, Charles'. Not a good track record either of them. They were obviously taking my lead.

In Berlin on the weekends the airline was usually operationally very quiet since it was mainly designed for the business people who worked during the week. All this changed, since we did notice that some UK charter airlines such as Dan-Air and Monarch would arrive on a Friday evening and operate a range of charter flights to cater for a growing holiday market. There was also a small outfit based in Berlin owned and run by an American pilot called 'Air Berlin' which boasted three aircraft that did charter work. Out of little acorns oak trees grow they say. Here was a chance for BA to enter this market and earn some money out of this holiday business. So suddenly we were off to Greece, Spain, Italy and North Africa for an 'away-day' at the week-end. It was a nice change to go from the world of the German businessman to the German party animals that would really let their hair down. There was a subtle difference between the German holiday passenger and the British one that I would occasionally fly out of Gatwick for Airtours. The Germans liked to party from the moment they got to the airport but never got out of order or abusive. I think it is the German discipline that keeps them in check. The Brits do have the habit of getting out of order and many a tricky scene would occur on, say, a Saturday night in Palma carrying the infamous 18-30s lot. I am not biased towards the Germans but I have always found them easier to handle when it comes to all things in the flying world.

In the August BA ordered 16 of the new 747-400 aircraft from Mr Boeing which would complement the remaining aircraft in the Long-Haul fleet. The original 747-100 aircraft were getting long in the tooth by now and were fast approaching their sell-by date but were still soldiering on. The difference between the new 747-400 and the older types was that the Flight Engineer was not needed in the cockpit since automation had taken over and it was down to the pilots to deal with all things engineering. The crew consists of only two pilots so what an advance on my dad's era. The downside was that it signalled the end of the Flight Engineer, delegated to history as a group of wonderful chaps who were, in my mind, the 'salt of the earth'.

As part of the commercial strategy of BA that was established as I mentioned before, it was felt that the earliest a businessman arrived in London the better for business. I would turn up on day one of, maybe, a six-day block and stay overnight in five different cities and arise with the larks every day to get these people to Heathrow. We had a union scheduling agreement at the time that entitled us to one clear day off in seven and two clear days in fourteen. The problem was that the 'one day off in seven' did not necessary mean at home. So what sometimes occurred was that you would crack on for six days and then end up in say, Madrid, for a day off and then repeat the process for the next six days. Of course, it all depended if the fleet was under or over established. The 737 was just about on the edge of being short of pilots for most of the time so, in consequence, we worked hard for most of the time. Of course, those of us who could fly both types of 737 were well in demand. The 'draft' flying of which I spoke earlier was always in demand and we generally made very good money so we were all quite 'happy bunnies'.

The family went to Majorca again for the annual holiday but this time we linked up with another couple, Alan and Caroline, and their three boys. Instead of the apartment on the west side we all went to an all-inclusive resort on the eastern end of the island. It was a deviation from the normal routine but in the end it was really good since the resort catered well for all age groups. The evenings were dominated by a large entertainment bar and club. At about midnight the 'Disco' would fire up. It usually started with the usual 'Techno Rock' stuff and a few of the young trendies would sort of motion and mumble around the dance floor. At some point a 60s record was played and all the more mature types, like us lot, would invade the floor and sweep the youngsters away. Paul and Jenny seemed to be totally gobsmacked that there was their dad gyrating around the floor like a madman swinging his arms all over the place. I think that, by now, they conjured up their parents as a couple of old crusties and only fit for making tea and doing things only old people do. With the holiday done and dusted it was back to the flying world and the first hints of autumn were in the air with the usual early morning mist and generally miserable weather.

In the September there was yet another hijacking saga with a Panam

747 being hijacked to Karachi, Pakistan. Twenty innocent people were killed but eventually the hijackers surrendered to the Pakistan authorities only to be released some months later. It seemed that there was some sort of collusion between the government and the hijackers. It created a feeling of mistrust between America and the Arab world which seemed to stick even to this day. The Americans, I felt at the time, were not, what you might call 'world-wise' since all their battles in history were either in Europe or the Pacific, and the Middle, Near Eastern culture was difficult for them to understand.

In the October President Reagan and the Soviet leader Mikhail Gorbachev met again for a summit in Iceland and actively discussed the start of the reduction of the nuclear arsenals that each country possessed. Things were certainly moving in the right direction in the world of 'East v West' politics. I personally think, as I mentioned before, that the Soviets were active in this field since the costs involved were spiralling out of control and only the US could maintain the expense.

Another interesting news item was the visit to China by HM Queen Elizabeth. This was the first ever visit by the UK royals and the by-product of it was the signing of a trade agreement which reflected well for BA in the opening up of a new route to Beijing. The other side of the coin was that China was seen to start emerging as a major world trading country. Look where they are today in the world pecking order.

On one of my night stops in Aberdeen I was invited to sit in the cockpit jump-seat of one of our BA helicopters and experience a ride out into the North Sea to one of the many oil rigs. I duly turned up and went out with the crew to a Boeing Chinook, which was the largest of the machines capable of holding some 40 or so passengers. I say passengers lightly since they consisted mainly of the 'Oily' who were the oil rig workers and mainly of Scottish origin. All on board had to wear a survival suit which was bright orange with the net result of looking like a bunch of 'EasyJet' employees on a day out. Once we all got into position complete with about 40 Oilys tucked up we started up and looking up I saw the large forward rotor start to swing around. Things then began to happen and the whole machine started to vibrate and get very noisy. Amazingly enough we started to taxi to the duty runway just like a normal aircraft. Don't forget I know nothing about helicopters except the fact that they managed to fly somehow. The Chinook that BA Helicopters used was a derivative of the military machine and could be simply described as an aircraft style fuselage with two massive rotors, one forward and one aft, above this fuselage powered by two engines at the rear via about five gearboxes. Not a pretty looking thing but did the job well. I understand that back in the Falklands campaign back in 1982 they managed to cram about 80 soldiers in one and fly. Not bad for a 45-seater.

We moved out onto the runway and, with little change in the noise level, it just simply lifted off the ground. The strange thing was that the Captain sat in the right hand seat which was alien to me. It was explained later that the reason for this is that all the activity like winching took place on the right hand side of the machine and so it was logical to put the 'boss' on that side. Anyway, back in the Chinook after a short while in the hover, as they called it, we turned to the north-east and climbed to about a thousand feet and set sail for the oil fields. After about an hour of noisy, shaking flight the Captain called me on the obligatory headset and told me that the rig was shrouded in fog and that we would be doing an instrument approach to it, whatever that entailed. The machine had the familiar radar set in the cockpit so I was somewhat in the know as to what was going on. The first thing that the guys did was to descend down to about 100 feet above the water and study the radar closely. After a short while an image appeared on the display.

"There she is!" the Captain announced proudly.

The next thing he did was to drive towards it albeit slowly.

What a strange thing to do! I thought to myself since it all seemed contrary to the world of aviation.

The radar was fine-tuned so that the display turned into a fast moving picture of the rig and nothing else either side of it. We seemed to be almost metres away from the rig when the Captain started searching visually out of the forward windows with my eyes watching as well. I had never seen a rig close up and my only picture in my mind was what I had seen on the TV or in the papers.

"Got it visually," was his next call.

I had not really visualised what to look for but suddenly I was looking up at an enormous structure of steel with seemed to dominate the field of view. The amazing thing was it towered above us. Having said that we were at about 100 feet so where else would it be? The Chinook stopped and slowly climbed vertically with the structure seemly being metres away. This was quite an experience I can tell you. Eventually we became level with the deck and then the Captain inched forward and hovered over the landing pad which to my mind was miniscule in size. He slowly dropped down onto this postage stamp and with a clonk we had arrived.

"Welcome to the North Sea, Gwyn," the Captain said with a grin as the Chinook was fixed to the deck.

"Wow, that was something else!" I said.

I decided to have a peep out of the main door since I had been cooped up in the cockpit for some time. As I opened the door to the cabin I was greeted by a cabin full of 'Oilys' who looked like they were off the film set of 'Braveheart' so I beat a hasty retreat backwards into relative safety. After about 30 or so minutes with the rotors just seemingly ticking over with the engines running the doors closed up and the Captain informed me that we were off to an adjacent rig to fill up with fuel and so the whole business started again and this time the new landing platform made the last one look like a playing field. How they managed to get this large machine measuring over 15 metres in length onto the landing pad was amazing.

We finally got back to Aberdeen in the early evening and then we all adjourned to the bar. The banter between helicopter pilots and airline pilots continued.

"I cannot imagine putting my wings on top of the fuselage and whizzing them around via a load of gearboxes and hoping that they will not hit each other or fly off and then expecting them to make us fly," was my statement for the day.

"Fancy sticking the wings on the side and sitting at the end of a piece of concrete and roaring along hoping to get into the air before the concrete runs out," was their reply.

"Each to his own!" I would have to say but nevertheless a pretty good day out for which I was most grateful.

It was a terrible shock when I heard in the news about ten days later that the Chinook that I had flown in had crashed off Sumburgh in the Shetland Isles killing 45 people in one stroke.

There but for the grace of God go I, I thought.

I actually made a point of going to the remembrance service held later in Aberdeen. I never ventured into a helicopter again from that day forward.

As the year came to a close in the December BA announced a tie-up with United Airlines in the States with the intention of combining schedules across the North Atlantic which was proving to a very lucrative market for airlines. There must have been up to 25-plus airlines all flying between Europe and America on any one day. BA, for example, had five services a day to New York alone and was desperate to get the Concorde there as well. We now covered maybe ten airports in America with some of them getting up to two services per day. With regards to United Airlines it seemed to fit but by now the place was full of regulators on both sides of the Atlantic who basically looked after their own country. For example, in Africa, where the routes were not so lucrative, the regulations were much more relaxed. Anyway, that was how I saw it. The tie-up was allowed with United under the title of 'worldwide marketing partnership' and lasted for three years. United cracked a deal whereby they could jointly use the new BA terminal at JFK with no recourse for BA to kick them out of it. Many years later BA did actually tie up with American Airlines very successfully but could not invite them to share the JFK terminal since United was still there and always will be. On the plus side the Concorde inaugurated a new service from Heathrow to Barbados. I believe the crews had about three days off when arriving in Barbados. Not bad after flying for only four hours. How the other half lived!

Xmas at home was the usual mix of parties and kids driving you mad. With Paul at the new primary school Moya and I had to endure the annual Christmas show put on by the teachers and kids. I say 'endure' with respect to the efforts made by the school staff but when Paul would come home a couple of days before the performance saying that he needed to be dressed as a shepherd complete with beard and walking stick then the stress set in. Jenny was also involved in her pre-school do as well, maybe dressed up as an angel complete with wings.

Improvisation was the name of the game! On the day of the 'do' all the parents would troop into the school hall and patiently wait for things to happen. There was lots of scurrying about by the kids and eventually the Head Mistress would walk up to the microphone only to find that it didn't work. In the end it all sort of worked out and as we spotted a bearded Paul looking a bit confused somewhere in the back row, we threw a small wave and all of the kids waved back. Having said that it was quite comical to watch Paul and Jenny pretending to be all angelic. Yea right!

The family had a small following of pets by this stage. We had a Bichon Frise dog called Tracey. She was a small bundle of white fur but most affectionate. The problem was that her spot at night was in the middle of our bed much to my annoyance. Mind you, when Moya was fast asleep my foot would wriggle under her and with a swift shove she would end up on the floor in a crumpled heap. Don't get me wrong about Tracey since I loved her as one of the family during the day but at night she was a right pain. She had an obsession about cats to the point that if, during the night, there was a cat fight in the garden or within hearing distance this small animal would fire up on both barrels and bark the house down sounding like a classic Alsatian-type guard dog. The funny thing was that she had no animosity towards our own cats, of which we had two called Tigger and Magic. In the morning they would lay out their night's catch in the kitchen and wonder why the victims would be scooped up and lobbed out complete with a vocal rendition as to why they should not live beyond breakfast. Feeding time was an interesting exercise whereby you would lay out three bowls of food. One was obviously dog food with the other two being cat food. The three of them would sniff at their allocated bowl and then musical chairs would follow with the cats ending up eating the dog food and Tracey eating the cat food. This tradition continued throughout their lives. As for me I decided to get a rabbit. So the cage was bought and in went a white furry male called Snowy. Dad had built a magnificent 3-storey townhouse for him and it stood proud in the garden. He actually became my sort of mentor whereby if ever Moya and I had a falling out off I would stomp out to my rabbit and tell him all about it. Don't think he listened too much and all he did was to twitch his nose but I felt good that someone listened to me without biting back.

In the meantime the house was slowly being enlarged by our friendly builder Alan with me seemingly to have an inexhaustible supply of money. I was starting to fall down the financial pit of life! The world of the credit card was starting to swallow me up!

The final bit of interesting news for the year involved an American pilot called Burt Rutan who resided in the middle of the Mojave Desert, north of Los Angeles. He was what can only be described as an eccentric in the world of aviation since he produced the most amazing one-off aircraft out of carbon fibre and flew them successfully. He catered for the world of the inventor and not the straight-laced manufacturer. One of his designs was an aircraft called the 'Voyager' which can be described as a rather insect-like aircraft with skinny wings and a pin-like undercarriage that looked too delicate to fly. Well, Mr Rutan took off in this spindly looking machine and flew it around the world non-stop in five days landing back where he started from. What an achievement!

And so 1986 disappeared.

In came 1987 and I had been flying for nearly 21 years with BA and was fast approaching 41 years of age. One dead marriage behind me and seemingly set to continue with Moya for many years ahead. Paul was six and giving us the usual headaches of growing up. Jenny was finding her feet as well and providing us with plenty of heartache. The problem with being a parent is that there is no manual to consult or training course available to deal with parenthood. Coming back to Moya I think that, as I said before, although on the surface things still seemed fine, underneath things were not too good but I was too dim to notice and try to make amends. Take me back to my head in the clouds.

The winter weather was playing its usual tricks and some of the days were stretched to the limit both in time and resources. Berlin coped very well again. In all fairness the weather in Germany was far more severe than in England. The Germans seemed to catch the snow as it fell. The main problem for me was the going back and forth to work. You would think that a quick hop onto the motorway and there you were at Heathrow. Not so since over the years the number of cars on the road had increased dramatically. In my childhood we had one car per household and mother made do when father drove off to work. What we had nowadays was a minimum of two per household and maybe three if the children were of eligible age. Now, where a wife was concerned, a small town type car would do the trick but there was this sort of rat race amongst a certain type of housewife since, at about this time, the famous 4 x 4 hit the market and it came in two sizes, large or extra-large. When dropping off the kids at school this flotilla of mechanised monsters would cruise up and down the road at the school entrance with the lady driver hoping to park the beast. Now, I am not one to criticise female drivers but to watch some of the attempts would be the highlight of my day. The other point was they had not travelled over the Alps or across the Gobi desert to get to the school gates but about half a mile down the road. In my day I biked to school complete with satchel strapped across the handle-bars. Times were changing fast.

In the January President Reagan had a prostate operation which caused a certain amount of concern since he was now becoming a popular and strong president but in the end all was fine. In the Middle East there were a series of spectacular kidnapping of leading figures. In Beirut, there was a Church of England envoy called Terry Waite who got himself kidnapped by a bunch of terrorists and remained so for four years. The Lebanon was considered a peaceful country and, in previous times, earned the nickname of the 'Switzerland of the Middle East'. Thanks to abortive Israeli invasions and many internal conflicts the Palestinians were pushed further north into the Lebanon having been thrown out of Jordan many years before. The result was a total cross-section of people all trying to live together, all harbouring differing views as to why they were there. As I said before I was now over 20 years in BA and still the Middle East cauldron was bubbling.

In the February BA was fully privatised and we all had the opportunity to buy shares at a discounted rate. This was the world of Maggie Thatcher whereby all things owned by the government were sold off to the private sector. With the BA privatisation the word was out that the initial offer to the public would be well oversubscribed. This meant, in effect, that the marketing price of 125 pence would be worth much more on the day. The object was to buy just enough to make a handsome profit on the day. There were many discussions in the crew room as to try to pin down what that figure would be with many different opinions. I opted for about £13,000 worth of shares which I could sell within a month and reap in a profit. So off to the bank I go and sit down with the bank manager with the object of borrowing the money for maybe two months at the outside. I must have been in a long queue of like-minded crew members since the bank manager commented about the never ending requests for the same sort of figure had come his way hourly. He did, however, come good and yes I did make a good profit on the launch. So there we were now flying for a completely private company with nobody to fall back onto if we fell. A bit of a sobering thought.

I did not see any real change at work but being free from the Governmental shackles allowed BA to show to the rest of the airline world that we were here to make money and that we had a healthy bank balance, so look out you lot!

The flying world of the 737 was generally routine with the aircraft performing well with all the engine problems well behind them and a series of new ideas being put into practice to circumvent the Air Traffic Control delays that were becoming commonplace across Europe. We started flying much lower or going by a total different route. For a while it seemed to work but then after a while every other airline followed our lead and the delays started again. The problem in Europe is based around the fact that there are a lot of countries within a small area and each wants to do its own thing as far as routing and timings were concerned. For example you might be off to Istanbul which may involve flying over, maybe, ten countries and the ninth one has some problem or other and bingo! All stops. The French were and always will be notorious for delays and industrial action. Right back in 1966 I can remember an early flight on the VC-10 routing via Germany to get round a strike by the French ATC lot. Now, I am not being rude about our French cousins since we are planning to build a tunnel under Channel to unite our nations.

Back to the 737 and how I said that the flying was routine, well every now and again something occurs to spoil it all. It was on a normal flight in the April to Stavanger, Norway when I had a bit of an 'event' you might say. As we levelled off at the top of the climb on the return flight back to Heathrow the forward galley stewardess came into the flight deck complaining of a vicious headache and dizziness.

"OK, you better go and sit down for the rest of the flight and I will get a nurse to meet you at Heathrow. We will be there in about one hour and I will get a priority approach," I said, bearing in mind that crew sickness whilst on flight is just as important as a passenger falling ill during flight.

After a while she called us on the intercom and said that the girls 'down the back', who were out in the cabin serving off the trolley, were complaining of headaches as well. This was becoming rather strange and well out of the ordinary so I got up and wandered back and as I walked down the cabin I saw the one girl on the trolley totally miss the cup with the orange juice. I must admit I did do a double take at this and then my head started swimming and the mother of all headaches started. What I was witnessing was Hypoxia or lack of oxygen to the brain.

Time for action was my immediate thought and I got hold of the cabin public address and told all the girls to get the trolleys stowed and sit down and strap in and to get on oxygen. Once I got back on the flight deck I told the Co-pilot, Marty, to turn back to Stavanger and to alert the ATC that we had quite a serious problem. We pulled the oxygen masks down and took deep breaths to clear our heads. It was a total mystery as to what the cause was but the priority was to get back on the ground and go from there. Both Marty and I were now on oxygen and all was good. The characteristic of the system is that to talk to each other you must use the microphone in the oxygen mask which produces a sound like a muffled succession of words which you have to really work hard to understand is English. OK, Marty and I could make out each other's words with the help of Italian-style hand signals but when the time came to tell the passengers what was going on nobody aft of the flight deck understood a single word and it came across as a rather blurry vocal rendition. The idea of the Captain's voice in times of crisis is to radiate calmness and assurance. From what I was told afterwards by the Cabin Crew the reverse applied with the passengers all looking left and right, up and down, and talking loudly to all around them as if this was their last hour on Earth. The funny thing was that not one of the passengers had the symptoms of these sickness phenomena. This was getting stranger by the minute.

Stavanger is partly a Norwegian military airfield so once we told them about the strange condition on board and the fact we needed to land soonest the military side got wound up and when we were on the final approach there was a helicopter flying either side of us and a blaze of blue lights on the ground. Once we had stopped on the runway passenger steps appeared and everybody was ushered off in double quick time. The Cabin Crew were taken to the airport sick bay to be checked over. The BA ground staff arrived including the local ground engineer and by this time all possible doors and hatches had been opened for ventilation. At first we thought it might be the bleed air from the engines and the engineer set about checking the engines over. The second thought was that one of the aircraft fire extinguishers had silently discharged; a check revealed that they were all reading correctly but we removed the lot just in case. It was at this point that the call of nature came and I disappeared into one the aircraft toilets. When I emerged I was struck by a headache. The engineer arrived and donned an oxygen mask (not because of me I might add) and went into the suspect toilet. What he found was that the Halon fire extinguisher that had been recently fitted below the sink had a broken seal. The seal was in fact a solder joint and it had cracked spilling out Halon gas which, being lighter than air, had floated into the cabin and settled in the upper areas and was responsible for the lack of oxygen when standing up and putting your head into this invisible gas. Amazing!

We then closed up the aircraft and went to the operations who were run by a Norwegian airline called 'Brathens SAFE' and I talked to BA at Heathrow and it was decided we should stay overnight and position the aircraft empty to Heathrow the next morning. The Cabin Crew would position home on another airline. Finally we all got together and off we went to a hotel for the night. By this time the Cabin Crew had recovered enough for a social gathering to take place in my room. It seems to be that whenever a non-scheduled event occurs 'down the route' it is an excuse for a social gathering, or as I tend to call it being 'polite'. In the morning we got a call from BA stating that we were needed in

Frankfurt as soon as possible since the scheduled departure aircraft had a technical problem. So off Marty and I went to Frankfurt with a load of cabin fire extinguishers as supplied locally since our original ones were all tucked up in the hold. Once in Frankfurt we had to talk to the Cabin Crew about the 'new' equipment we had on board and eventually we made it to Heathrow at about midday and all returned to normal.

In my flying career to date I seemed to have circumvented any major drama and the one just described was a one-off happening and hopefully never to be repeated or anything similar. Not a bad record after some 21 years of flying 'before the mast'.

Back home the usual half-term school break came along and so the drama of the caravan reared its ugly head again with a trip to the New Forest in Southern England which is between Southampton and Bournemouth on the South coast. Being a shorter run than to the other side of the world in Cornwall the exposure time was much less which was a true blessing. With Jenny coming up to four and Paul closing in on seven and not forgetting Tracey these short breaks were good fun but had the effect of testing my patience to the limit on occasions. The problem was that the kids were all 'up and running' all the time and by the time it came for a nice leisurely drink and a smoke in the evening I was totally burnt out together with Moya. I loved my kids dearly but what happened to the old routine of 'bed at seven'. No bloody chance with these two.

This period of flying and home life was a long cry from the dramas of previous years with my first wife and all the dramas that unfolded at that time. The 737 was becoming a 'cult' fleet and the work was hard but very satisfying. Of course, one can become too complacent with one's lot and so I felt it was time to expand my 'portfolio'. I applied for the position of 'Training Captain' and passed the interview with the Flight Manager OK and joined forces with Mike Williams whom I had known for many years. The first thing to do was to complete a simulator exercise to qualify ourselves to be able to sit in the Co-pilot's seat and instruct a new Captain in his rightful seat. OK, that was done OK and so off I went and joined up with a Training Captain to start the route flying part.

The 737 training department was mainly manned by ex-BEA types who, by virtue of their upbringing in BEA, had a completely different attitude and method than what I had known in BOAC. So off I went to Berlin for a five-day stint with one of the chaps. His first introductory words were:

"Whatever you were taught by your trainers in BOAC you have to forget since we in BEA know how training is really done."

That got my back up straight away as you can imagine. It had been quite a few years since BOAC and BEA had joined hands and here was a guy going on about how his lot always did it right and the other lot always did it wrong. OK, in the days of BOAC the trainers had a lot of shortcomings but they did the job and moulded me into a Captain by sheer 'Mental Brutality' but that was what they were briefed to do at the time and I feel that, maybe, they didn't do a bad job. I hasten to add that the normal line pilots I had met who had hailed from BEA were a bunch of very professional guys. I saw no distinction or bias as to whether a guy started life flying an RAF Tornado or was taught at some two-bit flying school on a Cessna as long as they did the job in hand. However, there was still that underlying tone of mistrust between BEA and BOAC to cope with. It went the other way as well. Tony applied for, and got, a conversion course on the 747 Classic which was the backbone of BOAC back in the old days. He witnessed the reverse of what I was experiencing with this Training Captain who had the pleasure of my company for the next few days. So the scene was set for, what turned out to be, a bit of a bun fight.

Day one started very early with a simple flight to Düsseldorf and back followed by a Hanover and back. From the moment we stepped on board with me in the right hand seat doing the Co-pilot's duties he started having a go at me. OK, I accept that not having been a Co-pilot for some ten years it did produce a few problems mainly around the paperwork and routine but give me a break please! This was day one of a change of direction for me. He continually harped on about how BEA had set the standard of Flight Training and that he had to extract the BOAC way of doing things out of me. In retrospect BOAC did it their way and BEA did it their way. So what! I do not rate myself as a super pilot but more as an average one who was looking for a new challenge. I don't think anyone who 'crossed the line' from Long-Haul to Short-Haul was guilty of announcing that the previous lot did it best. We just adapted to the new environment and got on with the job. Besides, I thought that we all flew for the same airline nowadays. By the time I had done four sectors with this guy I was burnt out and very confused.

The next few days and sectors followed in much the same vein with me getting more and more annoyed and not enjoying the experience one little bit. We finally ended up in Düsseldorf for a night stop before going back to Heathrow. Unfortunately there was only him and me to entertain ourselves for the night with mainly a lot of small talk. It was obvious to him that I was not enjoying it.

Maybe I am not cut out for this training business, I thought to myself as I listened to him rattling on about some incident on a Vanguard many years before where he saved the day.

Ah, we have a right John Wayne here! was my thought for the day.

We took off the following morning to Heathrow and as we settled in the cruise an amber warning light flickered very dimly 'on' and 'off' on the overhead panel on my side to indicate that there might be a problem with one of the air conditioning ducts. Having flown with Flight Engineers for a good part of my life I learnt from them an awful lot about how an aircraft ticks engineering-wise. This dim flickering light was quite common to the Boeing type of aircraft and was cured simply by cleaning the connection or 'Cannon' plug once on the ground. The secret was that if it brought up a light on the 'Master Warning Panel' (MWP) then there was really a problem. To put it in simple terms, the MWP was the display that ran independent of the system fault and needed action to be taken. So, there I was with this dim flickering light overhead and a simple check of other readings showed that there was nothing to worry about except a good clean once on the ground.

"Captain, we have a small indication fault here on the overhead panel that needs attention once we get on the ground. There is no master warning and I have checked the system and all is fine," I said casually to my beloved master.

He looked at the dim flickering light and went into 'John Wayne' mode by ordering me to start an emergency drill as if the bloody wing was about to fall off. Part of this drill was to shut down half of the air conditioning system which is not to be taken lightly at our cruising altitude. I was totally gobsmacked by his response but felt the best course was to just follow the drills and sort out my feelings on the ground. His next action I was ordered to do involved telling ATC all about our problem and to descend immediately and request a priority landing.

That's one way of getting out of any landing delays! I thought to myself sarcastically.

The next thing was that he called up the Cabin Crew to brief them all about the fact that he would do his best to get us all on the ground safely and alive.

By this time I was totally bemused by the whole business but what else could I do but to follow John Wayne's order? We finally landed on a wing and a prayer and taxied to the assigned gate in total silence to be met by a fleet of ground engineers who swarmed onto the Flight deck once the passengers had left. JW gave them the impression that the aircraft was doomed until the wing was removed and that he personally would supervise the complete operation.

"Was the light on fully or just flickering dimly?" one of the ground engineers innocently inquired.

Ah, a man after my own heart, I thought to myself.

Before JW could open his mouth I confirmed that it had just flickered dimly and that a clean of the cannon plug would do the trick in my opinion.

"OK, it looks like the old Boeing problem again. It happened yesterday on another aircraft and the cleaning did the job," he replied.

"You must have flown with Flight Engineers to know about the old plug cleaning routine then!" he added.

"One or two in my time when I was in BOAC," I replied quietly.

Total silence erupted now with the Trainer grabbing his briefcase and pole vaulting down the steps and yomping off in double quick time like a Royal Marine to the crew briefing room. I followed at a distance but, instead of going into the Crew room, I did a detour up to the Flight Manager's office and told the boss that I had resigned from the training scene with immediate effect and that was that.

"Why is that, Gwyn? I had great faith in you as a possible trainer. What happened?" he said with a quizzical expression on his face.

"Just put me back as a normal line Captain and I will then sit down and talk to you about life," I replied.

This he agreed to and then I made my way to the crew room for 'High Noon' with JW.

He was sat stony-faced at one of the desks and was completing a form about how he felt, in his terms, towards my possible Training Captain appointment. I sat down opposite him and opened the conversation.

"Don't worry about the assessment. I have already resigned as of now. I could go into all sorts of reasons for resigning but please accept it as gospel," I said carefully choosing my words since I knew that one day he may be my Checker on the simulator and the knives would be out. I think his expression was like someone who had had the wind just blown out of his sails.

"Could you please sign this adverse report," he grunted at me.

"Please leave it in my mail box for me to read later. I am off home," I retorted sharply.

A few crew members around the crew room started to take notice of these two statues facing off against each other across the desk. I needed to get out of there and simply got up and said my goodbye quietly and off I went to the car park without a glimpse backwards. When I got home Moya listened patiently to my ranting and raving suggesting that I just stuck to being a standard issue line Captain. Tracey must have noted my mood since she scurried away and hid under the settee. The cats had disappeared as well. Very sensible! Mind you, the rabbit got the full story as well and he just twitched his nose as usual. So much for my venture into training!

I went back to work as a normal line pilot a few days later and had a meeting with the boss and he accepted my explanation for my resignation. I filed the adverse report in the nearest rubbish bin and spoke to the ground engineers who confirmed my diagnosis as to the fault and to date it had not re-occurred. It is by strange irony that my replacement potential Training Captain got through the course OK but he too resigned within a month of taking up his duties. Funny old world don't you know.

So back I went to Berlin for a five-day tour and met up with John Brassington with whom I did the original 737 conversion and, apart from the fact that I was a bit miffed about what had happened with the 'Wonder boy trainer' I soon settled back in the old ways. By the time the tour was done I was a happy bunny with no regrets about what had happened. Of course, there were a few curious comments bandied around since pilots are worse than women when it comes to gossip.

In the May there was a very nasty air crash involving a Polish LOT airliner, an IL-62 at Warsaw, Poland in which 183 people died. The IL-62 was a Russian aircraft from the Ilyushin Company being a copy of the VC-10 excepting that they got the centre of gravity in the wrong spot and it had an extra undercarriage right in the tail to stop the aircraft falling over on its tail. What actually happened was that one of the engines caught fire just after take-off and set the engine next to it on fire as well which spread to the tail and a catastrophic breakup occurred. Fire is the number one fear of any pilot and is a well-known fact.

In the Middle East the US Navy ship 'Stark' was hit by an Iraqi Exocet sea-skimming missile. The ship was actually in the 'Persian Gulf' at the time and 37 sailors died. This act turned Iraq into a totally hostile place in the eyes of the Americans and suddenly there were a heavy load of US military hardware being flown out to the Gulf region and large airspace restrictions came into force. At the time Iraq was led by Saddam Hussein, who was basking in the limelight of seemingly winning the war with Iran and taking great pleasure in antagonising the Americans. The plot was thickening in the region.

On a more light-hearted note a German light aircraft pilot, Mathias Rust, flew undetected in a small Cessna aircraft all the way to Moscow without being intercepted. He actually landed in the middle of Red Square much to the embarrassment of the mighty Russian military machine. May was quite a month in the world.

My flying continued at a steady pace with time spent in my favourite city, Berlin, plus a good variety elsewhere in Europe with, maybe, half the month away. In Berlin we had a visitor to the city in the form of President Ronald Reagan who made it his policy to continue the verbal attacks on the East Berlin masters with the well-known phrase:

"Mr Gorbachev, tear down this wall!"

Things were starting to stir in the apparent thaw between the superpowers with total silence coming from the East which would have been unheard of a short time before.

"Could it be possible that the wall could come down?" was the question on many people's lips following his visit.

It was also in the June that Maggie Thatcher got re-elected for the third term so the famous four were still there and intact. At the time of her re-election I was the chairman of the Binfield Conservative Association so was involved in rounding up the party faithful to vote on the day at the polling station established in the Binfield Primary School. One of the people on the list was a Mrs. Bridle. It was her son Ron that was my best mate at school back in the sixties. I went round to her house and mentioned this fact to her and, low and behold, Ron and I met up some days later after some 23 years since we were last at school together. It was an emotional experience to say the least. We chatted for hours as to how our paths had gone after leaving school.

Within the UK aviation world the 'second force' airline formed some years before was in financial trouble. BCAL was losing money fast and BA, being freshly privatised, made an offer to buy them. Scandinavian Airlines also were interested but in the end after a certain amount of horse trading BA got its way and BCAL was ours. BCAL was very famous for its adverts referring to the 'Caledonian Girls' with music based around the Beach Boys song 'California Girls'. It is interesting to note that quite a few of the pilots in BCAL were ex-Hamble who had had the misfortune to leave before the end of their course but finally got into an airline. My old school friend Frank Brejcha was amongst them and I did catch up with him many years later. BA inherited a diverse fleet of aircraft that included the DC-10, BAC-111, A320 and a motley small collection of the older 747-100. BA instigated a plan of action and within six months the name of BCAL was gone forever.

The other thing that happened in Berlin was that Rudolf Hess, the old war criminal, who I mentioned before, died. Incidentally, back in the early 40s on the eve of war with the Soviet Union, he flew solo to Scotland in an attempt to negotiate peace with the United Kingdom, but was arrested and became a prisoner of war. At the time he was

Hitler's deputy which makes the flight even stranger. I was in Berlin the evening that the news got out about his death and so a couple of us got the crew car out and drove out to Spandau prison out of curiosity. Being the only inmate left there the event seemed very significant. The British Army regiment at that time was the Black Watch, which was a very famous Scottish Regiment. As we approached the prison main gates there were an awful lot of Berliner Police around the area and also a lot of British Army personnel with full arms standing at the gate. The presence of all this security became obvious when we got out of the car. On the road opposite the main gate there must have been about 50 or so German men all bedecked in the full wartime Nazi kit all singing at the top of their voices some rendition which was obviously associated with the wartime Nazi movement. It was a very sobering sight to see many of them all dressed in black like they were out of a movie set. There were TV film crews all over the place all filming the happening. We were looking at history and it was not a pleasant sight. As we watched the spectacle from a distance a bus load of police rolled up and the riot squad poured out and formed a line. They then walked, or rather, marched in definite unison, about 100 strong, towards this group of choir boys and the expression of 'no prisoners' sprang to mind. Within minutes the singers were totally crushed and dumped into prison vans parked around the corner and dispersed. It was all over so quickly but the worrying thing was that many of these protesters were too young to be in the war. What we were actually witnessing was a gathering of the Neo-Nazi lot who worshiped their heroes of the past. Mind you I had a great appreciation of the police after that. After an hour or so the party broke up and all that was left were a few soldiers at the gate. We wandered over and chatted about the events just witnessed. They were equally impressed with the police operation. They were actually ready for protesters. I asked what would happen to the prison now.

"Tomorrow, the bulldozers arrive and this place will be flattened within days and a shopping arcade is going up in its place," one of them said.

The shopping arcade is there today. Quite an experience!

With BA being fully privatised it was free to order aircraft as it felt like so shortly after the BCAL purchase they ordered 11 more Boeing 767 large twin-aisled aircraft to consolidate the merger since the older 747-100 that were inherited were really past their sell-by date and needed to be put out to pasture. BA now had a large second base of schedules to run out of Gatwick and a new workforce to induct into the company so a new series of one-day experiences were put on the agenda. Once again I trooped up to the Concorde Centre and tried my best to get the 'buzz' of the day. As before BA had dispensed with the outside contractors for the event and trained up some people within the company to run the show. I found it all very disappointing since I again felt the professional side had drifted away. I am not having another go at the company people who volunteered to run the show since they made it as enjoyable as they could. Later in the afternoon Sir Colin Marshall arrived and spoke for about 30 minutes about BA with regards to the present and the future. Once again, here was a gentleman who knew how to deliver a speech and he impressed one and all with his flow of words. Good to have him at the helm!

Back home in Binfield Moya and I decided that it would be good to get a nanny to help out with the kids. I know, it sounds a bit flash but there we are! There was a girl down the road called Hillary who lived with her husband Steve in a mobile home and she came along to say hello. She seemed to have all the right credentials so off we went with Hilary looking after the kids. She fitted in very well and she actually came with us when we all went off to Majorca again for the summer holidays. With Paul aged seven and Jenny at four Moya and I found them a little bit easier to handle especially with the help of Hillary. Mind you, there were times when Moya and Hillary got totally engrossed in something or other and it was left to me to sort the kids out. Not that it was a drama but the problem was, as I said before, that each age brings different problems. Consider:

"Why does Mary down the road get sweets when she gets home from school and I don't?"

"Because that is the way it is," you would reply trying to be all correct.

The kids would then give you that look that cannot be reproduced by anyone else except your own bunch. Jenny was a master of 'the look' and still is to this day. The net result was that I would go from being an authoritative figure seemingly in command to a gibbering wreck feeling like an evil ogre. They say that daughters can twist their dad around there little finger. They are bloody well right you know!

The summer drifted to an end and along came the autumn. So there we were in the October all tucked up for the night in Binfield and looking at the TV news when the weatherman Michael Fish comes on talking about the fact that during the night the wind would increase to, maybe, gale-force but not too much to worry about since this was to be expected at this time of year. He even answered a TV caller who said that there was a hurricane on the way.

"Don't worry, there isn't a hurricane on the way," he replied casually.

Did he eat his words or what! That night we had the mother of all storms that killed 23 people throughout Southern England and ripped trees out of the ground the like of which has never been seen before. I remember waking up to the sound of crashing trees outside. I looked out across our back garden and was totally mesmerized by the way the smaller bushes in our garden were all horizontal and the sky was full of flying debris. The whole family was up at this stage watching the spectacle and then the electricity failed which made it more eerie to look at. It lasted maybe two hours but boy, what a two hours. I was due to fly the next day and after breakfast I had a go at getting to Heathrow and came back after about ten minutes since Binfield had, effectively, been cut off by falling trees. I admired the council services who were struggling to clear the roads of all the debris of the fallen trees. There was a town in Kent called Sevenoaks which was obviously named but that morning it became known as Two Oaks since five of the magnificent oak trees had been uprooted during the night. A friend of mind was flying into Heathrow in the early hours and as he landed on the cross runway the wind speed recorded on his approach exceeded 70 knots. Fortunately it was straight down the runway and he stopped within metres after landing and then took two hours to offload a very grateful bunch of passengers. So much for Michael Fish and his forecast. It really was a wild night.

There was another interesting snippet of news also in October whereby an RAF pilot accidentally ejected himself out of a Harrier jump jet and landed safely. His aircraft however just kept going west and headed out across the Irish Sea and Ireland itself. The solution to what to do about this runaway mount was settled when another RAF fighter, the famous English Electric Lightning, shot it down west of Ireland. This was the only recorded action of one RAF fighter shooting down another in modern times. Embarrassing or what!

In the November we all went out to Zimbabwe again to coincide with Moya's birthday. We all piled on the 747 at Heathrow and as we backed off the stand I was listening for the usual sound of the engines starting up. Well, they started up OK and then they all shut down and we were towed back onto the stand.

"It looks like we have a problem. Could be a short one or it could be a long one," I said casually fearing the worst.

It was the long one with us all having to hand back our duty free items and get coached off to a hotel for the night. The problem was that in Zimbabwe we were all due to depart in the evening of our arrival up to the famous Eastern Highlands and stay in a bungalow in the middle of the sticks together with Leslie and Charles. With us not leaving until the next morning and arriving in the late evening then things could get a bit tricky. We did just that and departed the next morning arriving in the early evening. This was our third visit so we were pretty well up to speed with the arrival procedure but as we walked out into the arrivals hall there was no-one to meet us. As we stood there a bit confused an Air Zimbabwe ground girl came up to us and asked if we were the Mullett family. So we had made contact but the instructions were interesting.

"I have the keys of Mr Fricker's car here and he said that you were to drive home to stay overnight and then tomorrow drive east from Harare to Nyanga which is about four hours' drive. Once there drive northeast for about three miles and then take the small track off to the right on a left hand bend in the road. After about another two miles you will see the bungalow on the right hand side. If it is at night when you arrive it will be marked by a candle which will be put near the road." She said it all very carefully and maybe watched my jaw drop gently to the floor.

It was now about 7 pm and so we ventured out into the car park and there was David's car sitting all alone. We all piled in and then set off away from the airport towards Borrowdale. Being in darkness added to the occasion with the first obstacle looming up. We had to avoid Robert Mugabe's residence in the hours of darkness unless we wanted to get ourselves shot at by the 'Third Brigade'. Having previously only been a passenger at night Moya and I had to scratch our memory boxes as to how to get round the obstacle. We were only going to Borrowdale with a day of adventures to follow and what a start! Amazingly enough we got to the house in Borrowdale finally after a maze of detours. As we approached the gates the dogs let rip at this intrusion into their sleeping hours and I stood there not daring to go in. Moya just opened the gate and walked straight in and the dogs just shut up and wagged their tails. Perhaps they didn't like English men and doted on English women. The ever faithful Langton came up from his quarters and made us a pot of tea and a few sandwiches to see us through until breakfast. We did manage to extract from him the directions to take out of Harare to Nyanga and so the next day we all piled back into the car and set sail on the second part of the adventure. By this time it was late afternoon, for some unknown reason, and it would be dark within a few hours. With no mobile phone or the like we depended on everybody being in position at the bungalow with a beer as the reward for getting there.

We managed to find the right road to Nyanga OK, since there were only four roads out of Harare heading north, south, east or west. Soon it became dark and the African night seemed to be darker than dark with no moon out and the street lights totally non-existent. There was no luxury like the famous 'Cat's Eyes' to mark the middle of the road and suddenly you would find a couple of locals walking along in the middle of the road as if they owned the place.

Don't screw up out here in the middle of Africa, was my thought as we trundled along.

What was good was that both kids fell asleep in the back so no whining there. Moya and I just kept watching the road looking out for this or that. I am sure if we had hit a wild animal such as a rhino we would come off worst and the kids would certainly wake up. After a while there was nothing outside of the strip of road that fell in the headlights of the car. It was a very eerie feeling and what was worse was that this was a so-called A road. After about four hours the lights of a town showed up ahead which could only have been Nyanga since nothing had been seen except darkness since leaving Harare. Now comes the tricky bit. In the 'Lone Ranger' western cowboy film that I used to watch on TV as a kid his ever faithful Indian friend would say:

"Kimosabi, meet me at the junction just northeast of town at sunset."

The Lone Ranger always turned up on cue at the right place at the right time. Never did know what 'Kimosabi' meant though.

Anyway, there we were trying to find this road to the north-east so the first thing was to establish where north-east was. This is where my navigational skills could come to the fore, so we stopped the car and I got out and surveyed the night sky which, incidentally, was a stunning sight with none of that industrial pollution in the way. Being close to the Equator the night sky looked a bit alien to me so I had to do some serious bluffing so as to not lose face.

"Gotcha, you little bugger," I proclaimed after a while and, like a tour guide, pointed the way forward.

Amazingly enough the direction I was looking in coincided with a sort of road that led out of Nyanga. Bluff completed! So off we went down this excuse of a road which was actually made up of two narrow tracks left by numerous car tyres with an occasional passing point which covered both directions. Obviously a B road! I watched the miles tick by on the speedometer and when we came just short of three miles we did start to go round a really sharp left-hand bend and, low and behold, off to the right was a track that looked totally overgrown but had the marking of car tracks in the dust. Tracker or What! Stanley is my name!

We gingerly went down this track slowly with the trees and shrubs banging against the car. So we had gone from an A road which was sort of workable, to a B road that tested the nerves, to this track which was a total nightmare. I expected a bunch of baboons to leap out at any minute. Our only saving grace was that we were in a Mercedes which gave us a feeling of security. Mind you, it was a pretty old model and the locks didn't work too well and the steering was a bit dodgy but what the heck the engine sounded good and we felt safe.

As we trundled along I was really concentrating on not departing the track and bounced along in and out of the many ruts. My mind was all fired up that we had stumbled on an old road that had not seen a car or civilisation for about 100 years and we were heading for a local village that had been undiscovered for all that time and they didn't like white people. Suddenly, on a rock by the side of the road, there was a small plate with a lit candle on it and some lights off the right hand side of the track. Moya and I shouted at the same time as we both saw the candle. Torches were flashed all around us and a beer was suddenly thrust in my hand by David.

"Golly gosh, I think we have arrived," I must have said or something similar. Not a GPS in sight either.

At this point the kids woke up and piled out of the car as if nothing was wrong as to the drive we had just done. I suppose they thought it was like going into Bracknell. Nobody seemed to say anything about the journey but, having said that, who cared since we had arrived in one piece and the beer was flowing. It was an amazing habitat being totally out in the sticks with no electricity or running water. All we had were lanterns all over the place and a large wood burning stove in the kitchen. It came complete with a couple of local chaps who cooked up a fantastic meal that evening and, of course, being Moya's birthday the drinking went on well into the early hours.

The following morning when we finally struggled up we could take in the full picture of our surroundings. We were perched on the top of a hill overlooking a small river and with the most fantastic views of the true African bush which was quite captivating. The temperature was, maybe, a balmy 27°C with not a cloud in the sky. I wandered down to the river and found David and Charles slumbered in the shallows by the bank.

"This beats washing anytime and is a good wake-up tonic," Dave shouted.

So in I go and was the water freezing or what! It certainly did the job of a wake-up tonic. It was just a question of whether the heart could survive. As I walked, or rather shivered, my way back to the bungalow the smell of bacon and eggs drifted across the 'ether' and we all sat down to a breakfast to beat all breakfasts. It was like the egg has just been pulled out of an irate chicken whilst in the act of laying it. So yellow!

Afterwards, we all made our way back to the river and basked away in the sunny weather. A net was produced that housed the beer and wine and was thrown into the river to keep cool. All the kids paddled around in the river and the whole scene was just idyllic and what with the cooled refreshment made for a lovely lazy day. The following day we ventured into Nyanga and had lunch at the famous 'Trout Beck Inn' which was an old colonial hotel set in stunning grounds. After lunch we made our way to a famous landmark known as 'World's View' which involved a gentle climb up the hill to the lookout post. The view from the top was amazing since we could see all the way into Mozambique on one side and large areas of Zimbabwe on the other sides. Dave and Charles pointed out that in the 'Bush War' they were stationed there since it provided a superb view of Mozambique and any movements could be spotted easily and dealt with. They recounted a tale that, at one point in the war, they were sitting in a tree acting as forward lookouts for the Rhodesian artillery. They would call the gunners with their 'Left a bit, down a bit' sort of stuff and wait for the sound of the guns firing. They would hear the whistle of the artillery shell going overhead and watch where it landed. On one particular occasion the sound of the gunfire was totally different with maybe a puff instead of a bang and they realised that the gun had fired a dud. They leapt out of the tree and within seconds the dud shell neatly demolished the tree they had been sat in. Lucky or what! Back at the bungalow the ritual of having a bath was really something. In the middle of the kitchen a large tub, similar to what you might expect in the middle ages, was produced and the wood burning stove was put into overdrive with bucket after bucket of hot water was poured into the tub until full. You then climbed in and off you went scrubbing. In turn anyone wanting a bath just climbed in after the person in front had finished. It was a bit like a Tesco's check-out queue in the middle of Africa. Lovely soak though!

The following day we made our way back to Borrowdale and so we all packed up and away we went. This time I was a passenger and it was in daylight so that I could enjoy the countryside instead of glaring at the road ahead.

Our friend Beverly, Minyon's sister, arrived from London that day and joined us for the rest of our stay. She was the elder sister and did not get on too well with her younger sister so the atmosphere was a bit strained at times. Dave had a sister who lived at Que Que which was in central Zimbabwe on the road to Bulawayo. She was married to a Dave as well, who had played an active role in the Special Forces during the 'Bush War' and spent the time mainly in Mozambique doing whatever Special Forces do. Don't forget it was only a few years before that all this was happening and it was a pretty grim affair. Anyway, I was invited to take the kids down to his farm for the day while Moya and Co went into town and did their girlie thing. So off we went in the 'Merc' with the usual set of vague directions as to how to get there. Zimbabwe is a big country and Que Que is not just down the road. After about three hours of driving we found the place and then eventually found the right track and arrived at the farm. You know the film 'Out of Africa' with Robert Redford. Well, here we were seemingly on the film set of that movie with all the attributes that makes Africa a great continent. We sat on the veranda with Dave and his wife with a view that was rural to say the least with a well cultivated lawn stretching out into the grasslands of Zimbabwe with its rich red soil. Dave was a truly interesting character and resembled a true 'White African' if ever I saw one. He commanded all that we could see and shortly after our arrival we all climbed into his truck and had a drive round the estate. He didn't actually own it and, amazingly enough, it was owned by an Englishman. All Dave did was to run it for him. Jenny was smitten by the horses that were in the small paddock and one of the locals saddled up a pony and off went Jenny into the horizon clinging on for dear life with the local firmly gripping the reins. This might have been the trigger that started Jenny wanting a horse when she got older.

"Thanks, Dave, for putting the idea in her head!" I must have muttered.

While she was away riding the range Dave, Paul and I sat on the veranda drinking a couple of beers and taking it all in. He took Paul over to his 'den' and showed him the trophies from the Bush War. I would not like to know where or how he got hold of them and I certainly never asked.

Eventually Jenny got back from her Safari and we all settled down for afternoon tea with cakes baked by his wife plus beer of course. In the tropics it gets dark at about 6 pm and as dinner time approached out came the lanterns and we had a magnificent meal on the veranda. We seemed to have laid claim to the veranda but where else do you sit in the warm evening air? Dave said they usually slept outside when it got really hot but he had the habit of having a loaded rifle handy.

Not quite like Bracknell, I thought to myself.

After dinner it was back into the Merc for the long drive home. Once again I was thrust into the African darkness with no GPS in sight. As we drove down the track with Jenny harping on about the horse ride and Paul equally going on about the war trophies all I could come up with was an occasional grunt as I was totally engrossed in getting to the main road in one piece. Once on the main road towards Harare I settled down for the longish drive. To the local people a three-hour journey was nothing for them and I could compare it with a 30 minute drive in the UK. Anyway, the kids drifted off to sleep in the back of the car and I concentrated on keeping on my side of the road, avoiding the night wanderers and the occasional dog that ventured out. There was not much in the way of civilisation. There was a bit of traffic around and I would make sure that I gave them a wide berth. In the road ahead I would see a dim wobbly light coming towards me and I assumed that it was a man on his bike. The amazing thing was that as we passed each other there was a 'whoosh' since this little wobbly light was attached to a huge sixty-ton lorry on its way south driven by a local who was happy to drive by 'brail' to keep on the road. His speed was seemingly about 60 miles per hour and the first time it happened I flitted and scampered all over the road fighting the controls trying to avoid becoming mincemeat and the dust storm following him was something else. So every time I spotted an 'African Moped' coming the other way I pulled over and slowed right down to avoid being part of his underbelly. Eventually I got back to Borrowdale with about six African Moped encounters under my belt. I felt like stamping a sticker of a moped on the side door as a record. Once again it took a few beers to calm down or was that just an excuse? Our African holiday came to an end so off we all flew back to Heathrow with the usual gamble for seats and arrived in a cold November morning. The winter was fast approaching.

Once home I caught up with the news to find that there had been two air crashes that month since we had left. A 747 of South African Airways had crashed shortly after take-off from Mauritius on its way to Johannesburg. The 747 model in question was known as a 'Combi' whereby at the rear of the main deck cabin behind a thick curtain freight could be carried. There was a fire that had started in this main deck cargo compartment and very quickly enveloped the main cabin and the aircraft fell into the sea resulting in 159 deaths. The cause was never fully established and many theories were put forward. South Africa was, at the time, under international arms sanctions and one thought was that it was carrying illegal arms from the Far East since the flight originated from Hong Kong. A total mystery!

The second air crash involved a Korean Airlines 707 en-route to Seoul from the Middle East which disappeared over the Andaman Sea with the loss of 115 souls. It was established that a bomb had gone off on board. North Korean agents were suspected and finally two agents were arrested in Bahrain. One of them succeeded in taking cyanide and died but the other one, a woman, was sent to Seoul to face trial. Kim Il-sung was the North Korean leader at the time. She was initially sentenced to death but pardoned by the President of South Korea, Roh Tae-woo, and served life. It was ironic that the flight was flying between Baghdad and Bangkok via Abu Dhabi at the time. It might have been assumed that it was all part of the terrorism world of the Middle East but this incident put a new twist on it and expanded the evil trade to encompass the whole world. North Korea was then added to the list of countries that 'sponsored Terrorism' as the Americans put it.

So the year drifted to its end and in December they started to dig the channel tunnel. England and France united finally. This cannot be! So, in comes 1988 and I wonder what fortunes will come my way. I am now approaching 42 years of age. Where has it all gone?

In the January BA introduced a new cabin status whereby there was a new class known as 'Club World' and 'World Traveller' which covered the long haul scene replacing 'Business Class' and 'Economy Class'. In Europe there were now 'Club Europe' and 'Euro Traveller' replacing the same. It was a good move since it elevated the old 'Economy' tag and was very soon followed by many other airlines once again.

In Berlin there was, at the time, just one class operating which seemed to fit the bill. BA, however, introduced the 'Club Europe' product on the IGS and it was an amazing success. Physically, it consisted of a moveable contraption that hooked into the luggage racks. From it hung a curtain so acting as a divider between the 'Club Europe' and the 'Euro Traveller' section. The amazing thing was that the seats were the same size in each cabin and only the cabin service was different. Having mentioned the seats attempts were made in the 'Club' section to leave the middle seat free which was a bit tricky when the aircraft was full. Consider a sector from Berlin to Hanover which was about 35 minutes flying where the 'Club' fare was pitched at about ten percent higher than the 'Traveller' fare. The status of the German businessman was such that he must fly 'Club' since his position earned him that privilege so he was led to believe. So we would fly with an aircraft full of 'Club Europe' passengers on a 35 minute sector and they all got the same service. It was a stroke of genius to introduce this cabin distinction and the money just rolled in.

Also in Berlin the decision was made to replace the old Avro 748 aircraft with the latest technological wizardry from British Aerospace known as the Advanced Turboprop (ATP). Well, if we thought the 748 was a nightmare then the ATP was the sequel. The famous quote from one of the ground engineers fitted the bill when he said.

"If the people who designed the ATP had designed the Avro Lancaster all you British people would be speaking German now!"

His remark summed up the ATP. It seemed to be an aircraft that was put together by sub-contractors. Nothing on it was normal. Yes, it was very economical but that only applied when it actually got into the air. There was one occasion when I arrived in the afternoon from Heathrow ready for one of our famous Pilots' parties in the evening that Joe and I had organised. I was due to do a standby block starting the next day. As I walked into the hotel foyer there was the complete Berlin complement of the ATP crews all sitting around having coffee.

"So what has happened to your lovely machine then? Have they all broken down or what?" I asked with a certain amount of trepidation fearing that my party scene was starting to drift out of reach.

"Ah, Gwyn, they have found a common fault in the undercarriage 'up locks' or something and the whole fleet has been grounded until further notice," one of the pilots replied.

At that moment my bleeper started bleeping and I cursed the lot of them when I was told that although I was not on standby all hell had broken loose and I was soon on my way around the West German countryside picking up all the 'waifs and strays' left stranded by the non-arrival of the ATP. Cinderella cannot go to the ball!

"That's nice! I set up the pilot's party and instead of being there I am flying around West Germany sorting out your lot. Thanks a bunch. Enjoy the party!" was my announcement to the assembled gathering.

So off I go on my travels back to Tegel and find out that both me and my poor Co-pilot are off on a 4-sector guided tour around the network. We were due back at about 10 pm that evening that would get us to the party at about 11 pm so it was 'all systems go'. If ever an aircraft went round the network at speeds approaching supersonic it was ours. We had a lot of help from the various stations we visited and the airways were very quiet due to the time of day. On the last sector down the corridor to Tegel we met up with a Panam aircraft whose pilot was hoping to get to the party as well since they were on the guest list. We landed at Tegel at about 9:15 pm managing to shave about 45 minutes off the total time so we did get to the ball albeit a bit late.

I once had the dubious pleasure of passengering in the ATP when I travelled from Berlin to Nürnberg to recover a 737 that had diverted there from Munich. As we flew down the southern corridor at about 9,000 feet we found ourselves slap bang in the middle of the icing level. This level is defined as the height where the outside temperature is at about 0°C and the chance of ice accumulating on the aircraft is at its highest. I was sat near the front on the left hand side and as I looked out of the window I could see that we were flying in the bottom level of a cloud and the build-up of ice was amazing. Every part of the front of the wing and engine was coated with at least ten centimetres of the white stuff. The de-icing system was similar to that I had had before on the small light twin aircraft when flying for Howard Rose. This was modern stuff! Every now and then I could see the leading edge boots expanding and contracting. The propellers were de-iced electrically but they too had a thick layer of ice on them such that they appeared as a solid white disc sitting out there on the front of the engine nacelle. I was sipping a coke at the time and as we descended the ice flew off as we went into warmer air. Being seated right in line with the propeller the ice hammered against the window next to me and seemed like it would break the window and land in my drink.

Who needs ice in the coke when there are buckets of it trying to get in? was my thought for the day.

When we finally landed in Nürnberg I felt like I should do as the Pope and kiss the ground as I descended the steps.

In the news in January Mikhail Gorbachev, the Soviet leader, started to introduce reforms known as 'Perestroika' which was seen as a turning point for the Russians. Suddenly a free economy regime became all the rage and the complete eastern bloc was slowly being released from its shackles of communism. It was if they knew that there was no way of dominating the world so why not join them.

Back in Binfield we bade farewell to Hilary since she was now pregnant and felt it was time to leave. A few months later she let us know that she now had a baby girl and all was well. Moya and I decided to go down the 'Au pair' route and along came Anna who hailed from Germany ironically. She was very good and being German had the kids organised to a tee. Efficient or what!

Alan, our friendly builder, continued in the 'Mullett's Mansion Mode' with extension after extension. To finance it all I used a combination of my monthly salary and the good old credit cards. The era we were in was the land of easy credit. Pretty well everyday some junk mail fell through the letterbox advertising this and that credit facility either by the use of a credit card or a cheap loan. I needed the money so I became, what you might say, a total addict to the credit card. Moya was unaware of what was going on and I hid my secret from her very successfully. Stupid or what!

On one trip I did up to Stockholm we met up with a BAC 1-11 crew from Manchester and we all adjourned to the bar and chatted over a few drinks. Bearing in mind that I had never met either of the guys before, I nearly choked on my beer when the other Captain said casually:

"Your mother was Mauvis Emerson, wasn't she?"

"How the heck do you know this sort of info about my mother?" was my response tinged with a large amount of curiosity since these sorts of things are never talked about at work.

"Gwyn, I'm your second cousin, that's why I know," he replied.

I nearly fell off my chair since I never ever knew that I had any relative flying in BA. His name was Roger Dunning.

"I knew about you all the time but never managed to get to find you in BA but here we are, part of the family," he went on.

I was stunned to say the least and we chatted on for a good few hours about South Wales and all the family history. We were roughly the same age and he had grown up in the valleys of the Rhonda. He mentioned that we did meet once as youngsters at some family do. You see, where my mum and dad grew up, they were all part of a large family clan which reached out into the valleys of South Wales. It was funny that when I got home and met up with Dad and Thirza I mentioned my second cousin Roger Dunning and my dad went all strange and serious.

"We never talk about the Dunnings as part of the family since your cousin was born 'out of wedlock'," he said, as if I had mentioned a ghost.

What had actually transpired was that Roger's mother, who was related to my mum, never married and worked as a chambermaid to some gentry of the land and found herself pregnant due to the over-indulgence of her master and she was ushered away in secrecy out of prying eyes to have the baby. So all in all Roger did very well in getting to where he was today but it is amazing how my family history is steeped in intrigue.

It was by irony that we met once more shortly after that on a very sad occasion when my favourite Aunty, Moyna, died in Cardiff. What had happened was that she had been divorced about 15 years previously and had married her cousin. This might seem pretty weird, but it did happen in the close knit community of the clan in South Wales. Having said that they were well over 50 when it all happened and he had been widowed. They lived in Porthcawl, where I used to go to the beach as a kid, and had the habit of swimming every day in the sea irrespective of the weather or time of year. On that fateful day my Aunty Moyna was in the water when she suffered a brain embolism and was rushed to Cardiff General Hospital and put into intensive care on a life support machine. Dad, Thirza, Moya and I all went down to Cardiff almost straight away to see her to put our weight behind her recovery. Cynthia and Robin also came down from Manchester soon afterwards. Aunty Moyna was the youngest of Dad's family which made it even worse. I remember in the hospital reception area there were all the relatives gathered from Cardiff and the Rhonda Valley including Roger Dunning and his Mum. Moya and I made a point of going over to him and saying hello to him and his mum. The disapproving looks from the others really made me quite annoyed. There was no way that they were going to be left out in my opinion. Bloody hypocrites!

As for my aunty it transpired that there was no hope of any sort of recovery and so, later on that evening, the life support machine was turned off and she died. It was all very sad since, as I grew up, I always found her to be a lovely lady who would confide in my own mum about me and between them hopefully find a solution. Whether they succeeded or not I will never know. A strange thing happened after she was pronounced dead whereby there was a procession of all the relatives up to the ward to view the body and utter a few words. Dad joined in as well. I have to say I find that part a bit strange and I certainly was not in the mood to join in the procession. She was cremated a few days later at the same crematorium as my mum and so, memories were re-ignited about my lovely mum and how I still missed her terribly.

Back in Berlin we did have a small problem with the cars that we ran. There were two of them and they were both registered with British Military number plates for convenience as I mentioned before. The problem we had now was that the good old IRA had spread their wings away from Northern Ireland and they were targeting anyone to do with the British Army in Europe. In the March three of their 'warriors', for want of a better name, were gunned down on the main street in Gibraltar by the SAS and that got them really annoyed. In Berlin Mel Sawden received a letter from the military authorities making us aware that our cars were a legitimate target for the IRA. Being bold and defiant men we took the cars off the road straight away and started the process of re-registering them with German plates. The privileges were gone but, what the heck, we did not fancy facing a mad Irishman. So why did we drink in the Irish bars where you could not be more exposed – I will never know.

At Gatwick BA moved into the brand new North terminal with the complete operation now using one central point which really put Gatwick on the map. Quite a few Long-Haul services transferred to Gatwick including all the services to the Caribbean being flown by the 747 fleet. The crews involved earned the nickname of being part of the 'Beach Fleet'. I didn't get to Gatwick much myself but when I did I was well impressed with the new facilities. At Heathrow we were spread over two terminals, one being Terminal 1 that dealt with all the Short-Haul flights and the other being Terminal 4 that covered the Long-Haul flights with the odd Short-Haul one thrown in. In Europe there was Frankfurt and Amsterdam supporting Lufthansa and KLM in one massive terminal. Heathrow was losing the edge as a destination. The solution on the table was a new terminal on the Western edge next to the M25 motorway, dubbed Terminal 5, but at that time it was all a pipe dream with massive opposition from the local noise abatement lot and the environmentalists. What it needed was a few VC-10s taking off in succession to really stir them up if you want to talk about noise. Even the 737-200 version that I mainly flew was being driven out by the modern do-gooders. In my opinion, if you bought a house close to an airport then you knew all about the noisy aeroplanes so why kick up a fuss about them now.

Back in Binfield I took the bold decision that I had done my bit for society with respect to the family unit and decided to have the 'snip'.

"Why do I need to tell the world?" you might say.

The reason is that it did produce a rather embarrassing moment afterwards thanks to Jenny. As it was, the actual act was not at all as I imagined it would be and was quite straightforward. The aftermath is quite amusing thinking back since being the victim you tend to walk a bit strange for a few days and be very protective of certain areas of the body. So off I limp taking Jenny to the local school where she had been enrolled a few months earlier and for some unknown reason I went into the classroom with her. There was the young lady teacher strutting about calling her brood to order when Jenny piped up:

"My dad has just had something cut off to stop him having any more children and he says it hurts!"

Being kids of about five or so they asked me questions like:

"What happened to you, Mr Mullett?"

Or:

"Did you get any sweets afterwards?"

The young teacher obviously knew what I had had done and being of the spinster variety was embarrassed beyond. As for me I cursed the opening of Jenny's mouth and slinked off with my tail between my legs trying to be super-cool but still walking with a limp. They know what to say and when to say things to cause maximum effect!

In the April a 737 took off in Honolulu and during the climb the upper part of the cabin forward of the wing ripped away exposing the forward cabin to the elements from the floor level up. Unfortunately, the one fatality was the stewardess who was sucked away with the broken roof. The aircraft landed some 30 minutes later and amazingly held together with a rather cold and dishevelled bunch of passengers still strapped in their seats. The fault lay in a manufacturing error which caused premature erosion of the fuselage fixture points and hence the breakaway after take-off with a small amount of air pressure on the suspect joint. In our morbid sort of humour it was referred to as the only Boeing 737 'Cabriolet' version flying in the world. Could you imagine taking off and then 'whoosh' your roof has gone 'walkies'?

Spring in Berlin was always a pleasant time with the last effects of winter disappearing fast. It was at about this time that one of our more adventurous Captains, Dave Wood, known as 'Woodie', did a deal with a local marina whereby we had the use of a small yacht that, for a small fee, we could sail on the local Havel Lake. It was moored up in this small Marina in the Spandau area and was a 'coup' for us all. With the weather on the 'up' maybe three of us would climb into one of the cars, resplendent with the new German number plates, and make out way down the Heerstraße, picking up a good supply of on-board vitals on the way, just in case we got marooned for the night. Once on board we just sailed away for a lazy afternoon. Berlin is built on a sandy base so that if, by chance, the yacht touched bottom there were no vicious rocks to do damage. I remember on more than one occasion getting stranded on a sand bank and calmly sitting back, enjoying the sunshine, drinking a nice glass of red wine. It seemed that the pace of scheduling out of Berlin was not as hectic as in the past so we did end up with some actual days off in the city. All in all, the Berlin scene was the most relaxing part of my flying career especially in the latter years that we were there. Even the ATP, which seemed to be dedicated to ruining our life there, seemed to be acting more like a real aeroplane nowadays.

Joe Hall and I seemed to be running the 'Pilot's Berlin Fund' to everybody's satisfaction with very few moans. Amazing for pilots not to moan! We decided to expand our portfolio by setting up a similar boat scene in Oslo since we always seemed to have a day off there and with the hotel on the edge of a lake it was just what was needed. The fact that only the Flight Crew stayed in that hotel was on the plus side as well. I am not sure if Joe and I set it up but the hotel manager was quite happy to fund the boat, which was a small cabin cruiser, and to rent it out to us. The idea was that the Berlin Pilot's fund would subsidise the rental. The deal was put in place and the boat duly arrived and Joe and I flew out to Oslo to set up the charts since the channel to the open lake needed a careful eye. Joe, being an ex-Royal Navy ship's navigator, created a very detailed map showing which channel to follow and placed it prominently on view for all to see. It was a work of art! Now the difference between a Berlin lake and an Oslo lake is simple with Berlin having a forgiving sandy bottom and the Oslo one being solid and unmovable rock. So, the boat was moored up for all to use and a briefing was written in plain black and white. It was launched very successfully for a short while and the feedback consisted mainly about the location of nudist beach not far along the lake shore.

"Could we please have a set of strong binoculars please to view the local wildlife?" was one request.

'Wildlife' was not on people's mind and far from the actual purpose of the request. After about a week we got a call that the boat had hit a mysterious underwater rock and had been dragged into the mooring a bit waterlogged. It was established that this mysterious rock was uncharted and the insurance company duly stomped for the repairs. About one month later it was re-launched, complete with a brand new set of binoculars, and on its second outing hit another rock and was once again dragged back to the berth much the worse for wear.

"Enough is enough," the insurance company wailed.

All in all, the Oslo boat lasted about ten days before the hotel took it off us and that was that. The binoculars were never recovered.

Not one of our greatest ideas, I thought to myself.

Besides, the ATP lot started moaning that they never went to Oslo so that was that! Mission failure!

In the April there was yet another punch up in the Gulf when an American warship hit an Iranian mine and President Reagan hit back this time by destroying some oil installations in Southern Iran. It was felt that a war in the Gulf was inevitable. It was a matter of 'when' and not 'if'. The repercussions of this would be felt within the airline world sooner or later. BA was entering a downturn of business, in common with many other airlines at the time and was tightening its belt. On the 737 there was a campaign run by the management to pick our brains if we could contribute in any way towards cost savings. Our Flight manager was Roger Price at the time. He hailed from Hamble so we knew each other and got on extremely well. The way the exercise was done was for Roger to meet up with maybe four of us in a local bar and over a few drinks listen to him and he, in turn, would listen to us. Once again fuel costs were high on the agenda and from what I remember a few changes were made and some savings were achieved. Altogether it was a rather civilised way of meeting up with the bosses.

In contrast, on the fleet, there was also an undercurrent of discontent with some aspects of the way scheduling was working which, combined with other items, was creating a feeling of 'Why should we go out of our way when they don't help us at all?'. Our union BALPA had, amazingly enough, washed their hands of any problems on the 737 being more interested in the 757. Maybe it was because the chairman was not on the 737 and felt that with Berlin we had nothing to complain about. In the end we took matters into our own hands and I approached Roger Price and a meeting was arranged with his boss, Mike Jeffery, to have what could be described as a frank and open discussion. The venue was the BA staff college up near High Wycombe and I was asked to sort out six other Captains to come along for the day to include lunch. Now, we were talking! I did get a team together and we did meet for the day. All the cards were put on the table and we get some modicum of success out of the day.

Another change within BA occurred in the April when Airtours was renamed Caledonian Airways and adopted a new colour scheme which featured a smart blue tail with a yellow 'lion head' painted on it. The tailpiece earned the nickname of the 'yellow dog'. The stewardesses went back to the old BCAL style uniform with a crisp white blouse and tartan shirt. Boy, they looked good. Little did I know what was in store for me a few years later!

The order placed a few years before for the newer 737-400 came to fruition in the May with the first arrival from Mr Boeing. Since I was qualified on the 737-300 that we had on lease from Maersk it was not long before I did a flight in one of these new shiny all singing-and-dancing machines. The passenger capacity has gone up from just over 100 on the 737-200 to about 150. The old Super VC-10 had about the same capacity but had four engines and used about twice the fuel per hour to run. All this had happened in about 15 years of aviation. The technical advances made in the airliner world were becoming quite amazing. It is a bit like your PC nowadays whereby the moment your switch it on it is obsolete.

So, now it's back to Binfield and my rabbits. The original boy, Snowy, was still going strong and getting used to my ranting when the chips were down on the domestic front. He still twitched his nose in agreement when I expanded my side of the argument – or was it in disagreement?

At the back of our garden there was a small plot of land belonging to the local water company that once housed a small back-up pumping unit that was deemed surplus to requirements and was up for auction. I spoke to the bank about making a bid adding the figure to the mortgage account.

"Mr Mullett, we see no problem with that since we consider you a very good risk with an excellent credit rating," was their answer.

What an amazing reply, I thought considering that, by now, I was beginning to drown in my credit card debts.

So I duly put in a bid at the auction and was successful in buying this small plot of land. The advantage of the new purchase was that it gave me a rear drive to my house if that meant anything at all. The disadvantage was that it had a very steep slope downwards towards the rear garden so it was no good for a car to park let alone the mighty caravan. So in comes the builder Alan again fresh from a large first floor extension over the garage and demolishes the small pump building and cleans up the driveway and constructs a magnificent set of gates at the new rear boundary. At the same time he fills in a drainage ditch so that the rear garden flowed well into the sloping driveway up to the new rear entrance. Money no object!

I hit on the idea of extending the rabbit colony with two new cages and runs. So what I did was to make, or rather Alan did, a couple of horizontal concrete terraces on the driveway slope. So now it was time to get some more rabbits so that I could talk to the whole colony about my woes. I bought a female and felt that the time was right for Snowy to have a bit of fun. When I popped her in his hutch he moved like the speed of lightning and it was all over in a couple of seconds. They didn't even have time to get introduced or any chance of a bit of small talk. I blinked and it was all over. David Bowie summed it up:

"Wham Bam thank you ma'am!"

I separated them and kept a watching brief over the lady and, low and behold, a short while later as I was cleaning out her hutch I spotted a small bundle of fur. I gently explored it and there were two little ones barely 5 cm long buried deep in the straw. Mother and babies were doing well! In fact, the mother was very happy for me to very gently touch them in turn. She got an extra issue of food for that. I don't think the dad cared less either way. Nature at its best you might say. No maternity ward needed here. I suppose you could say that it was someone else to add to my audience when I felt I was losing the domestic argument. After a while the little bundles of fluff became little rabbits and it was very relaxing watching them leaping about the hutch that, incidentally, had a quite large run for them to enjoy the outside world. I had the vet check them out and discovered that I had a boy and a girl. So I had to do a bit manoeuvring to sort them out to avoid a complete football team arriving.

So there we were sitting in the lounge on one occasion when we spotted Tracey doing a runner around the garden like a dog possessed. I casually looked further to see what the commotion was all about and found that Snowy was on the loose together with the little ones that were, incidentally, called Penny and Tuppence and there was a right commotion going on. I sprinted, well nearly, to the back door with Moya in hot pursuit to try to restore some sort of order. I must have looked a right sight chasing Tracey, who was chasing Snowy, who was chasing Penny and Tuppence. All I was thinking about was that the cats could well be lurking looking for dinner. The amazing thing was that Penny and Tuppence shot back through their wire of the run and into the hutch with the mother thumping the floor as if she was saying:

"Now look here, Snowy, you had the pleasure of me but you leave my kids well alone!"

So I was left trying to corner Snowy with Tracey doing her ferocious bit and eventually peace was restored with all animals in their correct places. It transpired that I had left the hutch open and Snowy had done a runner. It all sounds a bit sad getting emotional about my rabbits but I did like them and found them a total joy to watch and look after. A total rebuild of the runs followed shortly in order to keep the little ones in.

It was also decided to build a flower border where the drainage ditch had been filled in and so the day came when a lorry load of topsoil was deposited at the rear entrance. I was not one for hard, laborious physical work since I was basically a lazy chap who would come up with ideas and then get someone else to do the hard work. Anyway, I started to shift this lot with my wheelbarrow and shovel it onto the proposed site of the new border. As time went on the wheelbarrow seemed to shrink in size and the pile of dirt got bigger. I must have been at it for a couple of hours when, low and behold, it started to rain. Now dirt when dry is heavy enough but add a bucket load of water and it seems that the weight doubles. It felt like it though plus the drive was turning to a mud slide. It must rate as one of the most miserable days of my life. I think Moya and the kids were out at the time since I had no-one to take it out on. The rabbits hid away to avoid the mutterings as I passed their pens with yet another load of dirt. My opinion of the plan for a new flower border was unprintable. It then got dark and there was this solitary figure still humping back and forth shovelling dirt.

Back in the flying world Berlin was still the main focus for me. As I have said many times the flying was good and the social side was good. The new 737-400s were proving themselves as a winner both in the noise factor as well as in the comfort factor. It was strange but the 737-200 was a very easy aircraft to land and invariably you could place it on the runway at the right spot very smoothly pretty well every time. I say that lightly since every now and again it would kick back like a mule and spoil it all. The 737-400 was proving to be the same but the 737-300 that we had on lease must have had a harder undercarriage or something because to get a smooth landing out of them was more by luck than by judgment. Strange but true!

Such was the modern world of aviation that the 737-400s came totally certified for low visibility approaches which on previous aircraft would have taken a considerable time to achieve. The downside to this was that most other airlines were obtaining these qualifications as an automatic right. In previous days when the fog came down BA was always cleared to make an approach and by-passed the opposition and took the glory every time. This advantage was pressed home by the PR department in no uncertain terms. Consider the domestic services which invariably brought passengers into Heathrow to connect with a Long-Haul flight and the fact that the weather had to be pretty extreme for BA not to arrive at Heathrow. With this modern automatic facility of being able to land in virtually the thickest of fog from day one for most of the airlines then it was:

"Please go to the back to the end of the queue and wait your turn," being the usual request from the controllers.

Back in Binfield with Jenny now coming slowly towards five years of age then it was a case of:

"Can my friends stay for a night's camp-out, Dad? Please oh pretty please."

It is that finger-wrapping thing rearing its ugly head again.

So what happened was that her bedroom was turned into a camp for maybe four of them to sleep. Sleep being the non-operative word since it was more like an all-night giggling session. In the morning her room was like a bomb site and by then the little darlings were too sleepy to do anything constructive. It was down to me and Moya to clear up the mess. Now, if that had happened in my younger days there would have been no way we could have avoided clearing up our mess. Times had changed out of all recognition! On another occasion a small one-horse circus rolled into town and I took Jenny and a couple of her friends to it. It was not really my scene but the kids seemed to enjoy it. So there I was with my little brood sitting on the circus bench clapping when I felt I should clap when the 'knife thrower' came on to do his act. Funnily enough, he was the clown in the last act but there you go. Anyway, he calls for a volunteer from the audience to help out and within seconds six little hands pointed at me accompanied by a lot of cheering. So I was dragged kicking and screaming into the ring in front of maybe 100 people to be 'sacrificed' publically.

This I am not enjoying! I hope he did not have a row with his girlfriend before the show... was my only thought.

Anyway, he led me to this large wooden cartwheel contraption and then set about strapping me to it so that I resembled a human cross with arms and legs spread out. I spotted a couple of knife marks where my body was and took a deep breath. He spun the wheel slowly and as he turned to walk away he said:

"Don't worry, mate, I have done this many times and never missed yet! You must remember to keep absolutely still for it all to work OK."

These words of comfort meant nothing to me and even Jenny and her friends went very quiet. The drum roll started and I just closed my eyes tensing my body like never before and wished I was somewhere else. There was a resounding squelch as each knife hit the wood and not me. He aimed lower each time and now I was getting a bit worried about everything that was dear to me. It was a bit like Brian Hanrahan, the TV reporter on HMS Invincible covering the Falklands conflict, when he made the famous statement:

"I'm not allowed to say how many planes joined the raid, but I counted them all out and I counted them all back."

Instead of planes I substituted knives. I counted six in his hand when he walked away and now felt six squelches in the wood. I opened my eyes to find myself upside down surrounded by six large knives, each one barely a couple of centimetres away from my fair flesh. There was large round of applause and I gingerly stepped down and took a bow and weaved my way to my seat. My little brood was very quiet for the rest of the show. I turned to Jenny and said:

"If I had been murdered out there I would have never spoken to you ever again!" with a smile on my face.

The gigglers were now all back to normal. Another camp-out that night I suppose.

Paul was now approaching eight and was establishing alliances with other boys of his own age. There was Mark, Chris, Barry and a few others who would all get together and cultivate the 'gang' culture just as I did at his age. There were a few bad apples out there but from what Moya and I could see it all seemed harmless enough. It even got to the point with the gang all going into Bracknell for a Saturday afternoon. In my day, we all would get on our bikes and go into town but nowadays it was the bus or one of the parents' car that would do the trick. We even enrolled Paul into the local cubs. He lasted about 20 seconds! He got bored I suppose. Of the two kids I found Paul easier to handle but Jenny, for me anyway, was always a handful. Loved then both equally though!

In the April we did the usual caravan trip to the New Forest with Chris and Elaine. I had by then bought another car in the guise of a MG Montego which was white with a 'go-faster' stabiliser on the rear boot lid and carried the famous MG motif. At the time it was the fastest production car around of its class and boy, did it move! When it was hitched up to the caravan it made light work of the extra weight with or without the wine bottles. Going backwards was still a nightmare! On one of the evenings by the caravan it was decided that we could all get together later in the year and drive down through France using the company of 'Eurocamp' to set up various venues on our French travels. Over a few wines later we organised the itinerary and planned the adventure for August that year. Moya and I had never been camping but it looked a lot of fun and not too much of a drain on the finances.

All in all 1988 was becoming a very mundane year with not too much happening of note. On the flying front all was fine except for the bi-annual simulator check, the annual route check plus of course the medical check that came around every six months. With regards to the medical check I was becoming a little paranoid about it. OK, I was fit and had no health-threatening ailments but for some unknown reason I began to really get worked up as the time approached. Yes, I was not exactly of the slim variety but the old blood pressure was spot on and the heart ECG always got the nod from the doctor. I still had the annoying pain in my left leg calf muscle but I felt that I could live with that and that there was no need to alert the whole of the medical profession about it. As it was I sailed through the medical checks with flying colours.

"What the CAA recommend is one glass of red wine per day to keep the arteries open," was actually quoted to me by my doctor. No specifications as to the size of glass though!

The simulator checks came and went with not too many problems. As I said before the bi-annual check was based over two days with the first day dealing with the mandatory items which we all knew well. The second day was being developed into a general training day. For example, the company introduced an exercise known as a 'Line Orientated Flight Training' (LOFT) whereby you had a route handed to you that was as realistic as it could be and you then made all the right noises to carry out the route. What then happened was that a realistic fault or a failure would be introduced to see how you would deal with it, together with your co-pilot and then take some sort of action. They actually had a CCTV in the 'box' together with a recorder so that afterwards you could sit down in the briefing room and go over the video and hear what you said, where and when. The best thing about it was that you were not scored on your performance but it was designed to, maybe, improve your thought process and I found it very useful except for my dreadful Berkshire accent which stood out.

"Gwyn, unfortunately everyone knows where you are in the air when you make a call because of your distinctive accent," I have often been told.

"Sorry, Mum," I often muttered to myself.

As for the annual route check then that could be tricky since it was happening in real time. Most of the checkers were good at their art but, having said that, there was the odd one or two who still lived in the old BEA days. Of course, it is like the first day away on a long trip, when the central heating packs up that a problem suddenly turning up out of the blue that is, maybe not an everyday route happening and you could spot the checker sharpening his pencil.

There was not even much to report in the news up to about June of that year when the only thing of note was the fact that President Reagan visited Moscow for the first time and on the TV there seemed to be smiles all around. The world was changing fast and Europe was right in the heart of it. The big four were certainly getting down to business and the cold war was top of the agenda. Helmut Kohl and Mikhail Gorbachev were particularly seen to be getting friendlier than ever.

"Could we be witnessing the beginning of the end of the cold war?"

Was the question on many lips and, of course, where was Berlin amongst all of this.

Also in the June the fancy new Airbus A320 crashed at Habshein, France whilst doing a low flypast for the crowds and failed to climb away and ploughed into a forest killing the three crew members. It raised certain questions about the flight systems of the Airbus range of airliners since the manoeuvre was apparently a very simple climb away after the fly-past. Airbus, as always, seemed to just flow over the queries as to why such a thing should happen. Perhaps it is the French way! Having said that the world of pilots was now becoming divided as to which way their loyalties lay. Me, I was and still am a total dedicated Boeing man. Suffice to say:

"I ain't going if it ain't a Boeing."

Another rather disturbing event took place in the June involving the USS Vincennes, which was cruising in the Straits of Hormuz, which lies at the eastern end of the Gulf with Iran to the north and UAE to the south. The ship picked up a radar contact flying out of Bandar Abbas, Iran and seemed to track directly to the American ship and actually started to descend as if replicating an attacking military aircraft. There was, at that time, no means of positively identifying it and so the US ship let fly a salvo of missiles and brought the 'intruder' down. It turned out to be an Iran Air Airbus A300 flying a scheduled flight to Dubai and 290 souls died. The Gulf at the time was a tinderbox just waiting to explode and this sort of action just added to the friction building up in the area. It is difficult to apportion blame here since the area was so volatile but what a tragic loss of life.

Amongst all of this tension in the Gulf area the Iraq-Iran war ended with Iraq being the victors but at a cost of over one million lives lost. The net effect of all of this for the airline world was a major beef-up in security and large areas in the Middle East becoming no-go zones both in the air and on the ground. It seemed to me that the focus of the world conflicts were pulling away from the old East v West theatre stage to a rather ugly back street illegal brawling club where there were no rules and anything went. This is borne out by the number of civilian lives that were getting destroyed in the eighties as compared with the seventies. This was particularly showing up in the airline world since, in the seventies, hijacking did not kill enormous numbers of people but in the eighties it seemed to be the norm for the perpetrators to kill as many as possible.

In the August we set out on our venture into France with Chris and Elaine's family and our two little darlings. The first night was planned at a place called Burgundy which was in central France on the eastern side. The car was loaded up as best we could; suffice to say there was a lot of kit travelling with us. The camp sites we had planned to stay at had the tent, obviously, together with cooking implements but that was all. It ended up with Paul and Jenny sitting on their duvets and every nook and cranny filled with something or other. Chris and Elaine had a similar problem but with a bigger car more space was available. Chris even managed to load his windsurfer on the roof rack of his car. We had a simple 'Citizen Band' CB two-way radio in each car so that we could keep in touch with each other. We must have left the house very early in the morning since we were booked on the Dover-Calais ferry at some unearthly hour. Mind you the full English breakfast while we crossed the Channel was very welcome. Once on French soil we made our way towards Paris and the famous 'Périphérique' that circled the city and headed southeast. The drivers in France were something else and I had to keep my wits about me. Mind you, Moya was a great asset in keeping me on the French side of the road and being my all-round lookout for trouble. Once we left Paris we drove on the famous 'Autoroutes' that wound their way down through the countryside. There was a speed limit of sorts but nobody obeyed it and it was a general free-for-all as to which lane and side the overtaking cars were coming from. It was quite something to look in the rear-view mirror and see a black speck some way back and then look again seconds later to see the bonnet of a Mercedes bearing down on you as if it were supersonic. One moved fast to get over and this blurred vision of a car would go past you at a speed of something well over 100 miles per hour. I was cruising at about 100 miles per hour and was left standing. Most of the routes were chargeable at the toll booths that were dotted about. It was annoying at first to have to fork out every hour or so but if you looked at the condition of the route and the fact that there was not a roadwork anywhere on all our travels through France it seemed very worthwhile. As well as the normal service stations there were rest areas on the route which became very welcome to stretch your legs and gather your thoughts. I think Paul and Jenny must have been supplied with games or something since there were not too many moans from the rear seats or maybe I just can't remember. After driving for some eight or so hours we pulled off the main route and weaved our way to the campsite at Burgundy and eventually found it perched on the top of a hill. I have to say the countryside was stunning to look at and the classic tree-lined avenues were something else. The tents were not too bad with two small bedrooms built-in for the kids and a larger one for Moya and me. The kitchen area was a bit basic but workable. Besides, by this time we had a few supplies in and we unwound very nicely over a glass of wine or two. I think we all slept like babies that night.

The following day we said goodbye to Burgundy and drove at a more leisurely pace to the famous 'Ardèche' area of south-eastern France where we would be staying for a couple of days. This region is famous for its wonderful scenery with rivers winding their way through the most beautiful valleys and gorges. It was really quite something to camp right on the river's edge and splash around in the water. The river was not deep and we spent a lot of time just relaxing. We ate locally most nights and I remember the food was totally delicious. The kids seemed to be totally chilled out as well. Chris and Elaine had Claire, about Paul's age, and Martin who was about Jenny's age. Of course there was the odd nuclear explosion but what the heck!

After a couple of days we headed south-west to a place just south of Perpignan called Saint-Cyprien which was on the coast and our home for the next ten days or so. As we drove through the town I was behind Chris at a set of traffic lights. On the green light Chris drove away and then 'Zappo' a lady driving one of the famous French cars, a Citroen CV6, hurled herself right into Chris's car and all hell broke loose. To witness it was quite a shock but worse was to come when the lady clambered out of the wreckage of her car and started yelling and screaming at Chris in French insinuating that since he was a tourist and an Englishman as well he had no idea how to drive and it was all Chris's fault. I got out and let rip at her in my basic French that she was the offender and to crawl back into her shell. She did not seem to have any concern for the kids that had been rocked about in the back of Chris's car. By this time a crowd had built up with a police car and an ambulance turning up. It was becoming a right circus with this lady still uttering forth. The policeman, or Gendarme, was trying to take notes both in English and French. While all of this was going on a couple of old Frenchmen wandered up and spoke to the Gendarme and his look at the lady said it all. One of them turned to me and said in his broken English:

"Monsieur, the lady was totally at fault. My friend and I were sitting over there at that bar enjoying a carafe of red wine and we saw it all. The lady is stupid!"

Well, at that point I declared undying love for all Frenchmen and took back all I had said about them in the past. The scene then defused with the lady being charged for jumping the lights but the main problem to us was what to do with the wreck of Chris's car. We were not far from the campsite so I ferried the kids and Elaine together with Moya there and let them sort out the arrival bits and wait for Chris and me to arrive. It took a fair while for Chris to sort out the paperwork at the police station and I managed to drive his car gingerly to the station for storage. We unloaded everything and put it all in the Montego with the exception of the wind surfer which we left in the care of the police and made our way to the camp site. We finally got sorted into the tents and a few glasses of wine were consumed while we had a planning meeting to put some sort of plan into action. Fortunately Chris had quite a high-powered position in his company, IBM Europe, and was on his mobile phone within minutes and, low and behold, they came up with a hire car arrangement for Chris to collect locally and to use that for the rest of the holiday and then drop it off in the UK when he got home. The only problem was that it did not have a roof rack to take the blessed windsurfer so Chris came up with the bright idea to put the thing on my roof rack and he could carry some of our excess kit in his newly acquired hire car. What could I say! I was not too happy with this thing that would stick out both ends of my car. Chris did not seem to have a standard issue windsurfer. It was bloody monster! The thought of dragging this all the way back to the UK did not appeal but I kept that to myself and poured another glass as some form of compensation.

As it was, after about two days Chris picked up a hire car which his company had sorted out for him and everything got back to normal excepting for my thoughts of the bloody windsurfer. We were staying at this campsite for about ten days so it gave us the chance to get organised around the tent and to use the facilities on offer. There was a swimming pool together with a small bar and café and the weather was quite glorious. Chris and I bought a small barbeque set and so it was our job to do the cooking while the two women dealt with the refreshments and keeping the kids amused. On one particular early evening while we were all sat around we noticed that the wind was picking up in speed and dust was starting to fly around everywhere. Chris and I had decided on the now famous barbeque but by the time we got it all set up the wind was really howling. Unbeknown to us a 'Mistral' was blowing. The 'Mistral' is a phenomenon peculiar to that region whereby a hot and dry wind that originated in the hills to the north would flow down the Rhone valley picking up speed as it travels along. By the time it hits the coastal areas it can have speeds of up to 80 kilometres per hour and can be very destructive. So there were Chris and I grimly going about our task of cooking and the rest of the mob all sheltering inside the tents which by now were 'shaking in their foundations'. Both Elaine and Moya were giving us a lot of verbal about the stupidity of trying to cook outside considering that the tents could blow away at any time and land in Algeria. We struggled on in our task and with me clinging onto the base and Chris holding down the meat. Finally, we entered the tent triumphantly with an assortment of cooked meats, and defied our critics. Having said that, there were traces of grass and the like all mixed up in the meal which made it all a bit exciting plus the fact that uneasy eyes were being cast around watching the state of the tent which, by now was being hammered by the wind. Fortunately there was no rain which helped a lot. In the end Chris and I ventured outside and lashed both tents with extra rope, which we had brought with us, to the two cars that were just rocking gently. It sounds a bit like 'Scott of the Antarctic' but it was a pretty viscous wind. Not much sleep that night I am afraid. In the morning we had a stroll around the site and found all sorts of damage from a fallen tree neatly bisecting a caravan to some people just sitting there on the plot where once a tent stood. In retrospect, the fact that we double-lashed the tents to the cars and stowed all the loose items in both car boots seemed to do the trick and we suffered very little damage. The barbeque must have ended up the sea since it was nowhere in sight. Apart from that one night of excitement the time spent in Saint-Cyprien was just what we all needed with blue skies, good food and wonderful wine. What more could you ask for?

At one point we travelled over the border into Spain and met up with Elaine's brother (I think) on the Costa Brava and spent the night there. I think the total sum of kids and adults numbered about 20 so it was definitely party time.

Eventually we had to move on and so we came to point of loading the monster on my roof rack. We had two suitcases as well up there plus now this extra thing. The Montego was not a small car by any means but the famous windsurfer actually hung over the front and back by a fair margin. I felt that we could become a bit top heavy so more stuff was piled inside to compensate. Finally lots of rope was employed strapping it down. We were ready to go! We said farewell to Saint-Cyprien and set sail to a small village called Beaujolais which is in eastern France just north of Lyon. We were now in wine country, as the name implies, and the countryside lived up to its reputation with vineyards, gentle hills and green valleys. This was rural France and really did captivate the imagination. Small rivers were running through the area and were as clear as crystal. OK, I am not a fan of the Frenchman but I have to say they live in a beautiful country. The monster was still in place on the roof as we arrived. Next to the campsite was a large lake which Paul and I strolled around and spotted large fish just lazing around below the surface. Later on that day, we assembled our fishing rods and just sat there watching the world going by. You could say we had both opened our 'Nothing boxes'. Whether we caught anything I can't remember but who cared!

We spent three relaxing days at Beaujolais but in the end we had to plan our run for home. We were not too far north of Lyon and the journey home was going to be quite an epic. On the 737 we would take just under two hours from Lyon to Heathrow so you can imagine the distance involved. Whilst driving quite long distances on the holiday Chris and I would chew away on caffeine tablets which did the trick of keeping us awake and alert. The downside was the fact that once we had arrived wherever we were destined for a deep sleep shortly followed. Anyway, we decided that with all the traffic problems we might encounter en-route to the ferry at Calais it was best to make our own way there independently and not as a tandem. So, we did our final loading session including the famous windsurfer and off we set for the long journey home complete with a full load of caffeine tablets at the ready.

The route was pretty straightforward once we cleared the backwaters and at one time I was pottering along at well over 100 miles an hour. The MG Montego had performed well throughout the holiday. Not quite like the Mini that I had driven many years before as a young Co-pilot. The problem with cruising along at this sort of speed was not the sheer sensation of speed but the fact that is was quiet and relaxing. I had forgotten about the load on the roof and at one time I leaned forward for a stretch. I happened to glimpse up and spotted the windsurfer virtually trying to jump out of its straps and go into orbit and fly gracefully into the local countryside. The fact was that this 'thing' was aerodynamic in shape since it was designed to glide through the surf. It was now trying to be a flying machine and, at the speed we were travelling, it was ready for lift-off. Besides, Chris would have been a tad upset if his beloved toy had ended up buried in some local cow shed. Could you imagine a herd of cows all standing in a row being milked gently when suddenly through the roof comes this flying wing complete with a bunch of suitcases attached.

"Not another bloody windsurfer!" the farmer would say trying to calm his flock which by now were totally entwined in pipework and undies with milk everywhere.

"Time for a break," I said with my heart in my mouth.

We hit the Paris area after about five hours with the speed now down below the hundred mark and with Moya's help we managed to navigate to the east of the city and picked up the road to Calais.

"Not bad at all without a 'Tom Tom' do I hear you say?"

Once clear of Paris it was time for a break and something to eat at one of the service stations. Whilst there, we were amazed to bump into Chris and Elaine having a break as well. Considering the distances and timing it was quite amazing to meet up like that. Bit boring but true!

"Windsurfer still attached," I reported to Chris.

So we then travelled on as a duo and made the ferry spot on time and eventually after nine hours of hard driving we made it back to Binfield and bed. It was with the greatest of pleasure to unstrap the monster and let Chris lovingly take it home. Apart from the odd problem I have to say that the holiday was pretty good but in the end it was wonderful to flop into our own bed and have no more driving for a while.

So, it was then back to work for me and with the schedules in full swing it was pretty hectic. BA came up with the idea that on the weekends the aircraft could be utilised for holiday charters on a similar scale to what was going on in Berlin. So it was on a Saturday night in Newcastle the crew assembled at about 9 pm and went to the airport to fly to Palma, Majorca and getting back at about 6 am. Such fun! In the crew room at the airport we mixed it with the charter crews who did this all the time. Not my idea of a Saturday night out spending it on the tarmac in Palma de la Majorca trying to get clearance back to the UK with a bunch of passengers who were the worse for wear. I felt sorry for the cabin crew who had to put on a smile for this lot. It was the Brits at their worst! On one flight I did with Les Johnson out of Gatwick we flew to Monastir, Tunisia in the late evening and

on the return flight as we arrived at about 5 am into Gatwick the
fog came down and even for us it was too thick to land. We made an
approach and broke it off at quite a low altitude and elected to divert
to Heathrow. The same happened at Heathrow with the fog and so
we decided to divert again northwards and opted for Luton airport.
Neither of us had been there before but it did not seem to present any
problems until we flicked through our landing books and, low and
behold, Luton did not feature. It would have been useful to have charts
for the approach and landing there since the fog was slowly spreading
north and we were running out of options. On the 737 all the spare
charts were all in a box which, in normal circumstances, could be
reached by one of us getting up and dragging the box out from under
the bulkhead. With the two of us totally occupied with the outside
world and getting routings, etc, together with a fleet of other aircraft
all doing the same thing getting to this box was proving a little tricky
to say the least. At this point the stewardess poked her head in the
cockpit to find out what was going on and before she could utter a
word there she was dragging this box out of its housing. With Les and I
watching the show outside with one hand and the other one dragging
all sorts of books, charts and manuals out of the box and throwing
them anywhere in the cockpit until we found the right books right at
the bottom. By the time we had landed with not too much fuel left the
cockpit resembled a mad professor's study. Now that was the easy bit
compared with trying to placate the passengers, who were now really
worse for wear, and tell them that they could not get off the aircraft
and go home which, for some of them, happened to be about two miles
up the road. We went over to the Monarch Airlines crew room to find
out what to do with this bunch of anarchists on the tarmac.

"Welcome to the holiday charter world where chaos reigns when it
all goes wrong!" was the greeting I got from a rather arrogant young
Monarch Airlines duty officer.

"Actually they are your lot, mate, since we are doing your flight for
you because you lot have run out of decent aeroplanes," was my reply,
betraying the fact that I was pretty burnt out from the various flight
distractions plus the fact that it was very early in the morning and I
was tired and grumpy.

Eventually coaches were organised to drive the passengers back to Gatwick. All in all we must have been on the ground for some four hours or so until we saw the back of the passengers. As for us, we got driven back to Heathrow arriving some 14 hours after we had set out from Gatwick. You might have gathered by this point that the holiday charter world is not for me.

On another occasion that year I did a strange holiday flight out of Gatwick whereby a complete crew crammed onto the jump seats of a Caledonian Tri-Star at about dawn and passengered out to Faro, Portugal and then stayed for the day and then flew that night to Belfast, Northern Ireland with a load of happy Irish people and then sat around there for a few hours before flying another bunch to Palma. Once there we were then taken again to a local hotel. We eventually passengered out back to Gatwick the next day all crammed onto the jump seats again on another Tri-Star. Apparently the unions had negotiated this trip as a perk for the Gatwick lot to compensate for the non-stop night trips that were all part of the holiday charter world. You can keep it!

"Take me back to Heathrow and Berlin anytime!" was my passing comment as I left the crew and drove home.

In the news that year was not too much to report that would change my world excepting that in the September the NASA space shuttle Discovery blasted into space signalling the return of the USA into space. Funnily enough, very shortly after that the Russians launched their own version, the 'Buran' which did three orbits before returning. No-one was on board and it was the only flight ever done by the Buran and the spacecraft was destroyed some time later. I believe that there is a mock-up of it in Gorky Park, Moscow.

In early November Moya got a call from Minyon about her 40th Birthday party that was set for that month and was there any chance that we could come out to Harare to join in the fun. Moya and I did a bit of manoeuvring around with the kids and off we went to Harare, childless, arriving on the Saturday morning for the party in the evening. It was one hell of a party as only they know how to celebrate birthdays. On the Sunday night we flew back to Heathrow. Is that flash or what! The only problem was that we nearly missed the return flight since we were so engrossed in a farewell drink at the airport that we missed the 'final boarding' announcement and had to hotfoot it across the tarmac to get on board. We totally missed the immigration and security channels and so the flight home was spent trying to work out how to deal with the lack of a departure stamp in our passports. When we got home I went to the Zimbabwe Embassy in London with cap in hand and explained to them what had happened. The amazing thing was that as I sat there in the waiting room the walls were covered in posters about Rhodesia and its former days. I found this all a bit bizarre considering the fight for independence that the new government had fought to get where they were today. Anyway, after many apologies and much humbling I was given a letter from them confirming that I had in fact left the country signed by the ambassador himself. I paid them a princely sum for their services and hopefully resolving the entry scene when we next ventured that way. Felt a bit of an idiot I did!

Also in November the month of birthdays passed with Paul reaching eight and Jenny getting to five years of age. Time flies when bringing up kids. They were both in the local school just up the road and, of course, the ritual of the Xmas school concert was looming.

It was on December 21st when the news broke that a Panam 747 with a flight number of Panam 103 had exploded over Lockerbie, Scotland. This was terrorism at its rawest. The flight had originated in Frankfurt, Germany and transited through Heathrow on its way to New York. The sequence of events was horrific when it was later discovered that a small amount of Semtex, which was developed as a potent explosive in Eastern Europe, was smuggled on board either at Frankfurt or Heathrow and ended up in a radio cassette player in a suitcase in the forward hold. Once it detonated it set up a chain reaction that literally blew the aircraft into five pieces and it crashed to earth on Lockerbie killing people on the ground plus all on board. The total loss was 270 people. The explosion actually happened in the hours of darkness and on the following morning the film footage was simply dreadful. The cockpit section with the Flight Crew still strapped in was lying on its side in a field as if the aircraft had been dissected fore and aft. As you could imagine the rumour network was doing overtime as to the perpetrators of this act and it seemed to lean heavily towards

Libya with the infamous Colonel Gadaffi and his bunch of hoodlums as the guilty party. Even today, the truth may never be known. The frightening part about it all was that the amount of Semtex used was small enough to fit inside a fountain pen.

"So where the heck does one go from here?" was the question on many lips of people in the flying world.

It was ironic that within a couple of days of Panam 103 the family attended the local church for the annual 'Christmas' service and I can remember sitting there listening to our local vicar, Owen, spouting on about 'love thy neighbour' and all that stuff.

What a load of rubbish, I thought to myself wondering why I was there in the church in the first place. As we left the church I did pass some sort of caustic comment which seemed to fall on deaf ears. Each to his own I suppose! I have to say the outrage of Panam 103 did upset me for quite a long time especially knowing that the truth will never be fully disclosed in my lifetime.

Unfortunately the incident put Panam in a very precarious position financially. It was a couple of years later when they went bust. Now, here is the irony of the collapse of Panam. Back in the 30s they were one of the main operators out of Miami, Florida to South America under the guidance of their illustrious chairman Juan von Trippe. Another fledgling airline of the day was a company called Southern Air Transport (SAT) whose headquarters were in Syracuse, New York and both of these airlines were lobbying the government to fly more services to South America. Panam got to the senators first and managed to convince them that they were the only airline to do the job. I am sure some dollars exchanged hands. The object was to crush SAT out of the airline world. It nearly did but SAT did survive and became Delta Airlines. When Panam had its terminal financial illness Delta was asked by the US Government if they could absorb Panam and save their name. Well, memories ran deep and so Panam was consigned to the knackers' yard.

"What goes around comes around," they say.

The aftermath of the Panam disaster stirred the airport security world to the point of paranoia and long queues at the security check points became the normal scene. Even as aircrew we were not exempt and I can remember having the most trivial items taken off me with the promise that they would be posted to my home address. Amazingly enough, the chances were that the confiscated items were in the hold of the aircraft that I was flying. I suppose that they had to be seen to be doing something but this was a total overkill.

All these new procedures greeted me as I went back to work after the Xmas break at the start of 1989. Great! If I recall the winter was not too bad with only the occasional bout of snow and fog about. That made a change from what I was used to. The IGS in Berlin was getting very busy with extra services being flown all over West Germany. West Berlin was becoming a city that was starting to attract various celebrities and I can recall Tina Turner doing a concert. She was certainly a stunner and the West Berliners loved her plus a few Brits like me.

In the January another airline disaster happened in the UK. A 737 of British Midland crashed while trying to land at East Midlands airport following an engine failure out of Heathrow. What actually occurred was that an engine vibration indicator, which was a small little display, showed up a fault in one of the engines but was missed by the Flight Crew who in fact shut down the good engine.

"How can they do that?" I hear you say.

It is like in your car when you accidentally select the reverse gear instead of the first gear when the car behind you is giving you hassle. Anything that is mechanical can be misplaced in the heat of the moment. The engines on the 737 in question were extremely reliable and so an in-flight shutdown was very rare. Anyway the crew elected to divert to the East Midlands airport, being their engineering base, to sort out the problem. They were, in fact, quite close to the airport so descended with the one engine at idle power not knowing that it was the broken engine that they were thinking to be the good one. As they came to the final approach they put up the power on this engine and of course it then failed totally so that they now had no engines working. They were unable to get to the runway and landed on the eastern side of the M1 motorway and bounced across the lanes and embedded itself in the bank on the western side. They were literally 600 metres from the runway. Forty seven people died that night. Absolute tragedy!

It takes an accident like this to highlight to the manufacturers that there is a strong possibility that they have got something wrong in the instrument displays that could be missed and it was not before long a new more prominent display was installed.

In Berlin there was a strange feeling that something was going to happen in Eastern Europe. Ronald Reagan and Mikhail Gorbachev were getting along famously and Perestroika was firmly in position. The two of them plus Maggie Thatcher and Helmut Kohl were talking quite openly about a new world order which may bring the east-west confrontation to an end. I was witnessing history in the making. In Poland, for example, communism was being challenged by the ordinary people. In the January Ronald Reagan was replaced by George H W Bush as president and he continued the rhetoric of his predecessor. It was like an unstoppable roller-coaster. Whilst not affecting us directly in Berlin on the IGS it was beginning to feel like the end of the road, for the Berlin as we knew it, was slowly coming into sight.

It was late one afternoon when I was at the airport there and just about to leave for the hotel when we saw an old Boeing 707 coming into land. When I say 'old' I mean that it was, in fact, of vintage class with the original Pratt and Whitney engines which dated back to the early 60s. It had no recognisable marking other than a German registration crudely painted on the rear of the fuselage. Having been accustomed to just BA, Panam and a couple of other airlines peculiar to Berlin it was quite an amazing sight. It parked on one of the outer stands and that was that. So when I came in next morning I was amazed to see this vintage 707 now completely repainted in the colours of Lufthansa. What's more the style was that of the original Lufthansa scheme that was around in those bygone days. It transpired that it was an ex-El Al aircraft, which was originally sold to them by Lufthansa and had been stored for some years in Israel. It was brought up to flying standard by an unknown organisation in West Germany. So there we were in West Berlin flying under the post-war agreement that denied access to Lufthansa to the city and on the tarmac was a 707 resplendent in Lufthansa colours. Cheeky buggers! The airport authorities felt obliged to allow it but had it towed to a less public part of the airport. The papers were full of the event and were predicting the end of the post-war agreement within months and that BA and Panam would be pushed out of the city.

It was in the March that I nearly met my maker. I was operating BA941 from Heathrow to Düsseldorf in the late afternoon on a Friday. The Co-pilot was Chris Challenger who, ironically, had come from the VC-10 having crossed the great divide like me some years before. I was in the descent and there was a small amount of turbulence so I had the passengers strapped in. As we passed 10,000ft I brought the speed down to the regulated 250 knots. We had just cleared the cloud cover and into clear skies and I was just changing a radio frequency when I suddenly looked up and saw a light aircraft about half a mile ahead coming straight at me descending at the same rate as I was. At our closing speeds we would have collided within a few seconds so there was no time for the standard recommended avoidance procedure of each aircraft turning to the right. I remember grabbing the control column and shoving it fully forward to go underneath the guy but at that instant he did the same. The force that I used disconnected the autopilot accompanied by the loud wailing sound. It was similar to walking along the road when someone comes the other way and you both try to avoid each other and end up meeting noses. So there I was heading steeply down with the opposition doing the same. I instinctively pulled the controls fully backwards to try to go over the top of him. So what did he do? You've guessed it! He did the same. So I just kept pulling back harder and harder until the control column was fully wedged in my stomach. This all happened over a timespan of about three seconds and he was looming larger and larger in my windscreen and there was nothing I could do about it. My aircraft reacted well to my demands and with the other aircraft about 200 metres away a small escape gap was forming and he passed under the nose with about three metres to spare. I actually saw the other pilot fleetingly. Seeing him up so close and passing just under me I fully expected him to hit us somewhere in the central section of our belly but suddenly we were in the clear with our aircraft now climbing skywards at an alarming rate. It took a couple of minutes to restore the aircraft to what could be considered a normal flight path. The time taken for my total gyrations in the sky covered a timespan of just under four seconds and that included going from pushing the controls all the way to pulling them all the way back. Such was my desperation to avoid ending up scattered all over the German countryside as a statistic. Once we got the aircraft under control it was then a matter of accessing what had happened behind the flight deck door during our escapade. It was a blessing that I had strapped the passengers in since all they would do is to bounce up and down within the confines of their seat. The Cabin Crew were all female and it was established that the two at the front had got through OK by just hanging onto the door handle although they did do an airborne ballet routine during the episode. The girls 'down the back' were not so fortunate and they ended up careering upwards and literally bounced off the roof of the cabin and then were thrown the other way as I reversed the controls. Clearly these girls were in need of some medical attention.

As for Chris and I it was now a matter of getting the aircraft onto the ground as soon as possible since it had been thrown about quite violently and unlike its military counterpart was not built for this sort of abuse and would need some urgent attention. I let Chris fly the aircraft as I needed a little time to access the scene and get the priorities right. There is an unwritten law in the aviation world that to use bad language over the radio was strictly not on but at that point I was running on 'adrenaline' at that time and let rip a few choice words to the controller on the ground in Düsseldorf as to what had just happened. This was followed by a sort of silence on the airways. The controller came back to me that he had, in fact, missed my close encounter and I was given a priority landing. I also called the company and let them know that the aircraft would be grounded once we had landed for engineers to check it out. The characteristic of the company frequency was that it was common to all the airports on the IGS so my call was picked up by the company all over West Germany so that Berlin operations were aware of what had happened and they, in turn, let London know what had happened. The weather at the time was pretty wild with a strong crosswind for our arrival but as I took the controls from Chris for the landing I just plonked it on the ground and both Chris and I breathed a huge sigh of relief. We taxied to the stand followed by a fleet of fire engines and ambulances. I had made a call on the cabin address informing the passengers that we had encountered some strong turbulence and not to worry. Once we disgorged our passengers the paramedics boarded to help with the girls who had been injured. The station manager was there too and he arranged for all the girls to be taken to the local hospital for checks. I have to say the BA staff were very good and even went with the girls to the hospital leaving Chris and I to gather our thoughts. Obviously there was a mountain of paperwork to complete plus talking to the Ground Engineers. Once we had finished on the aircraft we let the Engineers get on with their checks and made our way to the BA office. As we approached the office we were met by the Air Traffic Officer who was on duty when it all happened. He was in a bit of a state and apologised profusely for the incident. What had happened was that the light aircraft in question was tracking nicely to avoid us by a wide margin but had suddenly turned into our path. On further analysis it transpired that an RAF Tornado aircraft was in the area but much lower than either of us and it looked like the pilot of the light aircraft had spotted him and turned his aircraft for a better look and low and behold turned right into our path. He must have got one heck of a fright when he then looked up and saw me bearing down on him. Anyway, we talked for a while and both agreed that it was just plain bad luck that it had happened but good luck that we had avoided a collision. In retrospect when I looked back I cannot understand what made me suddenly look up but maybe my mum was just looking after me. Once we got into the office I just stood there and announced:

"Folks, I stopped smoking six weeks ago so I would like a cigarette and a shot of whisky would be nice."

Both items were supplied within seconds much to my delight. We then talked to Berlin and London about the incident and then Chris and I made our way to the hotel. Once there I put a block on the phone to stop nuisance press calls and then we both went out and devoured a few beers which I felt were very much needed.

BA rang me in the early morning to check if I was happy to fly to Berlin as planned or come back to the UK as a passenger. Nice option! I spoke to Chris and we both felt happier flying to Berlin as scheduled. It was a bit like falling off a horse when the first thing you have to do is to get back on. We checked with the injured Cabin Crew and found out that they were fine and on their way back home. The flight to Berlin went fine and after landing we met up with the boss and filled him in with the details. There were obviously various debates with the other pilots over a few beers but I wanted life to get back to normal as soon as possible and forget about my brush with death. It was ironic that my sister was reading the 'Daily Mirror' at home that day when she read about her brother 'desperately fighting with the controls and saving over a hundred people from certain death and was considered a hero'. The press people have a wonderful way of flowering things up. I did what any other pilot would have done in the circumstances. I must admit I did have some sleepless nights over the incident but in the end I decided to put my experience down on paper and that acted as a great therapy. It was a little while later that I was informed by the authorities that my air-miss was the closest encounter on record to date. I have to say that it was not a record that I enjoyed achieving as opposed to my previous 'Atlantic Dash' on the VC-10 some ten years earlier.

A few months later the German authorities held an enquiry and deemed that both pilots were at fault for not maintaining a lookout. What a load of drivel! How could I have kept this 'so-called' lookout when I was in cloud and the whole incident occurred within about five seconds of emerging into the late afternoon fading sunlight? I was so incensed with their conclusions I wrote to them in no uncertain terms that I would release my version of events to the press if an actual mid-air collision occurred in the future. Fortunately none happened. I was not even allowed to attend the enquiry in person. The light aircraft pilot attended and stated that he missed me by at least two miles.

"He's a bloody liar! I could pick him out of a line-up today," I said out loud.

I think it was the Germans protecting their interests that they decided the outcome of the enquiry. There was more fun and games to follow when, at about the same time, the Cabin Crew who had been injured on the flight went back to work. It amazed me that they stayed off work for all this time since, although injured, they were only superficial ones but there you go! Anyway, they had obviously lost income by staying off work and went to their union to see what could be done about their financial state of affairs. The union recommended them to sue me for not seeing the other aircraft earlier and within a few days my boss gave me a call that this action had been taken and a writ was on his desk. I am known for not mincing my words but I was speechless when I was told about it since, by good luck or judgment, I had saved their miserable lives and now they deemed it their right to splatter me all over the courts. The cabin crew with me that day were all based in Gatwick and I felt like going down the M25 and confronting them about it. Not a good idea! In the end BA offered me the facility of using the company legal department for consultation as to how to tackle the problem. It was agreed that I would counter-sue them for deformation of character and would settle for a vast amount of money from each of them. That did the trick and all court proceedings were dropped. In conclusion I felt absolutely outraged that these girls had taken this action considering the fact that, as I say again, I managed to save their lives not as a hero but as a by-product of someone trying to save his own skin and it left a mark on my relationships with Cabin Crew.

The other thing that happened was that BA decided that I was worthy of an award for my handling of the incident. Having done what any other pilot would have done I was a bit mystified as to why I would get this award. Anyway, I was invited to the BA headquarters and duly presented the award by Captain Colin Barnes who had the grand title of Flight Operations Director. It was all a bit of pomp and ceremony and Sir Colin Marshall dropped by to shake my hand as well. Together with the award was a free trip courtesy of BA to New York for two days with lots of goodies to go with it. So Moya and I turned up at the appointed hour and off we flew with Colin Barnes to New York. All in all there were about eight of us in the party. The complete weekend was organised by a specialist company in New York and I have to say the weekend was quite superb. On the first night we dined on the 83rd floor of one of the infamous twin trade towers and there we were all sitting around a large oak table with a view overlooking the whole of Manhattan. The food was incredible and only the New Yorkers know how to cook a T-bone steak to perfection. As the meal progressed we were formally introduced to our fellow award winners. Firstly, I remember there was a ground engineer who worked in the large 747 hangars at Heathrow. His speciality was the Rolls Royce engine and he had devised a simple device that cut the time down dramatically for the overhaul time of the engines. His device, whatever it was, produced large financial savings for the company and hence the award. The second award was to a stewardess who apparently stopped a fight between two aborigines while travelling in the crew bus somewhere in Australia. Strange but true! Anyway there were some speeches made and one of the guests was the BA financial director of North America. My Godfather, Bill McLaren, whom I had mentioned way back had held that title many years before and so I asked if he knew of him. In fact he knew my godfather well and so we ended up engrossed in conversation for some time. Bill had retired some time before and lived in Long Island, Connecticut enjoying life to the full. We actually spoke, maybe, two or three times a year.

On the following day we were given a guided tour around the top sights of New York in a very luxurious coach complete with hot and cold running bar. In the afternoon each of us were issued a stretched limousine and off we went to the famous Macy's for a spot of shopping. We parked right outside on 5th Avenue and the driver just sat patiently waiting for us. There was never a question of being moved on by the police.

"This is something else!" was my comment as we got out of our chariot.

In the evening we were all taken to Broadway and indulged in a theatre performance of the famous production of 'Cats'. Later that evening we dined just off Broadway at one of the most famous of New York restaurants, the 'Gingerbread Man'. On the following day, Sunday, we did a leisurely ride around Central Park in a horse and buggy and eventually in the evening we made our way to JFK for the flight back to Heathrow. All I can say is that it was a very enjoyable weekend in New York visiting places that I would never have been to on an ordinary trip.

So the April found me settling back into the less dramatic lifestyle on the 737. It was also in the April that BA introduced a new first class concept of fully reclining seats that converted into full beds. It was totally revolutionary and took the airline world by storm. BA had, by a stroke, enhanced the first class product to the point of luxury. Of course, all other airlines followed suit but once again BA held the lead in new products.

In Berlin, things on the political front were moving fast with the Polish movement, Solidarity, making a strong impact in the Eastern Bloc. Michael Jackson came to Berlin and performed a concert right next to the wall and the music drifted across into East Berlin and we saw film footage of many thousands of East Berliners gathering by the wall all dancing to the music. It was done obviously as a ploy by the West to further stir things up.

At about this time a new airline arrived in Berlin under the banner of 'Euro Berlin' and was 51 per cent owned by Air France and 49 per cent by Lufthansa. The aircraft flown were 737-300s and were leased from Monarch Airlines of the UK. So, those cunning Germans had got a foothold in Berlin and there was nothing we could do about it. The funny thing was that the crews were mainly English and we all met in the bar almost every evening to banter as only pilots know how to do.

Also, in the April there was a tragedy that happened at the Hillsborough football stadium in Sheffield, England when, during the FA Cup semi-final match between Liverpool and Nottingham Forest football clubs, a human crush resulted in the deaths of 96 people and injuries to 766 others. It remains the worst stadium-related disaster in British history, and one of the world's worst football disasters.

In the May, Hungary took the unprecedented step of dismantling 150 miles of border fence with Austria and thus allowing East Germans to travel freely to Austria. Once there, they were repatriated to West Germany via Munich. On the IGS we suddenly had many extra flights from Munich to Berlin carrying these refugees for want of a better name. These people lived in East Berlin and had gone all the way to Austria and then back via Munich to be in West Berlin. It was obvious that things were moving very fast towards the repatriation of the two Germanys. We also did the odd charter flight to Zurich to bring more refugees home to Germany. As for us on the 737, operating the IGS, it was becoming very clear that our days were definitely numbered and that the end of the cosy Berlin scene was nigh.

This move against authority by the people spread around the

world and in some countries the outcome was dreadful. In China, for example, the student movement rebelled against their masters by occupying Tiananmen Square in the centre of Beijing and in the June the government brought in the army to quell the movement and this resulted in total carnage with the final death toll varying from hundreds to thousands. Many students were crushed to death under the tracks of the tanks whilst they slept in their tents in the square. It was known in the media as the 'Tiananmen Square Massacre'. What it did was to highlight the culture of China which, on the one hand, was opening up its cities to the world of air travel and commerce with on the other hand crushing any reforms by the people.

In the July an aircraft accident occurred in the USA which changed the philosophy of the cockpit culture forever. A United Airlines DC-10 was flying over the Midwest of the USA when the centre engine just simply blew up and disappeared overboard. As it went it took out all of the hydraulic lines that powered the flying controls with it so suddenly the flight crew had no way of controlling the aircraft by the conventional means. They were left with the two wing mounted engines to attempt to fly the aircraft. In the cabin was another United Airlines DC-10 Captain and he entered the cockpit to help. Amazingly enough between the four crew members they managed to get some sort of control by using the engines to descend by simply slowing them down and the natural momentum of the thrust line being below the wing pushed the nose down. To turn, they simply pushed the power up on one side only. It sounds simple enough sitting here but up there it must have been terrifying; what they did was to work together as a team to get the aircraft to go where they wanted it to go. They elected to try to land at the quiet suburban airport of Sioux City. The airport was not really geared up for the big jets but eventually the flight crew managed to line up on the main runway and finally hit the ground, albeit a bit short of the runway, and then the whole aircraft cartwheeled across the airport finally coming to rest on the runway. One hundred and twelve people died that day but the amazing thing was the 184 people survived. The fire services in attendance rushed to the wreckage and were amazed when suddenly passengers starting walking out of the cornfield just outside of the airport boundaries. The cockpit was found upside down with the four flight crew members still alive encased in it. Whilst one could say that it could be classified as a simple aircraft accident, what it did was to highlight the co-operation between the pilots who worked as a team and not as individuals in managing the flight following this catastrophic series of failures. From this single accident the concept of a flight crew working as a team evolved and the title of 'Cockpit Resource Management' was born. This was later refined as 'Crew Resource Management' or CRM. Incidentally, the rogue engine was found 18 months later in a wheat field.

BA took this new CRM subject seriously and set about how to put the theory of it into practice. They employed an outside firm to begin a programme of educating its pilots to enhance the full value of this CRM. Maybe up to this point we, as Captains, simply behaved as we were taught according to our backgrounds. BOAC, for example, taught us to be the Captain and Commander with very little discussion amongst the other crew members if we decided a certain course of action. BEA might well have had different ideas of who did what, when and how. Other airlines could well have had totally different ideas altogether. The concept of CRM was to bring us all to the same standard of running the show. The programme devised was pretty extensive and we were all issued with a large folder that required us to hand out five appraisal forms to give to five co-pilots. They, in turn, completed them as to what their opinion was of your operation as a Captain. Brutal honesty was the name of the game. We had the same forms given to us to complete about a particular Co-pilot's operation. I can remember sitting in Berlin with a group of Captains and we put names in the hat of those Co-pilots whom we felt could benefit from this new buzz word 'CRM' and amazingly enough we were just about spot on with the names we had written. I fell in the category of the ex-BOAC type and so could well have come across as a bit draconian in the cockpit but to my defence that was the way I had been taught.

Eventually all the forms were collected and we then trooped off down the M4 to Newbury for a two-day symposium at a hotel where we would be digested and analysed as to how we were seen as Captains or Co-pilots. The side issue was that you put a bunch of pilots together for two days with free food and beverage then the whole thing becomes a bit social. There was, of course, a serious side to it with many presentations of various scenarios being acted out. On the second day the results of our assessment were handed out to each of us. Amazingly enough, I did not fare too badly in the role of a Captain and, in the eyes of the rest of the Flight Crew community, I was considered fine. A couple of the guys were visibly quite shocked as to their assessment and the idea was for them to change their attitude to fall into the required 'box'. All said and done I felt that it was needed so that we could all 'level the playing field' as they say but one thing is omitted in this new field. It is the Captain that holds the final responsibility in the event of an accident or incident so he must still retain a leadership quality. It was not long before the men in the CAA got hold of this new CRM issue and soon it became a compulsory subject for all budding pilots and so an empire soon built up within the corridors of power. Not a good thing! This was all very serious stuff.

Things were moving apace in Europe with Poland being the first of the Eastern Bloc countries to totally denounce its former military rulers and in the August it became a democratic country. Being on the border with East Germany all sorts of stories were emerging about the unrest just the other side of the wall in East Berlin. Although not directly affecting me in my work it was fascinating to know that, maybe, I was witnessing history in the making. The IGS was becoming very busy with a constant flow of government officials flying into and out of Berlin. The government was, at the time, established in Cologne and suddenly, with things starting to happen in the East, the talk of moving the complete government to Berlin was hot on the rumour network. Our talk was on the more depressing side concerning what would happen to us after the fall of the wall. The fact that the wall would fall was, by now, becoming a certainty and it was a question of 'when' and not 'if'. OK, the agreement for the allies to run the IGS out of Berlin was based on the post-war era and that was over 40 years old but the West Berliners were a resilient people and accepted the fact that the national airline, Lufthansa, was not in the city and that us and Panam were their only lifeline to the West. In fact, I had the sneaking suspicion that quite a few West Berliners were quite happy to keep things as they were since they were enjoying the financial rewards of living in an isolated city.

Back in Binfield the house had just about finished its transformation by Alan the builder and I was sinking further into debt to finance it all. Having said that, the house was looking pretty good with four large bedrooms, a large lounge and family room plus various extras. The summer passed well with a break in a holiday complex in Majorca with Chris and Elaine this time. Socially, Binfield was pretty good with most weekends, when I was home, being spent raving it up at someone's house. In hindsight, it was starting to get a bit out of hand with various relationships either falling apart or new ones beginning. I think it all came down to the fact that there were various couples who had been married for some time and these social gatherings were a chance to let their hair down, be it good or bad. There was Chris and Elaine whom we had been on holiday with twice now. As I said before Chris worked for IBM and was always ready for a party. Barry and Sue were our old neighbours from Knox Green. Barry worked as a printer in Uxbridge. Unbeknown to us at the time Sue was not happy in her marriage and seemed to enjoy the odd flirtation when the chance arose. Sally and Mike were new on the scene. Mike was a director of a laundry company. In the end Mike ran off with Barry's wife Sue and Sally ended up with Barry. Lynn and Chris were also from Knox Green. Chris worked for Unilever in Weybridge and Lynn worked in Lloyds Bank in Bracknell. Their marriage survived all the 'goings on'. I thought Lynn was lovely and Chris, being of Welsh descent, enjoyed a drink or two. Dave and Carol were there too with Dave working as an accountant. He was, in his day, a bit of a comic but eventually left Carol and died, as I mentioned before, many years later of the demon drink. Steve and Veronica were in the crowd as well but Veronica had her eyes on Dave which caused a few problems. Rosemary and Alan the builder were in the crowd as well but Alan kept a firm grip on what was happening. Caroline and Alan were all part of the group as well and well established friends of ours. Alan worked as an exhibition designer. Alan died suddenly many years later of a heart problem. Mick and Nicky were there too. Mick worked as a car panel beater locally. Nicky would let her hair down after a few drinks much to Mick's annoyance but they survived the test of time. Last but not least there was Mandy and Keith. Keith worked for Mandy's brother in a retail shop in Maidenhead. Mandy was the star of the group with great looks and a very flirtatious manner. When Moya and Mandy got together they were a formidable pair. In the end Mandy ended up leaving Keith and marrying Moya's brother Paul who had, in turn, left Mary, his wife. When I read back over this list it looks a bit like one big party 'Dynasty' style. Complicated or what! Maybe it was and we did not notice it at the time!

The party where Mike and Sue finally got together was held by Mick and Nicky. It was a fancy dress do with the lads all tarted up in short trousers and the ladies all kitted out in short skirts complete with stockings and suspenders. The party was in full swing when Sally and Mike arrived to be confronted by Barry's Sue grabbing hold of Mike and telling the world that she was leaving Barry for this man. This was like something out of 'EastEnders'. A slanging match followed with the party slowing up rapidly and in the end Sue stomped off with Mike. Sally and Barry were totally unaware of what had been happening behind their backs and so the party broke up soon after that with me marching Barry around the block to cool him off. To a stranger seeing two guys marching along in shorts and socks with their arms around each other it could well have been a case to make a call for the people in white coats to get here quickly since two of their patients had escaped. Yes, it was quite a party!

Moya's mum and dad were still surviving and living in Stanmore, Middlesex. Paddy had recovered from his various operations for his cancer but Mary was in a real bad way with the onset of Alzheimer's disease and was getting worse by the day. Paddy had to lock all the doors to keep her in and this lovely English rose was reduced to a non-person in front of our eyes. Our visits were becoming more and more upsetting. There was nothing that could be done and poor old Paddy had to cope with the trauma of his wife's deterioration plus his own health problems. He had the help of the local National Health Service but it was quite dreadful to watch both of them suffering like this. On one occasion Mary got out of the front door when Paddy was not looking and the police found her quite a few miles away and brought her back. How she had covered the distance in the time was quite amazing.

As for Moya and me we seemed to be plodding along OK but the spark between us was slowly diminishing. Maybe it was the lifestyle we were leading or simply we had fallen out of love with each other and that can produce an emotional roundabout. I had the guilt feeling about the money but it seemed that I could just about get along without arousing too much suspicion. I had by then established an office just off the kitchen and could hide away and sit and ponder my predicament. Yes, we now had a lovely house but at what cost? Maybe my marriage might fail over this screw-up of mine. All these things weighed heavily on my mind. As I have said before many times I was at my most relaxed with my head in the clouds.

I was flying a lot more in Berlin these days since my seniority number was roaring up the scale. One thing that became clear to me was that although the other Captains were at about my same level in the company there was a new younger input of Co-pilots coming onto the fleet. It occurred to me that it would be a good idea to form what you might call an 'Inner Temple' of seasoned pilots to help these new young pilots whenever they might get a problem or need some guidance. I sat down with my boss, Roger Price, and we established a simple procedure to follow whereby if one of the younger pilots needed some help they could come to this 'Inner Temple' of Captains and seek advice. I was given a free hand to choose the members of my group and later on the names were published and it worked very well. For example, one of the younger pilots contacted me about the fact that his wife had just walked out on him and he was due on the Simulator the following day. I called Roger and within minutes his Simulator detail had been postponed for a week or so to give him time to sort something out with the family problem. It worked!

I sometimes feel that pilots and marriages do not go together very well. I was not doing very well at it myself with one failure behind me and now a question mark on the second. I do stand corrected when I see some marriages lasting the passage of time, but it was quoted to me in later life that pilots are brilliant at their jobs but when it came to earthly matters they were useless. Not all of us are the same but I was getting the feeling that I was fast approaching that category. Serious stuff what!

OK, back to flying and Berlin. In the September Hungary pulled down the complete length of its border with Austria and what had started as a trickle of East Germans crossing into Austria and the West was now becoming an unstoppable flood. The East German authorities seemed powerless to stem the flow and in the October the Communist leader of East Germany, Erich Honecker, was forced to step down as leader of the country after a series of health problems be they of a medical nature or a political one. This left East Germany and, in particular, East Berlin, without an effective government. The people were openly demanding the fall of the wall. Mikhail Gorbachev, the Russian leader, visited East Berlin at about that time and urged the remaining leaders to open the wall. The intransigence of the East German authorities would not allow this to happen as they clung onto their crumbling seat of power.

CHAPTER 11

– THE FALL OF THE BERLIN WALL

It was on November 9th 1989 when I was in Berlin and in the evening we had retired to our usual watering hole. It was about 11 pm and we were quietly enjoying a beer when the barmen suddenly looked up at the TV that was behind us on the wall.

"Mein Gott, die Mauer ist gefallen!" he shouted.

"My God, the wall has fallen!"

The whole gathering of people in the bar swung around as one and the TV showed that the crossing point at the Brandenburg Gate between the two Germanys was open and that people were streaming through. Crowds of East Berliners were coming through and climbing onto the wall, joined by West Berliners on our side in a celebratory atmosphere. We were watching history in the making. We very quickly paid up, grabbed a taxi, and off we went to the crossing point but were stopped well short by the police. We walked with the crowds and witnessed the stream of people coming through the wall. There was an amazing party atmosphere and when we finally made it to the wall we found people with chisels hacking away at the brickwork. I grabbed a bit of the debris as it fell and tucked it away. I still have it today. On November 17th they actually started to dismantle the wall and there was a free-for-all in the trade for bits of the wall.

What had actually happened on the night of November 9th was revealed many months later. The ruling party members were attending a dinner in East Berlin somewhere. Erich Honecker was present and trying to rally his fellow guests to crush the 'freedom surge' of the people. One by one the people present left, leaving him all alone. The party broke up early and Günter Schabowski, one of the other party members, accidentally stated in a live broadcast press conference that new rules for travelling from East Germany to West Germany will be put into effect "immediately". Whether it was by accident or by design is down to speculation. Anyway, multitudes of people gathered at the Brandenburg Gate crossing check-point. Estimates of numbers vary but it was well into the thousands or even tens of thousands and the border guards were totally outnumbered. Calls were made to the military headquarters for guidance by these guards but no one answered since it was now getting quite late in the evening. In the end the border guards simply turned and opened the crossing point since they had really no choice. It was only the following morning that the East German rulers knew what had happened the night before. The rest is history. It was amazing for me to witness it all.

When we woke up the next morning you could not move for people and the famous 'Trabant' car made its début on the roads. The Trabant was the product of the East German automobile industry and was the mainstay of the transport world of the Eastern Bloc. It was actually made of a recycled material and driven by a simple two-stroke engine. The simple construction may have suited the roads of the former East but in the West there were stringent emission laws in place and suddenly this car cut right across these rules in a stroke with a trail of exhaust smoke and fumes behind it. The shops were full of 'East Enders' just staring at the incredible choice of goods on the shelves. The scene was quite amazing with all these people milling around just staring at everything Western. Suddenly Tegel was inundated with Lufthansa aircraft that had flown in. Even a 747 arrived in all its glory. It was really strange to hear the Lufthansa call sign over the air. When all was said and done all they were doing was exercising their right to fly to their forbidden city after many years but as I said it was very strange to see so many of their aircraft on the tarmac. I remember that evening when Joe Hall and I stood in the crew room in the hotel and looked out at the fireworks going off everywhere in the city.

"Time to leave Berlin," I said to Joe and at that point I decided that it was time to move on in BA.

So where to go? was my passing thought.

By this stage I was fully integrated in the world of Short-Haul and there was the 757/767 fleet that I could have gone to but that thought did not interest me. In the end the only credible option was to go to the 747-400 which had just been introduced onto the Long-Haul scene. The thought weighed heavily on my mind for some time.

I arrived back home after a couple of days and engrossed myself in the month of birthdays as a diversion. With Paul coming up to nine years old Moya and I decided to enrol him in the local Binfield boy's football club. The under-10s to be exact. I took the opportunity to help out with the supervising of the team and when home on a Sunday I would go down to the local football pitch helping out in trying to mould these young hooligans into some sort of team. They did try my patience on many an occasion but eventually we got a team of sorts together. The name of the team was aptly named the 'Binfield Moles' since the pitch we used was the refuge of, in my opinion, the complete Berkshire Chapter of these creatures. It was my job to prepare the pitch for any forthcoming match with like-minded teams in the area. So, off I would go the day before and mark out the pitch as best I could. These blessed little moles seemed to get turned on by tunnelling furiously around the centre spot. The only cure I came up with was to go to the local hardware store and buy a large collection of 'Mole bombs'. These were readily available in those days and, so equipped, I made my way back to the pitch and planted them around the centre spot. It seems a bit cruel to do this to them but my mind was focused on getting the pitch ready for the following day and, besides, they had the whole of the meadow to tunnel away in so why pick this spot? If you recall the famous English comedian Jasper Carrott did a sketch about getting rid of his moles in his garden by sitting in a revolving armchair armed with a 12-bore shotgun with disastrous consequences. Well, there I was performing a war dance around the centre spot shouting at the moles that they should kindly 'up sticks' and shove off my pitch or words to that effect. Smoke from the 'bombs' was everywhere. On one occasion, unbeknown to me, there was a small party of nursery school children being guided by their teacher on a sort of 'Nature walk' around the pitch. What she saw was this demented chap performing some sort of crazy war dance and shouting at something or someone below the ground.

Perhaps he has murdered his wife and buried her under the pitch and was performing the last rites! she might have thought.

I remember looking up and seeing her rounding up her brood and marching them out of the area as fast as their little legs could carry them. I expected, like Jasper Carrott, for the police to turn up at any moment and cart me away. I attempted to offer an explanation to her but she was long gone before I had a chance. Anyway, the little fellows did vacate the pitch for about a week until I had to do the same all over again. As for the football team Paul seemed to be happy as the goalkeeper and that was where he stayed for that season. I think in our local boy's league we fought bravely for the position of being bottom or next to bottom.

As for BA there seemed to be a period in late 1989 when they felt that they could buy the airline world. Firstly they attempted to buy into United Airlines and that failed for the simple reason that the Japanese bank they had chosen for the financial side of the purchase could not raise the necessary funds and so the plan floundered. Also they attempted a buy into Sabena Airlines of Belgium with KLM and the European Commission announced that the tie-up would not get approval so that failed as well. Not a good ending for the year for BA. Berlin was the icing on the cake for the European network for BA with consistent profits over the years from the IGS but now it was only a matter of time before the Berlin base had to be dismantled.

In the December the Cold War was officially declared at an end after some 40 years of stand-off between the super powers. 1989 proved to be an amazing year on the world stage and we all breathed a sigh of relief that maybe things might generally improve in the New Year with the exception of the demise of Berlin as we knew it. Having said that, the re-unification of Germany was a very significant event and defied all the odds against it ever happening.

The Christmas party season was upon us and so 1989 faded away with the arrival of a new year and once again world events turned a nasty corner. Read on!

1980 Piper Aztec G-ATFF

1981 A bewildered me with Paul

1981 BA 737-200 G-BGDB in BA colours

1984 737-200 G-BGDA in BA Landor colours

1985 Me and Jenny

1985 Moya, Paul and Jenny

1986 737-300 G-BOZB in BA Landor colours

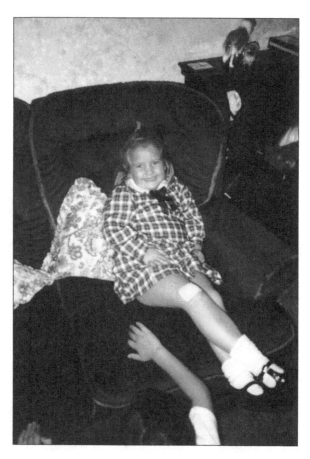

1986 Jenny complete with war wound

1986 The Kids

1988 737-400 G-DOCF in BA Landor colours

1989 My Award Presentation with Captain Colin Barnes

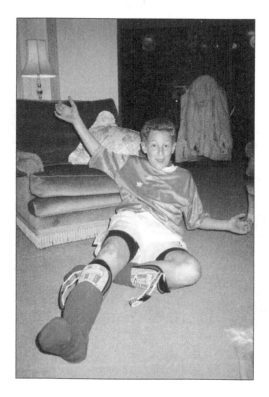

1990 Paul the footballer

So 1990 arrived with me getting to 44 years of age and 24 years in BA. The scene in Berlin was becoming stranger by the minute. Lufthansa was, by now, becoming established once the initial furore had passed. We were still operating our normal schedules on the IGS but had Lufthansa doing some flights on a random basis around the network as well. The downside was that the German Airport Authorities formally took control of Tegel airport and the route network that had been established into and out of the airport. Nothing changed straight away but with a lot of previously restricted airspace in East Germany now becoming available it was not long before the normal routine of visual short approaches were forbidden and we started doing long drawn out approaches under the strict rules of the German controllers. This elongation of the flight resulted in adding at least ten minutes to each arrival into Berlin which, in turn, disrupted the schedules a lot. Gone was the fun of real 'hands on' flying to be replaced by the rather boring procedures that only the Germans could devise. One good thing that was done was to eliminate the ceiling in the famous 'air corridors' which made the flights simpler to plan and operate. Apart from that not much changed at all in the life of BA in Berlin. However, that all changed when a new BA airport manager was appointed and his brief was to shut down the operation and to establish a new low-cost airline to fill the void left when we had all gone.

As for the rest of the Eastern Bloc each country in turn turned democratic and what was originally the huge Soviet Empire was dismantled bit by bit leaving only the, now familiar, Russian Federation remaining as the only foothold of the communists. The expression of 'Market Economy' emerged in the former outposts and would you believe it, in the January, the first McDonald's opened in Moscow. Stalin must have shuddered in his grave.

More and more of the new 737-400 aircraft arrived and some of the older 737-200 were being sold off to other airlines. Because of the noise issue with these older types the buyers were airlines based in South America where there was little legislation covering aircraft noise issues. The new Boeing 767 had also started to arrive in large numbers and was being introduced into the BA scene. It was all happening you might say!

The routes flown by the 737 were little changed from the previous year and, with the exchange of aircraft models, our workload was little changed either. I seemed to be averaging about 20 days a month away with three to four sectors a day being flown. In Berlin, again, we were chatting amongst the crews as to how to put our mark on this historic occasion and we felt it would be nice to do some sort of charity flight. Heads went down and what was decided was to fly out of Tegel airport with a bunch of West Berlin orphans and then fly into the Schönefeld airport in the former Eastern sector of Berlin to collect a bunch of East Berlin orphans from there and then fly them all up to the old North corridor towards Bremen and then to the South west towards Hanover and finally head east and back into Tegel. BA kindly donated a 737-400 for the flight and the pilots put up the cash for fuel and catering. I contacted BA in London and they shipped out a load of 'young fliers' packs which had games and all sorts of other goodies in them. I got together a flight crew consisting of myself, Julie Fisher as the Co-pilot and my very good friend Captain Roger Harben. Roger sported a very thick bushy beard and so looked just the part as the pilot in the cabin. The Cabin Crew were all voluntary and so on a crisp February morning we took off complete with the local TV crew on board to record the happy event. The weather was perfect with a clear blue sky and a thin covering of snow on the ground. When we landed at Schönefeld it transpired that we were the first Western airline to land there since its inception. The scene was a bit different to what we were used to with a load of older Russian aircraft littered all over the place. 'Interflug' was the designated airline in East Germany at the time and were dominant. As we parked on the tarmac we seemed to be surrounded by a great host of ground staff who, once the steps were put in place, all clambered on board to welcome us to the airport. The TV crew were all over the shop filming this and that. Suddenly out of the terminal a bunch of kids emerged and literally ran across the tarmac hotly pursued by two or three rather delectable Interflug stewardesses. This young mob invaded the aircraft stand and ran all over the place. It took the concerted effort of the ground staff to round up this herd and guide them up the steps. Boy, were they noisy. But why not! Pilots from Interflug came on board to have a look in the flight deck to wonder at our modern instrumentation. It must have been a treat for them since their machines were pretty old and rather basic. The stewardesses, whose job was to escort the kids, also came on board to wonder at the modern décor and equipment in the cabin. We must have been on the ground for some two hours or so but eventually we got everybody strapped down somehow in the seats. Roger and I exercised our charm on the Interflug girls and they came along for the ride as well. We finally took off and flew towards the North. The Air Traffic Authorities had given us clearance to fly the complete route at 3,000ft with the views quite spectacular. I think our young guests were more interested in the food side of the flight and Roger was doing a wonderful job in the cabin chatting to them all in their own language. Our cabin crew also did a wonderful job keeping the herd of young animals fed and watered. The noise of the kids was approaching decibel limits but was well worth it. What a treat for them! We were all enjoying it as well! The TV crew came into the cockpit and chatted away happily. They were very impressed that the Co-pilot was a woman and a cracking good-looking one at that. The camera seemed to pan in on Julie for most of the time. On the final leg from Hanover to Berlin we descended to 1,500ft and there was a rush on out in the cabin when it was announced that we were over East Germany. There must have been one hundred or so faces pressed against the windows. I turned the aircraft left and right so that all of them could see something below us. As I said the ground was covered in crisp white snow and looked like something out of a fairy-tale remembering that, for these unfortunate kids, this was the first time that they had been in aircraft let alone in the air. We finally landed back at Tegel. Once we had parked we filed each of our young passengers via the flight deck and assembled them in the terminal where Roger handed out the 'Young Fliers' packs to each of them. Their smiles said it all! We tried to persuade the Interflug girls to stay in the city for the night but they declined since their job, so they were told, was to keep their group in order and to deliver them back safely. That evening we all crowded into the TV room in the hotel and watched the local ZDF channel and there we were in all our glory. Obviously Julie had a bit of an impact on the cameraman since there were only a few shots of me and lots of her. Not that I am jealous you understand! It just goes to show the power of the female form!

Also in the news in the February Nelson Mandela, who had been imprisoned for some 27 years in South Africa, was released from jail by the South African president FW de Klerk. It signalled the end of apartheid and he went on to become the country's president from 1994 to 1999. The effect of this event opened up South Africa to the world and BA stepped up services to the country with the new 747-400 aircraft, including the first direct flights to Cape Town.

In my flying world I had now been on the 737 for some nine years and I was now looking at the prospect of leaving the fleet to go to the 747-400 since my decision was made up. As I said before every August a list is posted to all pilots detailing all the latest information about which fleet needs pilots and when to expect a conversion course. I would have to wait until August to be able to bid for the 747-400 for, hopefully, a move in early 1991. Not being a very patient person frustration was beginning to set in. OK, I loved the 737 but without Berlin I felt lost. As it was, the Berlin operation did not seem to be affected as quickly as I would have thought and it was a case of 'business as usual'.

With the wall down we were free to travel anywhere in the city so quite often we would go over to the 'Former East' as it had become known and look around. It really was quite a dismal sight. In the 'Former West' the road system soon became totally clogged up with cars and a simple journey to the airport from the hotel or the other way around became quite a nightmare. Quite often when we had an afternoon off we would travel down to the RAF base at Gatow to play some golf. The route involved us going west along the main east/west highway called the 'Heer Straße' which was nowadays clogged up with cars continually. I recall driving back one day and was crawling nose to tail when I heard a screech somewhere behind me. I looked in the rear-view mirror and there was a Trabant snaking its way towards us obviously without brakes. We all braced for the impact but amazingly enough it skimmed down our side without making contact and embedded itself into the back of a large Mercedes car just ahead of us. All stopped! We got out to survey the damage and it seemed that the Trabant attacker was reduced to a smouldering wreckage with the driver just sitting amongst it with only the steering wheel for company.

The victim of the attack seemed to have got away with just cuts and bruises. David fought Goliath and failed. The downside was that it added a further hour to our journey back to the hotel. Nearly missed dinner!

In May of that year it was formally announced that all evidence of the wall was to be demolished both within the city limits of Berlin and along the complete length across Germany. There were some 140 kilometres of wall within Berlin and many more across the rest of the country so it was going to be a monumental task. With usual German efficiency the Germans go to work and within a few months all traces of the wall were gone. At Potsdamer Platz the final traces of Hitler's famous bunker disappeared under the hammer drills and it seemed as if that period of history was being finally eradicated.

The spring arrived and so did the sun with balmy days. Spring is my favourite season since it feels like brushing out of the old and bringing in the new. Moya and I were still drifting along seemingly OK and the kids seemed to be fine at school. Of course, there were the odd dramas to deal with but they all seemed containable. I think at this stage Moya was beginning to smell a rat as far as my finances were concerned since she began to ask a few questions about them but, like a total prat, I breezed over the questions as if all was well. It was not that I was unable to pay the ever mounting debts but they were soaking up all the money coming into the house. My head was well and truly in the sand. Having said that we did have a good time financially and even Moya and I managed a week away in Antigua without the kids. The caravan scene was still there but, with the kids getting physically bigger, the space available was becoming a bit of a premium. In the end we decided to sell the caravan. Although we had had many good times in it I did not enjoy the getting there and getting back. I seem to remember that Chris and Elaine sold their one as well.

In Berlin, as I said before, the borders were now open and so on a rare day off, my good friend Gordon Dobie and I set sail one day to explore the former east. We decided to drive down to Leipzig and then turn eastwards to try to find the town of Colditz which was famous in the last war as the prison camp which housed the prisoners who had all managed to escape from other prison camps. The theory being that they would put all the 'bad boys' in one high security prison. The reverse in fact happened, whereby they put all the brains in one spot and the escape plotting became a daily routine. Up to 36 'home runs' were actually made from the prison, being the highest recorded from any camp during the war. The prison was actually the castle that overlooked the town of Colditz. It had high walls all around it and seemed to be escape-proof.

We left Berlin on a cold and miserable morning. After about two hours we were heading east out of Leipzig and the weather was really miserable with heavy rain. We encountered a Russian military convoy which was slowly making its way back to Russia. With no more borders to protect the presence of the Russian military in the former east was no longer required and so they all went home. There must have been thousands of Russian soldiers based in the area and it seemed that all of them were on the same road as us. The amount of hardware was quite amazing with many tanks and armoured vehicles just plodding along. The roads were constructed such that a huge centre section was built-in to accommodate the weapons of war heading to Berlin and the west if it ever came to it. We must have passed at least five kilometres of transporters of all shapes and sizes and it sort of summed up the dismal day and surroundings. Eventually we found the town of Colditz by accident since it was not shown on any map that we had picked up en-route. The town was an equally dismal place and totally dominated by the castle. We stopped off in the town square for lunch and were amazed to find that the local people were very curious about our West German currency. Maybe this place had been left out in the cold when the wall came down. In the afternoon we managed to rustle up a guide and were given a tour of the castle. It was quite an awesome place with high walls looking down on the town and I wondered how it was ever possible to escape from it. The guide took great pride in showing us all the tunnel entrances and confessed that there were more of them undiscovered. There had even been a glider built on the fourth floor of one of the blocks designed to be launched once the gable end wall was demolished. Unfortunately, once the war was over many of the items used in the various escape attempts, including the glider, were destroyed by the local people. The famous fighter pilot Sir Douglas

Bader was incarcerated in the Castle after many escape attempts. The place was eventually liberated by the Americans. The guide was quite a jovial character and when the tour was over we all went back into the town square for coffee and cake. I asked him about what he thought of the wall coming down. He replied in impeccable English.

"In October of last year they delivered my Trabant after a three-year wait. What use is that car now once it has been banned for polluting the world? I want a Mercedes instead," he said with a note of resignation in his voice.

We finally bade farewell to Colditz and made our way back to Berlin passing the same Russian convoy. What a miserable existence these people must have had in the former days.

Another place to visit was the town of Potsdam, situated to the south of Berlin. It boasted the famous castle of 'Schloss Sanssouci', which was an inspiring place to visit. The castle is set in large grounds and originated back to Frederick the Great of Prussia. He was finally buried in the grounds with his beloved dogs. History lesson over! All I can say is that it was lovely to stroll around the grounds and when you entered the buildings you took your shoes off and donned oversized slippers so that you just slid along polishing the floor as you went.

Besides all of these leisure activities we did keep up a steady pace of flying as the summer moved in. In the July BA ordered a second batch of 747-400 aircraft which bought the total order to over 40. This aircraft had to be the one for me and I eagerly awaited the bidding form to put my name down for the fleet. I finally put my name down for the 747-400 in the August expecting a course in early 1991. I was now ready to go to pastures new.

However, all hell broke loose in the August when Iraq, fresh from its victory over Iran, invaded Kuwait. The invasion was led by Saddam Hussein who was becoming a pretty evil guy having crushed his own people in the Northern areas with poison gas as an example to others who might oppose his regime. The world stood still once again. Within BA the effect was to immediately shut down the routes to the Gulf area. It all happens so quickly that some flights were turned back while en-route to the area, except one.

BA Flight 149 was operating a flight from Heathrow to Kuala Lumpur,

Malaysia via Kuwait and Madras, India. Flown by a 747-100 Classic aircraft, G-AWND, the flight never travelled on after stopping at Kuwait several hours after the Iraqi invasion during the early hours of 2nd August 1990. The aircraft operating the flight, and its passengers and crew, were detained by Iraqi forces and many of them became part of the 'Human Shield' which was put in place by the Iraqis so that high value military targets had innocent foreigners sitting on top of them acting as a deterrent. One passenger, a member of the Kuwaiti Royal Family, was killed by the Iraqis, but most of the remaining passengers were later freed, although at least one died during captivity. The aircraft, still at the airport, was destroyed by the Iraqis. Allegations that the airline deliberately did not divert the flight, so as to insert British covert operatives, formed the basis of at least one court case.

Though it did not affect me directly since I was working my passage in Europe the effect on the economies within BA soon came to the surface. Once again the Middle East had raised its ugly head and this time it was enormous. BA made good money in the Gulf area and suddenly it seemed that we were heading for financial problems. In September President George Bush stated on TV for the entire world to know that Kuwait would be returned to its rightful owners with the use of force if necessary. The up-and-coming conflict would make the Falklands conflict look like a walk in the park. Pretty well every Western nation was seen to join the coalition army to rid Kuwait of the Iraqis. BA did its part by flying a lot of the military people involved all over the place. I was not directly involved in any of this except that in Germany a lot of British military personnel were stationed and the UK-bound flights were completely full with all sorts of people. It was obvious that this military build-up could not happen overnight so we just had to sit back and await developments. Interesting times!

In the October, Germany formally announced the total re-unification of the country with all the barriers now removed and the states of West and East Germany were annulled. We continued flying as if the wall was still there with or without Lufthansa. The new manager in Berlin openly stated at a meeting that the presence of BA in Berlin would not be an option in its present form in the future and he was actively engaged in closing the base within the next few months. This meant

that all the people employed in Germany that worked exclusively for
the IGS would be made redundant. We had some 200 plus Cabin Crew
based in the city that had all been groomed in the BA mould. They
simply worked out of Germany and not the UK. It was a known fact at
the time that there was a Cabin Crew shortage at Heathrow. The Cabin
Crew in Berlin who felt happy to move to LHR applied for a transfer
via the normal channels. The shock came when they were all asked
to apply to the BA Cabin Crew recruitment centre as if they were new
applicants. How crazy was that! These crew members had been working
for BA for maybe 15 to 20 years and operated the flights the 'BA way'.
They looked very smart and were generally in very good shape to do
the job. It seemed to me that this was bureaucracy gone mad. As pilots,
we felt it was time to act to try and play our part in securing these
people a job within BA. A small group of us decided to try to tackle the
appalling manner that BA had handled this total rejection of any form
of transfer to LHR for those who wished to do so. Besides, it would save
BA a large sum of redundancy payments which in Germany can amount
to large figures per person due to the strict regulations. We met up
with the Berlin management and it soon became obvious that we were
talking to a brick wall. We approached our own flight management
and, although sympathetic, offered us no solid help. In the end four of
us went to meet up with the head of BA Cabin Crew recruitment in LHR.
Having never seen inside the workings of Cabin Crew I was amazed
at what I saw. I found that the layering of the management structure
seemed to be out of control with managers for this and managers for
that.

"I bet they have a manager for 'teaspoons western routes' or the
like," I muttered as we sat there patiently waiting for someone to, at
least, talk to us.

Eventually we were ushered into an office and sat around this rather
ornate oak table. After a while we were joined by two ladies who were,
in title, the head and deputy head of Cabin Crew recruitment. It became
quite obvious that they were not interested in having their boat rocked
by a bunch of pilots. OK, I can understand their thoughts but our main
argument was that it would be cheaper for them to transfer people
within the company rather than do the whole recruitment process

from scratch. After a sort of debate they finally agreed to interview those who had expressed a desire to move to LHR and so we thought that we were finally getting somewhere. Back in Berlin we passed the message on and shortly after that letters started arriving inviting those who wanted to move to come over for an interview. So far so good!

Those who accepted the interview invite trooped over to Heathrow and started the process but it soon became obvious that the interviewing staff just had no idea of the origin of these people from Berlin. Questions were asked like:

"How do you feel about wearing a BA uniform?"

And

"So, what is your job when you are back in Berlin?"

"What are these people up to with these stupid questions?" was my statement of the day.

In the end the acceptance rate was extremely low and it seemed that the recruitment people had totally misunderstood the Berlin situation. Apart from the financial implications, the ones that did apply were very dedicated people and loved BA. To our simple pilot's mind, it seemed to be the obvious solution whereby those who wanted to go should at least be given the chance to show their skills. So, it was back to the drawing board for our campaign.

We contacted the BA Chief Pilot and met up with him at Heathrow to put our case again for the transfer of some of the Cabin Crew to Heathrow. We were beginning to sound like a scratched record by now but persevered in our endeavours. He arranged a meeting with the head of Cabin Crew and, so, off we all trooped again into the devil's cauldron and, once again, put our case to him. There was a lot of 'head nodding' and notes written during this meeting. Our case was based around the question:

"Why not come over to Berlin and sit as a passenger 'incognito' on a flight where one of the applicants was working and see how he or she behaved in the cabin and mark him or her accordingly?"

To us it seemed the fairest option.

It was finally agreed that a recruitment team would come to Berlin and conduct more interviews. It was felt that to sit in the back of the aircraft watching what was going on was deemed unnecessary. So, off we went back to Berlin with the news.

You may wonder why I got so involved with the Berlin based Cabin Crew since I had had that bad episode with Cabin Crew following my incident in Düsseldorf. The Berlin Cabin Crew were a totally different bunch of people to the Heathrow ones and I found that, over the years, they were a very professional group of people, well turned out for their duties, did not mind going that extra mile to get the job done without any recourse to their union and very rarely skipped a duty for whatever reason.

So, a few days later a group of people from the BA Cabin Crew selection department turned up in the hotel lobby of our Berlin crew hotel and started the interview process all over again. Again, very few people were selected for the move to Heathrow. Same result!

It was at this point I got a call from the BA Chief Pilot saying that I was to stop trying to stir things up within the Cabin Crew community and that in effect I was to 'wind my neck in'. I would be in deep trouble if I continued to keep up the rhetoric. So that was that, we had to stop the campaign or I would be out of a job. In retrospect, I think that there was an underlying plot to totally break the Berlin base down to nothing since it suited the management politics at the time and the financial implications of such a move were justifiable. I also learnt at a much later stage that Lufthansa wanted to buy the complete IGS operation as a total package and simply put our staff in Lufthansa uniforms. If you think about it, we had the infrastructure and the know-how to run the operation. BA, for some unknown reason, turned this down. What do I know? I was a simple pilot trying to help my colleagues. So, the saga of the transfer ended on a very sour and unhappy note.

With the prospect of a full scale war now brewing up in the Middle East the fleet plans within BA were thrown into disarray. The bidding list I had completed for my transfer was now put on hold and so my transfer would have to wait. It was not a total disaster for me since the European scene was pretty much unaffected by the goings on down in the Gulf region. It was very frustrating though.

In the November, Maggie Thatcher, who had led us for over ten years was ousted from office in a sort of inner sanctum rebellion. What a time to do it with most of our military assets on the way to the Gulf! Her appointed successor was John Major who at first seemed to be tailor-made to fit into her role but in the end I felt it was a non-event. The events surrounding her leaving were very sad, but inevitable.

As the winter approached so did the weather with early snow and all sorts of freak happenings around the world weather-wise. The birthday month duly passed with Paul now ten and Jenny seven. The Binfield Moles football team were soon back in action with Paul still established as the goalkeeper. I can remember the family all trooping up to the football field and cheering the team on. I had the exalted position of being a linesman for the team but I have to confess that I was not very good at it, being accused a few times of being too biased to my own team. Can't think why?

To cap it all in the December the Channel Tunnel broke through from either end and there we have it – the English and French nations were joined together as one. The thought of the onion man on his bike came to mind again!

As Xmas approached the usual spate of delays and diversions occurred within the flying world. I decided at that point to buy one of these new all-singing, all-dancing mobile phones so that all around me could keep in touch as to exactly where I was and what I was doing. Bearing in mind this was the first generation of mobile phones it would be called a relic of the past today. It was referred to as 'the brick' and you have to believe me when I say that it was about the size and weight of one. The network that it used was totally inadequate to deal with the demand. The display was a simple non-LED one with the illuminated display numbers draining the battery at break-neck speed. I seem to remember that its battery life was measured in minutes and sometimes by the time you picked it up to answer a call it went flat. This happened on more times than I care to remember. If you managed to squeeze it into your pocket you walked with a permanent limp. It had no memory so you had to carry an A4 folder with all your precious numbers listed. So there I was entering the electronic era of the mobile phone world. It could be put in the same class as the first PC that I bought at about the same time, being the famous Amstrad beast complete with discs that had to be loaded before you could access any sort of program.

So there I was with a couple of new toys to play with and slowly the frustration of computer buffs set in as only anyone who uses a PC or mobile phone knows.

"What the bloody hell is it doing now?" is a common phrase that comes to mind.

And

"I didn't mean to delete that. Now I have to do it all over again!" was another common utterance.

So Xmas came and went with the usual happenings, not forgetting the school Xmas concert.

In comes 1991 and with tensions building up in the Gulf Region there was with a certain amount of trepidation as the New Year started. There was a request from the Flight Management at about this time for volunteers that, in the event of a major war against the Iraqi forces occupying Kuwait, the fleet would act as 'airborne Ambulances' ferrying wounded from an RAF base on the island of Cyprus back to the UK. The word was out that maybe Saddam Hussein might use chemical weapons against the Coalition Army and there could well be hundreds of casualties. I think, in retrospect, that it would have been easier to ask for the people who would not be interested in the operation because the fleet office was swamped with calls of unequivocal support, including mine.

My flying went on as normal but there was a large amount of air traffic passing through Europe on their way to the bases now opened up in the Gulf Region. Even the old RAF base in Bahrain that I remembered way back on the VC-10 opened its doors and now housed a squadron or two of the latest military aircraft that the RAF could muster. The BA charter company, Caledonian Airways, got in on the act with delivering personnel and goods to the area. My very good friend Ian Munroe, who had by now got his command on the Lockheed Tri-Star aircraft, after many years as a co-pilot on the 737, got involved with some flights out of Cyprus to Saudi Arabia. We chatted about it quite a bit when the two families would meet up for dinner.

"The problem is that the RAF estimated the weights of the bits and pieces we carried in the aircraft hold and we were obviously much heavier than they had calculated and the beach at the end of the runway looked pretty close as we got airborne before we had even pulled up the undercarriage," he said on one occasion.

"The other thing that was amusing was that the aircraft we used had first class, club class (the old business class) and world traveller (the old economy class). What happened was the officers went First Class and the Non-commissioned ranks above a Sergeant went Club and the remainder slummed it down the back. What's more the soldiers all carried their own 'body bags' to make it easier to administer."

He then added:

"And they all drank tea like it was going out of fashion."

"No British Soldier goes to war unless he has had a cup of tea!"

Now where have I heard that before? was my thought of the day.

It all started as Operation 'Desert Shield' in the January and our ears were pinned to the radio or TV at every opportunity. I tried calling home a few times whilst I was away but usually I could only get a couple of sentences out before the battery in the infamous 'Brick' died. After about one month the coalition forces crossed the borders into Kuwait under the banner of 'Desert Storm' and it was all over by the beginning of March. Kuwait had been liberated. It was a very clinical operation but with a rather inconclusive ending since all it did was to push the Iraqis back into Iraq which enabled them to still be a menace to the whole of the Middle East. It could be summed up by six months' preparation and three months' action. A lot of tea must have been drunk out there in the desert.

I am sorry if I have deviated from my flying story but a world event like this could not go without mention in a certain amount of detail. Besides, BA took an enormous financial hit over the whole period of the Gulf War. As history will show it actually became known as 'Gulf War 1'.

Things slowly got back to normal as the war wound down and all the people involved returned to their homes or bases.

It was in the March that the IRA got to work as well just to add to the fun by lobbing some mortar shells at the Prime Minister's house in London and also scattered a few around the ramp at Heathrow Terminal 4 where the big boys were parked. Total chaos followed with cars on fire in the nearby hotel car parks from where the mortars had been fired. Terminal 4 was evacuated and Heathrow was closed. I was at the time plodding up from the Mediterranean somewhere and ended up in Paris for the night. Where's my mobile phone?

Back home Moya confronted me about the ever increasing credit card debt. In modern terms it was not a huge amount but within the Mullett household it became a massive issue. Can I blame anyone but myself for getting into this mess? Moya was not a happy lady and that was an understatement. The main problem she had was that I had buried my head in the sand and not told her earlier. What a prat I was!

Once the dust had settled Moya decided to go back to work to help the situation and to give her something else to think about apart from the idiot she had married. It was an extremely low part of my life and it looked like the marriage was going to suffer because of my actions. Our relationship did deteriorate and we were heading for the rocks. There was nothing I could do to save the scene except to just grin and bear it. So, in the end there was a sort of stalemate in the house with each of us doing our own thing. The other thing that was decided is that we would sell the house and move to a smaller one. So, we went to the local estate agent and started the process. When I look back many years later I could honestly say that, yes, I was a total dirk to get into that sort of mess. I think it all stems around the fact that I hated to say 'no' where finances were involved and it finally kicked back at me big time. The actual figure involved was, as I said, not much in modern terms but it was the fact that I had kept the situation to myself and not shared it with Moya. Enough said!

Part of the debt accrued was, in fact, a sum of money I had raised to help my dad with his finances since he had been on a BA pension that dated back to the early sixties and its value had fallen over the years. In the seventies we had inflation running at nearly 30 per cent and money values fell dramatically so he was getting pretty desperate and was very grateful for the money I gave him. All I did was to simply agree a percentage of the value of his house as collateral. It all sounds very generous on my part but it simply added to the melting pot.

We did get a sale for the house quite quickly with a couple just down the road and agreed a house swap with a financial settlement being paid to seal the deal. The new house was a good deal smaller than what we had but it kept us in the area and hopefully would be cheaper to run. So, off we went to 5 Pitts Close and hopefully things would ease off and Moya and I would, maybe, get back together properly. Massive mountain to climb though!

The kids seemed to be fine with the move since they had not lost any of their friends and as long as they had a bedroom then all would be fine. I find that kids seem to have an in-built 'survival gene' which cuts in at times of crisis with the parents. They are cleverer than we think and we should not underestimate them.

Moya got a job at Heathrow in Terminal 1 joining the BA ground staff doing the complete package for departing passengers from check-in to boarding. By now there was a sort of truce in the household and things did start to get back to normal. Within BA, the pension scheme was rehashed whereby an alternative scheme was offered which was not as good as the original one but included a cash settlement to transfer to this new one. The figure involved was just about the same as the debt I had and so, with not too much thought, I transferred and I ended up back to square one financially. However what cumulative effect it had on my marriage only time would tell. Not a nice period in my life and I have to thank Moya for her tolerance during that time in getting through it and dealing with a stupid husband. Someone, take me back into the clouds please!

Back in the flying world in Berlin the German Government were coming to grips with the influx of the people from the Former East. The Trabant car, which was the symbol of former times, was banned due to its ability to pollute the world and there was a programme put in place to scrap them. The problem was that the car body was not made of metal and could not be easily recycled so the scientists came up with the idea of a 'laboratory produced' micro-organism that could literally eat the car body shells leaving the metal bits for recycling.

My flying was still pretty well centred round Berlin and what was the IGS which we still flew every day as if nothing was happening. With Lufthansa on the route as well the potential passengers had an ever-increasing choice of flights and so passenger numbers started to drop dramatically. The Gulf War 1 also took its toll and BA cut back on many routes within the network. Ireland totally disappeared off the timetable being one of the major casualties. A campaign was instigated to get people back flying whereby on April 23rd of that year all seats were given away free. It was an amazing campaign and pretty bold but it worked. There are some clever people about to think up these things. The Atlantic routes were the most rewarding financially and came in for a complete revamp. So all in all BA did a good job in getting people back into the air.

With my 747-400 conversion course being pushed back into1992 I just simply settled down again and awaited developments. In retrospect, when I think back to the time just after the wall came down I expected the whole operation in Berlin to fold up within weeks but we were now over 18 months after the event and nothing had changed so let's just sit back and enjoy it. Besides, the famous ATP that served some of the smaller routes out of Berlin was being sent back to Scotland and a farewell party needed to be organised.

All crew parties, as I maybe said before, were held in the British Officers' club in the Former West and Joe Hall and I duly trotted up there to book the place for the night. Since BA had a strong link to the British military lot in Berlin we never had any problems sorting out the booking for any specific date. It was normal courtesy to invite the Officers since it was their club and by chance a Scottish regiment was in residence and so we managed to procure the services of a Scottish Piper which Joe and I felt was fitting since the ATP operated the 'Highlands and Islands' services for BA and the crews had very much a Scottish flavour to the point that no one could understand them most of the time. The evening arrived and, as usual, the German Cabin crew arrived looking as lovely as ever. Wow – they were a stunning looking lot of ladies! There must have been well over 100 people at the 'do' plus the usual contingent of British Officers strutting around. At one point Joe and I took hold of the proceedings before they became uncontrollable and we produced a rather fancy party balloon in the shape of a parrot and ceremoniously deflated it while the piper played the 'lament' on his pipes. There was not a dry eye in the house as we bade farewell to the famous ATP or 'Parrot' as it was known. The party then really got going in full swing. I went up to one of the British officers and asked if the piper, who was of lowly rank, could have a drink on us.

"Good God, no! This is the officers' club and not for other ranks. Put him in the kitchen with maybe one drink if you must," was his curt reply.

Amazing, we are all on the same side and this is how they treat their soldiers, I thought to myself.

Anyway, I duly led him into the kitchen together with a bottle of whisky being the definition of 'one drink' in my mind, and left him to it. This was one happy Scotsman. About an hour or so later the most dreadful wailing sound came from the kitchen and we found the piper in a very bad way suffering from the effects of the bottle that was rattling about somewhere empty on the floor. The officers turned up and took stock of the scene and hijacked the company stretcher that was propped up against the wall and deposited the hapless piper on it complete with his bagpipes and marched him through the main hall to great cheers and calmly up-ended him on the lawn in front of the club. The piper moaned and muttered something in some unknown language and calmly turned over and fell into a coma-type sleep. The officers returned to the party and it must have gone on well into the early hours. Fortunately the following day was a Sunday so not too many 'earlies' to deal with.

Back home in Binfield things seemed to have settled down a bit but the days were different with Moya working all week and catching up with the house on the weekend. A sort of truce was in the air. The problem I have found over the years is that if, between partners, the trust and respect of one of them is broken, it is a long, long road to re-establishing it and sometimes is never fully restored with dire consequences. This was the situation I had with Moya whereby if certain topics were not talked about then all was fine. The social side still seemed to be out there but even that was becoming a bit of a strange happening. I would say that it was becoming very 'cliquey' with an undercurrent of innuendoes and familiarity. I think the title of 'Binfield' should have been changed to 'Sinfield'. Paul would be 11 this year and our thoughts turned to his next school and in the end we settled for a local school in Bracknell. A lot of my colleagues opted to send their children to private schools but I was of the opinion that, even if I had the money, this was not the course to take. In later years I did find out that some BA pilots' children who did go down the 'private' road ended up no better off that those who didn't. As for Jenny she was still in the local primary school, causing havoc as usual. She was coming up to eight years of age and any thoughts of her further education were far from our minds.

"Let's get this bit done first without any dramas shall we?" was a comment frequently made.

The au pair scene was still very much in evidence with a girl from Yugoslavia called 'Zocchi'. What actually happened was that Zocchi was with a family in nearby Reading and when we called the agency for a replacement au pair, since the present one had decided to go home, we were told that she was having massive problems where she was and we were welcome to rescue her and take her on. So the scene was set, watches were synchronised, for an agreed rendezvous place and time for the pick-up. Off I went in the car and finally found her standing on the roadside waiting for me. Not exactly James Bond stuff but once she got into the car and we were up and away she broke down in tears explaining in her broken English that she was scared that if the family she had run away from ever found out where she had gone things could get a bit nasty. She then asked me for a cigarette.

This is my sort of girl! I thought to myself as I drove her home looking in the rear-view mirror all the time expecting the bad guys to be chasing me.

We eventually got home and she was welcomed into the family and did become one of our favourite au pairs amongst all of them. No baddies turned up either I am glad to say! She must have stayed with us for quite a while. She was not that good around the house clearing up after the kids but both Paul and Jenny thought the world of her.

It was in the May that there was a tragic air crash when a 'Lauda Air' Boeing 767 was climbing out of Bangkok and one of the engines went into reverse and the pilots lost control and 223 people lost their lives.

"How could that happen with all the modern protection safeguards?" was the obvious question.

It transpired that the activation of the reverser system was electronic as was its protection system and it was this that had broken down. It was ironic that the engines prior to this version were protected mechanically and could never have physically broken down since it needed to be physically on the ground to activate the reverser system. So much for the modern 'appliance of science' method!

The summer schedule for the 737 was pretty hectic with nearly our full quota of 737-400s arriving during the late spring. We still retained some of the older -200 versions so in reality we were now flying more aircraft than ever. The -300 versions that were leased from the Danish company Maersk were returned during the year since the future use for them in Berlin was becoming a big question mark.

BA introduced a night stop for us in the French city of Lyon and I must say it is a beautiful city and, by chance, I was in the city on 'Bastille day' and we joined in the celebrations including a spectacular firework display. It was only marred by the fact that we had to be up at the crack of dawn the following day to go back to Heathrow. It was with irony that a few years before Moya and the kids plus Chris and Elaine's lot had camped not far from where we were.

In the June Boris Yeltsin replaced Mikhail Gorbachev as the Soviet leader so the original instigators of the new world order were all but consigned to the history books. In the Middle East the Gulf War 1 did little to the Iraqi high command and airline traffic in the area was still being disrupted with Saddam Hussein still spouting off about all things warlike. After 25 years in BA the Middle East was still at the forefront of the news. Although not directly affecting me on the 737 the thought occurred to me that we have not seen the end of this guy and things would fire up again at some time in the future.

Now here is a little anecdote for one to ponder over. I was sitting in the famous crew room at Heathrow and chatting amongst a few other pilots about the question of:

"What was the most money you ever spent on a night stop?"

Various figures were quoted ranging from 30 pounds to, maybe, 100 pounds. A voice piped up from another quarter:

"One hundred and fifty thousand pounds or thereabouts."

All stopped and the hapless guy simply said:

"Well, I was on this night stop in Amsterdam when I met this stewardess on the crew and I ended up getting divorced for her, costing me that amount of money."

It just goes to show that I was not the only one who had wife problems, albeit for different reasons. Statistics have shown that Pilots are pretty well at the top of the list when it comes to the divorce rate. I wonder why? Perhaps it is that we are so involved in our profession that we miss the obvious on the home front. There again, what about other professions like doctors, dentists and the legal profession? Where do they fit into the equation? Surely we cannot all be bad? Then my mind drifted to the 'goings on' in Berlin with other pilots and that fact seemed to answer my question somewhat. That is enough of the philosophising and ramblings of a 45 year old pilot. By the way, it seems that large amounts of cash are mentioned frequently in my life and to my defence I confess that pilots are paid quite well for their endeavours. Who am I to judge as to what I should earn? I think that it comes down to the 'supply and demand' issue. Enough said again.

In Europe the Balkans exploded in racial conflict and brought the spectre of war closer to home than ever before. What happened was the collapse of Yugoslavia with Croatia and Slovenia declaring their independence and old hatreds flaring up into open hostilities. Massacres were committed just at the other end of Europe and once again military intervention was the only solution with NATO taking the lead. They finally acted only after many people had died. Zocchi, our beloved au pair, had by this time gone back home to complete her education and we did wonder how she was coping with it all. Her home was right in the middle of the war zone. It was quite extraordinary to have such carnage so very close to home.

My flying progressed at a higher pace than ever with a very busy summer schedule since most of the passengers lost in the early part of the year due to the Gulf War 1 had returned with seemingly, their brothers and sisters, to add to the ever swelling number of passengers. There were many Air Traffic Control delays again throughout Europe and the pressure on the resources was getting ever harder. When you consider the number of people involved in just getting one aircraft to depart on time it needs just one hiccup and it all goes for a ball of chalk. There are cleaners, engineers, fuelling staff, dispatchers, check-in staff, cabin crew, baggage handlers, the famous toilet service people complete with their 'Honey Wagons', push-back crew, operations, crew dispatch, flight planners and finally the pilots. I am sure I have missed out a sheet load of other staff but it just takes one passenger to wander around the airport shops and completely lose track of time. So there you are sitting there all fired up to go when the dispatcher rushes on board and comes into the flight deck with the words:

"Captain, we are missing one passenger!"

You have a take-off time or 'slot' that needs you to be off the gate within three minutes. So you call up the Control Tower and in a sort of desperate, but trying to be calm, voice to enquire when the next slot to Rome will be available and you can feel the mood of despair across the airwaves since your gate is needed for an incoming aircraft in five minutes.

"Standby Speedbird 'XXXX' and I will get back to you as soon as I can," he calmly replies.

Meanwhile the whole of the Terminal check-in staff for your flight, which could include Moya, are checking every corner, nook and cranny, airport shop, coffee shop and even the toilets for the missing passenger. Their time is limited since they are needed at a gate right at the other end of the Terminal to check in another flight that is chasing its own slot. Suddenly this excuse of a human casually turns up as if nothing was happening and is kindly asked to get on board.

"Or you will be publicly hanged," was the muttering under many a breath.

So you plead with the Control Tower that you could make the famous slot with about ten seconds to spare to be told that if you don't you have a three hour delay. The challenge is on!

The moment the door closes the aircraft pushes back with the dispatcher just about hanging onto the doorknob as you see him out of your windscreen pausing to wave goodbye and then turning on his heels and running to the next drama. The engines are fired up within seconds and you must remember to actually check the aircraft is clear of the ground crew before you give the throttles, now re-named thrust levers, a 'Ferrari-style punch on the gas' and leave the ramp like a scolded cat on heat. You hair-pin the taxi routes remembering to get the checks done and all the time looking at the clock which seems to march along in double-quick time. You have all points along the runway covered for potential take-off spots and then the Cabin Service Director steams into the cockpit with thumb held high and the Control Tower see this 'Formula-One 737' on the starting grid with about ten seconds to spare. So off you go to somewhere in Europe well knowing that you may have to repeat the feat maybe three more times that day. Life was fun in the 737 'fast lane'!

I did a rather simple flight to Bologna in Northern Italy one sunny morning and sat patiently on the ramp waiting for the passengers to arrive for the return flight. The dispatcher came rushing up to me explaining that there was a retired BA Captain hoping to fly with us back to Heathrow and could he please use the Flight Deck jump seat to get home. I casually asked his name and low and behold it was the famous Captain T who, if you recall, was my first trainer I encountered on the VC-10 when I was at Shannon. He was famous for walking across the ramp smoking one of his cigars and was responsible for the high jinks that happened on my very first flying detail.

"Well, what a turn-up for the books," I said with a sarcastic smile.

"Please let him know that he will be OK for the jump seat but I do not want to see a cigar anywhere near his mouth," I followed up to the rather confused dispatcher.

Captain T finally arrived on the Flight Deck with all smiles.

"Good to see you after all these years, Captain," he said, not remembering me in the slightest I am sure.

"Hi, Captain T. If you recall you took me under your wing back at Shannon in 1966 when we nearly stalled into the ground," I replied with a smile.

Either he didn't remember or didn't want to remember, but anyway I then gave him a bit of a safety briefing and away we went. He was chatting all the way back to Heathrow about the fact that he was a pioneer on the Concorde and that is where I should be instead of on the 737. I am sure he still couldn't remember me when he got off at Heathrow.

"I suppose I will get like him one day?" I said jokingly to the Co-pilot as we made our way back to the crew room.

"What do you mean 'will get like him?' You are already," he jokingly replied.

Cheeky sod, I thought.

Back home is Binfield we seemed to be the refuge for the local au pair community since we had by now two or maybe three of them staying with us. One particular French girl seemed to have the appetite of ten of them and it became a battle of us and the fridge. Paul and Jenny had never had it so good. Moya and I were sort of getting along OK but the spark had gone and it was only a matter of time before something would happen to us.

In the July BA ordered 15 Boeing 777 aircraft, being the first twin-engined aircraft to accommodate over 300 passengers and fly a long way. The peculiar thing about the 777 aircraft was they came with General Electric engines and not the normal Rolls Royce ones and by an amazing coincidence BA had sold its large engine overhaul centre in South Wales to General Electric at the same time. Funny that!

In the August a British Computer Scientist, Sir Timothy Berners-Lee, invented the world-wide-web, www, or w3 and the revolution in on-line information started. I wonder if he knew what he had unleashed?

The November birthday season arrived with Paul arriving at the grand age of eleven and Jenny attaining eight years of age. Paul had by now moved schools from the primary to the secondary one which was in Bracknell albeit a year early for some unexplainable reason. In my youth this school had a pretty bad reputation in the area but nowadays it seemed to be OK, not the greatest but, hopefully, would do the job of educating Paul to what was known as GCSE standard. It was pointed out that if any of the pupils showed any signs of brilliance then it would hopefully be picked up by the teachers and catered for. Paul didn't seem to have any passion for anything in particular. Having said that, I did take him to the Golf Course on a few occasions and I was amazed to see that, even at that young age, he had a talent for the game. I watched him and saw my mother's approach to the game. Maybe this was where his talent lay. As for Jenny we had no idea at all. It was a simple as that.

Also in the November two Libyan officials were named in the bombing of Panam 103 and were arrested and sent for trial in Scotland. Freddie Mercury, of the pop group Queen, died from Aids which was a tragedy since his voice was stunning and his charisma on the stage could never be duplicated. At the other end of the scale the business rogue, Robert Maxwell, was found to have fallen off his boat and drowned in very mysterious circumstances. What a villain this man was! He was the boss of the Mirror Paper Group and even poached the employees' pension scheme to get his money. After his death there was a massive shake up in the business world to prevent this sort of pilfering of other people's money. I am sure it still happens nowadays though!

So here I was entering the last winter season in Europe since it looked likely that I would definitely be moving fleets in 1992. I had really enjoyed the 737 and would be sorry to go but, with the demise of Berlin as we knew it, it was time to move on. It was at about this time that I got a call to come into the simulator and act as a 'stand-in' whereby a new Co-pilot was converting onto the aircraft having only just joined the company and one of his details was to fly with a standard-issue line Captain so as to get away from the training Captain scene. So I rolled up at the appointed hour and low and behold the trainer was my old school mate Dave Hanks. It was some 27 years since we had been at school together. The simulator ride was generally focussed around what we had both been up to in the intervening years with the 'victim' enjoying the freedom from the training regime. So there we were with two of us from the same school flying with BA. Dave had got married and stayed that way all his career. Wow, what a star!

Back home Moya's birthday started the Xmas festivities off as it always did and so we moved into the December with the news that the old USSR was now officially known as the 'Confederation of Russian States' with Boris Yeltsin at the helm. Xmas was spent at home as usual with yet another refugee au pair and so 1991 came to a close.

In comes 1992 with the usual hangover from the party activities of the night before. As it was with my seniority I was able to do all Berlin trips until the end of my time on the 737 and so it was Berlin every time for me and it was an excellent ending to my time of some 11 years on the fleet. Funny, I was only going to stay for a few years but I ended up staying a lot longer. Gatwick was once more under the BA limelight with concerted efforts to establish the base as a profitable centre. All of the Caribbean services were operated by the 'Beach Fleet' of the 747 Classics and some new long haul destinations were added but it was the short haul side that was dragging profits down at Gatwick. It did not concern me too much being a Heathrow guy but nevertheless was part of the complete BA picture.

The weather in Germany was not bad considering that the winter was upon us and so I just sat back and enjoyed the company of fellow pilots and, of course, the Berlin Cabin Crew, for whom I had a great affection. In world events the Americans and the Russians agreed to stop targeting each other with the massive arsenal of missiles, bombers, submarines etc. At their peak I am sure that both of the superpowers could have wiped each other off the map many times over. It was amazing to think that up to then there were bombers of both sides airborne loaded up with nuclear weapons just cruising around ready to strike.

It was in the February that the European Union signed up to the infamous 'Maastricht Treaty' setting out the framework of Europe. Our then Prime Minister, John Major, signed the treaty on behalf of the UK and I am sure that he did not expect it to come back many times to haunt us as it did.

"Do politicians ever read the small print?" I asked myself.

I don't, so why should they?

The question I have often asked myself about England and Europe is that perhaps the English are not natural Europeans since they stem from being part of a huge empire that encompassed the globe. In other words, we do not like being dictated to by a bunch of Bureaucrats sitting in Brussels. We like to do the dictating! Take, for example, the English are used to the rather strange units of weighing things in pounds and ounces which does not have any simple multiples but it works. Along comes Brussels with their grams and kilos which in reality is a simpler form of measure, being based on units of ten, and all hell breaks loose when Europe insists we adopt their measures with shopkeepers and market traders risking jail rather than sell a 'half kilo' bag of tomatoes instead of a 'pound' bag.

"Who is the more awkward, us or them?" is the question of the day.

Also in the February the western alliance under the guidance of NATO decided that it was time to tackle the Balkans crisis and marched in en-masse complete with helicopters and other fancy military hardware and began to sort out the mess that had been on our doorstep for some years. It seemed to be successful since it has been quiet to this day but still has a large contingent of western armies keeping the warring sides apart.

In the BA scene the company formed British Airways Regional to run services out of Birmingham, Manchester and Scotland. The move was designed to make the regions profitable. In Scotland the last of the Avro 748 aircraft were finally replaced by the famous ATP.

In March I settled down to my last month on 737 since I had been given a 747-400 course start date in the middle of April and I had some leave to take before then. I was so used to the Short-Haul scene by now and especially the Berlin operation that the thought of going back to a life of long haul did not seem too inviting.

"Onwards and upwards," I said to myself.

The confirmation that the Berlin operation was to close became fact when in March British Airways bought a small airline operating out of Stuttgart and formed Deutsche BA (DBa) which was intended to replace the IGS as a wholly owned German company. The base was to be Munich and so the countdown to the end had started. Quite a few of the Berlin ground staff were offered the chance to move to Munich and Mel Sawden was asked to head up the new operation. The remaining staff members in Berlin were offered the usual severance deals ranging from retirement on a BA pension to a lump sum offer. The cost to BA was very high since the laws in Germany were very much in favour of the employee. I seem to remember that only about 12 or so of the cabin crew actually moved to London and joined BA mainline. By that time there were well over 200 cabin crew based in Berlin. Taking into account some of them were ready to call it a day and a few went to Lufthansa it would have been very nice if BA had seen the light and offered to transfer more to London since the financial implications were now being exposed. BA seemed to have money to burn closing the Berlin operation.

As the month progressed I found myself saying farewell to the various outstation staff that I had met over the years that I had spent in Germany. This might all sound a bit melodramatic but the IGS was something special for the pilots and many friendships were formed between the flying staff and the ground staff. You could say that we depended on them for good efficient transits and they depended on us to get the aircraft to the stand on time. In Berlin I put a notice on the crew board that if anyone was interested there were drinks on me at a local watering hole on one of my last evenings in Berlin. I had saved some of my precious allowances and on the appointed night I duly turned up with a crisp 1,000Dms note in my pocket. I was overwhelmed with the number of people who went out of their way to come along. The drinks flowed and it was quite an emotional night for me. It was even more emotional when I gave the waiter the crisp note and he arrived back with about two pence change. That was the first and last time I ever handled a large denomination note, albeit only for a few hours.

I had the pleasure of operating the IGS in Germany for nine years and formed some wonderful friendships in that time together with some very enjoyable flying experiences. I could name all of the people that I had met on my Berlin travels and I place them amongst some of the nicest people around. I will name a few for the record.

Amongst the ground staff I had two very good friends, Steve Davies and Jack Jones. Steve was English and Jack was Scottish. They both worked in Operations at Tegel and there was always a good banter to be had with them. I did hear of a tale about Jack Jones which I found quite amusing. It was just before Xmas and Jack had been home to Scotland. On his first shift after returning he proudly presented the other controllers with the mouth-watering thought of genuine Scottish mince pies. He then went into the crew room and popped them on a tray and put them in the oven for about ten minutes to warm them up. In the meantime some flight crew came and went in the normal course of events. When Jack went to retrieve his prized mince pies the cupboard was bare. It was pretty obvious that one of the flight crew had nicked the lot. Apparently, Jack turned into a 'raging bull' and cursed every pilot ever put on the Earth and questioned their family origins. I could imagine the next crew to arrive got the full brunt of this modern day 'Braveheart' in no uncertain terms.

Another person worthy of mention was Allan Stilwell or 'Stonker' to his friends, who worked in customer service at Tegel. Always one with a witty remark and his history goes back to the VC-10 when he was on the ground at Heathrow.

Amongst the Berlin based cabin crew, what can I say? The girls were all lovely with some being lovelier than the others. There is one worthy of mention who became a favourite of mine. Monika was one of the girls who caught my attention whereby she actually moved on from being a stewardess and changed careers to become one of the controllers working with the likes of Jack Jones and Steve Davies thus breaking the mould of what can only be described as a male-dominated section of BA. Well done to Monika! Amongst the male members of the cabin crew I single out Ian Baxter. Ian came to Berlin as part of the British Army and decided to stay on after his demob. You could not meet a more honest guy than Ian. Many years later in my retirement we rekindled our friendship and will stay that way for a long time yet.

It was finally in the late March that I left the 737 fleet for challenges elsewhere. I had completed some 6,300 hours in total on the aircraft and about 6,000 landings. I might add that not all of them were good.

As for me it was now the 747-400 to get to grips with!

CHAPTER 12

– FLYING THE 747-400

With my technical course not starting until the end of April I spent a week taking stock of the Binfield scene. Moya and I were just drifting on getting nowhere and it seemed that maybe we might end up separated which I found hard to digest but had become resigned to the fact that our marriage was not as it once was. The social scene around us did not help either with a few goings on as I said before, which are not worthy of mention – suffice to say that things were not good. I was now 46 years of age and in nine years I would be retiring from BA. The thought of the cost of a divorce was not good with Paul approaching twelve years of age and Jenny nine. I accept that I was to blame for a lot of the problems between Moya and me but once you slip down that slippery road it is difficult to climb back up. OK, enough said!

While the time drifted along towards the start of the course the IRA reared its ugly head again and let rip a bomb in central London killing three people. Events of this sort will never change and rarely make the headlines on the second or third day after the incident. This was the sort of world we were now living in. There were riots in Los Angeles caused by the alleged assault on an African American guy, Rodney King, by four LAPD Policemen who were acquitted after a rather short trial.

Before the course start date I arrived at the fleet Technical office and collected a wheelbarrow load of books plus the programme of events for a bit of light reading. I was amazed to see that a lot of the systems on the 747-400 were similar to the 737-400 with the exception that there were two more engines. It was a well-known fact that the conversion from a 737-400 to the larger 747-400 was easier that going from a classic 747. Having said that the figures quoted for weights etc were very impressive when compared with the old classic 747 that I flew many years before as a co-pilot. An example of this is the maximum take-off weight which was over 75 tonnes heavier that the original machine plus the fact that the range of the -400 (as it was now known) was well in excess of even the most adventurous classic. The -400 was designed to fly non-stop to all points in the Far East, Africa and South America carrying a full load of about 55 tonnes of passengers and freight. It even carried up to ten tonnes of fuel in the horizontal stabilizer to get the most out of the aircraft performance. All I can say is:

"What a machine!"

The day finally arrived when I turned up at Cranebank and got teamed up with a Co-pilot and off we went into the electronic world of the training system by now established as the latest state of the art and technically fail-proof. Fifteen days were allocated to cover the complete technical side of the -400 which made for a pretty mean pace on a daily basis. There must have been about ten of us altogether on the course and most of the others were from the long haul scene. The old tensions were still there in the frequent coffee breaks and some of them even took a dig at me for 'crossing the line' some years before. Captain Tony Hanson, who had joined me on the course from the 737, took even more verbal hits than I did. I got fed up with it all and by day three I fired back on both barrels and things did quieten down from that point on. As I said before, the fact we had come from the 737-400 did pay dividends and by the time the second week finished Tony and I were pretty well on top of the beast. We completed the technical bit by the end of the third week and then had a further two weeks dealing with the performance of the aircraft and the on-board safety equipment. It was back to life-rafts and emergency radios to name but a few of the fancy equipment that is needed to satisfy the rare occasion that you ditch in the middle of the North Atlantic after all the engines have mysteriously fallen off. The phrase:

"I didn't ditch last trip!" springs to mind.

Once again we all piled into the famous smoke tunnel complete with the hated self-contained breathing kit that we had all come to love and hate. The health and safety people had been in and the slide down from the upper deck door was deemed to be not a good idea which suited me. Hated heights anyway! It was towards the end of May when we finished the ground school side of the conversion course and had a week or so clear before the dreaded simulator course which consisted of 14 separate sessions in the 'box'. It was also in May that the new space shuttle Endeavour flew into orbit to mark the return to flight of the shuttle fleet after the Challenger disaster.

The simulator course started with the usual briefing as to how we were expected to progress over the next 14 sessions. I have to say that the instructors were all about my vintage and came from various backgrounds so there was not that pressure inflicted as in previous times. Nevertheless, there was a lot of content and it needed a 'heads down' approach. I had joined the 737 fleet back in 1981 and spent some 11 years on the aircraft so the 'grey matter' needed to be stirred up somewhat. As the simulator course unfolded we were informed that we would be the first course to be known as a 'Zero Flight Time' course. What it meant was that the simulator was certified by the authorities to be of sufficient standard that the requirement for base training on the real aircraft was no longer needed. To put it in plain simple language: the first landing I would make would be with passengers on board.

As I got to about session 12 then I teamed up with Tony and we started practising for the final detail when a 'man from the ministry' would be on board to witness us doing simulated circuits at Shannon so that he would be happy that we could be released to line training. Once again, I felt like a guinea pig and it took me back to the VC-10 command course when I had two of them watching over me. This feeling was further confirmed when the instructor declared:

"OK, Gwyn I will put you up first for the final detail if you don't mind. They only need to see one of you."

Thanks a bunch! I thought.

Was that a sly grin I spotted on Tony's face or not?

So the big day arrived for the final and crucial session and we all gathered in the briefing room to be greeted by my instructor and two of the ministry men. I was amazed that they did not resurrect the original pair that had followed me around many years before. Anyway the scene was set and off we went to a simulated Shannon airport and the instructor threw in a bit of breeze right across the runway just to add to the fun.

Bloody masochist, I thought.

I have to say that the realism of these modern day simulators is amazing to the point that I even felt a slight thump as I drove over the centre taxi lights.

I got airborne and did a reasonable visual circuit as the first one of, maybe, six to keep everybody happy. As each circuit was completed then more and more bits of the aircraft fell off so that in the end I was doing an approach on two engines. After we stopped on the runway it was time for a break and the usual 'head nodding' exercise started up.

"OK, Gwyn that was fine and everybody seems to be happy," the instructor said as we gathered around the coffee table.

The other two gents seemed in agreement and after a session of form filling and signing they both disappeared and we could then relax a bit. The final session in the 'box' was with Tony repeating the exercise but with the watchful eyes gone it all went very well and so there we were signed off the simulator part of the course and ready to do battle down the route.

It was in early July when I did my first line training trip and the amazing thing was that Pete Dyson, my old friend, was the training Captain. He had stayed on the classic when I went off to the 737 and progressed in the training department and here he was a fully qualified training Captain looking after me on my first trip. Tony was on the trip as well and we were due to go to Philadelphia and then do a shuttle to Pittsburgh after a day and then back to Heathrow. I was to do the bit out to Pittsburgh and Tony was due to fly the return two sectors.

"We also have got the two CAA inspectors with us to check out your landing, Gwyn, as a follow up from your simulator session," Pete said casually.

"Didn't think that they would leave me alone for long," I remarked.

Anyway, after the niceties were completed we all made our way over to the 747-400 that was poised ready to go at one of the gates at Terminal 4. After the usual pre-flight organised chaos that I remembered from my previous times in Long-Haul we eventually taxied away to the duty take-off runway with all eyes on me as I came to terms with the sheer size of the -400. It had been 16 years since I last sat on a jumbo so I taxied with a certain amount of caution.

We took off OK and made our way westwards towards the Irish west coast in the Shannon area for our step into the North Atlantic and I was staggered by how automated the whole operation had become. The last time I flew to the USA was on the VC-10 and back then one of us had to make a few radio calls to get our assigned route across the Atlantic and then do a marathon cross-check so that eventually all was declared in order. Nowadays a small gadget on the centre consul is used to transmit the requested routing, height, speed and times and within a few minutes it spews out a paper sheet with all the actual clearances on. It was simply a question of pressing a few buttons and away we went. By the time we got to the Shannon area it was all done and dusted with Pete and me settling down for a bit of lunch and a chat about what each of us had been up to in the intervening years. Pete had actually moved away from London to Shrewsbury and was seemingly well sorted in the matrimonial department and had even bought a small twin-engined light aeroplane, a Dornier DO-27, for his fun and games.

The gadget of which I spoke earlier was now being utilised to get weather reports, company business, engineering things etc. The technical name for it is the Aircraft Communications Addressing and Reporting System (ACARS). It allows the operations side back at base to keep an eye on the engineering side of the aircraft as it flies to its destination. It does pretty well everything needed on board except making tea. Gone were the days of listening and writing down weather reports via a scratchy radio.

After some seven hours we were flying in the New York area and being sequenced for our arrival into Philadelphia and the old familiar chat with the American controllers came flooding back into my memory box.

"Turn left, turn right, go down, slow down or speed up."

Eventually we lined up for the landing and all eyes were watching how I would fair considering that this was the first time I had got behind the wheel of the beast after the simulator. Well, I have to say that I smacked the aircraft well and truly into the runway and I pushed Philadelphia about six feet further down towards the centre of the earth. Teeth shook and silence reigned.

"Golly gosh, that was not good!" I think I uttered as we careered down the runway.

The CAA inspectors were in a state of shock and, as we turned off the runway, Pete said:

"Gwyn, welcome back to the 747 fleet. That was quite an interesting start to your line training but I know it will get better."

He then turned to the two shell-shocked inspectors and, with a totally relaxed voice, explained that he knew me well enough to write that landing off as a 'one-off' and that the system of 'zero flight time' was to be deemed a success since all was good until the last three feet of the approach and landing.

"Thanks, Pete. Beer coming your way soonest," I must have muttered.

A rather white-faced Cabin Service Director (CSD), as they were referred to nowadays, arrived on the flight deck to check for dead bodies and assured us that apart from six miscarriages, four heart attacks and a few passengers praying to their makers all was OK back in the cabin. I crawled off the flight deck with my tail between my legs and endured a barrage of comments from all around me and eventually we departed for the hotel and the safety of my room. As it was, it was only the flight crew who stayed in Philadelphia since the cabin crew went on to Pittsburgh. After a quick shower we adjourned to a local bar and the inquest continued but more based around the saying:

"If you can walk away from a landing it was not that bad!"

I have always maintained that even the smoothest of pilots 'screw up' occasionally and it is the pride that is damaged mostly. Anyway, I had completed my first sector back on long haul and the route training part of the course had started.

The following day we flew the route to Pittsburgh and, low and behold, I greased it onto the runway and there were smiles all round, especially from the two pairs of eyes that seemed to adopt the 'brace' position before landing.

"My honour is now restored!" I announced to all around me complete with a grin from ear to ear.

Pete was pretty chuffed too since it confirmed to the CAA inspectors that all was well.

Tony then flew it back to Philadelphia and so he started his bit as well. That night a few beers were drunk by Pete, Tony and myself since the CAA guys stayed on board on their way back to London. After a day off we then flew ourselves back to Heathrow and so my first outing was completed.

The next trip was of a similar vein with a stopover in Montreal and a shuttle to Detroit and back. The trainer on this occasion was one of the old-fashioned overbearing types that I thought had disappeared many years ago.

"So, you are ex-short haul are you then?" he asked in a superior sort of tone.

"Were you ever in BOAC?" I asked politely.

"No, I came in after the merger," he replied.

"Well, I was in BOAC well before you joined the airline which says something!" I sarcastically replied.

It did set the tone for the trip at that point. The problem is that sometimes I have this habit of 'opening my mouth before engaging my brain' and then spending the rest of the time under self-inflicted pressure to perform.

Anyway, there were now just the two of us since Tony had gone off on his own training schedule and so it was small talk all the way. Fortunately by now I was feeling reasonably comfortable with the aircraft and so he had very little to bite on or to criticise me for. We landed at Montreal and again I seemed to get the landing right. The French influence in Montreal was, by now, worse than ever and when I plonked my Canadian passport down on the immigration counter the officer started yakking away to me in French. I just shrugged my shoulders and let him ramble on until it was obvious to him that I spoke only the Queen's English (well nearly! Sorry Mum). He mumbled a few English words and let me pass. In the evening I went on my own to the area of the city on the banks on the St Lawrence Seaway and enjoyed a night of good music and local beer in one of the many bars scattered along the waterfront. The shuttle to Detroit went fine and, finally, after another day off in Montreal we set sail back to Heathrow. On the flight back I got a call from the CSD that there were a couple of stewardesses from Berlin down the back that knew me and could they come and visit the flight deck. I got the 'nod' from old boring features and up they came. I forget their names now but it was great to see them and there were hugs and kisses all over the flight deck much to the annoyance of my trainer who seemed to survey them with his glasses perched on the end of his rather elongated nose. After they had left the atmosphere was pretty subdued and so I kept myself busy to pass the time.

It was very shortly after this trip was over that Moya was informed that her mother had died. She had had Alzheimer's for many years and was in a small hospice at the time. It was tragic for this nice English rose to go this way but, in some ways, it was a great release for Moya's dad Paddy. He struggled himself with ill-health for many years and to have to tend to Mary as well was an ever increasing burden on him. In 1991 he had got Mary put in a hospice for fellow-sufferers and it was in there that she died. It was unfortunate for me that I was in the middle of my training flights and I did ask at the training office whether I could get some time off for the funeral but they were not very co-operative about it since they seemed to think that, since it was not immediate family, it was not important enough to warrant any changes. Had I been on the 737 I am sure they would had helped out. Paul was 11 at the time and was well aware of what was happening so I told Moya that Paul would represent me at her mum's funeral. She was not impressed but what could I do? What I promised to do was to go into a church in Singapore and pay my respects.

After a few days I found myself with the same trainer on a long flight to Singapore. Wow, this was going to be fun. The normal crew complement on these long range trips was made up of two Captains and two Co-pilots but on this trip it was me and my wonderful trainer who were to be the main crew plus another Captain and Co-pilot who were to be the heavy crew. Both crews were present for the taxi-out and the take-off and once in the air the heavy crew retired to the bunks. These bunks are situated at the back left-hand side of the flight deck and face fore and aft. There are two beds in there bunk-style. They come complete with small pillows and a flimsy blanket which just about covers 50% of the average sleeping body. They have got to be the most uncomfortable place to try to sleep in. There is a heat control for the victim in the lower bunk to use if needed but with two heaving hot bodies in there the temperature soon climbs the scale and the air becomes pretty thick and dry. I think I came out of the bunk on many occasion more knackered than when I went in. The flight on this occasion to Singapore was about 11 hours so I would end up with just under five hours' so-called rest time. The -400 is by rights a heavy aircraft. On this flight, for example, we would have about 140 tonnes of fuel on board which incidentally was very close to the weight of a fully loaded Standard VC-10. With a passenger and freight load of, maybe, 55 tonnes then the take-off weight could well be over 380 tonnes. The figures are pretty awesome if you consider that manned flight had only been around for less than one hundred years. In fact, the ground distance covered by Orville Wright back in 1903 is less than the interior cabin length from nose to tail. You would imagine that to fly at these sorts of weights would require a lot of physical strength but the way the controls were rigged this heavyweight mass of aluminium could be controlled with the lightest of pressures with just one hand actually on the controls. Such was the advancement of aviation. Compared with the original 'Classic' 747 this machine was a real Ferrari of the flying world. Mr Boeing certainly knew how to take the original design and work on it to produce a pedigree version to be proud of.

We took off late at night which was quite normal for the ultra-long range services and so at about four in the morning the crew change-over occurred with four guys falling over each other with half of them trying to get dressed and the other half undressing to hit the bunks. There were arms and legs all over the place. So, in I clambered into the bottom bunk and tried to sleep for some five hours. It is funny but the best sleep for me was about one hour before I had to get up. The heavies pressed the wake-up chimes at the appointed hour and I struggled up with bleary eyes and then opened the door into the flight deck to be greeted with, what seemed, about one million candle-power of sunlight straight between the eyes. You are by now somewhere over Malaysia heading southeast towards Singapore. Everyone was talking at once:

"Good morning Gwyn. The weather at Singapore is fine and sunny with some thunderstorms around."

And:

"Do you want some breakfast?"

All I cared about was whether I would ever see again! Tea was requested by the bucket load and so the ritual dressing and undressing started again with the heavies trying to get in the bunks for a final doze before landing.

We eventually all got into our proper places and so the arrival into Singapore was talked about between me and the trainer in great detail. Back on the 737 we all knew where we were going and any pitfalls that might be in our way and any arrival briefing could be dealt with in a few minutes but was equally concise as the elongated one I was now supposed to issue. Not that I am here to criticise but the Long-Haul side of BA was still a bit in the old BOAC world. The Short-Haul side of BA has developed many procedures that could have been implemented in the Long-Haul scene but were rejected on the basis of the 'Not invented here' syndrome. Off my soap box now!

We finally landed in Singapore in the middle of the afternoon after some 11 hours' flying and taxied to the gate to be relieved by a new crew that would take the aircraft on to Perth in Western Australia. The aircraft stayed on the ground normally for over one hour and the Cabin Crew was obliged to remain on board until their new crew arrived. Suited me! What it meant was that only the Flight Crew got off and went through the formalities to collect our suitcases and drive off to the hotel. Don't get me wrong, I do not dislike all Cabin Crew members, but after my near-miss incident some years before I felt a certain hostility towards them as a group. I do, however, have many good friends amongst their ranks and treasure their friendship.

Once I had arrived at the hotel and I got to my room I was totally and utterly burnt out. This was my first ultra-long range flight and as far as I was concerned I needed to sleep until pick-up for the flight home in a couple of days. Fat chance of that!

The modern hotel bedroom is a far cry from my early days in places like Lagos. They are bedecked with background lights and fancy switches all over the place. What happens is that you managed to crawl into the bed and hit the switch by the bed thinking that all the lights would go off. What happens! Another hidden light comes on somewhere over the other side of the room and so you abandon that switch and choose another one and the TV starts up. As for the TV the first job was to find where they had hidden the remote control and then it seems to have a never-ending list of menu pages starting with the screen saying:

"Welcome Mr Mullett, we hope you have a relaxing stay".

"How can I, since I spend most of the time thumbing through the menu screens until I finally get to the TV channels and then find that I have accidentally paid for a 'pay-movie' without knowing it," was my comment of the day.

In the bathroom the bath accessories needed a full six-week conversion course to understand how to get a simple shower. A well-known crew trick was to leave the shower head all loaded up ready to go and as you delicately leant over the bath and managed finally to switch on the bath taps a deluge of cold, miserable water descends on your head from above. I hate it when that happens!

So, back to my attempt to sleep for two days. After about two hours I woke up and started to panic as to where I was and looked around the room at all the strange bits and pieces, wondering exactly what was going on. It took enormous brain power to work out exactly how I got here and what country I was in and as for the time of day that was totally beyond me. The room was in semi-darkness but that did not mean a thing to me. Was it morning or evening? So much for the delights of ultra-long range sector flying.

"Take me back to four sectors out of Berlin any day," I muttered to myself.

"At least I knew which way up I was," I added.

After a struggle I managed to get up and sort things out only to find I had only been asleep for a short time and it was early evening. There was a loose arrangement with the other flight crew members to meet about that time in the local bar called the 'Lock, Stock and Barrel' so I decided to get dressed and go out since there was no point in trying to go back to sleep. Besides, I was hungry! If you consider that up to then I had eaten one meal on the aircraft which, in UK terms, was taken in the early hours and now it was the middle of the afternoon in the UK. So off I went and found the bar in question and found a couple of the other pilots sitting quietly drinking a beer. There were also some other crew members around so it was bit of a lively place with the usual airline chat. Crews tend to stick to company issues which might seem a bit boring but with BA getting so large there was plenty to talk about. The main talking point at the time was the fact that BA had agreed to code share with USAir in the States and the hot topic at the time was whether the USA and European governmental bodies would agree without any large concessions. These ruling bodies were all powerful and were becoming politically motivated to the point of obsession. The other news within BA was that Lord King had announced that he would be standing down after 12 years at the helm. He and Sir Colin Marshall were responsible for turning BA into a very vibrant company after many years of neglect. They were also responsible for getting BA onto the stock market through a very successful privatisation process. I don't think I heard of any bad words spoken about either of them. So, the 'hangar doors' were pretty busy that evening. Being creatures of habit we all then went and ate at 'Fatties' which pilots had done so for the last thirty years or so. Dad even mentioned the place when he went to Singapore back in the days of the Comet 4 when he was a Flight Navigator. I eventually got back to my room at about midnight which was early evening in the UK and attempted a fresh attempt at sleeping.

I finally did get some sleep and got up mid-morning only to find I was starving hungry again. In the UK it was the early hours but nevertheless I could have eaten a horse as they say. This is the point when the body metabolism goes totally up the creek and I found that I was eating a full meal in the Far East and the body was totally mystified as to why the body was throwing a bucket load of food in it when it should be sleeping. Anyway, I was hungry and that was that. After satisfying the need for food I went to the church just across the road and sat quietly contemplating the passing of Moya's mum. She was, as I said before, a lovely English rose and to end her days in such a sad way was difficult to comprehend. I drifted in thought back to my mum and how she had been struck down in a similar manner. Life just is not fair sometimes. After the church I grabbed the local English newspaper, the 'Straight Times' and settled down in the local Starbucks for a coffee and a read. In the news the headlines were all about Iraq and the fact that the US government insisted that Saddam Hussein

was hording some pretty horrible weapons of war. These so-called
weapons became known as 'Weapons of Mass Destruction' or WMD
for short. Having shoved Iraq out of Kuwait a couple of years before
Saddam had retreated to lick his wounds and you would have thought
that that was the end of it all. Don't forget this was the Middle East
though and anything could happen and probably would. George Bush,
the US president, started to push the western nations into action and it
looked like a second 'Gulf war' was brewing. John Major, the UK prime
minister at the time seemed to be sucked into the hype and so setting
the scene for this new confrontation.

The change in Singapore over the past 25 years that I knew it was
incredible. Now there were shopping malls, huge food courts and
skyscrapers all over the place. Gone were the shady alleys with the
equally shady stalls run by the elite of the local stall keepers who
ripped you off with a smile on their face. Where had 'Change Alley',
'Bugis Street' and the 'Satay Stalls' all gone? They had been swallowed
up by progress as they call it.

By then early afternoon had arrived I was feeling very tired again
and so off I went for a longish sleep back at the hotel. The time change
between the UK and the Far East was a killer both for the eating and
sleeping needs. You ended up eating in the middle of the night and
sleeping during the day. I finally struggled up in the early evening
and made my way to the same bar as the night before and the ritual
of the 'hangar doors' and 'fatties' started all over again. This time my
boring trainer graced us with his presence and seemed to spend most
of the time having a go at all these Short-Haul pilots coming over to his
beloved -400 with their so-called quaint ideas of how to get from A to B.

"Don't knock it until you have tried it," I was going to say but decided
against it since he was running the show.

I think that the fact that I was in Long-Haul on the VC-10 before he
even joined BA annoyed him somewhat but what can I say. Keep quiet,
Gwyn, or you will really get his back up, was my thought for the day.
Besides, we were due to fly home the following evening so the time
exposure to this guy was not too long and could be endured.

The next day was spent mainly in bed since the trauma of the sector
to Singapore was nothing compared with the thought of the return

flight to Heathrow. A short meteorology lesson follows. Generally, the usual direction of the wind over the earth is from West to East. Consider a normal flight time from Heathrow to New York might be anything up to eight hours since you are battling against the wind but on the return back to Heathrow it could be as short as six and a half hours. Transfer that to a ten and half hour sector from Heathrow to Singapore and it could be converted into anything up to 12 hours going back.

I duly pitched up in the lobby at the appointed hour and my trainer greeted me with the news that the flight time going home would be very slightly over 13 hours since we had to do a big re-route away from Northern India due to a tropical cyclone that was in our way and we would be routing over the 'Gulf' hence the long flight time. The time in the UK was early evening which meant that the flight would be in darkness all the way through the night.

When we got to the airport we joined the throng of people who were all going somewhere that night on an aeroplane. This was a far cry from the time years ago when I first went there on the VC-10. The whole airport complex was huge and incredibly modern with never-ending gate concourses. The -400 was waiting for us at the end of one of these and finally we climbed on board and my beloved trainer and I went over the fine details of the flight plan. To put the modern aviation scene in perspective, the weight of the fuel to get us to Heathrow that night was more than the total all-up weight of a Super VC-10 as opposed to a Standard VC-10 on the way here. In turn, the maximum fuel load of the Super VC-10 was more that the total all-up weight of the Comet 4 that my dad flew. This all happened over about 25 years. I wonder what the next generation of heavies will do to these statistics?

The take-off weight for the flight was just under four hundred tonnes which is pretty mind-blowing and you would expect the aircraft to struggle at that weight but surprisingly enough it handled pretty well and actually climbed very nicely which is a tribute to the design and, of course, the Rolls Royce engines out there on the wing. We turned to the north-west out over the Straits of Malacca and set course towards the south-eastern coast of India. After about 30 minutes or so the heavy crew disappeared into the bunks and left me and my trainer to tidy up the paperwork and get the aircraft to fly as close to the computed figures as shown on the flight plan as possible. As we approached India it was quite amazing to hear all the other airlines going our way. Now, India is a wonderful place but its air traffic control system was, at that time, stuck in a time warp. If you look at Europe or America you have excellent radar coverage and systems that allow aircraft to fly pretty close together all going the same way at the same height with a time interval of, maybe, five minutes between them. Now, back then with the Indian authorities they would only allow 20 minutes between aircraft flying the same way at the same height. With this fleet of aircraft approaching the Calcutta area all destined to arrive in Europe early the following day then you could imagine the chaos that was about to descend on us. Just to add to the fun Calcutta did not possess any radar that would help to sort out the various conflicts. So, you switched to 'Calcutta control' frequency and awaited your fate. It was like a massive jigsaw puzzle with aircraft being fitted in where there was a space and then trying to cling onto that space like it was a 'life or death' situation. The task in hand was to try to keep as closely to the flight plan or 'script' as possible since that gave you a chance of arriving in Heathrow with enough fuel left in the tanks to cover any contingencies.

When we finally got a chance to talk to the Calcutta controllers after trying to find a slot in the constant radio chat we were told to descend about 10,000ft and then to slow up to fit into their jigsaw. All our careful planning went out of the window at that point. So we struggled through India debating with every controller whether there was a chance to get back to original height and always they came back with a profound 'Negative'. Since you were 'away from the script' all you could do was to watch the fuel consumption rise and this had, of course, an effect on any precious fuel that you had planned to still have when you arrived in the Heathrow area. Fortunately at this time of year the weather at Heathrow was usually pretty good and the fact you would be arriving very early in the morning with few arrival delays did help the situation. In the depths of winter it could be a different scene.

Eventually we cleared India somewhere near Bombay – or Mumbai as they call it now – and it was time for the change-over of the crews so the ritual of dressing and undressing took place. I climbed into the bunk and seemed to pass out for ever but after about one hour I woke up nearly passing out since the small switch controlling the heat had been left on and there I was in this sauna. The small blanket was thrown off and the search for the half-size pillow commenced. As I said before these bunks had to be the worst place invented to try to get some beauty sleep. Having said that they were much better than trying to sleep in a cabin seat.

At about one and a half hours before the planned arrival into Heathrow the alarm call sounded in the bunks, which seemed to coincide with the deepest sleep of all, and it was all change once again complete with a totally blank bleary expression which only tea can cure plus maybe a bacon sandwich to wash it down.

"Bloody hell, it is still dark out there," I exclaimed as if it had been that way for days.

Me and old 'boring' got into our seats finally with about an hour to run to the landing and we then started the obligatory briefings and other items which he seemed to find essential for me to digest. We were by then in the Frankfurt area which was home territory to me on the 737 but all that was irrelevant since, according to him, the -400 was a completely different operation to the little old 737. I am not wishing to be arrogant but to me an aircraft is an aircraft whether it is one hundred tonnes or three hundred tonnes. They both do the same thing getting from A to B.

Just keep quiet and try to look interested, was my thought of the moment.

Somewhere over the channel we started our descent and I was amazed at the number of other airlines doing just the same, all going to land at Heathrow considering it was about 4:30 in the morning. We finally landed just after 5 am and made our way to our gate at Terminal 4. We finally got off the aircraft after about 45 minutes with my beloved trainer detailing my every move but finally giving me the 'tick' in the box regarding the long-range operation side of things. My thoughts were based around my lovely bed waiting for me back in Binfield. I finally fell into it at about 6:30 in the morning and must have slept for, maybe, two hours when the clatter of kids getting up, 'Tracy' barking at full power at some imaginary cat and other unidentifiable sounds disturbed the slumber. I can't blame them at all since I had arrived at some unearthly hour and the daily routine must go on.

If you can't beat them, join them, I thought to myself.

And so up I got and groped my way downstairs and grunted the odd reply when confronted with a question.

In early August I finally got cleared on the -400 to fly on my own. So there I was commissioned, as they say, as a fully-fledged Captain on the aircraft. The course had taken just over four months to complete which is, in relative terms, pretty short compared with previous ones.

My first flight was to Johannesburg, South Africa, and I duly turned up at the appointed hour to be met by the other two crew members. When we arrived at the aircraft we found a technical fault which seemed to be totally alien to me. The way the -400 displays fault is via a message on one of the centre CRT displays and it is up to the Engineer to interrogate the on-board computer to look for a remedy. In the past they got their hands dirty crawling all over the aircraft pulling this and pushing that. Not so with this aircraft since the engineer would use his delicate fingers to run over a few buttons and hopefully the fault would go away. In my case, it didn't go away and so there was lots of head scratching going on. At that particular time we had a Technical pilot on the fleet, Dave Fleming, who was a complete genius when it came to anything technical. He never seemed to sleep and even Mr Boeing would call him to help with a problem somewhere in the world.

"I think we better call Dave Fleming," the Engineer announced.

By this time we were about two hours late departing and, since we only had three of us flight crew, we were approaching our flight time limit and so things were beginning to hot up. If I recall, the fault was somewhere on one of the undercarriage legs.

"Just go to the undercarriage leg in question and give the bundle of electrical cables a good shaking and the fault will clear," was Dave's reply.

Could it be that simple? I thought as the Engineer scurried off the flight deck to do the 'shaking'.

It was, since within a minute or so the fault just disappeared off the screen.

"Dave, you're a bloody genius," I said to him on the mobile.

Dave's origin was Short-Haul and we talked for a while about the old rivalries between the fleets. The next question was how to make up some time en-route to keep the flight crew within their time limits. So what we did was put on a load of extra fuel and fly at a much lower altitude since we could go much faster lower down. I think the extra fuel figure involved would have taken the 737 from Heathrow to Istanbul. The cost of fuel in those days was about US$1,200 per tonne but if you compared that with the cost of putting the passengers in a hotel for the night and delaying the flight some eight hours the expense of the extra fuel was justified. Besides, Dave fully approved of my plan. So off we charged to South Africa at double quick time and managed to shave a good slice off the flight time off and landed in Jo'burg just within our time limit. Saved a lot of paperwork as well!

With the first trip under the belt I then tried to settle down into the Long-Haul scene after many years away and I have to say I did find it difficult. It had been some 12 years since I had flown the VC-10 with its gentle meandering route structure and suddenly here I was being thrust into the world of keeping airborne for well over 12 hours on some occasions plus a time change that defied belief. The other side of the equation was that I was at the tender age of 46 and the wear and tear on the body was more aggressive than if I were 20 years younger. I began to notice that the waistline was expanding more and more. Back in Germany I used to eat well and invariably consume three meals a day plus a good portion of refreshment for want of a better word. OK, I was never built like an Adonis but I was not in too bad a shape. On the -400 you would spend many hours in the seat and, if not there, in the bunk. Eating was very sporadic with some days I missed out altogether on the culinary delights of life since I spent it either horizontal in bed recovering from a long flight or getting ready for the next one. As for the bar scene the consumption was nowhere near as high as in Berlin.

"So why am I putting on all this weight?" I would shout at myself when I spotted my profile in a mirror.

"Life just isn't fair," I would say with a note of depression in my voice.

Back to BA – in the September of that year they bought into a French Airline TAT and so now had financial interests in one airline in the

States, one in Germany and one in France. Expansion or what!

Shortly after my first 'solo' I flew as the heavy crew to Singapore and then on to Perth, Western Australia. It took just over three hours to fly from Singapore to Perth so it was a pleasant change. The only downside was that we had only about 12 hours there before we set sail back to Singapore. The route took us up the Western coastline of Australia and did give us some spectacular views of the rugged terrain and offshore islands to the west.

How could a country as vast as Australia be defended effectively? It's so bloody big! I thought to myself.

We then would have a couple of days off in Singapore followed by the long trek home. I found that the most social of my fellow crew members were those whom I knew when I flew in Short-Haul. Funny that, since my origins were the VC-10 and Long-Haul.

Hong Kong was next on the agenda with its famous 'Chequer-board' approach into Kai Tak and it was pretty spectacular hauling the beast round the final bend at about five hundred feet hoping to land it on the numbers before screaming to a halt to avoid a dunking in the harbour. The last time I had done the approach was in the VC-10 and now here I was sitting on top of this five-storey house trying to be Mr Cool while white-knuckling the controls. It is a general rule that if you slipped in a bit of rudder while turning it was not considered good airmanship but I found that a little push here and shove there did wonders for keeping you in the right 'slot' albeit with a distinctive sideways lurch followed by the odd comment like:

"Nice one, Gwyn!"

Or:

"That was different!"

Anyway it seemed to work and we plonked onto the runway somewhere about the right place.

The last time I was in Hong Kong the ramp area was about half the size of what I was looking at now. Back then, there was usually only us and Cathay Pacific, the local airline, as the only inhabitants. When I looked at this present day ramp after landing it seemed huge and tightly packed with all sorts of airlines and the majority of aircraft were of the -400 size. It was like some huge jigsaw or 'Sainsbury's car park'. The moment one aircraft departed its spot another one slotted in. The terminal was equally 'jigsaw-style' with what seemed about two million Chinamen hustling and bustling around. Outside of the airport the harbour seemed to have shrunk to half its size, which it actually had due to an aggressive land reclamation programme that only the Chinese could carry out.

The crew hotel was the 'New World Harbour View' which was pretty well central on Hong Kong Island. In the VC-10 days the Hong Kong and Shanghai Bank behind the hotel was the tallest building on the Island but this was now being totally dwarfed by the skyscrapers I was looking at now along the harbour front running from the Central District where we were now and all the way to Causeway Bay to the east.

The normal routine followed, beginning with an attempted sleep lasting maybe three hours, followed by a wash and clean up in a sort of daze and then a meet up in the bar about 20 seconds before the end of 'happy hour' much to the annoyance of the bar staff. Crew, being creatures of habit, would then set sail about an hour later for 'munchies' at the local Chinese restaurant 'King Lao' on Lockhart Road. It was a well tried and trusted place and, I have to say, the food was spot on. Once done, my thoughts would drift back to my bed but the usual suggestion was:

"Anyone fancy 'Joe Bananas' for a nightcap?"

Joe Bananas was the local nightspot boasting good music and gave an instant green card to any BA crew members bypassing the queue of hopefuls who would glare at this bunch of 'Brits' sailing past them. Inside the atmosphere was pretty electric with good music, a small dance floor and a more than adequate bar to tend to our every need. There is this expression of 'going through the sleep barrier' well known to crews based on the fact that if you are continually occupied then sleep is generally forgotten. Joe Bananas was just such a place to forget about sleeping and so the evening would drift on into the early hours when, finally, the body would scream for attention in the exhaustion department and off you would go back to the hotel, thankfully quite close, and then go through the ritual of trying to find your room. All you had in your hand was a flimsy piece of plastic showing that, at least, you were in the right hotel. At this point the brain box kicks into action and you confidently strolled past the reception area with the knowledge that you had your room number 'in the bag'. You get yourself upstairs and, with total conviction, slide the plastic card into the slot. Nothing happens except a red light flicks on. Not a green light anywhere!

"Perhaps I put it in upside down," I say to myself.

Again the red light flashes again like a traffic light at you. Not a green light in sight.

By this time you are totally worked up and resort to all sorts of combinations to get the green light on.

"Perhaps I swiped it too fast," I mutter to myself.

After numerous permutations and combinations the blood pressure is rapidly rising and so off you go back to reception ready to rip the reception staff apart since they obviously supplied you with a duff piece of plastic.

"This miserable piece of plastic does not open my door," you say with air of impatience and superiority.

"Please sir, what is your room number?" is their automatic response.

At this point another bit of the brain box shudders into life and you then realise that you had been trying to 'break and enter' the room whose number is very similar to the number in the hotel that you stayed in on the last trip in Singapore. In fact, it was the same number exactly.

"Please sir, what is your name?" is the second response.

You humbly give them your name trying to be all smiles and apologetic and then you look around and, low and behold, there is another retiree from Joe Bananas doing just the same as you. When you finally get into your room at the first try all you see is the bed calling out to you to 'come on in'. You dive in and then go through the ritual of switching off the room lights which I described earlier and then finally you just pass out, hopefully for a day at least.

On the second night the scenario is repeated with the exception that you carry a large piece of paper with your room number written on it. Simple but effective! Back to the 'King Lao' for second helpings followed by Joe Bananas yet again. Life at that time for me was simply based around eating and drinking (not in total excess I might add).

The route back to Heathrow was normally about 13 hours but for a while there was a problem with the Russians not allowing us to overfly their country so we would route down over Vietnam, Thailand and the Gulf area with a flight time of over 14 hours. That made it an exceptionally long night since for the first three hours or so you were heading southwest and not west. Long nightshift I reckon!

The departure from Hong Kong at night was a pretty colourful affair with all the advertising neon lights plus numerous other ones lighting up the night sky as you groped your way towards the south-east after take-off through the gap between the mainland and Hong Kong Island known as the 'Lie Yue Mun' gap. After about three minutes you then turned to the right and flew just to the south of Hong Kong Island heading west. Not that you had much time to enjoy the view since the aircraft was usually at its heaviest weight and it was 'heads down' concentrating on the instruments until safely clear of the high ground to the west and southwest. It was always good to climb away nicely leaving the lights behind since any problems occurring before then would have been pretty exacting to deal with. Having said that this was what being a pilot was all about, ie plotting for the worst case and ending up not having to get to use it.

Once settled down in the cruise it was the usual scene with the heavy crew getting into their 'Jimjams' and disappearing into the bunks in the hope of getting some sleep for a few hours. The route south-west took us down to a point just off the North Vietnamese coast and you were generally greeted by a mass of lights that were maybe one hundred in number and seemingly about ten to 20 miles off-shore. The lights were all part of a very large fishing fleet with each boat having its own one that attracted the fish so I have been reliably informed. The lights or boats seem to extend as far as the eye could see in all directions and confirmed the fact that, in the Far East, the staple food after rice was fish. It was quite extraordinary to me that there were so many fish around to sweep up into these boats. Or were there?

The route then traversed Cambodia and Laos and finally the northern areas of Thailand flying close to Chang Mai. We finally turned north-west, which was generally in the right direction and then we awaited our fate as to what the Indians would like us to do to ruin our finely tuned plans which up to that point was pretty well 'on the line'.

The arrival in the India airspace coincided with the 'all change' scene with the usual chaos. Then would follow the usual routine of trying to sleep whilst hearing the engine note change signifying that the Indians were doing their best to ruin what had up to this point run like clockwork. The usual wake-up call in the Frankfurt area would arrive with the cautious look around the flight deck and in particular the fuel situation and relief all around that the high jinks with the Indians did not upset the flight too much. The arrival at Heathrow at the crack of dawn would be an accumulation of over 14 hours of pretty exacting work and by the time I got home the bed was calling out for me to join it as soon as possible, family willing of course.

Another route that was pretty interesting was non-stop from Heathrow to Buenos Aries, Argentina. At the time it was the longest non-stop route flown by a commercial airline. Once again, we would depart late in the evening and with a scheduled time of some 14 hours settle down for a long night. The route took us south-west from Europe and then south just off the West African coast with the landfall being on the northern coast of Brazil at a place called 'Fortaleza'. Now, Brazil not only boasted superb footballers but is a huge country and it took at least two and a half hours to fly from the northern coast to the southern border with Paraguay. The problem with Buenos Aries was that the arrival time was at about dawn and the weather was not the best together with the fact that the airfield approach facilities was not too well equipped to deal with fog. In consequence, at about two hours before our arrival it was a case of keeping up with the weather and also the various alternative airfields that we could divert to if needed with our main one being Montevideo in nearby Uruguay. The battle of the River Plate springs to mind at this point! Anyway, the actual numbers of diversions carried out were small in comparison with the normal arrivals, so invariably you would arrive at dawn and get to the hotel ready for the sleep of a lifetime. Thinking back it was only ten years since we were at war with Argentina so you might expect a somewhat frosty reception but I found the local people very friendly and all talk of conflict seemed to be forgotten. The other fact that was pleasing to the brain was that the time change with the UK was only two hours which was a very welcome bonus.

The social side of the city was pretty good and would start with a meal that, even today, makes my mouth water. South America is known for its beef and here was no exception. It is quite amazing to watch the way the local people start the evening at about 10 pm and sit down and order a piece of beef that spreads out beyond the plate, being about 3cm thick. This beef was known as 'Lomo' and comes in various sizes starting from a 'Mini Lomo' to what seems like a complete side of a cow. To add to the Lomo were a variety of side dishes plus a large helping of the local red wine. Now, if you listen to the so-called nutritional experts of the world what they were doing was the biggest no-no ever known to mankind. So why do these people look so fit and healthy? I found it quite amazing. As for me I could just about struggle through my Mini Lomo complete with grilled garlic, vegetables and red wine. No kissing me tonight! After the meal we would waddle off to some bar in the local area and I would end up in bed 'wallowing in my juices' as they say. At that time we only did three services a week so we would have a few days off to enjoy the city. Golf was always on the agenda and quite often we would join forces with another airline crew who stayed in the hotel and off we would go over the railway station, complete with golf clubs slung over our arm and go a few stops down the line to a local course and enjoy the day which was usually full of inter-airline banter which would spill over into the bar after the match. On one occasion with a Lufthansa flight crew we stayed longer than normal after the game and were told in broken Spanish that the last train had just left and the whole area was off to bed. Using our skills of negotiating, which amounted to generally very little, we managed to sort out a couple of local guys to drive us to the hotel.

All well and good you might say.

The problem was that neither of our drivers had ever been to the big city so it was a case of 'the blind leading the blind'. We eventually got dumped at the hotel after a guided tour around the city and the re-negotiations over the price commenced. Beat Lufthansa on the golf course though!

Eventually after a few days we flew all the way back to Heathrow, virtually on the same route and I have to say of all the routes we flew the route to South America was amongst my favourites.

My time on the -400 moved on through the year and in the October there was a very nasty air crash in Amsterdam involving an El Al 747 classic freighter which had a double engine failure just after take-off and hit a block of flats whilst attempting a return. It left 43 people dead with most of the fatalities on the ground. There is controversy to this day as to exactly what cargo it was carrying. El Al operated a fleet of old 747 aircraft that had been converted to freighters and flew with little or no markings that could identify them. A lot of their routes were to non-descript airfields and the whole operation seemed to be shrouded in secrecy in line with the whole of the Middle Eastern scene.

With the month of November approaching and the family birthday time arriving things at home were seemingly coming to some sort of peak with Moya and me at odds most of the time and the whole thing getting worse by the day. Paul was coming up to 12 years of age and Jenny getting towards nine years of age. Jenny seemed to be developing an obsession with horses, which I can see is normal for a girl of her age but bordered on the expensive option as far as I could see. Paul was well involved in the village 'gang culture' and would spend a lot of time with other boys of his age doing their thing just like I did when I was at his age. You could say when looking into the family from the outside that all seemed well but behind closed doors things were a lot different. We had, by then, a French au pair called Ludivine and she seemed to be the one in the middle when Moya and I were having yet another conflict. Moya was happily settled in her work with BA ground staff at Heathrow but things were brewing up for the big showdown.

Back in the flying world Los Angeles often featured on the agenda. I always found the west coast of the USA a fascinating place. At that time BA operated two services a day with the -400 so there were was plenty of scope to get trips there. For me, one of the main attractions was the obsession I still had and will always have for all things aviation. California offered a kaleidoscope of places to see and do. Whenever I was there I would usually hire a car and set off, with or without company, north to Mojave, in the desert, to look at the old airliners that had been parked there in storage since their glory flying days. There could well have been over one hundred of the old 'girls' parked there in the dry, hot heat of the desert to await their fate. There were some airliners from the early sixties there such as the 707, Convair 880s and DC-8s all neatly parked in rows with the faded logos barely seen but readable on the fuselage side. The Convairs, for example, were bedecked in their original Trans World Airways (TWA) markings and must have been there for at least 20 years even when I saw them. They even had an ex-Swissair Convair 990 Coronado, which was the fastest airliner in its day and probably still is, parked up with power available to electrify the interior as it would have been many years before. The trip out to Mojave would be an all-day affair with a return to the hotel feeling pretty exhausted and a good night's sleep was on the cards.

In the USA President George Bush, who had led the western effort in the deserts of Kuwait a short time before, lost out to the Democrat Bill Clinton in the presidential election. Now, here was a character of a man who came from the quiet backwaters of Arkansas to become the most powerful man on Earth. He was a total contrast to George Bush whereby he came across as the original 'smoothie' with his long suffering wife, Hillary. Time will tell and it certainly did. Back in England there was a massive fire at the Queen's residence in Windsor. It was Windsor Castle that was going up in flames and pretty much every fire engine within 50 miles was called in to tackle the blaze. There was a wonderful picture in the press of Prince Andrew with a column of helpers carrying a huge rolled up carpet to safety. The cause was, in fact, a stray flame from a canister being used in some restoration work in one of the rooms. There was a funny side to the whole business when I chatted, by accident, to one of the firemen involved. Apparently every fire service is financed by the local councils and some units are better equipped than others. Consequently, when they all combine together for a fire like they had at Windsor Castle there is a tendency for equipment to be laid out all over the place and when it is time to go home all sorts of items end up in the wrong fire engine either by accident or design. At some later stage the ritual of going around and trying to recover bits and pieces takes place but usually becomes a lost cause. The fireman I spoke to talked about leaving one of his colleagues guarding the engine to watch out for this illicit trade. So there is this poor guy acting as a policeman instead of a fireman.

In the December my flying continued towards the Christmas break in the knowledge that I would be at home for the festivities whatever they held for me and Moya. Also, in the December BA bought the remnants of one of the oldest established independent airlines, Dan-Air. The price paid was a symbolic £1 but included the debts built up by them. The name of Dan-Air traced its history back to 1953 and it was sad for the flying community to witness the demise of 'Dan-Dare' as it was nicknamed with affection. Also in December the European and USA regulators reported their decision regarding the proposed tie-up with BA and USAir and demanded too many concessions from the two airlines and the proposed deal was considered null and void. It was also announced that Prince Charles and Diana were to part company. It was an inevitable end to a fairy-tale wedding and I have my own feelings about it all but nevertheless not a good time for the Royal Family. The Queen summed it up in a speech referring to the year as an 'annus horribilis' since in the March Prince Andrew had split up with Sarah, in the April Princess Anne had got divorced, in the November Windsor Castle had caught fire and now in December Prince Charles was to part company with Diana.

And so 1992 came to a close and in comes 1993 and yet another personal crisis looming. It all started in the early January when Moya and I agreed that, in both our interests, I should find somewhere else to live for a while so that there might be a chance of restoring the marriage to what it once was. I called my old friend Ernie Sailor since he mentioned once that he owned two other houses in addition to his own up in Edgware, North London. So, in early January I put all my worthy possessions in the car and bade farewell to Moya, Paul and Jenny and made my way up to Ernie's and moved into the house next door. It was an absolute thermal shock to the system having come from a nice warm house full of familiar bits and pieces to a house that had been empty for a few years and was damp, cold and with no heating of any kind. I remember I went over the road and got some fish and chips and made up a bed in the lounge keeping warm with a single bar electric fire. I really fell down to earth with a bump and fell totally dejected. To add to my misery I was allocated the dreaded reserve line for the whole month of January whereby I was constantly put on standby with very little hope of actually flying anywhere. I still had the dreaded 'brick' mobile phone and that stood on its charger as the only means of talking to the world. Ernie's wife, Valerie, was a wonderful lady and very comforting to me as she realised that I was not at all happy with my lot. I would class it as the one of the lowest points of my life to date and I dreamt of that phone call from BA calling me out anywhere to get me out of my misery. I would add that it was totally self-inflicted and that I had to endure the pain of it all. The hardest part was to start all over again with even the basics of life such as salt and pepper and to get to grips with feeding myself. After a short while Ernie got the central heating back working and I was able to move the bed upstairs and, at least, get some semblance of order back into my life. I spoke to the kids a few times which was really hard. Heat was beginning to come back into the house and the damp was going, albeit slowly. I spent quite a bit of time next door with Ernie and Val and started slowly to feel a bit easier about it all. I visited home a few times and found that extremely hard when confronted with the old home comforts. Moya tried her best to make me welcome but with both of us being the source of the problem it was pretty difficult.

On about the tenth of January the 'brick' fired off and to my delight I was off to Los Angeles the following day. I was talking to my old friend Ian Munro that evening and it transpired that he was operating a flight to Los Angeles himself on the same day as me and why didn't I come down to his hotel in the evening and join him for a few drinks?

What could be better than to be amongst friends? I thought to myself not knowing what was in store for me in Los Angeles.

So, off I go to Los Angeles arriving in the mid afternoon with Ian and Co arriving later that evening. I pottered around until I got a call from Ian that he had arrived and got myself organised with a taxi and off I went to his hotel which was quite a bit south of where we were. In fact, US$140.00 taxi fare's worth south.

Good start, I thought shelling out a fistful of dollars just for a drink with Ian.

Anyway, I met up with Ian and he had his wife, Pauline, with him and part of the crew so a social scene was forming. Ian and Pauline knew Moya and about the breakup and we had a few words but left it at that. After a while we all decided to abandon Ian's room and go to the local bar frequented by the airline crews that stayed in the hotel. It was also decided that I would stay overnight and sleep on the sofa in Ian and Pauline's room so the scene was set for a social evening which for me was well needed considering my miserable home life.

Once established in the bar more of Ian's crew joined us and as I chatted to them I spotted a rather nice girl by the name of Johanna. I was, at the time, wearing a T-shirt that had the name of the local bar in Berlin known as the 'Eierschale' where we would quite often end up at back in Berlin.

"My mother used to go to the Eierschale in Berlin," Johanna said casually.

"How old do you think I am then?" I replied.

I was bit taken aback by her referring to me in her mother's generation but then, maybe I was when she revealed to me later that she was only just 29 years old. I also detected a slight hint of a foreign accent.

Careful, Gwyn, you could be accused of cradle snatching here, was my thought of the moment.

It was only a fleeting thought since I continued in 'chat mode' with this Johanna. I found her quite mesmerising when it transpired that she was German, born in Munich, raised in Switzerland and Berlin and finally moving to Italy for her main education. She further explained that she was shipped out to England when she was 19 as an au pair and eventually joined the student world getting various qualifications along the way and had finally fulfilled her dream of being a stewardess and seeing the world. As the evening progressed then it became obvious that there was a buzz between us and maybe, just maybe, something a little bit more than casual bar chat. I won't bore you with the finer points. Johanna, or Jo, was on her last trip with Caledonian Airways since she was off to Goa, India for a six month flying contract with an airline called 'Goa-way' flying to various airports in the region.

On the following day Ian drove me back to my hotel with Jo in the back for company and it was the first time that she realised that I was not just a friend of Ian's but a BA Captain in my own right. She was rather taken aback seeing my uniform hanging in the cupboard as I collected a few items together for a second night stop down south.

What an amazing turn around in my life, I thought to myself as we travelled back.

Anyway, the second evening came and went and it seemed that Jo and I were pretty well in tune with each other and enjoyed each other's company. On the third day I set sail back to my crew hotel via the bus which, in its own right, was a bit of an epic since I ended up in 'downtown LA' whilst changing busses. Not the nicest of areas since most people glared at you with that 'what are you doing in my territory, man?' look. I eventually made it back to my hotel and shortly after that flew back to Heathrow and Edgware, my new home, with thoughts of Jo fresh on my mind.

Within a couple of days I was off to Hong Kong and so life slowly began returning to normal. My visits to Moya and the kids became part of the routine but there was a certain amount of pressure being put on me to set up some sort of monthly payment to Moya to help with the cost of Paul and Jenny. This did cause a massive amount of friction between Moya and me and of course, I had to pay Ernie some money since staying in one of his houses was not a charity hand out. So, once again, my finances were being squeezed on all fronts. I was slowly getting my house in order towards the end of 1992 when this lot 'hit the fan'.

In the world of BA another tie up with USAir was announced which, maybe, might suit the regulators and actually involved money being invested by BA into USAir and new transatlantic routes being opened up using USAir flight and cabin crews. The Atlantic routes were historically the most lucrative of areas and BA was hell bent on exploiting the potential profits that could result from a tie-up with an American airline. At the same time BA paid Virgin Atlantic Airways a handsome sum in settlement of a libel action bought by Mr Branson.

I did catch up with Jo just a couple of days before she went off to Goa and her new adventure with 'Goaway' airlines. The aircraft they were to operate on was a Fokker F-27 and apparently six stewardesses were recruited, including Jo, to run the cabin service. Anyway, it was a bit of a strange farewell, since we had only just met, when we parted company and went our different ways. Maybe we could meet up when she gets back to the UK after her Indian adventure. As for me, I concentrated on the flying world and as many visits to Binfield as I could make. The poor old MG Montego was certainly doing its thing in keeping up with all the driving that I was doing. I was pushing it a bit I have to admit since I was missing the kids desperately and would fly all night, then drive one hour up to Edgware, get changed, drive maybe two hours to see the kids for the morning and then drive two hours back again. It was a punishing schedule but necessary.

In the February I was in New York and was watching the evening news on the TV when a news flash came up whereby the famous World Trade Centre buildings had been subjected to a car bomb explosion in the basement. It killed six people causing little damage but highlighted the new world terror tactics that were being adopted.

Also in February, Lord King finally retired as the Chairman of British Airways and became the first-ever President of BA. Sir Colin Marshall was appointed as chairman and Robert Ayling became Group Managing Director. The name 'Ayling' became synonymous within the BA management circle as I shall recall as time progresses.

In the UK the IRA finally hit rock bottom when they set a bomb off in the garrison town of Warrington, Lancs and succeeded in killing two children as their trophy.

Within BA the news was out that the regulators had approved the tie-up with USAir as proposed in the January and so, finally, BA got the transatlantic link-up with an American carrier it had been seeking for many years. The company also bought a 25% stake in Qantas adding to their ever expanding airline acquisitions. The final item in a busy month for BA was the inauguration of flights from Birmingham, Manchester and Glasgow to New York plus a direct flight to Los Angeles from Manchester. On the -400 we suddenly found that one or two of our aircraft had a strange logo on the tail resembling some weird Chinese symbols that were actually representative of British Asia Airways. This wholly-owned subsidiary was set up to allow BA to operate to Taiwan via Hong Kong without any interference from the Chinese government since it was a fact that within a few years Hong Kong would be handed back to the Chinese.

As for me I continued to get more acquainted with the routes and the aircraft itself. I did notice that the relationship between the flight crew and the cabin crew had hit rock bottom on the -400 with a new pecking order amongst cabin crew management being created daily so it seemed. By now we occupied a brand new building on the north side of Heathrow, aptly called the 'Compass Centre', where all operational bits and pieces were moved to. It housed the complete Flight and Cabin Crew management plus a host of other departments that, up to that point, were scattered all over Heathrow. It was a Goliath of a building and lent itself to be used to expand various departments under the banner of 'the bigger the better for us'. Hence the Cabin Crew Empire expanded to such a point that it totally occupied about half of the total floor area of a complete floor. To me, as a common pilot, it was like a no-go area but always worth a small peep to check the ever-expanding number of desks and titles. As for my own Flight Crew management we seemed to be squeezed into the end of one of the floors with everybody seemingly on top of each other. One of the proposals put forward was that the Captain of the flight would venture forth and introduce himself to the Cabin Crew while they were being briefed by the Cabin Service Director (CSD) in their briefing room. Well, that was fun! First of all you had to find where they were and then you entered into the world of the CSD's briefing.

"I am sorry, Captain, but would you mind waiting a few minutes whilst I brief my crew about a very important aspect of the flight?" he would say with an air of self-importance.

I would stand there like a prat whilst he would witter on about some new piece of paperwork or something like that. Being slightly behind the CSD I could survey the crew members all sitting there with paper and pencil poised plus the obligatory mobile phone resting on the table. Eventually my cue to talk would be signalled by his Lordship and I would generally try to humour things up a bit with such expressions like:

"If at any time you feel the need to talk to me about any aspect of the flight, problems or complaints that you might have please just give me a call and come on up to the flight deck where a friendly ear will be waiting. Please don't forget to bring a cup of tea with you since I cannot think straight without a cup of tea in the hand."

Well, that went down like a lead balloon with the CSD and I could feel the hairs on the back of his neck bristling up like a boxer dog.

Again, I would hasten to add that I have a lot of good friends amongst the cabin crew population and the majority of them are excellent people but a few of them tarnished their reputation. This equally applies to my lot as well. Human nature I suppose. Anyway, this practice of saying hello in the building before getting on the bus withered away and the first time we would generally meet up was going to the aircraft. Even that was a bit tricky since the advent of the smaller, more compact mobile phone was upon us and it seemed that these things came with Velcro tape to permanently stick them to the ear. I found it quite amazing to think that one would have the desire to speak to someone who had only just dropped you off, maybe two hours before. Amazing new world we were now entering!

Another destination that the -400 went to was Japan. BA in those days went to three destinations in Japan namely Narita, Osaka and Nagoya. Narita was the most frequented with two services a day. In the days of the VC-10 we flew into the airport of Haneda being close to the capital, Tokyo, but as 'out of town' airports became the order of the day based on the ever increasing noise lobbying then the airport at Narita became the main outlet for Japan. It was situated about 75 km to the east and lay on the coast with the water being on the northern, eastern and southern sides. Ideal for the noise lobby but the area was plagued with consistent bad weather as in strong winds and generally wet conditions all year round. The runway was in the direction of north-south and usually the final part of the approach was dogged by turbulence and pretty uncomfortable conditions. As for Narita itself it was once a sleepy farming village which suddenly had an airfield built around it. There could be up to ten airlines staying in the place in any one night so the centre of the town transformed itself into a social scene with bars and cheap beer. Just what aircrew thrived on! Invariably crews from the various hotels that lined the road from the airport to the town would descend on the town square in the early evening and adjourn to one of the local bars. The favourite one for BA was the 'Flyer's Bar' and the evening fun and games would then begin. At some stage we would eat but as the hour approached midnight crews would assemble in the town square and climb aboard a bus that would take us to the local Karaoke bar. To describe this venue as a bar would be an understatement since it consisted of two 'Porta-cabins' bolted together and placed in the car park of the local 'ANA' hotel. Conditions were pretty basic but as you arrived the place would light up to the sound of some pretty relaxed stewardesses from Virgin singing their heart out to a chorus of 'Like a virgin'. It was the sort of place where you felt the best course of action was to quietly sit in the corner and watch the idiots singing their hearts out. Good plan you might say but once a few drinks had passed the lips there you were screaming down the mike trying to emulate Frank Sinatra's 'My way' to the delight of anyone who might happen to be listening at the time. The bar, or 'The truck' as it was known as, laid on a bus in the early hours to drop the various refugees off at their various hotels on the assumption people on board could remember where they were staying. So that sorted out the first night and normally the second night was spent quietly since on the third day it was back to Heathrow.

Osaka was situated south of Tokyo and was the business centre of Japan. BA flew there three times a week with each flight continuing on to the city of Fukuoka on the west coast. At the time BA was at odds with the Russians about overflying rights so the route took us northwest from Heathrow right up over the Arctic and then down over Anchorage, Alaska and then on across the northern Pacific area to the northern Japanese island of Sapporo and then head south to finally arrive in Osaka. The route was very long when heading west into the prevailing winds and I have a personal log book entry showing a flight time of 16 hours and 15 minutes. We had double crews and ended up usually doing three-hour shifts so as to break the time more realistically. Osaka itself was a pretty lively place with the usual 'downtown' social scene of bars, fancy lights and restaurants. There was even a bar called the 'Pig and Whistle' which became synonymous with aircrew. The one advantage of the Osaka trip was the flight time lent itself to large inputs of cash since a lot of our variable pay, as you might call it, was based on the length of the sector and also the destination. Japan, and Osaka in particular, had a good pay allowance structure plus the longest flight time on the fleet and so was a much sought after trip. I was reasonably placed in the pecking order so I would get one of these lucrative trips at least once a month. It was well needed since I was now forking out cash like it was going out of fashion, helping Moya and the kids and trying to get some sort of domestic life for myself.

Now, Nagoya was the other end of the social spectrum of Japan with absolutely nothing to do there except ferment since the town was in the middle of the countryside with the highlight of the day being the street lights coming on. OK, there were a few bars around but they were run in the very traditional Japanese way. The other problem was that BA only operated there once a week so the stay there was about six days. OK, the money was good but the place just drove you mad with boredom.

So there I was in Hong Kong quietly dozing in my room in the hotel when the phone rang once and then the sound of a fax coming through started. I will point out at this stage that the rooms in this hotel were equipped with a small telephone exchange complete with this fax machine that was now jingling away. I wandered over to the machine expecting to see a fax from BA or the like. Surprise, surprise it was a hand-written fax and as I ripped it out of the machine I noted that the header was the Holiday Inn hotel in Mumbai. It was, in fact, a fax from Jo! You could have knocked me over with a feather as to how she had found out where I was and which hotel I was in since from the moment she went to Goa some time ago communications were virtually impossible. The answer lay within the words that she wrote whereby one of the other stewardesses with her in Goa had a pilot boyfriend on the -400 in BA and knew me and the name of our hotel in Hong Kong. The rest was pure chance that I might be there.

What a clever lady, I thought to myself.

As I read on it seemed that the job in Goa was nothing like she imagined it would be since the aircraft involved was a real old rust bucket and the whole operation was run on a shoestring by some unscrupulous Englishman who deemed it his right to break any contract that might have been signed by anyone unlucky enough to sign up with his airline. Having said all of this Jo was having a great time in Goa. There were six girls in all and they found accommodation just up the road from the famous Bogmalo Beach. The schedules were totally random and they spent a lot of the time on the beach waiting for the aircraft to arrive before one of them would go back to the small hotel, change and go to work. The only destination of any real importance was Mumbai where they stayed in the Holiday Inn on Juhu Beach hence the origin of the fax. It was ironic that back on the VC-10 I had stayed in the same hotel under its old name of 'Sun and Sand'. Anyway, Jo had written about three pages so that sorted me out when I finally flew out that night back to Heathrow and disappeared into the bunk complete with fax for a read. It appeared that her contract was coming to an end within a month and she would be back in the UK shortly after that. The other story she related to me was about the arrival in Goa of the Royal Navy Type 42 Destroyer HMS Nottingham. The ship was on a goodwill visit and the request went out for some pretty girls to come along for a cocktail party. By this time Jo and Co had befriended a bunch of guys who were working for British Aerospace while they set up the 'Sea Harrier' ship-borne fighter for the Indian Navy. So the request for the girls did not go unanswered and Jo and one of the other girls were duly picked up and off they went to the Port of Goa and enjoyed the evening being entertained by the officers of the ship. Apparently, the evening was a fantastic insight for Jo into the hospitality of the British. The drinks flowed well too! Enough said.

During May BA completed some domestic take-overs whereby Brymon Aviation, who concentrated their route structure out of Plymouth in the West Country, and Maersk Air, concentrating on Birmingham, became part of the company under the banner of 'British Airways Express' and eventually encompassed another UK domestic airline, CityFlyer Express so that the majority of the UK domestic scene had aircraft in BA colours together with flight and cabin crew wearing BA uniforms. It was hard work keeping up with it all.

The months rolled on and it was soon approaching June when I got a call from Jo to say that she was now back in the UK and staying with some friends down in Kent. I was not around for a couple of days but finally I got down to meeting her to be greeted by a creature that had a suntan like no other and looking really healthy after her Indian adventure. There was nothing left to say except:

"Jo, do you fancy staying with me for a few days up in Edgware?"

The answer was "Yes" and so Jo and I embarked on our own adventure which would change both our lives.

"Let's just take it by the day OK," was my final word on the subject. Yea right!

And so my life with Jo started in Edgware. She moved all her worldly belongings in and then she got to work finding temporary work in London and surrounding areas. She was not a shirker and pulled her weight workwise. Jo was an only child with German parents now living in Italy in the north-west of the country near the city of San Remo. Her father was an artist and quite a successful one at that with the gallery for his work being in nearby Genoa. Her mother was only about seven years older than me which I found a bit daunting.

As for Moya I felt that it was time to act and so we discussed divorce proceedings. Whether I was right or wrong I will never know but what else could I do? Our conversations were very limited and usually ended up in a slanging match. I would point out at this stage that I am not very good when trying to cope with a personal crisis. Add to that the attempt to say the right things on the phone was beyond me. I introduced Jo to the kids which was a bit strained since Jo was an only child and did not relate to children through no fault of her own. Paul seemed OK but Jenny was really struggling with the break-up of her mum and dad and found it very difficult to handle someone new in my life. Paul and Jenny would come up to stay in Edgware sometimes which always seemed to be full of drama. I think, in hindsight, that I should have understood their feelings a bit more with regards to the whole situation. To them it was only a short time before that I was living in the same house as them and we were a complete family and now the whole business was totally disjointed.

As for my flying I just plodded on as normal earning my keep and seemingly paying everybody around from Ernie, for the house rental, to Moya for the kids. Jo was holding her own financially and applied to be a stewardess with United Airlines based in Heathrow. One of my flying colleagues ended up with one of our German stewardesses and she too applied for United Airlines. Low and behold they both got accepted and off they went to Chicago for a six-week training course together. This was in the late June so all seemed set for Jo to get back into harness again. It was, however, not to be since, after about five weeks, I got a call that she was on her way home having left the course. To this day, it was not clear exactly what happened but apparently it was the overbearing attitude of one of the instructors that finally broke her. I was not around when she got home and when I got home a couple of days later there she was complete with a temporary job to go to in London.

This girl is made of strong stuff, was my thought for the day.

It was at about this time when the new US president Bill Clinton flexed his muscles and fired off some cruise missiles into the centre of Baghdad and the war of words between east and west fired up all over again. Not that it ever stopped that is!

Back in BA the new approved agreement with USAir went a step further with the launch of flights from Gatwick to Pittsburgh with USAir aircraft plus their cabin crew bedecked in BA uniforms. During the year Baltimore and Charlotte were added to the bunch of new routes. To round it all off BA also opened a new maintenance base at Cardiff Airport in South Wales to deal with the heavy maintenance work envisaged for the -400 since there were plans to have a fleet of over fifty plus.

As for me and Jo we seemed to settle down to our new life together and Jo became close friends with Ernie's wife Valerie. At the time there was an offer through the Sainsbury supermarket chain such that you could exchange shopping receipts for BA tickets. Jo, at the time, was not eligible for BA staff tickets since she had to be registered with me for one year minimum. So it was off to Sainsbury's every day to collect discarded bills lying around in the empty trolleys. It did not take too long before the first ticket to Berlin rolled through the letter-box and Jo went off to see her grandparents in Berlin. As flight crew I had a perk of the job whereby we could hitch a ride anywhere on the European network as an extra crew member and so it was easy for me to go with Jo to Berlin and meet her grandparents. They lived close to the airport in an apartment and Jo's grandfather was retired having worked all his life at Siemens. When I did meet them I found him a really nice old gentleman with a twinkle in his eye for his granddaughter. As for

Jo's grandmother I was not too sure what to make of her. She seemed to be very dominant and hugged the conversation, albeit in German. I remember being in my uniform, since that was the only stipulation for the 'extra crew chitty', and the grandfather fussed around me like I was some sort of celebrity. In the end we made a few visits to Berlin as the year wound down. It was ironic that I knew Berlin better than Jo considering she had spent some of her upbringing there and Jo knew London better than me despite me being an Englishman.

I did get Jo registered as my live-in partner within BA so that in the spring of the following year she would be eligible to fly with me on staff travel. With regards to the kids back in Binfield I did see quite a bit of them when I was at home and a sort of routine was established. I have to say that Moya never once used the kids as a weapon or denied me access at any time which was great. Having said that, our personal side was getting pretty strained. She had by then found a new male friend, Ray, who worked on the ramp at Heathrow and had, in fact, moved in with Moya after a while. The problem with all of that was the attitude of Jenny since, in her mind she wanted Moya and me back together and considered both Jo and Ray as threats. I cannot blame her but it was not to be. In consequence Ray got the full wrath of Jenny when he was there and Jo got the same when we both appeared together. It was not an easy time for any one of us and it put a strain on all of our relationships. What was nice to think was that Berlin was not too far away and with Jo being a German from Berlin it seemed that I had not lost that link to the city.

The news towards the end of the year was interesting with the famous Palestinian leader, Yasser Arafat, meeting up with his Israeli counterpart, Yitzhak Rabin in New York under the guidance of President Clinton for a historic meeting. The other equally interesting item was about Boris Yeltsin quelling a coup attempt in Moscow by standing on a tank whilst it fired into the famous White House in the city. The pictures came live from Moscow in graphic detail showing the final assault by the loyal military and ending the coup very decisively. In the world of computers and mobile phones Microsoft announced a new operating system known as 'Windows 3.11'. Wow, was it impressive at the time! And just about within my technical knowledge. I remember being in Los Angeles and my computer-mad Co-pilot showing me with great pride the first '1 Gigabyte' hard drive and a knockdown price of about $300.00. As for the mobile phone scene my 'brick' was consigned to history and was replaced by a more compact one. It still had very limited battery life but at least it could fit into my pocket without destroying it.

The birthday month of November was a bit of a muted affair with both Paul and Jenny getting two separate do's – one with Moya and Ray, and a second one with me and Jo. Having never been in the position of being separated from my kids I did find it very hard to cope with and, in line with a lot of other couples in the same predicament, found that to compensate by spending money on them seemed to ease my conscience somewhat. I know that it was not the right thing to do but at the time it seemed the only thing to do.

Jo and I spent our first Xmas together and I bid to be home for the holidays spending most of the time commuting to Binfield trying to spread myself across two families.

1993 ended with a new relationship to deal with plus an old one to sort out. It was quite a year in my life.

In comes 1994 and a sense of intrigue as to how things would develop. Jo seemed happy enough with temporary work contracts in London and more than pulled her weight in the newly established home that we had set up in Edgware. Back in Binfield I was kept on my toes with the demands put upon me by the kids. I decided to go down the road of separation and divorce since I found no other real solution to our predicament and so Moya and I sat down across the kitchen table to try to hammer out a financial solution that would be acceptable to all parties. Eventually we found one and so we started the arduous task of getting the ball rolling with the courts.

I continued to earn my keep on the -400 and found that the routes that seemed to suit my mood at the time were the ones that ended up in Australia either via Singapore or Bangkok or the South American ones. In BA the deal with USAir moved up a gear with up to 65 routes being linked together or 'code shared' to be correct. The routes involved were the domain of the old 747 classic aircraft. As for the -400 it never got involved in the routes to the 'Eastern Seaboard' as they were referred to. Examples include New York, Boston, Chicago, Philadelphia, Detroit, Toronto and Montreal. Having done a lot of those routes back in the old classic days I was happy to leave them well alone. Give me Bangkok or Singapore any day.

In February in the world of space the Russians seemed to steal the show for long endurance flights with Valeri Polyakov starting a marathon 15 months in orbit in a Soyuz spacecraft. Only 33 years ago Yuri Gagarin made just one orbit which shows the incredible advances in space travel. Also in February the first seeds of an end to the war in the Balkans were sown but not before four Serbian jets were destroyed by American F-16 fighters. It always seemed to take a worsening situation to produce a result but that is the way it is.

Within the pilot community on the -400 there emerged a 'have you got?' or 'I got this in Hong Kong last trip' split. I am referring to the latest in the computer or the mobile phone world. As for me, I was not in the computer world and just about struggled with the mobile phone so I was in the 'have not' group. It was in the March that a small American company, Apple Computer Inc, launched the first Macintosh model of a PC that revolutionised the world and put the personal computer into the category of 'every household should have one' class. The world of the home PC had started. So where did that leave me with my rather cranky and temperamental Amstrad machine? I thought I was in the 'buzz' but when I listened to any pilot who was in the 'must have' group I was like a fish out of water and nodded when I felt it was appropriate as he opened his latest gizmo on the way back from Hong Kong and spouted forth a load of technical words that seemed to be in a different language to any other:

What's a bloody PowerPC Microprocessor when it's at home anyway? I thought to myself as I nodded an approval to this over-active Co-pilot whilst he fired off on all fronts.

Now here is a question:

"When did that ever-smiling Italian TV Tycoon, Silvio Berlusconi, come to power?"

March 1994 is the answer. Amazing!

In the April I was scheduled to fly to Nagoya when I heard on the news the night before that a China Airlines A300 Airbus had crashed just off the main runway during an overshoot there killing all 260 people on board. Amongst our passengers the following day was a complete team from the UK accident investigation branch who had been called in on behalf of Airbus to help with the investigation as to the cause of the crash. My thoughts went back years before when I was in Lagos with a team investigating the Nigerian Airways VC-10 crash. As we landed in Nagoya the only evidence of the crash site was a few bits of twisted metal and a blackened smudge in the grass just to the left of the runway as we slowed to a halt. Aircraft are made mainly of aluminium and so burn furiously when ignited leaving very little residue. Anyway, it was a bit of a sobering thought that so many people had died in such a small area. We stayed in Nagoya for the standard five days and met up with the investigation team most evenings since they stayed in the same hotel. These guys are amazing to listen to once you get past the casual references they made about the victims of any accident like this one. When we flew home we took the team with us since their part was done.

It was in the May when Jo finally qualified for her first trip with me on staff travel and so off we went to Hong Kong with Jo nicely tucked up in her first class seat. The flight to Hong Kong was uneventful with Jo popping up every now and again to say hello. We had the usual double crew which, in relative terms, was luxury for a ten-hour flight. When we landed I had Jo sit behind me and it was quite something to see her expression change as we approached the runway from a strange angle. I purposely didn't let her know about the rather strange approach to the runway and so it was quite amusing to see her straining in her straps to see what I was up to and where exactly we were going. We got to the crew hotel, which by now had changed to the Excelsior, overlooking Causeway Bay, at about mid-afternoon. Jo had been tucked up in the First class cabin for the flight so was well rested and pretty excited about being in Hong Kong for the first time and I was feeling not too bad so we took a stroll outside the hotel to the local shops and Jo's eyes lit up with all the colours and styles she was confronted with. This was a side to Jo that was slowly emerging, whereby her instinct for anything 'arty' filled her mind with all sorts of ideas. Her father, Otto, being an artist had instilled in her the basic concepts of his work and skills from a very early age so that Jo had all the ingredients of an artist but had never had the chance to bring it to the surface since up to that point her whole life was based around survival and where the next rent money was coming from. It was difficult to bring her down off her 'high' but eventually we got back to the hotel when it was time for Jo to learn about my social skills based around the famous 'Charles Dickens' bar in the hotel and how to arrive and do a double order of drinks just before the clock hit 7 pm when the 'happy hour' ended. We joined the rest of the crew and ended up in the usual Chinese restaurant and it was a rather nice feeling to have Jo alongside so that she could sample the lifestyle that I could only talk about up to then. Of course, we ended up in Joe Bananas for the usual late night fun and games and eventually got back to the hotel in the early hours.

Amazingly enough, we were up quite early the next day and, after a quick coffee input, we took the subway to the Central District and got on the double-decker bus to Stanley, which was on the south-eastern tip of Hong Kong Island. The bus ride was quite an experience in its own right and the best spot was upstairs in the front row. The driver seemed to put the bus into all sorts of spots that a bus does not normally go and get away with it. The route runs near to the coast and one of the most memorable bays is Repulse Bay, named after the famous Royal Navy Battle Cruiser that sank north of Singapore in 1941 due to overwhelming Japanese airpower. As we drove along this bay a newly constructed block of apartments came into view just inland from the shore which had what appeared to be a huge hole constructed in the middle of the structure.

"The hole is constructed to allow the dragon to come down the hill and escape," I said to Jo pre-empting her question.

All I could think of is that someone told me about it and it must have sat in my brainbox ever since.

We finally made it to Stanley by about late morning. The thing about Stanley is that it boasts an old-fashioned Chinese market which is world famous. It sits on the edge of a bay and, amazingly enough, a local garrison of the British Army was established just outside of the town. Anyway, Jo and I wandered through the market place with a lot of 'Wow. Look at that!' and 'What a fantastic place!' emanating from Jo.

After a couple of hours we then got onto another bus and went westwards along the coast to the old fishing village of Aberdeen. Here was the famous floating restaurant or 'Jumbo' as it was known. There was a small boat that took us over to the restaurant and we settled down to a well-earned lunch. Well, for me it was, due to the fact that being awake during the day was pretty well unheard of when flying on my own. Jo seemed to be enjoying every bit of it and I have to say it was really nice to see that she was like that and not the sort to take everything for granted.

We finally got back to the hotel in the late afternoon and, after the obligatory sleep we set sail again to the Dickens bar for part two of our stay. That evening we dined just over the road at the Royal Hong Kong Yacht Club. This place was established many years before as a small island connected to Causeway Bay by a rickety old bridge. It became the club and restaurant where anybody who was anybody had to be seen. It had a real old colonial English style about it and a dress code that went with it. Nowadays it was all part of the island but still retained its traditions and to eat there, while overlooking Hong Kong harbour with the airport on the far side and all the night water activities going on, was pretty magical. It was the sort of place where a tie was required to get into the dining room and if, by chance, you didn't have one, a selection would be produced as if out of thin air to keep everybody happy. Needless to say the food was quite excellent and the company pretty good as well. Eventually we got to sleep quite late and the next day was spent with me in bed and Jo looking around the local shops and darting down alleyways to see what was around. All was brought down to earth in the evening when the crew got together in the lobby and off we all went to the airport for the long flight home. Jo got a rather nice seat again and so slept her way to Heathrow whereas I was doing the business upstairs in the Flight Deck with the usual mini-dramas of the flight to deal with. We eventually got home in the very early hours the next day and drove back up to Edgware. Jo really enjoyed her first trip with me and it seemed to set the trend for a few more in the future.

It was also in the May that three-times Formula One world champion Ayrton Senna was killed in an accident during the San Marino Grand Prix in Imola, Italy. The whole of Brazil went into mourning since he was a national hero. In May the Channel Tunnel opened for business enabling passengers to travel between the two countries in 35 minutes. This was maybe the start of a love affair with the French but, then again, maybe not. In South Africa Nelson Mandela was inaugurated as their first black president and the country re-joined the British Commonwealth. A lot happened in May.

Jo and I continued our rather basic existence in Edgware which was interrupted by the visits to Binfield and the kids. At one point Jo actually met Moya and feathers did not fly which I think was down to the sheer sense of the situation. Jo accepted my past with Moya and the kids and, as I said before, Moya never once used them as any sort of weapon. I remember the first time that the two women in my life met up since Thirza had come over to Binfield and sat in the lounge totally confused as to how these two women could calmly sit down over a glass of wine and chat as if they were old friends. Confused me as well it did!

In the world of BA it transpired that during the summer months the whole of the Club Europe brand was to be upgraded with all sorts of goodies such as new leather seats, lounges within Europe and a new buzz word evolved called 'Fast track'. The background to this was to provide a special routing from check-in to boarding for the business community to make them feel special. The figures involved for upgrades nowadays run into millions with this one set at about £70m. In real terms I could have bought over 20 Super VC-10s at 1960 prices for the same figure. It is amazing how the world was using the figure of a million as the benchmark price of anything to do with company finances. In the same breath it was decided to dispense with the First Class on the 'Beach Fleet' Caribbean services and increase the Club World seating to compensate. Both of these changes seemed to do the trick since all of the other airlines did the same and followed BA's lead. Having bought into Qantas some months back it was decided to combine the scheduling, sales and marketing on the so-called Kangaroo Route from the UK to Australia. I found it quite amazing that on a route such as Heathrow-Bangkok-Sydney that good money could not be made. Every time I flew the route the aircraft were jam-packed in all classes and staff travel was a nightmare. Being a simple pilot might have a bit to do with it, besides me and finances never did get on anyway.

With the Berlin scene well and truly put into the history books it was a real treat to hear about a bar in the city that Ian Baxter had bought with his wife and that every month he established a 'BA re-union night' so off Jo and I went to Berlin and met up with some of the ex-IGS people and so the party started again. It was a great shame that I did hear much later that the bar had collapsed financially and cost Ian dearly including his marriage. Bloody shame!

My route flying continued on the -400 and, with more aircraft being delivered, the tempo of work increased. Jo was still going for temporary work in London and all in all life was pretty hectic. I was in Los Angeles on one of my trips when the local TV channel was interrupted by a live broadcast of the famous National Football League star OJ Simpson in his Ford Bronco car being chased by the police and then being finally arrested for the murder of his wife and another person outside his mansion. He had become famous as an actor as well so it made it all a bit of a curiosity. Don't ask me how he did it, but he was acquitted of the charge much later after a trial that seemed to occupy prime-time TV for days on end. It was strange watching American Justice in action as if it was a daily 'soap opera'.

With my usual route being the flight through Bangkok to Sydney it was only a matter of time before Jo came along on one the trips so in the August off we went to Bangkok with me driving and Jo passengering. I had warned her beforehand that I felt that Bangkok was a bit of a vice-den and that maybe she might feel a bit a bit awkward about being there, seeing it all.

"What a fantastic place," were her words as we wandered out on the first clear day.

She readily accepted the seedy side of it all and revelled in the colours, sounds and smells of the city. When we went out in the evening to the downtown area where all the girlie bars were Jo seemed to take all the sights and happenings in her stride and it was hard to keep up with her as she darted in and out of the various stalls in the late evening. We always found time for a pause for refreshments though. It was a little bit like going out with my best mate for the evening. The evening usually ended up with a rather hairy ride to the hotel in the back of a 'Tuk-tuk' which was the local delicacy for a taxi. What it was, in fact, was a three-wheeled motorbike contraption with the driver perched over the front wheel motor-bike style with two seats sort of attached behind him with the hapless couple clinging on for dear life. The whole thing had a roof of sorts but was open to the elements elsewhere. So there you were careering down the road with your faithful driver beating six bells out of the two-stroke fuming piece of engineering pretending to be an engine weaving in and out of the traffic as if he had just fired off the starting grid at Silverstone. By the time you arrived at the hotel it took a firm tug of at least two of the door staff to release your grip from the handle that had been your life-line for the journey. If you recall the film with Jack Nicholson and Shirley MacLaine 'Terms of Endearment' where Jack takes Shirley for a spin in his sports car and in the end Shirley's beautifully manicured hairdo sort of ends up a bit wild then you might understand what I mean.

On the day of departure to Sydney I went off for a rest and Jo explored the local area and came back raving about some grubby little alleyway just around the corner that was, to her, a goldmine of inspiration and all sorts of assorted items tucked up in some grubby looking plastic bags. So there I was assuming that Jo would hate Bangkok but, in reality, the city, warts and all, gave her a real buzz. So, having finally dragged Jo down from above we joined the rest of the crew and off we went to Sydney. The flight time was about eight hours and with only two of us in the flight deck it was a bit of a workout. We were due to arrive at Sydney just after 5 am and not a minute before. The position of the airport was such that all the local politicians and people of importance in the city lived in the local area and it had become a haven for the noise lobbyists with huge restrictions placed upon the airport to the point that the radar people would send you on a conducted tour of the local beaches rather than allow an aircraft to even think about landing before 5 am. We were not even allowed to use reverse thrust just in case we might disturb the beauty sleep of some boring old politician. Bring back the VC-10 I say and give them both barrels.

Anyway, we finally got to the hotel at about 7 am and after a quick change and a clean of the teeth we went off to Circular Quay, which I mentioned way back as the ferry terminal with the bridge on one side and now the opera house on the other side. I remember back as a young lad staying in Sydney when my dad was posted there and the opera house was just a shell and lay derelict for many years due to the fact that the engineering side of the construction was proving just about impossible to do, but here it was in all its splendid glory and creating a structure worthy of any city. Anyway, the intention of coming down to the quay was to indulge on a real Australian breakfast with all the trimmings including champagne and orange juice or 'Buck's fizz'. It was a great way to unwind after a longish flight and set the scene nicely for a full day's snoring.

In the evening Jo and I went down back to the quay and climbed aboard a small harbour cruise ferry and enjoyed the delights of good food and stunning views of Sydney and the surrounding areas at night. All I can say is that it was a perfect introduction to Australia for Jo. All that was required was to get rid of that broad Aussie accent and all would be perfect!

On the following day we all gathered together again and off we all went back to Bangkok. We took off in the early afternoon so had a grandstand view of the country as we made our way northwest towards a place called Derby which was right up in the top left hand corner of the country. It would take us about five hours to get to Derby such was the size of the continent. Most of it was desert, once you got away from the coastal areas. We arrived in Bangkok at about 11 pm and so the race was on to get to the hotel and hit the bar for the late night 'happy hour'. Usually made it by the skin of our teeth! After another couple of days with Jo seemingly becoming obsessed with anything Thai and having itchy feet all the time we finally climbed aboard the aircraft and flew overnight to Heathrow. Jo and I eventually got back home in the late morning and so another trip was all done with Jo along for company and, I have to say, I did enjoy her company.

In the August the Provisional Irish Republican Army announced a complete cessation of military operations. This was a courageous step for the 'Provos' as they were known and maybe, just maybe, it heralded the start of the end of the hostilities in Northern Ireland after many years of conflict. As one conflict seemed to be getting resolved the reverse was true in the Middle East with Iraq threatening all sorts of things in response to the sending in of United Nations inspectors to search for the infamous WMD. They put extra soldiers on the Kuwaiti border and the Americans did likewise on the Iraqi border. I would have thought that Gulf war 1 would have done the trick in getting the various factions to run for cover and thank their lucky stars they were alive to tell the tale. Not so with the defiant Iraqi high command as they continued posturing as if nothing had happened. It is amazing to me how one person can influence the minds of the complete population. Amazing! Towards the end of the month a happening occurred in the Gwyn and Jo household which makes the previous news items pale into insignificance. We were off to Italy to meet the parents. It was with a certain amount of trepidation that we boarded the flight to Nice one sunny afternoon.

A little insight into Jo's upbringing might be useful at this stage. As I mentioned before Jo spent her first six years living a true 'Heidi' lifestyle high up in the Swiss Alps having moved there very soon after being born in Munich. At that point, her father got a teaching position as a professor in Berlin so the family 'up sticks' and moved to Berlin. It was here that Jo started her real education, German style, until the age of about ten when the family 'up sticks' again and moved to Italy. It was here that she was expected to continue her education under a completely different regime with the language being the first thing to conquer. This nomadic upbringing must have created a feeling of 'not belonging anywhere' in Jo's world and, in consequence, she did not have a happy upbringing. The other side of the equation was the fact that her father was quite old when she was born and a lot older than her mother. He was an architect by profession but in later life his world was dedicated to painting and so he would be in his own world with his paints and canvasses to the exclusion of everything around him. That left Jo's mother to carry the burden of all things to do with the family side of life. I think that like most families – and mine was no exception – there was always a certain amount of built-in conflict when it comes to growing up within the family. I think that as far as Jo was concerned this conflict was pretty strong to the point that, at the tender age of 19, she was shipped out to England as an au pair. Having said that her education in the world of art and the understanding of it was exceptional since her dad would talk to her from a very early age about the complete 'who's who' in the art world. He also showed her the basics of art and how to do this and that with colours and brush. This talent is something that one is born with and can be developed as Jo did with her dad. Boy, has she got a talent for all things arty! So, in summary, her relationship with her mother was one of constant conflicts, and a challenge with her father as love, understanding, mutual tolerance and preserving a good amount of emotional closeness became increasingly difficult as Jo grew up and even more so when Jo moved away.

So, we finally landed in Nice and after going through the usual formalities there was Jo's mum standing there waiting for us. I have to say that she was really lovely and welcomed me with a huge hug. The drive to Jo's home in Italy took us east along the coastal motorway and, as we passed the Principality of Monaco, we pulled off the motorway and made our way towards Monte Carlo and ended up at a restaurant overlooking the harbour and enjoyed a very pleasant drink in the late afternoon sun, watching the hang gliders floating aimlessly in the air and drifting gently with the sea breeze. We eventually got to Jo's house in the village of Pompeiana which was a few kilometres south along the coast from San Remo. Jo's dad, Otto, met us and I was introduced to him. I found him a fascinating man although there was no way we could communicate. He obviously doted on his daughter and was totally contrary to what I had expected. The other introduction that was essential for a peaceful stay was the guard dog, Bello. Dog he was, guard he was not since he could well have licked any intruder to death. He was the same breed as Tracy, being a Bichon Frise and was quite a character. Mother went fussing about in the kitchen and within a couple of hours we all sat round the table enjoying a superb meal with Bello lurking under the table somewhere. Jo's parents had basically two houses to their name. The first, or larger one, was what we were sitting in now and next door was a much smaller one which they had acquired some years before. Jo and I stayed in the smaller house so it was really nice to be able to say 'goodnight' and disappear into the night.

The next day Jo took me around her old haunts including a walk up the hill behind her house amongst the flowers and fruit trees. This was rural Italy and it was a pleasure to get the feel of the place where Jo grew up right down to the village square totally dominated by the church as you would expect. Otto took great pride in showing me all Jo's early attempts at painting. He was the original hoarder. I know now where Jo got it from. As for Jo's mum, on the surface all seemed fine and dandy but I was sure that there was conflict lurking just below the surface. Anyway, after a couple of days we went back to Nice airport and Jo and I flew home and off I went back to work.

Cynthia, my sister, came down for a few days to stay with Dad and Thirza and so the time came for Jo to meet my side of the family. So off we trooped to Wokingham and arrived for dinner. Dad had a habit of putting on some classical music as we all sat down after the usual introductions. For my sins, my knowledge of the classics is sadly lacking so I would just sit there and endure it. Not so with Jo since her background in the arts flowed out and very quickly she commented to my dad on the choice of music. If I recall, he was playing the 'Planets Suite' by Gustav Holst and before anyone could say anything Dad and Jo were engaged in a conversation about classical music and everybody else was side-lined. Was I impressed or what!

Anyway, with all the family introductions out of the way it was business as usual with me flying and Jo getting agency work in London. In the November it transpired in the news that the former US President Ronald Reagan had been diagnosed with the dreaded Alzheimer's Disease. He did so much to change the world events and it was cruel to be struck down like this.

Within BA the Concorde service to Washington, the US Capital, was discontinued after 18 years and, at the other end of the scale, GB Airways became a franchisee of BA operating scheduled services in full BA colours and crew uniform. BA was slowly completing its stranglehold on the UK domestic scene.

Also in November I did manage to get down to Binfield to see both kids for their birthdays. Paul was 14 and Jenny was 11. As I said before I found that throwing money at them was my attempt at compensating them for what had happened. Jenny was still taking the separation very hard and it was like her world was falling apart. Paul seemed to cope but I never knew what lay behind the façade. Unfortunately there was no going back since Moya and I would still be faced with the same scene as before.

"Where would that take us?" I often said to myself.

I flew to Nagoya just before Xmas and was due to return on Xmas Eve to be followed by a flight to Caracas, Venezuela on Xmas Day. Jo was due to fly with me on the Xmas Day flight and we would be back early January. Great planning on my part but I forgot one small but significant detail which was the English weather. The aircraft that was due to fly out to Nagoya for us to fly back on Xmas Eve got stuck, along with quite a few other aircraft, on the ramp at Terminal 4 at Heathrow due to the arrival of freezing fog. This phenomenon, in simple terms, is fog which freezes on contact with anything solid. It virtually stops an aircraft in its tracks and nothing moves until the temperature rises a degree or two. It is quite rare to get this happening but it did on that day. To add to the fun the auxiliary power unit that provides power for the aircraft on the ground sensed these conditions and stopped working as well. So on the tarmac were a number of -400s going nowhere, especially to Nagoya.

I had the dubious honour of collecting the crew together and giving them the sad news that we were going nowhere that day. The hotel management was, I have to say, very sympathetic, and arranged for us to have a 'party' room for the evening and laid on coffee and cakes. Unfortunately these things do happen in the airline world and you just have to make the best of what you have got around you. I spoke to Jo and gave her the bad news. She sensed something was afoot since she said that the landscape out of the lounge window was pretty bleak and that the TV was full of the dramas about the weather. I also spoke to crew scheduling and it was confirmed that the Xmas Day flight was not for me but, after a lot of shuffling about they confirmed that I was off to Hong Kong on the 27th provided I got back from the depths of Japan in time. The freezing fog that had stopped Heathrow in a flash disappeared in an equal flash and finally our aircraft arrived in Nagoya very early on Xmas Day and we all finally got home very late on Xmas Day. So, off Jo and I went to Hong Kong for a few days including New

Year's Eve and so a rather eventful 1994 finished on a happy note.

In comes 1995 and maybe this year might hold the clue to my future. Within BA I was extremely happy with my lot having been a Captain for just under 20 years and in a very good position on the famous seniority list so that I could just about pick and choose where I wanted to go. With six years to go until retirement the pension due at that time was extremely attractive and was solely due to the fact that I had kept with BA all of my flying life and would retire after 34 years plus a few months. The only downside of the equation was the fact that I had, by now, two failed marriages to come to terms with in all senses including the financial one. OK, the pension would be very good but with Jo now well established I had a lot on my plate as to how to maybe start again on the property ladder at the tender age of 49 in a few weeks. Not easy!

I went back to work with all sorts of thoughts buzzing around in my head. One thing that was certain was that I could not stay renting a house for ever. Great with Ernie next door and Jo got on with Valerie very well even to the point that Jo had invited her to go to Berlin with her when she went next time. As for the flying, I was generally going to the Far East or to South America each month which financially was the best trip sequence to extract the most out of the 'pot' as they say.

It was in the March when BA sold the charter company of Caledonian Airways, including the five remaining Tri-stars, to a company called Inspirations. It was back in 1969 when Airtours was founded becoming Caledonian Airways many years later and now it was gone. I understand that the airline continued for a few more years before it too was absorbed in Thomas Cook. Jo had the privilege to fly with them a couple of years ago. The 'yellow dog' on the tail was finally painted out.

It was also in the March that the first American Astronaut to fly in a Russian rocket blasted off from the Baikonur Cosmodrome in Kazakhstan. This was the start of co-operation between Russia and the USA in the world of space. It coincided with the Russian Cosmonaut, Valeri Polyakov, having just completed over 366 days in space aboard the Mir space station. He actually did 438 days in total before returning to Earth. That is more than a year in space for one man which, by anyone's standard, is amazing.

On one occasion at home in Edgware Jo and I sat down and talked about how we going to handle the coming months with respect to where were we going to live?. It seemed to me that we were pretty well an item and 'we' as opposed to 'me' was the in-word. What we did was to try to itemise our priorities together and we kept coming back to 'somewhere permanent' to live. I felt that I needed to be close to Paul and Jenny.

"Not too close but not too far" was the way I put it.

So what I did was to check with the bank as to how I would stand if I wanted a mortgage and what sort of limit would I be looking at? I had been with the same bank for many years and so hopefully, had a good rapport with them. In the end I must have, since I got a good response and so I could set a budget as to what I could afford. Jo and I then went down to the Binfield area and started looking around for somewhere to put down roots. The village next to Binfield, Warfield, had a new estate of houses and flats of different shapes and sizes being built and so we put down the deposit on a two-bedroom flat. The moving date was some time in the August so there was plenty of time to plan. The finances all came together to my amazement – we were all set to get back on the property ladder again. The agreement with Moya was all done and the courts had the paperwork in place with the hearing set for June or thereabouts. This summer was going to be pretty busy.

I did a trip to Narita in March and awoke to the news that in Tokyo there had been a Sarin gas attack on the Subway carried out by members of the Aum Shinrikyo religious cult and that 13 people had died and over five thousand were injured. Why is it that religion, in some form or another, always gets involved in attacks like this? was my thought for the day. Take Northern Ireland as another example, where Protestants and Catholics freely admit killing each other if given the chance. By the way, in the March, for the first time in 26 years, no British soldiers patrolled the streets of Belfast. On my soapbox again trying to understand why it took such a long time to maybe start the healing process. Enough said!

On my return from Narita I was told of the untimely death of Phil (Rocky) Reynolds who was on the 737 and whom I had known for many years. I mentioned way back that he had married Lisa, who I also mentioned even further back. He actually committed suicide and it transpired that it was all down to women trouble. Jo and I went to the funeral together with my old friend Joe Hall, and found it all quite upsetting to see a man do this to himself and leave two young boys to survive without a father. What a tragic ending to a life. Having said that I feel that to leave two young boys like that is a pretty selfish thing to do whatever the situation.

In my flying world I did a flight to Mexico City. We had a couple of days off so myself and the two Co-pilots plus one wife went for a day out to the famous 'Sun and Moon' pyramids, about two hours' drive out of town. The driver seemed OK and the car was one of those large American Cadillac sorts. Anyway, apart from one of the Co-pilots being bitten by the local donkey all seemed fine until it was time to go home. Our driver had spent the day with other drivers and consumed copious amount of the local speciality, Tequila, and was well out of sorts for the drive back. I sat in the front and spent most of the time doing the steering and screaming for brakes when needed. It came to the point when we were in agreement to lob him out and somehow get back on our own. As we came around a corner we ground to a halt after much screaming and steering and joined the most beautiful traffic jam we had ever seen. We then spent the next two hours crawling along with numerous attention-getting schemes to keep him awake. We finally got deposited at the hotel and he sat there all angelic waiting for a tip for the wonderful experience of driving in Mexico. My language was pretty blue and he must have taken offence since he attempted to roar off the starting grid only to end up embedded in the back of a taxi within about five seconds. Yes, quite a wonderful example of driving in Mexico!

On the departure from Mexico we found ourselves too heavy for the take-off. Let me explain further, if I may. The -400 is a magnificent aircraft with lots of power and can pretty well manage any airfield on the BA network with a full load of freight and passengers. What is peculiar about the Mexico City airport is that it lies in a valley running north-east to the south-west and is surrounded by mountains on pretty well all sides. The normal departure was to take off towards the south-west and, at a relatively low height, do a complete about turn and head north-east out of the valley, this being the safest route. On this occasion we had a full load of passengers plus about 20 tonnes of local fruit in the holds. The route was a new one for BA and so nobody on the ground really thought too much about what weight we would be and just shovelled the fruit on. What we decided to do was to taxi out to a remote part of the airfield and to sit tight and wait for the temperature to drop a few degrees since it was early evening. After about an hour of sitting tight the temperature dropped enough and we were ready to go. So we lined up on the runway and hit 'the pedal' and waited for the aircraft to start its take-off roll. We pretty well used up every inch of runway and staggered into the air leaving the runway end a blur just below the windscreen as we slowly started to climb away. Then we came to the turn to get us on the way out of the valley. By this time, the temperature had gone up a couple of degrees, which was detrimental to the aircraft performance and, combined with the fact that we were turning, stopped any climb that might have been there. We flew over a village half way round the turn and the sensitive radio altimeters started to get agitated showing us that we were very low and all that it needed was a small descent and we could have been in a dangerous position so I very gingerly pulled the nose up and, low and behold, we got a very small climb showing. As we straightened up from the turn then the climb rate slowly increased and we ascended ever so gently out of the valley. I had great faith in the engines since they had been kept at full power for over ten minutes to get us safely up and away. As for the controller who told us that the temperature had dropped enough for us – I put him in the same category as the taxi driver.

This particular flight from Mexico to Heathrow proved to be quite an epic since it was later in the flight when I retired to the bunk for a couple of hours' sleep that my body decided that it did not like the pre-flight sandwiches that we had eaten before departure and so off I went to the toilet feeling very sorry for myself. Things got worse when I struggled back into the bunk and, not wishing to be too dramatic, I was not a well 'bunny' and I finally curled up on the flight deck floor and told the two Co-pilots to get on with the rest of the flight on their own and that I would be playing no part in it at all. All I wanted was to be somewhere else and spent the time on the floor devouring gallons of water – or so it seemed. Fortunately, there was a procedure in place within BA to deal with one of the crew members being incapacitated, with the only additive here was that it was the Captain that was 'out to lunch' as they say. Anyway they did a splendid job and we arrived on the stand to be met by a full team of medical staff who climbed on board the moment the doors were opened. They were complete with a portable stretcher and I reckon enough equipment to perform major surgery. The passengers must have got quite a shock seeing this lot arriving and an even greater shock when they all went in a bee-line for the flight deck. Anyway, by this time I was feeling a little better and it was decided that open heart surgery was not needed and I finally struggled up and was taken to the BA medical centre in the Terminal complete with all my worldly possessions and collapsed in the company bed for the sleep of the century. I called Jo and let her know what was going on and just managed to stop her getting on the bus in her dressing gown to come to see that I was still in one piece. After a sleep of many hours I slowly came to.

"Funny sort of hotel room!" I muttered to myself as I surveyed my new surroundings.

At that point a nurse arrived complete with the best cup of tea I have ever tasted in my life and then 'checked my vitals' and said that Jo had been ringing up a few times and all that was reported to her was that I was still asleep. Even after ten hours I was still asleep. The body is quite amazing when all it needed was sleep to repair itself. Anyway, it was, by now, late in the afternoon and I have to say BA were pretty good and laid on a car to take me home to Edgware where a very serious Jo took me in and got me back into bed to continue my slumbers for another ten hours or so. Not bad sleeping with 20 hours completed after only being home from my travels for one day. Yes, that was quite a trip that I did to Mexico. The place did not feature too much in my social diary after that.

It was shortly afterwards that Jo and I made another visit to Italy and Jo's parents. On this occasion the four of us travelled to Genoa and I was introduced to the owners of the art gallery where Jo's dad exhibited his work. They had a small cottage-style house sitting in the hillside overlooking Genoa and we were all treated to the 'lunch of lunches' as only the Italians could conjure up. I seem to recall at least six courses. They also had a small number of other guests for the lunch which included a retired English professor so that I could chat away to him in English and not feel too left out. It took a mean two-hour walk in the afternoon to get over the fantastic food and the amount of it. We all got back to Pompeiana in the late evening. It was shortly after Jo and I got back to the UK that it transpired that Jo's dad was not well and that he was beginning to go downhill quite fast. Jo had a very close relationship with her dad and his illness did upset her immensely. People get old unfortunately!

In the June BA announced the transfer of flights to Central and East Africa to Gatwick to free up valuable slots at Heathrow since it was fast becoming a very popular destination for many airlines but was equally fast running out of terminal and runway capacity. For example Panam and TWA held precious slots for the transatlantic route but in the end conceded them to United Airlines and American Airlines. These two airlines, in turn, pushed the UK Government for more access to Heathrow. This push coincided with a new UK/US agreement being negotiated which would allow BA more access flights into the USA. Within Europe the airports were getting bigger and bigger with Frankfurt and Amsterdam leading the charge. The amazing thing was that Heathrow was still the most sought after destination from all points of the compass. At Heathrow there was still talk of a new terminal being built specifically for BA combining all European and Intercontinental flights under one roof. It was a pipe dream in a lot of people's eyes since the environmentalists and anyone who fancied it climbed aboard the band wagon and forced a public inquiry on the issue.

Also In June progress was being made on two domestic fronts with a court date set for the divorce petition to be heard and the move to Warfield seemed to be getting nearer. Both items were due to be set for August so we were on the way as they say.

The other sad news in June was to hear of the death of another very good friend, Mick McKeon, who was on the 737 and just about to start a -400 course. He was killed in a car accident while walking along his local road near his home. Mick hailed from the 707 in BOAC and was a great character, and could only be described as a very loveable

Irishman. I was also told about Pete Brown, who was a training Captain on the 737, whom I knew reasonably well, who had died whilst on a walking holiday in Scotland. The 737 was still, even after leaving the fleet, like a family and to hear of these events was pretty sobering. I could not make the funeral of Mick but Joe Hall made it OK and told me afterwards of the many people that made it and the whole event was quite moving.

In the news a hijack attempt in Japan of an All Nippon Airways 747-200 with 365 passengers was thwarted by the police and ended without injury. In the world of space the US shuttle Atlantis docked with the Russian Mir space station for the first time further cementing the co-operation of the super powers.

In the July I took Jo on a trip with me back down to Australia but this time we went through Singapore instead of Bangkok. Once again Jo seemed totally enthralled by anything Eastern and it was good fun having her along. In Singapore we met up with an Australian, aptly called Wally, who tried to sell us a short holiday break on the Indonesian island of Batam that was about 30 minutes' boat ride away. The small resort was known as the Turi Beach resort. On our return to Singapore from Sydney we went over to the resort on the ferry and, I have to say, it was small but an enchanting place complete with swimming pool plus an excellent restaurant. Sometimes resorts like this turn out to be a disappointment or a 'poser's paradise' but this place was neither and Jo and I felt that a few more visits would be made as time went on. We finally returned to Singapore and caught up with the rest of the crew and off we went on the usual 13 hour jaunt back to Heathrow.

I did one more trip in July to, of all places, Mumbai and it was there that I caught up with Joe Hall who had just converted onto the -400. He lived at Abingdon, Oxfordshire in the UK and so we arranged to meet up on our return so that I could introduce Jo to his wife, Gisela, a fellow German lady.

It was also in the July that the war in the Balkans hit a new low when Bosnian Serbs marched into Srebrenica as Dutch peacekeepers left and committed horrific crimes that became known as the Srebrenica Massacre. I have to confess that I found the politics of the area incredibly confusing and it seemed that there were numerous conflicts happening in the area which seemed to be based around old scores that needed to be settled. It felt like that game at the fair where you try to hit the head coming up only to find another one popping up elsewhere.

So, the month of August arrived and Jo and I moved into a first floor two-bedroomed flat in Warfield which was about three miles from Binfield and the kids. Being a new place it came with all the small problems that seemed to be the norm but it was in a nice location being about three miles from Bracknell and that provided an outlet for Jo and her agency work. A new supermarket was opening in the September just down the road. So here I was back on the property ladder and the place suited the pair of us perfectly. When we moved into Warfield I finally succumbed to the computer world and bought a new all-singing, all-dancing piece of kit that came with the latest and greatest software known as 'Windows 95'. Jo was quite up to date with the modern computer scene and so it was down to her to 'educate' me as to what to do after I had taken the bold step of switching the thing on. She must have been very patient with me and that is all I can say.

It was in the August that the official divorce for Moya and me came through and so I was a free man again.

Not for long, I thought to myself.

So there you have it with my second marriage officially 'up the creek'. This one was particularly difficult since I had Paul and Jenny to consider and not just Moya. My mum would not have been too chuffed with her son's performance in that department.

"What is it with me that I can cope with a very exacting professional career but fall down hard in the relationship career?" I said to myself in the mirror at the time.

Perhaps I was not built for the emotions of marriage. Yes, my first marriage to Pam was a total disaster for many reasons but with Moya I would have thought I would have learnt all the lessons to make it work but I didn't. Maybe it was the money issue or was it something else?

Anyway, philosophising is now over and a new era in my life was about to start because I asked Jo to marry me and she said "Yes". So the plans were put in place for the forthcoming wedding day and Jo came up with the suggestion that to marry in 1996 on my 50th birthday in

January would be ideal since I could not ever forget that date. Right, the date was sorted, now to sort the venue. What better place to tie the knot than in Los Angeles, where we first met? Even better than that, we decided to marry on the old Cunard liner 'Queen Mary' that was tied up permanently at Long Beach in the city and would be perfect. I can remember back to my Hamble days seeing her sailing past my window on her way to New York. Ironic or what! So there you have it with the place and time sorted so it was now down to getting the organisation in place to make it happen. This task became a bit daunting and required a lot of resource management as you might say but slowly it was seen to come together.

So, all in all, August was a busy month for all of us. Jo and a stewardess friend Christiana were invited to go to Beijing and stay with the British Airways airport manager for a week so off they went and by all accounts fun was had by all. The city was full of sights to see and explore from the 'Forbidden Palace' to the 'Great Wall of China' and so Jo indulged for a week away from all of the goings on back home to do with our forthcoming wedding. Me being close to the kids did have its advantages and disadvantages. The journey time, compared with Edgware, was minimal but created a scene whereby it was easy to drive over and collect the kids from school as a daily routine By this time Jenny had moved on to her secondary school and for a while she went to the same one as Paul. So it was off to collect the pair of them at just after 3 pm and operate a taxi service for the next couple of hours.

It was at about this time that we heard about a colleague of mine, Ted Barber, who was a Captain with me in Berlin on the 737. Jo had, by that time, accepted the fact that the 737 family in Berlin was very close to my heart. Ted was married to a Danish girl, Inga, and their relationship was a bit of a roller-coaster. Inga was a stewardess on Short-Haul and I had met her a few times so I knew that their scene was not brilliant. Ted had left the 737 for a conversion course on the -400 earlier in the year and this coincided with the total breakdown of his marriage. The pressure on Ted was just too much and he was taken off the course and stood down. Roger Price, our old fleet manager on the 737, arranged for Ted to be sent to a clinic in West London since Ted had, by this time, suffered some sort of complete mental breakdown, and needed

help. At this point Joe Hall and I were brought into the picture to try
to talk to Ted and help him where we could. His best friend, Brian
Horne, was also heavily involved so the three of us would ring Ted
daily. Ted was eventually released from the clinic but remained stood
down, since he was still on heavy medication. Joe and I visited him on
various occasions and it seemed that, maybe, Ted was slowly on the
mend. He had two sons who were at the time applying for university
and their entrance exams were due shortly. It was a total emotional
shock when we were told that Ted had taken his own life the night his
sons had completed their entrance exams. I was in Los Angeles at the
time and Joe was in New York. Joe actually rang my Jo from New York
and she had the presence of mind to hold the news about Ted until I
got home off the trip. Ted was a very popular Captain on the 737 and
also well regarded amongst the German cabin crew though not in any
way sinister. They just loved Ted! It was as simple as that. The funeral
was a pretty dramatic affair with a lot of flight crew and German cabin
crew all paying their respects. Ted was the final sad chapter in the year
with Rocky, Mick and Pete all gone. It was quite a tough year on the
emotions I have to say.

In total contrast I was on a trip to Hong Kong shortly afterwards
with a computer-crazy co-pilot who introduced to me the latest gizmo
on the market called a DVD or 'Optical Disc Computer Storage' media
format to give it the correct title. He said that it would not be long
before the '3½ Floppy Disc' would be done away with to be replaced by a
built-in CD/DVD player. I nodded when I felt it was the right time to do
so. He also talked about a new web site that had just come on the scene
called 'eBay' where you can trade anything for anything. I nodded
again in sympathy hoping not to betray my ignorance.

Trading on the internet eh, it will never catch on, I thought to
myself.

Boy, did I eat my words!

I also did another trip to Los Angeles so was able to go to the Queen
Mary and started to get the ball rolling for the forthcoming wedding.
In addition to the plans for the following January we also decided
to have a church ceremony a week later in the UK and then go off to
Phuket, Thailand for the honeymoon. The planning committee moved

up a notch to cope with it all.

It was in the September that BA announced yet another revamp, with this one costing £500m with a complete new Club World and First Class product. The name 'First Class' got shortened to 'First' for some unknown reason but people in that department are more privileged than I as to wonder why. A new initiative was also launched known as the 'Executive Club Frequent Flyer Programme'. As I commented before the figures quoted seem excessive but I have to say that whatever BA did most of the other airlines followed suit so they must have got something right. At the other end of the world Qantas and BA finally started operating the 'Kangaroo routes' under a joint venture as proposed many months ago.

Seoul, South Korea featured as a new route with the start of the winter schedules with the -400 operating three direct flights a week. I operated one of the first flights there and found the geography of the place quite amazing with the city and airport situated about 60 miles from the 38th parallel border of North Korea with all that that implied. From June 1950 until July 1953 the two Koreas were at war and, although the United Nations had committed just under 350,000 soldiers to the conflict, the original 38th parallel border remained. With no official piece of paper stating that the war was over, the area became known as the 'Demilitarised Zone' or the 'DMZ'. Since 1953 there has been a huge military presence in South Korea consisting mainly of American soldiers whose job was to deter the North from having another go. This short piece of history puts the capital of South Korea, Seoul, in its correct context as a military city dominated by the Americans. The social area of the city was called 'Itaewon' and you could be fooled into thinking you were in some sleazy downtown American city. Eating in Seoul was quite an experience with the famous Korean barbecue being the main ingredient. What would happen is that you would all sit around a table as normal and in the middle would be a hole. After a few minutes of trying to analyse the hole and the menu the waitress would suddenly plonk a real live barbecue bucket complete with red-hot coals into this hole. Various small dishes, containing strange bits of things, would then turn up. The menu at this point was totally irrelevant since you would be completely mesmerised by what was happening on the table. I use the term 'waitress' lightly since they were generally of the more mature variety with the standard Far Eastern smile built-in. Anyway, after a few minutes she returned with a plate of beef that looked a bit dubious. She then proceeded to attack the meat with a large pair of scissors cutting it into small pieces and throwing it on the grill. Within seconds the grilled meat was removed, plonked in your bowl and away you went adding all the strange looking ingredients plus a good portion of rice. The drink that traditionally went with the meal was a local concoction called 'Soju'. All in all, the meal was totally different but a real treat of an experience complete with the mature waitress.

It was in the November news that the Israeli Prime Minister Yitzhak Rabin had been assassinated at a peace rally in Tel Aviv. In the Middle East Israel was considered the most stable of the countries and then this happens. In the Balkans, agreement was reached to end the conflict, and NATO, under the name of the Implementation Force (IFOR), went into the region to keep the peace. In the UK the infamous Rosemary West was convicted for the murder of ten women and girls and sentenced to life imprisonment. She was only the second woman in history to be given a mandatory life sentence with the other one being Myra Hindley convicted years before for the 'Moors Murders'.

In BA the first Boeing 777 arrived and entered service on the Dubai route. This aircraft was to be the first of the 'big twins' in the fleet.

Just before Xmas I took Jo with me on a trip to Kuala Lumpur, Malaysia with a return on the 2nd January 1996 so there we were together for Xmas. I flew to Djakarta, Indonesia on New Year's Eve and so the scene was set for a crew party in the evening. Between us we arranged with the hotel to have one of the large convention centres for the event complete with a music station and a manned bar. KLM were in town as well so it was brewing up to be a quite a do. It was decided the theme would be fancy dress so while we were on our shuttle during the day Jo, plus a few of the other wives and girlfriends, got together and made up the various outfits for the night. I was dressed as 'Onslow' from the famous TV sitcom 'Keeping up Appearances' complete with the famous string vest and beer cans dangling around my neck. Jo went as 'Er indoors' complete with a headscarf Nora Batty would have been proud of. The party was a brilliant success with nearly all of the participants dressed in fancy dress. Fortunately we did not have to fly home until the 2nd January so a quiet New Year's Day was had by one and all. And so 1995 ended with a few solid achievements being notched up.

So, 1996 arrived and all sorts of plans we had were slowly being put in place. The only small thing that seemed to be niggling away at us was that Jo had developed a really nasty cough that didn't seem to want to go away. Also, she seemed to be losing a lot of weight. In retrospect alarm bells should have been ringing but, at the time, there seemed to be a simple reason for the situation with the cough being put down to the cold weather combined with the air-conditioning in the various hotels we stayed in 'down the route'. The weight loss was put down to pre-wedding nerves. I did one more flight to Los Angeles in early January and tied up the loose ends at the Queen Mary so all was set for our wedding later that month. We did invite four other couples to our wedding. There was Dick Carter and Evelyn whom we had befriended when both girls went to Chicago for the United Airlines training. Dick had, by now, converted onto the -400 and Evelyn was flying as a stewardess with United Airlines. There was Jo's old friend, Juliet from Caledonian Airways and her new man Stratos the Greek. They were both flying as cabin crew in BA. There was my old friend Joe Hall and his wife Gisela. Finally there was Brian Horne, who was still on the 737 and his lady friend Patricia who was a stewardess with BA.

Within BA there was a change at the top with Bob Ayling becoming the Chief Executive with Sir Colin Marshall, recently knighted, switching to be the Chairman on a part-time basis. The 'Ayling Era' had been ushered in with the first business being done as the USAir deal goes under the microscope with maybe a better deal with American Airlines being on offer as the year progressed.

In the world of mobile phones Motorola introduced the most compact one to date known as the Motorola StarTAC for want of a better name. These new phones had come a long way from the old 'Brick'. As the phones got smaller then they got smarter. I remember having just arrived at Bangkok and as we emerged out of the Terminal expecting to see our crew transport sitting waiting patiently there was not a bus on sight. I suggested going back into the terminal and trying to find a BA person when the Co-pilot simply consulted the famous briefing sheet and took out his mobile phone and dialled the number of BA operations here at the airport. Someone answered him within seconds and the phone was handed to me to talk to them to get find out where the bus was. This was my first introduction to a new phone facility called 'Roaming'.

"Thanks a lot for that. I must get roaming installed on my phone as soon as possible," I said in a total state of confusion since I had, by then, only just managed to load my 'contacts list' after many attempts.

In parallel with this explosion of new mobile phone technology a rather nasty medical condition came along as well. What happened was that the vertebrae supporting the neck drooped and created a forward facing curve that, in effect, made the head point downwards. Depending on whether the patient was right or left-handed then the arm in question would also assume a right-angle locked position with the palm uppermost. The focal point of the eyes appeared to settle at a point in this upturned palm which, by design, was physically adapted by generic movement to fit one of these new slim-line mobile phones. The patient could walk for miles with this head-down affliction as if guided by telepathy. Every now and again an involuntary jerk of the affected arm would occur and it would adopt a second fixed position whereby the mobile phone would be pressed, as if powered by hydraulics, into the ear of the patient and talking would commence. The art of conversation outside of this limited application was generally non-existent since the head was unable to assume its normal pose to find out who was talking to them. There was a third fixed position whereby the spare hand, be it the left one or the right one, would extend a digit and commence to tap the keyboard as if sending a morse-code signal like my dad did many years ago on the 'Strat'. In fact he would have loved to be involved in the modern version of his old art of communications. The final conclusion after my personal exhausting research was more frightening since it seemed to affect young people first and only hit us oldies when all those around us seemed to have the head-down disease and conversation became limited to the odd grunt. An example of this is the bank queue and there I was, patiently standing in line and suddenly some tune of no particular origin starts up and the chap in front of you goes 'head-down' and you find yourself involved in his personal life whether you like it or not even to the point where you knew who he is talking to intimately. The fact that he is in the queue becomes irrelevant and he needs to be prompted to move forward. At this point he glares at you for daring to interrupt his so-called personal chat which, by now, has done the complete rounds of the bank with everyone waiting for the "Will she or won't she" answer. Drives me mad it does!

Anyway, back to Jo and me when, on about the 24th January we flew to Los Angeles and settled into our cabin on the great ship and started to put in place the final bits prior to the big day. Perhaps the story behind this great ocean liner would be appropriate to set the scene.

Quote:

"The Queen Mary's creation and launch was nothing if not extraordinary and her story is rich with history, elegance and grandeur. From the time her construction began in 1930 in Clydebank, Scotland, the Queen Mary was destined to stand in a class all her own. Despite suffering economic setbacks during the Great Depression, which stalled construction on the ship for several years, Cunard Line spared no expense on building the Queen Mary – which was originally known as job #534. Legend has it that the board of directors at Cunard had decided to name the ship the Queen Victoria, which would have been in keeping with the tradition of Cunard ships having the 'ia' suffix (Mauretania, Aquitania and Berengaria). As per protocol, legend states that the Cunard directors went to ask King George for his blessing of the ship's proposed name saying, "We have decided to name our new ship after England's greatest Queen," meaning Queen Victoria, the King's Grandmother. Upon which the King is reported to have stated:

"My wife (Queen Mary) will be delighted that you are naming the ship after her."

On May 27, 1937, the Queen Mary departed from Southampton embarking on her maiden voyage. She boasted five dining areas and lounges, two cocktail bars, swimming pools, a grand ballroom, a squash court and even a small hospital. The Queen Mary had set a new benchmark in transatlantic travel, which the rich and famous considered as the only civilized way to travel. She quickly seized the hearts and imaginations of the public on both sides of the Atlantic, representing the spirit of an era known for its elegance, class and style. For three years after her maiden voyage, the Queen Mary was the grandest ocean liner in the world carrying Hollywood celebrities like Bob Hope and Clark Gable, royalty like the Duke and Duchess of Windsor, and dignitaries like Winston Churchill. During this time she even set a new speed record, which she held for 14 years. But when the Queen Mary docked in New York in September 1939 that would be the last time she would carry civilian passengers for many years. As World War II started, the Queen Mary's transformation into a troopship had begun. She was painted a camouflaged grey colour and stripped of her luxurious amenities. Dubbed the 'Grey Ghost' because of her stealth and stark colour, the Queen Mary was the largest and fastest troopship to sail, capable of transporting as many as 16,000 troops at 30 knots. After the end of WWII, the Queen Mary began a 10-month retrofitting process, which would return the ship to her original glory. On July 21, 1947, she resumed regular passenger service across the Atlantic Ocean, and continued to do so for nearly two more decades. The increasing popularity of air travel helped signal the end of an era for the Queen Mary. By 1965 the entire Cunard fleet was operating at a loss and they decided to retire and sell the legendary Queen Mary. On October 31, 1967, the Queen Mary departed on her final cruise, arriving in Long Beach, California, on December 9, 1967. She has called Southern California her home ever since. The Queen Mary is now a floating Hotel, Event & Wedding Venue, home to three world-class restaurants and an icon in Southern California."

There was many a time while I was at Hamble back in the '60s when I spotted her funnel going past the window from my room on her way to New York.

After breakfast on our first clear day we made our way to the actual wedding venue which was at the stern of the ship on the promenade deck. It was originally called the 'Edward VIII Chapel' since it was used frequently by none other than Edward VIII and Mrs Simpson on many of their transatlantic voyages. It was now known as the 'Royal Wedding Chapel'. The sheer decadence of the ship was something else. This was

British engineering at its very best. The ship was over 65 years old and there she was as good as ever. When the ship arrived in Long Beach in 1967 the city of Long Beach assumed responsibility for her and she sort of bumbled along. Howard Hughes's 'Spruce Goose' was on the shore next to the ship and in the early nineties both of these creations were looking their age and the future for them was in doubt. An investment company, of Japanese origin I believe, came to the rescue and the 'Spruce Goose' was sold and shipped up to Oregon for display. The 'Mary' was totally refurbished back to her glory days and so there we were in 1996 soaking up the atmosphere of what it must have been like in those bygone days. We did the tour of the ship from the front to the back or from 'stem to stern' as they say in nautical terms. On the promenade deck overlooking the bow there was a bar which seemed the ideal venue for dinner and a few drinks. It even had a small smoking section for us.

Before we could indulge in the social side of the ship we had to do a visit to the local marriage registration office to get the paperwork out of the way. For the Port of Long Beach this office was at the Court House on a small island offshore known as Catalina Island. So off we went with a suitcase full of paperwork just up the quayside to a jetty and climbed aboard the 'Catalina Express' Hydrofoil to take us to Catalina Island. As we left the jetty we cruised gently past the Queen Mary and Jo and I just sat there with our mouths open and jaws drooping looking at the ship that we were to get married on. Once clear of the breakwater the hydrofoil lifted out of the water and there we were doing about thirty-five knots with not a ripple in the glass of something that we were drinking. Within about 30 minutes we berthed on Catalina Island and made our way to the Court House and were confronted with a setting that could have been taken out of the very old TV series of 'Peyton Place'. It was like going back in time. There was not a computer screen in sight and all we could hear was the sound of typewriters being driven expertly by a bank of ladies who seemed to be in a '60s time warp. So I boldly stood at the counter and one of these 'Dolly Parton' look-alike ladies came up and spoke to me. Once she picked up my English accent then a big beaming smile broke out and off we went with our details while she patiently typed them all down very carefully and when completed she ripped the required piece of paper out of the 1920s machine and asked for a couple of signature plus the fee of about fifty dollars. I calmly asked whether they took credit cards to be confronted by a speech about the ethics of credit or cash. Back in the days of 'Peyton Place' there were no credit cards hence the speech. So cash it was! Anyway, the whole procedure took about 30 minutes and so off we went then back to the dock for our return voyage. As it was, there was available on the Catalina Express an upgrade to First Class with your own small cabin at the bow overlooking the 'driver' in his cockpit, plus a bottle of bubbly to see you on the way.

"Sorry, but this just has to be done to celebrate the completion of the paperwork," I said as we settled into our own exclusive cabin.

The trip back was equally exciting but with the additive that we were invited to sit in with the Captain as he fired us across the water back to the 'Mary'. The bubbly was not too bad either. We even spotted a couple of dolphins leaping out of water not too far away. What an amazing and romantic start to our wedding plans.

"Now, where is that Promenade bar to carry on the celebrations?" was my request when we got back on board the 'Mary'.

The next day, the 26th was technically my last day of freedom as a single man but with Jo there it felt like any other day. Throughout the day our various guests arrived on the ship and by the early evening we were a complete wedding party. As you might imagine the evening was a pretty social affair and eventually we all ended up in our cabin toasting whatever came into the mind at that moment. The porthole was pretty popular with the smokers and if viewed from the outside it must have appeared as a sort of foggy smog arising from a spot on the starboard side about mid-ships.

So the big day arrived and with the ceremony set for the early afternoon we all had plenty of time to get spruced up, clear the throat and get ready. Joe Hall and I sneaked off for a quick calming drink in the now familiar promenade bar and when I got back to the cabin Jo was not at all pleased with my antics – but after a soak in the bath we were all set to go. The actual ceremony was conducted by the ship's Chaplain and reflected the American commercialisation of what can only be described as a solemn affair. Anyway, under American law we were pronounced 'man and wife' so it was done and dusted.

Afterwards we went to a pre-arranged afternoon tea at one of the many restaurants and in the evening we ended up in the main restaurant called 'Winston's' which was on the upper deck and boasted views over Long Beach and beyond. The meal was pretty good and there were a few toasts and speeches as the evening carried on into the early hours.

The next day was 'wind-down day' and we were all due to fly back to Heathrow that night. Various couples went their own way leaving Joe, Gisela, me and Jo to fill in the day and finally we made our way to the airport for our return flight. The only downside was that Jo and I were on the 'lowest of the low' priority for getting on the flight but amazingly enough we got presented with a pair of club boarding cards and so our adventure to Los Angeles ended in style and we got back to our cosy flat the next day ready for the second part of the wedding in about a week which was the church blessing at the local church in Warfield. All I can say is that the planning to sort out the wedding in America was pretty mind-blowing in its concept but it all went like clockwork even down to the size and shape of the wedding cake. Well, the simple task of arranging a church blessing in the UK pushed Jo and me to the limit of patience and endurance. Everything was within arm's length but anything that could go wrong did go wrong.

It all started a few months before in 1995 when we decided to have a church blessing after our return from Los Angeles. So I naturally contacted my old vicar, Owen, from Binfield and invited him over for tea. When I suggested that it would be good if he could do the honours and conduct the church service at my old church in Binfield, Owen coughed politely and said that he would find it quite awkward to do so since I had been married before and he knew Moya and the kids. He went on to mention that his friend Brian Reardon was the vicar of Warfield, and suggested that I kept quiet about my past then he would do the service in the church at Warfield. Brian, it later transpired, was an ex-pilot so off we went and met up with him at the church in Warfield and 'mum's the word' it was and so the initial plan was put in place. I was quite shocked at the cost of the service being somewhere approaching £500 without heating – which was £30 extra.

Church of England PLC, was my thought at the time.

Jo chose a piece of music 'The March of Triumph' by Aida which she felt would fit the bill as she walked down the aisle. The organist sort of grimaced a bit and muttered something about the normal wedding march being what he normally did. Simple and effective!

Not a good start we thought but let's plod on to the next task which was the meal after the wedding. Having been a few times to eat in a small restaurant in Binfield called 'The Wooden Hut' we felt it would be a good idea to use that venue for the sit-down meal. OK it was not cheap but it could nicely house about 30 of us so that part seemed to go fine.

Next, there was the venue for the evening bash that would be needed for maybe one hundred people or so. Various places were checked out and each one had some sort of problem like 'too small, too large, too narrow, too wide, too isolated and of course too expensive'. Eventually we found the Thames Hotel over at Maidenhead which was as close as we could get to what we wanted. We sat down with the manager and agreed a figure for the do in the evening to include about six rooms for accommodation for people staying overnight.

Jo's mother kindly financed the wedding dress and it was down to Jo to get it sorted. We decided on two bridesmaids for Jo, one being my old friend Debbie Meyeur from Binfield and Jenny. We found a wedding dress shop and from the outset it tested Jo's patience to the limit both in time and quality of work. The problem that did not help the scene was that, unbeknown to me, Jo was losing a lot of weight which she put down to pre-wedding nerves. Her coughing was not abating either but I think that we were so wrapped up in the planning that both points were ignored or put into the 'pending tray' for later.

We also found a local professional photographer to do the pictures so that was another tick in the box. The car for Jo was also sorted being a friend of a friend.

So, there we had it by the end of 1995 with the 'Queen Mary' all sorted. In the UK the church was sorted, the meal afterwards was sorted, the evening bash was sorted, the hotel was sorted for overnight guests, the photographer was sorted, the car was sorted and finally Jo's dress was sorted. All the invites had all gone out as well.

"What could go wrong?" was my statement of the day. Read on.

So, back to our arrival from Los Angeles as husband and wife and, after a good night's sleep, we sat down to finalise the details for the church. I rang Brian, the vicar and all seemed in order.

"What time will the bell ringers turn up?" I enquired casually.

"What bell ringers?" was his reply with a sort of innocent air to his voice.

"The ones I ordered and paid for in your invoice," I replied whilst stirring in my seat.

"Oh, I had forgotten to order them. If I give you their phone number could you please ring them to get them organised as I am rather busy," he said rather sheepishly.

Right, so off I go on the hunt for the famous bell ringers and after numerous phone calls and coffees I managed to get through to the boss of the bell ringers.

"This is not very good to give us such short notice for a wedding do when we haven't even had a chance to practise yet! Please remember that for next time," she said as if I had asked to borrow the crown jewels for the night.

"What do you mean by 'the next time'? Hopefully I will only have one wedding and one church do unless she knows something I don't know?" I chuckled to myself.

Jo called the organist to confirm the music she had chosen.

"Sorry, but I didn't have time to practise that piece. You will have to settle for the standard wedding number," he said casually.

"Just how long does he bloody well want?" was Jo's comment as I restrained her from lobbing the phone out of the window towards the horizon and beyond.

Not a good start to what was supposed to be a relaxing time for the next few days.

There was more to come on the Wednesday, three days before the event – the hotel manager rang up and asked me what the time our DJ would be arriving and what did he require from the hotel.

"If you go back to our first meeting it was agreed that you would supply the DJ for the night playing a mix of 60s and 70s music," I calmly replied whilst reaching for my ever-ready cup of coffee.

"I am sorry about that, Mr Mullett, but I thought you were supplying the DJ and we will now have to try to get one organised at short notice which could be a problem," he replied with a note of desperation.

"Thank you for that. All I can say is that we do need one for the night since small talk can only stretch so far," I replied, gripping my coffee cup with a shaking hand.

I put the phone down and went for a walk around the block to recover. When I got back Jo said that the man had called back and needed to talk to me urgently.

"Right then, here we go again into battle," I said as I dialled the number.

"Mr Mullett, there has been an enormous booking mix-up with the rooms you wanted. We have, in fact, double-booked the rooms for a party of Welsh Rugby supporters next Saturday night since they are playing England at Twickenham that afternoon. What would you like us to do?"

Deadly silence issued from the flat for a few seconds as I stared at the phone in total disbelief. Jo sensed the pressure build-up and cleared all coffee cups and anything fragile out of my range and then scurried off into the kitchen.

"What would you like me to do? Now there's a statement of all statements," I murmured to myself while entering a few seconds of self-briefing before replying.

"OK, let's look at what we have got to date to see what recovery action, if any, can be taken. We now have a reception at your hotel mixing it with a load of Welshmen who will no doubt drink themselves stupid either in commiseration or happiness according to who wins on the field. Either way, they will consume the same amount of booze and knowing Welshmen quite well they will start singing at some point with all their hearts and lungs. Their singing will rise to such a pitch and volume that they could well drown out the music being played by the DJ on the proviso that we actually have a DJ on site in the first place. It could well come to a head and people might consider creeping off to bed only to find that their room is full of Welsh Leeks and maybe the odd refugee spread-eagled across the bed snoring gently mumbling about the green, green grass of home. Got any suggestions, then?" I said calmly looking around for a coffee cup to demolish. There were none!

"Mr Mullett, I am very sorry for this mess. I will call you back as soon as we can sort out a solution. Please be patient for a short while. Again, I am very sorry for this," he replied with a note of panic in his voice.

I put the phone down again and went for another walk around the block at a slightly higher tempo this time! Jo stayed in the kitchen where she felt safest.

It was in the early afternoon that the hotel called me and announced that they seemed to have solved the problem.

"Yes, we do have a DJ sorted for you OK. There is a small hotel down the road that is willing to put up some of your guests that we cannot accommodate. Your room is booked plus the one for your mother-in-law as well and we will endeavour to have the Welsh lot in a reception room for themselves away from your reception and we will let them know not to interfere."

"What can I say? It seems to be a sort of compromise so we will have to go with it," I replied in a rather dejected tone.

We also agreed a discount on the total price as a compensation for their total mishandling of the complete business.

At about this time Jo went over to check progress on her wedding dress. Debbie picked her up in her car and off they went to the wedding shop. There was a problem with the sleeves that required some unpicking of the thread. Not an easy job but when you consider the cost of the dress it seemed only right to have it as close to perfection as possible.

"Well, that's a lot of work!" was the comment of the shop owner in a rather dignified manner.

"That's what I am paying for!" replied Jo.

Not sure whether I mentioned it before or not but for someone to speak in direct tones as opposed to waffling on is, in my opinion, the better option.

I don't know what it is about wedding shops that seem to prey on the emotions of the bride-to-be and hopefully the rich mother. It seems to go along on the principle of:

"This will only happen once in your life so why not spend just a little bit more on the dress and you will look absolutely beautiful on the day."

Happiness all the way to the bank I would say.

The two final bits of the jigsaw were paying the photographer and getting the flowers organised. Both of these items cost an arm and a leg but finally we seemed to have got there. Financially the cost of the church blessing in the UK far outstripped the wedding in Los Angeles by a large margin. Considering that the wedding took place on the Queen Mary and there were a few extras to cater for including a fantastic dinner on board plus accommodating a few guests I would have thought it would have been the other way round but no, the UK side of the deal was very expensive even though it was a small local church and a small hotel. Anyway, there was no turning back now.

On the afternoon before the do Paul and I got on the train and went off to Abingdon where Joe and Gisela lived to stay the night so that Jo and her mother who had now arrived from Italy could have a sort of family evening together in the flat. It was very unfortunate that Otto, Jo's dad, was too ill to travel to the wedding of his daughter but I know he wished her well.

On the morning of the church blessing, which was exactly a week after the wedding in the States Paul, myself, Joe, Gisela and their son Stephen all drove down to the Warfield church. It was a cold February morning so I had hoped that the heating that I had paid for had been put on early but as we entered the church the temperature could only be described as sub-Arctic and we actually could see our own breath steaming away. Anyway, onwards and upwards, as we took our allocated seats and waited for the action to start. Brian Reardon, the vicar, turned up and switched on the heaters which seemed to be buried somewhere high in the rafters above us. Dad and Thirza turned up complete with overcoats since they must have known something about winter weddings that we didn't. At the appointed hour Jo and her mum arrived and 'walked the aisle' to the sound of 'Here Comes the Bride' played by the rather reluctant organist. The ceremony got underway with Brian running the show. When it came to his small sermon he spoke of the comparison with the day to a girl in the local area suffering from a virulent cancer and I have to confess, as did Jo, that I did not see the connection between the two. After the service Jo and I ventured outside for a photo-shoot and low and behold the bells were firing away on all cylinders. The fact that Jo looked absolutely frozen to the spot did not detract from how radiant she looked. I was told later that the wedding dress was held together by a few safety pins. Wow!

As Brian made his farewells he flicked the heating off. It must have been on for only 40 minutes at the outside which made it rather an expensive luxury. We all finally made our way over to the Wooden Hut for the 'wedding breakfast' and maybe we might have a chance to relax a bit and de-stress from the whole business. There were, maybe, 30 people all sat around the tables and what we failed to think about beforehand was the fact it was great to eat there as a foursome with good food and a reasonably effective service, but multiply that by seven or so and things start to get a bit lop-sided. Jenny wasn't well so she was dispatched home by Debbie and so the service started in a sort of 'disorganised chaos' way. Eventually everybody got something put in front of them albeit hot, warm or tepid. The speeches were a little disorganised and mine was not the best since I confess, with all the things happening in the past few days, little time was allocated to thinking it through. Finally we were all done at the Wooden Hut so off we go to the famous Thames Hotel in Maidenhead for the evening party complete with half the Welsh Nation singing their hearts out.

Can't wait for the fun to begin, I thought to myself as we were driven to the hotel.

At the hotel we got to our room and Jo made sure her mum was organised in her room and then we made our way down to the reception room. The Welsh lot were there getting slowly tanked up and the best bit about it was that to get to our reception room you had to go through the 'Welsh Male Voice Choir' ensemble and soon they realised that there was a wedding reception next door. Well, this brought out the best of the songs that they could put together directed at the antics of the 'first night' of married bliss. The DJ started up and seemed to be playing all the really old 60s stuff as if stuck in a time warp. What we wanted was a mix of 60s and 70s music but what we got was non-stop Adam Faith and Cliff Richard. As the evening progressed more and more guests arrived and the tempo of the Welsh singers and Adam

Faith got faster and louder than ever. The whole do was slowly decaying into a standard boozy night at the pub and the fact that Jo and I were meant to be the centre of the celebrations became totally irrelevant. When it came to the buffet we had organised it was consumed within seconds and Jo mentioned that, at one point, she wandered up for a chicken's leg or the like to find the table bare. She was not amused since it had only been laid out what seemed minutes before.

Eventually, we all crawled off to bed complete with the odd Welsh refugee struggling to sing and walk at the same time. Jo and I ended up having a big argument which was a result of all the tensions and pressures of the past week finally coming to a head.

Nice way to start a married life, I thought to myself.

I think we must have slept 'back-to-back' that night.

"That was the week that was!" I have to say.

In the morning all was a bit subdued at breakfast with the events of the past week catching up plus a bunch of hung-over Welshmen looking the worse for wear. Eventually everybody disappeared from whence they came and Jo and I got back to the flat in the early afternoon totally exhausted but relieved that it was all over. Mother was duly dispatched back to Italy. The final item on the agenda was the honeymoon which would be very welcome after all the trials and tribulations of the past two weeks.

The following evening we made our way to Heathrow and climbed aboard the flight to Bangkok and onwards to Phuket for two weeks of total nothing. On the following afternoon we arrived at the Laguna Beach Hotel in Phuket. The hotel was idyllic, being perched on the edge of the sea at the head of a bay with a lagoon behind it complete with a water taxi that would float you between any one of the four hotels that straddled the bay. I have to say that we had struck gold in our choice of honeymoon hotel and enjoyed the facilities on offer. The swimming pool came complete with a swim-up bar plus happy hour being at 4 pm precisely which seemed to coincide with one eye opening following an afternoon nap by the pool. The beach was fantastic to stroll along with Jo eyeing up coloured sea shells that were scattered everywhere. There was nothing nicer than sitting at the beach bar enjoying a cocktail as the sun went down in the west. The food was equally good but needed a careful eye to avoid the rather spicy additive known as Lemon Grass. The name sounds a bit nondescript but, as Jo found out, as an additive to a Mango salad it can bring tears to your eyes. As it was the two weeks did pass in total relaxation. The only downside again was Jo's persistent cough and the fact that her weight seemed to be falling off her. We actually sat down and discussed the problem at great length. I think we again talked ourselves into various reasons for it but decided that on return Jo would go to the doctor as soon as possible and seek professional advice.

We got back to the UK in late February and so it was all over bar the shouting. Jo's parents and grandparents had been extremely generous to us as a wedding present and so we went out and bought a second-hand car in the shape of a classic Mercedes saloon. It was bright red in colour and very quickly became our pride and joy. The other thing that happened involved a good friend of ours, Sally, who by now had married Barry, who was originally married to Sue who had married Mike who was Sally's original husband. The saga of Binfield was very complicated! Anyway, Sally worked as an agency nurse at a local hospital owned by a private health company in the name of the British United Provident Association, or BUPA for short, and she offered Jo a private health scheme at extremely good rates. I felt it would be good to put Jo on this scheme as the National Health Service, good as it was, had extended waiting times and many other problems were starting to creep in.

In the news there was an air crash report of an unauthorised charter flying German tourists back from the Dominican Republic to Germany. During the take-off the Captain's airspeed indicator packed up and the crew seemed powerless to deal with, what can only be assumed a simple instrument failure, and crashed into the sea with all 189 people on board. This accident was clearly avoidable and should never have happened. Were we now seeing a trend for cheap non-regulated airlines trying to get in on the market?

Jo did go to the doctor and initial diagnosis was based on the fact that maybe she had become asthmatic and the cough was the result. She went back again after a few days since the pills subscribed had no effect at all. On this occasion she saw a different doctor and it was suggested that Jo should have a chest X-ray. This was set up for early March.

I went back to flying with a simple Hong Kong route at the end of February returning in early March in time to take Jo to the local hospital for her X-ray, the results of which would be sent to our local doctor. It was a few days later when I was sitting at my desk checking through the paperwork for Jo's membership to the BUPA health scheme to which she had been accepted. I remember Jo was still sleeping when the phone rang. It was Dr Tong from the local surgery.

"Mr Mullett, I have just received the result of the X-ray and I am very sorry to say but Johanna is extremely ill and I need to see you both here as soon as possible," he said.

My mind went into overdrive and I very quickly woke Jo up and within 20 minutes or so we were at the surgery. We had only been back off our honeymoon for about a week and had been married for a little longer. Jo even had her suntan still and we were now here to find out what was wrong with Jo since it appeared that it was very serious.

Dr Tong explained as best he could but a lot of it went over our heads. The simple fact, if I recall, was that Jo had a collapsed lung and the working one was being engulfed by some sort of 'thing' that was also wrapped around the windpipe and the heart. In simple terms Jo was a medical disaster and her future was very much in doubt. The 'thing' was in fact a Blastoma of the cancerous variety and immediate action was required to quell its growth.

Jo and I were shell-shocked as you can imagine and a plan of action was needed as quickly as possible. Dr Tong was very professional is his assessment and suggested that the first course of action was to see a specialist. It was at this point that I remembered the BUPA membership that had accepted Jo that morning and when I mentioned that to Dr Tong he grabbed the phone and arranged for us to see a Dr Lyle, who ran a clinic in nearby Reading, that afternoon.

So off we went back to the flat and sat down to talk about the morning's events and come to some sort of understanding as to what was happening to Jo. There she was with her suntan still in place and a shiny wedding ring on her finger and now facing all this. We drove in silence to see Dr Lyle at the Reading clinic. I think we were both deep in our own thoughts. Anyway, we saw Dr Lyle and he surveyed the X-ray as only a doctor could and then sat us both down. His first words echoed Dr Tong's.

"Johanna, what you have is very serious and we need to get it sorted as soon as possible. Please accept the fact that for the next few weeks you will be pushed and prodded all over the place. First of all we need a deep scan or MRI to really look at this thing and then go from there. I see you have private health insurance and that fact will help speed the whole procedure up."

We got back home in the late afternoon and sat down again and talked and talked about what was happening. The word 'Cancer' is a frightening word to anybody but to a person as young as Jo it was doubly frightening. What we did was to repeat the word over and over again during our long chats and that seemed to act as a therapy. It was a start anyway. We eventually crashed into bed through total emotional exhaustion.

We had a couple of days before the MRI scan at a hospital in Frimley, about one hour away, so we busied ourselves with all sorts of things so as to take our mind of things. I went up to Heathrow and met up with my Flight Manager, Geoff Smith, to ask for some time off. After I had explained what was going on he simply said:

"Gwyn, you are off the roster until your wife gets better."

"Thank you Geoff" were the only words I could think of saying.

BA might, in some people's eyes, be full of faults, but in times of family crisis they come up trumps as they did on that day.

The other thing to do was to let friends know what was going on. Joe Hall's wife was very happy to talk to Jo's mother in Italy to let her know what was going on since, both being German, the language problem would be solved. I was learning that at times like this true friends come to the surface and other friends disappear below it.

We had the scan done and returned to Dr Lyle and he confirmed the extent of the problem in greater detail. Arrangements were made for Jo to have a small 'exploratory' operation in a local hospital within a couple of days. I am very sorry if I am dwelling on the happenings to Jo but they are still very vivid in my mind and very difficult to summarise in a couple of sentences.

So, within a couple of days, Jo was wheeled into an operating theatre with a very emotional pair of newlyweds saying words of strength to each other. This was all new ground to both of us! The conclusion reached by Dr Lyle afterwards was that he could not draw too much from the small 'procedure' as he called it and that he felt that a hospital that specialised in this sort of condition was needed. The hospital he had in mind was St Anthony's in North Cheam, south-west London. Arrangements were made for Jo to become a resident there within a few days. By this time it was well into March and only one week had elapsed since the initial shock and time seemed to stand still.

It was that night that Jo nearly died on me. The fact was that she could only sleep upright and so a bed was made up in the lounge on the settee propped up by cushions. It was at about midnight when I felt a dead weight on top of me on the bed and I struggled to come to and found Jo collapsed on top of me. I put the light on and found that Jo had very shallow breathing and her lips were blue. She was dying right in front of my eyes. Some sort of instinct took over and I slapped her on the face shouting at her at the same time. I raced to the phone and dialled 999 for the ambulance to be told that, being a Saturday night, there would be a delay in getting there of about 30 minutes.

"My wife will be dead within ten minutes," I shouted down the phone.

I then went into automatic mode and dragged Jo down the stairs and carried her 'fireman style' to the car. I started up and drove like the wind with Jo struggling alongside with me slapping her to keep her awake. I arrived at the local hospital within about 20 minutes and carried Jo into the reception area and just kept going until I found the casualty ward and laid Jo on a bed and shouted for help. A lovely petite Irish Sister came over to find out what I was shouting about and took one look at Jo on the bed and did her own shouting for assistants. Within minutes Jo had an oxygen mask strapped on. Various other things were going on that were beyond me but slowly but surely Jo came back from the 'edge'.

"Fricking heck, don't ever do that again on me. The new 'Merc' is just about burnt out from that drive," was all I said when Jo was fully with it.

I had a smile from ear to ear at the time. I eventually took her home at about 6 am. Jo was by this time totally pumped up with steroids. What a night that was!

After a few days we arrived at St Anthony's Hospital and Jo got organised with a room. We were then introduced to a Professor Treasure who was one of the top consultants in the field of lung problems. He looked at the MRI scan that we had with us and arranged for a more comprehensive examination after he had studied the scan in more detail. It was at this point that it all seemed too much for Jo and me to come to terms with since I would have to leave her there and go home alone. The journey home was my most miserable and loneliest experiences to date. The flat was totally empty and devoid of any character. I spent a fair amount of time on the phone talking to people about what was happening with Jo. To be the 'communicator' was quite a responsibility and quite exhausting. Nothing whatsoever compared with what Jo was going through I hasten to add.

The next day I was back at the hospital and we had a meeting with the Professor and he said that a further exploratory examination was needed to find out exactly what was happening and which way to go. This was set up for the next day. It actually involved a small incision in the neck enough to put a camera down into the chest area. And so I duly turned up at the appointed hour and Jo was wheeled down to the operating theatre for the second time within a week. Supportive words were exchanged again. Later that day the Professor met up with us in Jo's room.

"I have done a very detailed examination of Johanna and have found that we have to do a major operation without delay since it is too late for chemo or radiotherapy. I have to consult over the next two days with some colleagues since I need some guidance as to exactly how to perform the operation since it is a first one for me," he said to a rather stunned husband and wife.

"Professor, please give me your opinion as to the chances of success of the operation?" Jo asked, breaking the silence.

"I would say the chances of success are good," the Professor said with a sort of reassuring smile.

All this happened on a Thursday and it was suggested that Jo go home for the weekend since the operation was to be set for the following Monday. Whilst Jo was getting herself ready to go I wandered down to the reception area for a coffee when Professor Treasure cornered me.

"Mr Mullett, I have to tell you that the chances of your wife pulling through this operation are very slim. I couldn't say that back there in front of your wife. The operation is very complex and I have to talk to a surgeon in America who attempted it but lost his patient. I am very sorry to tell you this," he said in confidence to me.

So there I had it with now Jo full of joy as to the thought of coming home and me having to put a brave face on it all.

The weekend was one of the hardest to deal with since Jo was very confident that within a few weeks she would back to her normal self and me trying to seem to be very confident as well. The words of the professor were, however, very heavy on my mind. On the Saturday evening Jo was dozing gently on the settee with me in the other room. The night was particularly still and devoid of any wind at all. Suddenly Jo shouted for me to come into the lounge and I found her in tears but smiling like a Cheshire cat.

"I woke up to a warm breeze flowing across my face as if someone was blowing into it. What do you think it was?" Jo asked curiously.

I thought back to my near miss that happened in Germany some seven years before and how something or someone had made me look out of the window at that crucial moment and helped me avoid smashing into another aircraft.

"I think my mum just popped down to give you a bit of reassurance before the operation," I said with tears in my own eyes.

Good old Mum!

Later that night I had to call the doctor out since Jo was struggling for breath again and we ended up checking Jo into St Anthony's in the early hours of Sunday morning instead of the Monday. Another weekend of the most difficult happenings when you consider that only just over two weeks before we were both relaxing on the beach in Thailand without a care in the world.

It was on the Sunday that I got a call from Moya that she was going into hospital herself on the Monday for an operation on her Gall

Bladder and that the kids were fine but would appreciate a call to check that all was well. She also sent a message to Jo, via me, to wish her good luck the next day. So there it was with my wife and ex-wife both in different hospitals both undergoing operations in the next week.

Jo's operation was set for early on the Monday and I remember the Sunday night's sleep was totally disjointed. I woke up early on the Monday feeling that I had done ten rounds with Mike Tyson. I made myself copious cups of coffee and virtually sat by the phone waiting for it to ring with the Professor at the other end with any news. It finally rang at about 3 pm with him saying that the operation had gone well but took six hours and that Jo was in Intensive Care and that the next 24 hours would be crucial for her recovery.

"It is up to you whether you want to see her but be warned that she has tubes sticking out everywhere," he said.

Stupid statement I have to say since within a couple of minutes I was off at the double up to North Cheam to see Jo.

Not being a frequent visitor to hospitals let alone Intensive Care it was quite a shock to be met at the door of the ward and be invited in quietly and to see Jo asleep amongst what seemed to a complete DIY plumbing kit with tubes all over the place.

"Jo's doing fine at the moment but sleeping, which is the best cure at the moment. The body is clever, you know! It needs her asleep to start the recovery process," the nurse said quietly.

Jo looked absolutely lovely just lying there totally oblivious of her surroundings. Her new shiny wedding ring was taped onto her finger since she had refused to take it off before the operation.

"Would you mind un-taping the ring before she wakes up and let her know that I popped in," I said to the nurse.

I left the hospital with the feeling that Jo would make it through and all it would take was time.

My day was not over by any means, since I had told the kids to be ready for me to drive them over to the hospital in Windsor where Moya was for them to see her before her operation. The traffic on the way home was pretty thick and it was heavy rain but finally I got to the kids and off we went to see their mum. When we got to the hospital I stayed in the car whilst Paul and Jenny went inside. Being the first time in that most important day that I could actually sit back and take stock I just crashed out asleep in the car somewhere in the hospital car park.

The following day I made my way to see Jo and found her propped up in bed slurping on a cup of tea. She even had some lipstick on. What a recovery! This girl was made of steel! The professor joined us soon after I arrived and said that the recovery was going much better than expected and that Jo plus tubes would be moved back into the general ward within a few days. This was great stuff for Jo and there were smiles all around. What had transpired was that this 'thing' was in fact wrapped around pretty well everything in the chest cavity and was on the point of closing off the windpipe, hence the problem Jo was having with her breathing. He went on to suggest that it was, in fact, the remains of Jo's twin which she had carried since birth. Jo was also the owner of a third Kidney which could well have originated from this twin. What an amazing story.

After a few days Jo was moved back into her original room and her remarkable recovery continued. Moya had her operation at about this point and she too was recovering well. On the following Saturday I picked up Paul and Jenny and took them to see their mum. Because of the timings I kept them in the car and took them with me up to see Jo. When we arrived I left them both in the car while I made my way to see Jo. After I got back to the car neither of them were around and the car was locked. I found them sitting in the reception and so I casually walked up and asked Paul for the car keys.

"I don't know where they are, Dad. I just locked the car as normal using the door lock as you always do it," he said.

I got as far as saying "But..." when it dawned on me that the car was locked with the keys still in the ignition inside. This was not a Ford or anything similar. This was a Mercedes which had the reputation of having a pretty secure locking system.

What to do apart from killing my son? This was midnight on a Saturday night in the middle of London and it was getting cold and starting to rain. I went up to the night porter and asked his opinion and whether he knew any good locksmiths around the area. He looked at me as if I was from a different planet. Maybe he knew of some dodgy sort of character who specialised in opening up cars in not a legal sort of way and there was this country bloke meekly asking for a local locksmith.

"Try the police, sir. They are always doing this sort of thing," was his final word.

I called them and they arrived shortly afterwards.

"Please, sir, can you open my dad's car before my dad kills me?" was the passionate plea from Paul.

So there we were all standing around my car in the car park with the police shoving and poking with a coat hanger trying to get the internal handle to move and the door to open. After about an hour there was a cry of success as the door opened. I do not know who was the happiest, be it me being able to drive home or Paul knowing that his life had just been spared. It was about 2 am when we finally got home and into a welcome bed.

As the days progressed Jo seemed to improve continually and even got to the point where she sent me flying down to Singapore and back so as to not lose touch with the flying world.

It was in early April that she was transferred to a local hospital in nearby Reading for two weeks' convalescence and finally after a visit by Dr Lyle she came home. It marked the end of a very trying time for Jo and me in the medical sense and now it was a question of the taste of home comforts to complete the recovery task. Moya survived OK as well so they were now both out of hospital. Jo, in fact, made remarkable progress considering what had been done to her in the operation and on another visit to Dr Lyle it was confirmed that the lung that had packed up a long time before had started to function normally. We have nothing but praise for the various elements of the medical profession who helped put Jo back together.

It was not long after this that Jo paid a solo visit to see her dad in Italy who, by now, was losing his health fast and was being tended to by Jo's mum around the clock. I actually went back flying and all seemed to settle down for a while.

In the news there was the headline which was all about a tragedy in Scotland whereby an unemployed shopkeeper walked into a Primary school in Dunblane and shot dead 16 children, one teacher and then himself. It was a singularly dreadful thing to happen in this so-called modern world.

In the May Moya called me to let me know that there was a health problem with Paul whereby he seemed to have his hands shaking all the time. The doctor had suggested that the problem was based in the brain signalling system so off Moya, Paul and I go to a health centre somewhere and sat quietly while Paul had an MRI scan on the brain. The consultant confirmed to us that all was well with Paul's brain and that the shakes could well disappear over time. This they did and all was well. It just seemed to add to the string of incidences that year with Jo, Moya and now Paul.

It was also in the May that a ValuJet Douglas DC-9 crashed just after take-off from Miami, Florida killing 110 people due to the unscheduled ignition of some improperly handled oxygen canisters in the cargo hold. This was the first crash caused by these types of canisters and heads were scratched as to what had started the disastrous fire. Tests were carried out and it transpired that once ignited they burn without let-up since they have their own oxygen supply and nothing can stop them. Up to that point we were vaguely familiar with a class of cargo that we might carry known as 'Hazardous Cargo' which was very lucrative for the airline but it did open a can of worms in the legislative world.

Within BA various alliances were being formed with other airlines. A code share was announced with American West out of Phoenix, Arizona and Canadian Airlines in Canada. In Denmark Sun-Air signed a full franchise agreement with BA and became BA Express operating out of Copenhagen, Oslo and Stockholm. The code share with USAir was gradually fizzling out and being replaced by a new code share agreement with American Airlines. The various departments in BA who dealt with all these agreements must have been working flat out to keep up with it all.

As for me, as a simple Captain on the -400, it was all a bit beyond me but in the same breath quite intriguing how the airline world was changing very fast with the advent of all these alliances and I did wonder where it would all end.

It was in the July when Jo got a call from her mother in Italy to say that her father had died and so I managed to get Jo on an aircraft that afternoon to be with her mother. Jo loved her dad dearly and was very sad when she visited him in the May and knew the end was not far off but when it did actually happen it was still a great shock. Jo was still in the recovery mode and found it very hard to cope with the funeral in the Italian heat but cope she did.

With me now being quite high on the seniority list I could pick my trips well and as I said before I spent most of the month going to either the Far East or to South America. I somehow got a flight to New York thrown in since we were now doing a few flights to the 'Eastern Seaboard'. It was quite ironic that the night after I left New York a Trans World Airlines (TWA) 747 classic literally exploded off the coast of Long Island after departing for Paris with 230 people dead. There was much controversy as to the cause with an explosion in the big centre fuel tank being the favourite. Nevertheless it brought into play the whole question of operating old aircraft. It is amazing to think that the original 747 aircraft which revolutionised air travel were now considered in the vintage class.

As for Jo her recovery was moving apace and it came to the point when we visited Dr Lyle again for the three-monthly check and as he pondered over the X-Ray declared Jo fit with two fully working lungs and not to see him for another six months. Wow and double Wow!

To celebrate this milestone I took Jo on a trip with me down to Sydney via Bangkok and great fun was had all round. Apart from a very sensitive left-hand side she seemed to be coping very well. The scars left from the operation healed well leaving a faint line. The funny thing was that she became very sensitive to any changes in the weather with the scars letting her know in no uncertain terms that it was about to rain or just about to stop. The amazing thing was that no medication was prescribed during her recovery since it was decided to let the body get on with it.

In the August Boris Yeltsin got re-elected for another term as President of Russia and a chap called Osama Bin Laden called for the removal of American forces from Saudi Arabia. He actually declared a 'Jihad' or 'Holy War' against the Americans and this single act started a string of events as time went on that changed the world. On the UK domestic front in the August the Prince and Princess of Wales were formally divorced.

As the summer progressed then so did my old complaint with my left leg which seemed to be getting worse. I visited the Chiropractic on a few occasions and expected, as always, for the leg to improve but nothing really happened. It all came to a head when I had taken Jo on another trip. When we got home in the early hours I carried a rather heavy suitcase up the stairs and then it happened. I suddenly found that I was unable to walk without the most excruciating pain from my leg similar to having cramp. What's more I could only walk completely bent over. I attempted to climb into bed but found the pain just too much lying flat so I retired to the famous settee and waited for the doctor to visit. He eventually arrived and diagnosed me with an acute disc problem in the backbone and all he could do was to prescribe me strong painkillers and suggest a specialist's visit. I was due to fly within a couple of days and so I called BA and got taken off the flight. It was fortunate that, once again, I had private health care with BUPA and so an appointment was made to see a specialist in Windsor within a couple of days. The visit there was a pretty painful affair starting with the taxi ride being like going 'to hell and back' with every small jolt seemingly being magnified many times and letting me know all about it. The specialist chap kept sticking needles into my knee which was pretty painful. He then described the course of action that, if a back operation was needed, bearing in mind that the main nervous system was very vulnerable and the slightest slip of the scalpel and that would be the end of my walking career. Needless to say he did not impress me at all. I decided at that point to forget any operation and live with the pain if it meant that maybe I could keep the legs working OK. He did send me to the local hospital in Windsor for a procedure known as a 'Venogram' to check for any blood clots or the like in the suspect leg. It was there that I met a Dr Giassi, who hailed from Sri Lanka and he performed the small operation and declared my leg in good condition with no blockages or the like. He suggested that I have an MRI scan of the back as he was certain that I had a disc out of place which was transmitting a nasty signal down the nerves and ending up in the calf muscle in the left leg. The scan was set up and in the meantime I got to grips with the walking stick that had been given to me many years before by David and Minyon in Zimbabwe as a memento. The scene with BA was that I was now deemed long term sick and in consequence my flying licence was made invalid which meant that I had to prove to the authorities that I was medically fit to fly when the time came.

At the time I didn't really take much notice of the implications within BA since I was concentrating more on getting back on my legs. Jo was a massive help but even she had her limitations when it came down to the basics of life. I really must have looked a sad sight hobbling around the place. As for sleeping and resting the most comfortable position was lying on my back on the floor with my legs up on a chair. A bit tricky for drinking and eating but somehow I managed.

It was at about this time that dad was admitted to a hospital in nearby Reading for a further operation on his prostate so another additive came into the medical equation. He did have the operation but there were complications to do with his heart so he was destined to remain in hospital for more tests. It was really sad that with me being a full nursing case we were unable to visit him.

The day came for the MRI scan and so off we went for the nightmare of a taxi ride to a hospital in Windsor and then to try to lie still while the equipment did its work. Whilst I was getting dressed Dr Giassi came in and announced that he had found the suspect disc and that if I was available that afternoon he could get it sorted. He implied that it would be a simple deal. This was music to my ears. So off Jo and I went plus walking stick up the road to yet another hospital. Now it is easy enough to say 'get it sorted' but in reality the procedure was far from simple. Firstly, after leaving Jo in the general waiting room, I was led into a small operating theatre and got changed into one of those hospital gowns with the open back. I was then asked to lie flat with my head down on this sort of contraption and then literally bolted down so that I could not move a muscle. Dr Giassi explained that he had to put a needle into my back at the spot where the damaged disc was and then pump in some fluid that would deaden the area so that natural healing could be allowed to repair the damage. The downside of it all was that he had to stick the needle in without any anaesthetic since he needed to check my reaction all the time being very close to the central nervous system. Sounds very dramatic but I can assure you that it bloody well was.

So there I was strapped down like a stuffed pig ready for the spit and then suddenly I felt the first prick of the needle going in. They say that at times like this one should think of something nice to detract from the pain. Yeah Right!

As the needle went deeper Dr Giassi disappeared behind the all too familiar lead screen and took an X-ray to check where the tip of the fricking needle was. All of a sudden the needle must have hit the right spot since my left leg sort of went into spasm and jerked in its restraints. Now I know why I was strapped down so tightly. This was accompanied by a sort of whimper from me. Dr Giassi ran behind the lead screen again and consulted the X-ray again while asking me how it was feeling. My words are unprintable at this point but I did apologise before using a certain choice of words. He must have pumped in the required solution since all pain was gone and I was left there as a pathetic gibbering wreck. I was unstrapped and in my haste stood up only to collapse sideways since my left leg was totally numb and did not even feel to be part of my body. I was helped to the changing room and was left alone to get dressed.

Now this is going to be a big challenge! I thought as I grabbed the coat hook above me.

This coat hook leapt out of its housing in the wall and proceeded to dump a load of plaster on my head. At this point Jo came in and looking at this wreckage covered from head to foot said:

"Come on, boy, time to get you home before you destroy anything else."

I eventually got home and slept for maybe 14 hours or so. When I woke up there was still no feeling in my left leg. Dr Giassi did say that it could take up to three days to recover but as usual I was impatient. Being numb there was no pain so I just had to wait. On the third day I started to get some sort of feeling back much to my relief. Still no pain! On the fourth day I could actually walk on two legs minus walking stick and there was definitely no pain so 'cautious optimism' came into play. I visited the hospital for another MRI scan and that confirmed that the suspect disc had somehow slipped back into place. The conclusion was that for a little pain there followed pleasure.

Within a few days I had seemingly recovered to the point that I visited the medical section of BA with the object of getting my licence back. I met up with Dr Green, since he was my usual man for all things medical with me for maybe the last ten years. After some pretty strenuous tests on the leg plus a full medical I sat there as he phoned the authorities and pronounced to them that, in his opinion, I was fit to get my licence back. They were happy, Dr Green was happy and I was really happy. The next thing was to get flying again and so a simulator detail was set up to check the leg out.

During the next few days we did manage to get into Reading to see Dad. The ward he was in must have been one of the most depressing places with peeling wallpaper and a generally uncared for look. Dad seemed to be OK and told us that he was lined up for another operation but the problem was that his heart was showing signs of wear and tear and they were not happy until it had stabilised.

"Hang on in there, Dad," I said to him knowing that his heart was not in good shape and would not, in the opinion of the doctor I spoke to, ever stabilise.

So sad!

I reported to the BA Training centre for my simulator check session.

"Hi Gwyn, I am here to do your check. Which leg was the problem?" the trainer said as we sat down.

Like a prat I told him the truth that it was my left leg. I say that since as the detail progressed he threw everything onto that leg so that it took the strain and hopefully would not buckle under the onslaught. Finally after it was all over he said:

"Right, Gwyn, you seemed to have coped well with the leg so I am happy to release you back on the line for a route check. Does the leg hurt at all?"

"No problems with the leg except maybe the odd small ache which would be quite normal for anyone going through that session," I replied casually trying to cover up the fact that it hurt like hell.

It was now October and I finally did a route check to Seattle, USA and returned home completely cleared and I waited for the November roster to come out and get back into the flying circuit.

In BA another franchise agreement was signed up with Comair, a regional airline in South Africa, and their aircraft were repainted in BA colours. DBA which, if you recall, was the new airline in Germany following the closing of the Berlin Base, sold some of its fleet to a French company leaving them with an all-jet fleet to compete with Lufthansa out of Munich.

In the news, Bill Clinton won a second term at the White House after defeating the Republican Bob Dole.

Jo and I made regular visits to see Dad in hospital. We met up with Thirza and she told us that the specialists said that Dad was not fit enough for an operation and he was being kept in to monitor his heart which was obviously not in good shape. It was like a medical merry-go-round where the only loser would be my dad.

It was in the November that I got my first trip back and it was a simple out and back to Kuala Lumpur (KL) in the Far East. The departure was set for the late evening and it was fitting that Jo would come along on the trip as well to celebrate the return to good health for both of us. In the morning of the departure day I went to the hospital to say farewell to Dad and he seemed quite chirpy and we both sat on his bed chatting like old friends. Any tension that there ever had been between us was long gone and I said that once we were back we would be down to see him.

That evening Jo and I set sail to KL and arrived on a sunny morning with all sorts of plans as to what to get up to during our three days off. When we got to our room the message light was flashing and so I casually called the operator to cancel it when the message came up to ring BA operations as soon as possible. This I did to be told that Dad had taken a turn for the worse and was in fact dying. Arrangements had been made for Jo and I to fly back to Heathrow that night and a standby Captain was on the way. I sat on the bed in total disbelief since it was only a few hours before that Dad and I were chatting away like old friends and now this had happened. I put a call through to Thirza and my sister Cynthia answered.

"Please get home as soon as you can. We all need each other at the moment," was all she said.

I gave her the flight details and Jo and I just muddled our way through the day until we were picked up that evening. It was ironic to note that when my mum was diagnosed with the brain tumour I had to call my dad home from Singapore on British Eagle and now I was being called home for my dad from the same area.

We got home and virtually just dropped our bags off at the flat and then made our way to the hospital to find out what was happening. Dad had suffered a heart attack and was now in a specialist intensive care ward and he did not look at all good. He soldiered on for a couple more weeks and was then transferred back to a general ward since there was nothing more they could do and it was just a matter of time. Once again BA gave me time off to sort things out.

It was during this time I had a rather interesting incident at the hospital. Believe me, I am not a religious person, but suffice to say that I find the inside of a church or the like very soothing and peaceful. At the hospital there was a small chapel and quite often I would wander in and sit quietly and close my eyes and try to relax. On this occasion I was actually staring at the floor when the biggest pair of men's boots came into my view. What's more a second equally big pair arrived next to the first pair. I looked up and found myself staring at, what seemed to be, two giants of men of African origin. What was I to think?

That's nice, I thought, I come here for a bit of peace and I am about to be mugged by a couple of thugs.

One of them held his hand out and shook mine, or rather crushed it, and they told me they were local Baptist Ministers looking after problems amongst their own kind in Reading. They had seen me sitting there looking rather sad and felt that a friendly hand would help. They were right and it did! We must have chatted for some minutes and finally they stood there offering a prayer for my dad. I found the whole encounter quite bizarre but also quite amazing. There were two total strangers not even of my colour saying lovely things about my dad.

It was in the early December when my dad finally died. The good thing was that he did not suffer pain. The family all gathered for the funeral and Cynthia and Robin stayed with us. Afterwards we all went back to the bungalow in Wokingham and had a few drinks to toast his life.

For us, 1996 had been our own personal 'Annus horribilis' what with Jo going down, Paul having a problem, Jo's dad dying, me going down and now my dad dying.

"Roll on 1997," I proclaimed.

There were a couple of aviation related accidents that occurred in late 1996 that were of interest. In the November there was an in-flight collision west of Delhi whereby a Saudi Arabian Airlines 747 that was departing out of Delhi collided with a Kazakhstan Airlines IL-76 which was arriving into Delhi on the same route and 349 people lost their lives. It later transpired that the air traffic controller did not have a full read-out on his screen as to the altitudes of the two aircraft since his system was not that modern and neither aircraft had any on-board avoidance equipment. There was a language problem with the IL-76 and so, by an amazing twist of fate, they collided head-on in cloud. In the December there was a bizarre hijack when an Ethiopian Airlines 767 was forced to fly out over the Indian Ocean until it ran out of fuel and astonished holidaymakers on the island of Comoros watched as the aircraft ditched in front of their eyes just off-shore. Many people were saved but 125 died that day. Not a good ending to 1996. Within BA the final divorce from USAir was completed in the December and the marriage with American Airlines was started.

And the other thing that happened that year was Jo and me getting married. But we were both glad to say goodbye to that year and things could only get better.

As 1997 arrives an interesting final note to 1996 was the fact that during that year we had visited eight hospitals. Not the greatest of achievements that I wish to remember. It was amazing to think that I now had just over four years before my retirement based on the fact that at the age of 55 BA retired you. There was a bit of a stirring within the union to get this increased to at least 60 since in the modern world the age of 55 was not considered too old to keep flying but, of course, it brought in a bucket load of emotions whereby the younger pilots felt that if the older ones stayed on for another five years or so then they would be deprived of command possibilities. However, for those who felt like flying on after 55 there was a spot opening up with Singapore Airlines who were more than happy to get fully qualified -400 pilots for little cost. As for me I had not really thought much about the retirement issue and was more focused on the present.

Thirza had decided to sell up and move in with her son Alan who lived down Bristol way. I did find Alan a bit of a strange guy and I have to say not my cup of tea at all. Anyway, the sale went through and off went Thirza into the sunset.

My flying went back to some sort of normality with the usual mix of the South American and Far East routes each month. Jo had a medical check-up and it was celebrations all round since she had finally been given the all-clear. Together with the fact that I was now in 'good nick' it made the celebrations even more worthwhile. I do find it quite amazing that when a crisis hits a family of the sort that Jo and I had been through your true friends are always there with full support and some friends who you would have thought would be there for you just disappear as if you had some contagious disease. It happened with Jo and me and we found it quite amazing. People like that are not needed.

In the February a sheep arrived on the scene in Scotland called Dolly. What was amazing was that Dolly had been successfully cloned, whatever that involved, and lived to a respectable age of six. In the same month BA formed a new franchise with British Mediterranean Airways to cover routes to the quieter parts of the Middle East and Africa. Way back on the VC-10 we would fly regularly to Khartoum in the Sudan usually direct from Heathrow maybe four times a week. Nowadays it was a small Airbus 320 with two stops en-route twice a week. It shows the changing world of aviation that we were now living in.

I did do a trip to Los Angeles late in February and did my usual thing of hiring a car for the two days there and making my way up to the desert storage airfield at Mojave which was about two hours north of the city. On this occasion I saw the old Caledonian Airways Tri-stars all lined up and looking very sad with the engines rattling away in the desert wind. A couple of days later whilst taxiing out at the airport for the flight home I was asked to hold my position and wait for a Tri-star coming from the left. When the aircraft came into view I could not believe it.

"That is one of our old Caledonian Tri-stars you see in front of your eyes. I am absolutely sure I saw that one rotting gently up at Mojave a couple of days ago," I exclaimed.

It looked in a dreadful state with the faded colours and generally totally scruffy appearance.

"I can't believe that it is actually carrying passengers!" I added.

We followed it onto the runway and I expected to see bits of aircraft scattered all over the place having just witnessed the Tri-star take off.

In the May Tony Blair and his henchmen won a landslide victory in the UK General Election and the Conservatives, under John Major, were relegated to the opposition benches after 18 years in power.

Life in BA started to turn a little strange with the new CEO, Bob Ayling, in charge and it soon transpired that life under Sir Colin Marshall had been far more agreeable. OK, it was not for us as employees to stir things up but in the June a new colour scheme, or corporate identity as it was now known, was announced with images on the aircraft tails from around the world which could only be described as designs Andy Warhol would have been proud of. There was no 'Britishness' to the designs and the general feeling amongst us was one of embarrassment. Consider the British businessman flying back from some far flung spot in deepest Africa and finally arriving at the departure airport with the thought of seeing a British Airways aircraft resplendent in something that reminds him of a nice cup of tea parked on the tarmac. What does he see? He sees this aircraft that someone seems to have tipped a load of coloured paint pots all over the tail and, in his haste, dismisses it as some wild airline of dubious origin sitting out there only to be told that that it was, indeed, his aircraft to take him home. Fortunately they kept the tea cups white!

"What was wrong with the so-called Landor colour scheme that we had previously?" we exclaimed.

It is said that imitation is the finest form of flattery since both British Midland and United Airlines decided to incorporate grey in their own colour scheme. Mr Branson took full advantage of the situation by incorporating a rather stylish union flag on his aircraft and I have to say that the result was rather impressive. This single act by BA management to try to transform the image of the company with these designs seemed to totally undo any faith we had in our leaders. Enough said! By the way the estimated cost of the repainting was well over £60m on a good day. There was one of the designs known as the

'Chatham Historic Dockyard' which was chosen for the Concorde fleet that at least had a certain charm about it and once all the hype had passed then a decision was made to repaint all the aircraft in this theme.

What a waste of money was my only thought.

Jo came along on a Singapore trip with an onward flight to Perth, Western Australia. In Perth we were due to have about 15 hours off and then return to Singapore. So what did we do for all that time? Yes, you've guessed it. We did absolutely nothing. Not even a foot ventured out of the door since we slept for most of the stay. I had all sorts of plans but they all came to nothing. Lazy or what!

With regards to Paul and Jenny their education seemed to be a bit mixed up. Paul was now approaching 17 and he felt he wanted to leave school and make his own way in the big wild world. I found it very difficult to fully understand his reasoning. When I was his age I had a clear idea of what I was going to do for the rest of my life but with Paul he didn't seem to have any idea as to what he wanted to do or where he was going so he took the chance of leaving school after doing his state exams in the June. My only thought was the fact that the world out there could be a lonely place without any real qualifications but he had made his mind up. As for Jenny she did have problems in the Bracknell school she was in and so we moved her to one in Wokingham and she seemed to settle down OK. She hated school with a vengeance and so any chance of skipping it for the day was music to her ears. There was a time when Moya got a letter from the local education people expressing their total dissatisfaction at Jenny's attendance record. Maybe with both of them there seemed to be no goal to go for or super job to attract them to keep them on the education trail from an early age. Was it the fault of the modern system they were in or was it the fault of Moya and me as parents? I was not at home living with Moya as parents and so that fact alone could have influenced their thought processes. At one point with Paul I said that if he did not get a job within a couple of weeks then I would put him in the army. He got a job within seconds!

As the summer progressed I found that I had no lack of passengers on the various trips that I did. Jo was always welcome, which went without question, but I did a Hong Kong trip in early July and took

Paul and Jenny along for the ride. I remember putting them both on the flight deck for the famous landing. In the middle of the final turn I squinted back at both of them and all I could see was a couple of bottom jaws scraping the floor. As with Jo I had not bothered to tell them about the approach and surprised both of them to the point of them being speechless. What an achievement that was! We had a couple of days off in Hong Kong and so I managed to pack in a few sights for them including the famous Temple Street night market complete with a bowl of Chinese noodles to munch on. By the time they climbed aboard for the return flight they were totally burnt out and slept all the way home. Perfect!

At the end of July Hong Kong was in the news when the Island, Kowloon and the New Territories were all handed back to China since the lease had 'expired' to put it in simple terms. Prince Charles flew out to do the official bit and the ceremony was quite spectacular with both sides having reached an amicable agreement some months before. It would appear that nothing would change and that BA would still fly there as normal. The only change was that a new airport was being built on the western side of one of the islands and would be ready in 1998. Its name would be the Chek Lap Kok Airport.

In the world of space NASA landed on the surface of Mars with the Pathfinder space probe. It consisted of a lander, renamed the Carl Sagan Memorial Station, and a lightweight wheeled robotic Mars rover named Sojourner. It took seven months to get there and marked the first serious exploration of the 'red planet'. Things had certainly moved on from Sputnik.

It was now mid-summer and I decided to take Paul and Jenny plus a friend each off to Majorca for a week's holiday. I used a rather obscure travel agent that had Paul and his friend flying out of Bournemouth and me, Jenny and her friend flying out of Gatwick but coming back to Manchester. We found a place on the eastern end of the island called Cala D'or and that seemed to fit the bill. When we got to Gatwick we waited for our call to depart and when it came in we made our way down to the departure gate and boarded a bus to the aircraft. We passed a multitude of aircraft of the Tri-star size expecting the bus to stop at one of these aircraft. Right at the end of the queue of the big boys I spotted an ex-BA BAC 1-11 sitting quietly all alone.

"Dad, I'm not getting on that little thing. It's just too small for me," Jenny exclaimed.

She was looking in horror at this small aircraft bedecked in the colours of 'European Air Travel' (EAT) and based in Bournemouth. Once on board we were greeted by a cabin interior that had not changed since BA days. It could only hold about one hundred passengers so it was not long before we were up and away to Majorca. Considering that we were in the peak month of holiday travel we had the minimum of delay and I have to say it was really nice to fly in the old aircraft with a really nice cabin crew to look after us. Once we landed it was again not too long getting off and getting our bags instead of the usual 'bun fight' when over three hundred people were all trying to get their bags all at the same time. We got to Cala D'or and had a pretty lively week with 'Good Old Dad' picking up the tab. Paul was nowhere to be seen as he stayed elsewhere but turned up like a bad penny when short of funds. We finally got home after a drive from Manchester in the middle of the night and a pretty exhausted dad crawled home to a very welcome bed.

In early August I did a flight to Seoul and learnt of an accident involving a Korean Air 747 that had hit a hillside whilst attempting to land at Guam in the Pacific with 228 fatalities. The finger was pointed at the pilots since they seemed to have set up an approach path which was doomed from the outset plus the weather was not good with heavy rain and thunderstorms. It is a well-known fact that an aircraft accident is never caused by one isolated item but a succession of smaller and, sometimes, quite trivial items that when strung together create the catalyst for something catastrophic. For example, in this accident the Captain was due to fly to Dubai on the day but was re-scheduled for this flight since he was short of duty rest. In other words he was tired. The aircraft usually assigned to the trip was an Airbus A300 but was substituted by the 747 at the last minute. The Flight Crew were unfamiliar with the airport at Guam and the charts they used were out of date. If you take each event on its own it is quite insignificant but put them all together and you have a recipe for disaster. I am by no means as clever as the accident investigators whose job is to get the answers but having built up over 30 years of flying experience I have certain thoughts when it comes to things like this.

On 31st August Jo and I woke up to the dreadful news that Diana, Princess of Wales, had died following a car crash in Paris the evening before. It was one of those days that I will always remember. It was on a par with remembering where you were when President John F Kennedy was assassinated in Dallas some 34 years ago. I have copied a quote below:

"On 31 August 1997, Diana, Princess of Wales died as a result of injuries sustained in a car accident in the Pont de l'Alma road tunnel in Paris, France. Her companion, Dodi Fayed, and the driver of the Mercedes-Benz W140, Henri Paul, were also pronounced dead at the scene of the accident. The bodyguard of Diana and Dodi, Trevor Rees-Jones, was the only survivor. Although the media pinned the blame on the paparazzi, the crash was ultimately found to be caused by the reckless actions of the chauffeur. An 18-month French judicial investigation concluded in 1999 that the crash was caused by Paul, who lost control of the car at high speed while drunk. His inebriation may have been made worse by the simultaneous presence of an anti-depressant and traces of a tranquilizing anti-psychotic in his body. Dodi's father, Mohamed Al-Fayed (the owner of the Hotel Ritz and Harrods) claimed that the crash was a result of a conspiracy, and later contended that the crash was orchestrated by MI6."

The above is an official statement that shows how controversial the whole episode became with claims and counter-claims flying around. The plain fact was that Diana had died and the country mourned. The fallout around the world was amazing as I found out when I flew to Hong Kong within a few days and read in the local paper that the Island of Hong Kong had run out of flowers and that you could not get anywhere near the British Embassy for crowds of Chinese people paying their respects. That was amazing since only two months previous we had given Hong Kong back to the Chinese. In early September Jo and I watched the state funeral on TV and found it all very moving. The pomp and ceremony was to the highest standard that only the British know best.

All was quiet on the BA front for a change with no franchise activity going on and with me flying the normal monthly quota. Although the

-400 was a brilliant aircraft, the fleet itself was very large and so there was a decision made that we would do more of the standard three-day trips to America taking over from the classic. Since I was now pretty senior on the fleet I felt that this decision would not affect me too much and I could just keep plodding the long range destinations which, as I mentioned before, were the most lucrative trips money-wise and I needed to keep ahead financially. The short 3-day trips were, in my mind, not very lucrative and extremely tiring. BA, however, felt that the work patterns should be constructed with both long-range and short trips included so that everyone on the fleet had an opportunity to sample both types. I was of the opinion that I had earned my position in the pecking order and after 30 years plus 'before the mast' I should be able to choose where I wanted to go and what sort of trips I would do. Sounded like a bit of a 'Left-Wing Coup' to me. The other thing that happened was that BA felt, in its wisdom, that the exclusive crew toilet at the back of the Flight Deck was surplus to requirements and if it was removed then another row of club seats could be fitted which created more profit.

"Is there any real problem without the crew toilet?" I hear you say.

OK, there was a normal passenger toilet available just outside the door so why the fuss?

If you consider human nature when applied to a passenger who has just woken up after maybe seven hours asleep in his seat and it is one hour to landing. The first thought he or she has is to go to the toilet and 'freshen' up before the arrival. Multiply that by maybe, 15 and it is quite normal for a queue to form for the 'freshen up'. He or she gets to the head of the queue and suddenly a pilot, who might not be looking at his best, thunders out of the flight deck and mutters something that only he understands and shoves his way ahead of this rather confused passenger into the toilet apologising that he has to 'freshen up' now and not in ten minutes. Not good in anyone's eyes I have to say.

"OK, get us up earlier," I again hear you say.

The amazing thing about that theory was the fact that whenever we got up for the final bit before the arrival there was always a queue. It was bit like a bank queue as well since you felt that it would be common courtesy to let one passenger in before you but they seem to take forever to 'freshen up'.

The subject even came up before the union and they didn't seem to be too interested about the 'Crew Loo' issue so at that point a few of us, including myself, resigned from BALPA in protest. In the end it was the adverse comments from the passengers affected that got the crew loos re-instated. In their haste to remove the loos they disposed of them and so when they refitted them they had to buy new units so the exercise was a pretty costly affair.

It was in the October that a chap called Andy Green became the first man to go supersonic on land when he broke the sound barrier for the ThrustSSC team led by Richard Noble at Black Rock Desert, Nevada.

It was in the November that BA decided to launch a new low-fare short-haul airline out of Stansted to compete with the new breed of airlines that were springing up all over the place. These airlines prided themselves on a low cost base which equated to low fares and were beginning to nibble at heart of the BA short-haul business. It was a bit like the day when Virgin Atlantic came on the scene and started carving into the long-haul business that BA had built up over many years. The name of this new airline was 'Go' and an old friend from many years before, Ed Winter, became the front man for them.

As the year drew slowly to and end I reflected on the year and the fact that there were no real dramas in my life compared with the previous year and nowadays my life was pretty normal finally after many years of turmoil. It was a nice feeling. Jo and I spent our New Year's Eve in Sydney.

And so into 1998 I go with thoughts more and more about the future with only three years away from retirement or the 'big one'. As I mentioned in my ramblings in 1997 my life could not have been more routine as it was now and I hasten to add it could be misconstrued as a bit boring. On the contrary, to me life was far from boring with the -400 routes expanding to cover more destinations than ever before. BA had link-ups with American Airlines and Qantas which pretty well covered a large percentage of the route structure. Within Europe the same was happening with Finnair coming on board and included DBa which BA now owned outright. More Boeing 777 aircraft were ordered instead of the -400 and so it seemed that the -400 was going a bit out of favour due to the improved economics of the 'big twin' concept.

In the late January Jo and I went back to the same honeymoon hotel in Phuket for a lovely cough-free two week holiday. It was heaven to be back there with no worries this time round.

It was in the February that I turned up for a trip to Beijing to be met by a chap from the airport police who explained that we had on board a 'Chinese Gentleman' who was being escorted back to China for whatever reason. The problem was that this was the third attempt to get him on board an aircraft since, on each of the previous occasions there had been a battle of wills at the aircraft door resulting in him not going.

"Sir, I can assure you that this time he will be on board and we have arranged for a couple of security guys to sit with him all the way to China. In fact, we have two sets of guys looking after him," he said with an air of total confidence.

So off we go to the aircraft and after a chat with the ground staff it was decided that, since we were only half-full in the World Traveller section all passengers would be seated towards the front and our guest and his escorts would be seated in the last row so that they could not disturb the other passengers. We finally departed and, with a three-man crew, the routine settled down with one of us in the bunk sleeping and the remaining two of us getting on with the job. The route took us up over the Baltic, entering Russian airspace near to St Petersburg and then generally headed east towards China. We were about one hour east of St Petersburg and my crew meal had just arrived when the CSD came onto the flight deck with the news that one of the passengers, a young lady, had made her way to the back of aircraft and was trying to engage our guest in a meaningful discussion as to why he was being escorted to China. Our guest was getting pretty agitated and the two security guards were working hard to keep things peaceful. The Purser in charge of the cabin was trying without success to get the young lady back to her seat and so the CSD got involved and hence I got involved. I took a loving look at my crew meal and bade it farewell as I donned my full 'Admiral of the Fleet' uniform and made my way to the rear of the aircraft. We had, in fact, put on the seat belt sign so that everybody should return to their seats and belt up. As I approached the battle zone it was pretty obvious that this young girl, whom I would judge to be about 20 years of age, was in full flow verbally accusing the security guards of ill-treatment towards out guest and that it was obvious to her that whatever crime he had committed he was facing the firing squad in China. The fact that I was standing there in all my finery made not the slightest difference to her. Now there is a code as to how to handle a situation like this which involves being very nice and polite. For example, if a passenger is drunk it is deemed not right to say:

"Sir, I do believe that you are as drunk as a skunk and you really hacking me off. No more drinks for you until we throw you off this aircraft when we land."

What you should say is:

"Sir, I do believe that you are slightly inebriated and I would very much like to provide you with the personal services of me, the Captain, to take you back to your seat and I would strenuously suggest that a nap would be the best policy before another drink."

Now this young lady was being so verbal and aggressive I felt that the more direct approach was the order of the day. What I did was to get very close to her left ear so that only she could hear my golden tones. I have forgotten exactly what I said but it went along the lines of ordering her back to her seat and to basically shut up and stop causing me hassle. To add to the short sharp speech in her ear I must have said something about landing within a short period of time and throwing her off the aircraft personally if all else fails. All I got in response was a load of pretty bad language and since her father was a personal friend of Bob Ayling, the BA Chairman, she would make sure that I would get sacked. In response to my comments about landing and dumping her off she just laughed at me and dared me to do it.

"That was the wrong thing to say, young lady!" I said.

I asked the security chaps to get a full team together with two of them watching the guest and the other two watching this young thing.

"Any move by this 'thing' and you are quite entitled to physically restrain her on my authority," were my last words as I made my way back to the flight deck.

I was not sure if I was allowed to say that but I was pretty angry by now. It had no effect on her since she curled up on her seat and started reading a book.

"We will be landing within an hour," I added.

On the flight deck I woke up the sleeping Co-pilot and we started negotiations with the Russians to turn around and head back west. We looked at all the options and elected to land in Helsinki, Finland. The worse thing about it was we had to get rid of about sixty tonnes of fuel to be able to land at Helsinki within our weight restrictions. With the price of fuel in 1998 this amounted to over $70,000 plus all the other charges so we were looking at close to $100,000 for the sake of one stupid girl. What was even worse was that I had missed my crew meal. We landed at Helsinki at some time in the middle of the night and with BA operations fully in the loop we soon found ourselves on a gate with, what seemed to be half the Finnish police force, waiting to board. I left them to it and sat in the Flight deck sorting out the planning for the resumption of the flight to Beijing. This was going to be a long night even for three pilots sharing the workload. After a short time a call came though that my presence was required at the rear of the aircraft to officiate in the departure of the girl. By the time I arrived, so too had her boyfriend, who was trying to calm her down since she was really firing on both barrels and refusing to move. I turned to the nearest policeman and said:

"Please remove this passenger from my aircraft now!"

At this point the girl lashed out at the policeman with her foot and hit him hard in the spot where a man does not like to be hit. Well, about three other policemen just physically lifted her off her feet and carried her horizontally through the door. I told the boyfriend to get off as well since she could well need some help and that I would make sure that she would be banned from flying on BA ever again. After about an hour and the liberating of a large strong drink to help the poor policeman regain his manhood we departed for China and eventually landed there about four hours late after some 14 hours' duty. Never did get my crew meal on that flight! We had a couple of days in Beijing and we met up with some of our passengers in the bar of the hotel being generally the only hotel that catered for westerners. Amongst our passengers were a collection of travel agents from the UK and the enforced diversion was the chat of the night amongst them.

When I got back to Heathrow I met up with my flight manager, Geoff Smith, and we went through the whole episode. The girl's father was, as she said, a friend of Bob Ayling and questions were being asked as to whether I had been a bit heavy-handed in the treatment of her. I stood my ground and Geoff was quite happy that I had done the right thing. The case was closed. It was with irony that a few days later Jo and I went to a party of her old Caledonian stewardess friend Juliet and as the evening went on I heard behind me somewhere a girl describing this flight she had just done to China and how this Captain had ordered an arrival en-route to Helsinki to drop off an unruly passenger. I swung round to be confronted by one of the travel agents who was with me on the flight. What an amazingly small world!

So, there I was sleeping peacefully in my bed in Buenos Aires and I woke up for some unknown reason and looked around and suddenly sat up and realised that the room was enveloped in smoke and the end of the bed was hardly visible. The smell was pretty awful and I quickly realised that something, somewhere was on fire. Now, I am not known for my speed but on this occasion I was fully dressed within seconds and groping around the room trying to find the source of the fire. I opened the door to the corridor and, low and behold, the whole place was enveloped in this thick acrid smoke. It is quite amazing when faced with the situation how you go into automatic mode and I vividly recalled my last BA Safety Equipment training day. Into the bathroom I went and soaked a towel in water and using that as a breathing filter I got into the corridor and, together with my torch, groped my way to the lifts where I remembered there were the emergency stairs. As I made my way I banged on other doors to get people up and moving. At the lifts I was amazed to see some people actually pressing the button and seemingly waiting for the lift to appear. My language was pretty colourful when I told them, in no uncertain terms, to use the staircase since the power might fail as they travelled down in the lift and they could well be fried alive. This was serious stuff. In the end I got into the emergency stairway and, being on the sixteenth floor, I knew that I had a fair way to go down until safety. I was joined by a multitude of hotel guests in various modes of dress and slowly we all descended downwards. The dim lights in the stairwell failed after a short while so there we all were in total darkness and hanging onto each other for mutual support. The hotel sprinkler system had by this time started up and water was cascading down around us making the whole experience pretty sobering. As we passed the twelfth floor the smoke had got into the stairway and was pretty thick. I was really getting worried that we were descending into the fire but we slowly crept on downwards with people clinging onto each other for dear life. All it needed was one person to trip or lose it and that would have been 'one step beyond'. The smoke gradually cleared and the lights came on suddenly to everybody's relief. The next thing I saw was the door sign that said 'Lobby'. A cheer broke out and we all emerged into the lobby like a bunch of refugees.

Having recovered somewhat from my rather dreadful experience I spotted some members of my crew and we all adjourned to the bar and watched the spectacle of the local fire brigade scampering around with reams of hosepipes all over the place. To give them their due it must have been very difficult to locate the source of the fire. The hotel manager came over to us and explained that the day before they had had the air conditioning people in to sort out a problem on the twelfth floor and they were using an arc welder and it looks like, unbeknown to them, some of the installation had caught fire and smouldered away producing the thick acrid smoke during the night.

"Don't worry about it and please, have a drink on the house," he said casually.

Having crawled down the stairs in very difficult circumstances only minutes before I was not in total agreement with his words – and that was being polite.

Not a nice experience I have to say and, hopefully, never to be repeated. The amusing side was the various outfits that people dressed themselves in when you might say they had a 'timer up their backside'. I felt all right in just a tracksuit which must have been lying on top of my suitcase. After a few calming drinks and breakfast we were given the all-clear and I returned to my room, via the lift this time, and surveyed the devastation that I had left. It looked like I had literally carved a path from the bed to door. Slept well though!

In the April there was news that the IRA had finally entered peace talks with Tony Blair's government and it looked like the end was in sight for the Northern Ireland troubles. It was just under 30 years since the British Army had attempted to restore order in the province so this 'Good Friday' agreement was very welcome. At the other end of the political spectrum President Clinton ordered the military to 'take all necessary appropriate actions to respond to the threat posed by Iraq's refusal to end its WMD program'. In other words Iraq was still top of the agenda in the Middle East.

The work load on the -400 was on the move upwards and I was forecasted to do just below 900 hours' flying time in the year which was the maximum allowable under the current legislation. This limit became evident when I was taken off a trip to the Far East at the last moment. On the -400 it was quite easy to get to these limits since the flights we flew were constantly of long duration. No wonder I felt tired most of the time or, maybe, it was age catching up with me.

I did a simple trip to Kuala Lumpur and met up with another crew and there was my old school friend Frank Brejka complete with daughter. Frank had gone to Hamble after me and ended up in BCAL for his sins. Since he was caught in the downturn in the aviation world Frank was still a Co-Pilot when I met him but later on he became a captain on the 757/767 aircraft and so, he too, made it to Captain during his career in BA. After the merger he moved aircraft and there he was on the -400 unbeknown to each other. It was 34 years since we had left school. As we chatted it turned out that Frank and the women in his life seemed to mirror my escapades so we chatted well into the night around a common theme. As a matter of fact Frank, Dave Hanks and I had all gone to the same school and we had all ended up in BA which I feel is not a bad achievement. If you recall I had met up with Dave back on the 737 and now all three of us were on the -400. Not bad I say!

In the late spring the low-cost version of BA got off the ground out of Stansted with 'Go' operating a fleet of seven 737-300 aircraft that included four of the original ones that we used in Berlin some years before. In the Far East BA decided to dispense with all but Narita in Japan and increase that service to two a day. Seoul also came in for the chop but extra flights to Australia via Kuala Lumpur were launched and we went back to Nigeria after a break of over a year so the net effect for the -400 operation was not much. We still worked hard.

I was fortunate to be one of the early arrivals in July at the new Hong Kong airport at Chek Lap Kok and suddenly overnight the famous curved approach to the old airport was assigned to the history books. I have to say the engineering feat of building the new airport was, without question, quite amazing. To drill out two long runways and a huge terminal in the middle in the time taken was amazing. There was also a new road connection including bridges and tunnels to the city centre plus a new train line put in. The whole new facility was very impressive and once the few teething problems were overcome it worked like clockwork. In addition to the terminals a new huge cargo ramp was also constructed plus of course a large engineering base for Cathay Pacific Airlines. It was strange to look out of my window in the Excelsior Hotel and not see aircraft landing and taking off at the old airport. Apparently the cost of building the new airport was less than the real estate value of the old airport such was the value of property in Hong Kong. It also was a known fact that the top half of a hill to the north of Kowloon was demolished to provide the base rock for the new runways being built. You have to hand it to the Chinese when it comes to building projects like this.

In the August I caught up with Ian and Tony, my long lost friends of many years. What had happened was that Tony and Ian had drifted off to different aircraft after getting their commands, like me, many years before with Tony going off to the Classic 747 and Ian going to the 757/767 fleet. I had gone to the 737 and now it transpired that all three of us were on the -400. It was really good to catch up after all these years. Tony was still married to Margaret and had four kids by now and Ian was still with Sue without kids. Ian was not far from retirement since he was the eldest of the three of us so it was decided that it would be great for the three of us to do a trip together. This we did with Tony and I being the drivers to Buenos Aires and Ian came along as a passenger using staff travel. It was fantastic to sit by the river on the Tigre Delta and chat about the old times over a beer or two remembering it was 34 years ago when we had first met on our arrival at Hamble. It was amazing to think that all that time had passed by.

The three of us had been Captains for well over 20 years just to add to the statistics.

Another new route came our way with the withdrawal of the classic 747 on the Caribbean run out of Gatwick. It was not long before I had Jo on board for a trip to Barbados and the flight itself brought back memories of when I navigated, or so I was led to believe, the VC-10 on the inaugural service for BOAC. All we did now was to follow the 'Magenta' line on the display and that was that. If I recall back to that infamous trip we ended up very short of suitable alternates at Barbados. With the -400 the world was our oyster with so many places to choose from plus of course about 350 passengers to wine and dine whilst en-route. There was something magical about sitting in the cool evening air sipping a rum punch, listening to the crickets chirping away and the sound of the ocean not far away. Talking about listening, it was becoming obvious to me that my hearing was not as it used to be and I was starting to suffer from 'Tinnitus' or whistling in the ears. I had just done my six-monthly medical that included a hearing test and Doc Green remarked that I was starting to get what was referred to as 'High Tone Deafness' but not to worry since it would not affect the flight deck scene where normal tones were the order of the day. He went on to say that all pilots who were of my vintage on the Long-Haul side of aviation suffered the same and, like me, Tinnitus was sometimes a side effect. Having said all that the noises were not that loud but just a bit irritating. I seemed to remember my dad suffered the same as he got older. Back in Barbados on about the third day I would fly to another island and back in the afternoon and then enjoy another two days lounging around in the sand and sun. This was definitely the life for a pilot of my vintage.

In the world of space the American astronaut Alan Shepard died. In 1961 he was the first American in space aboard the small Mercury capsule with the flight lasting minutes and ended up flying to the moon ten years later on Apollo 14. He was famous for the fact that he smuggled a golf club to the moon and whacked a golf ball many miles across the moon's surface.

In the August BA ordered 59 new Airbus A320 aircraft with 129 options. This in itself was a remarkable turnaround for the company which, up to that point, had always bought Boeings. They also ordered 16 more 777 aircraft from Mr Boeing with 16 options and cancelled the final orders for the -400. These aircraft would be powered by the new Rolls Royce Trent engine which would give the aircraft the range of the -400 that I flew. The big twin was starting to make its mark.

As for me I just plodded along keeping my nose clean and even found time to take Paul on a trip with me to South America and even Jenny got a ride to New York with me. It was in the September when New York was in the news for a different reason. A Swissair McDonnell Douglas MD-11 crashed just off the coast shortly after taking off. Two hundred and twenty nine people died that night. The reason was traced to faulty wiring in the flight deck ceiling behind some insulation and seemingly impossible to extinguish and the fire spread very quickly and the flight crew lost control. It was the In-Flight Entertainment wiring that had actually caught fire. It was another unavoidable tragedy.

Also in the September American Airlines, BA, Canadian Airlines, Cathay Pacific Airways and Qantas Airways announced the new 'oneworld®' global alliance. What it meant was that all of these airlines could integrate their resources and produce a world-wide product with an example being a timetable and ticketing as one flawless item. Once again BA was seen to lead the aviation world with this alliance and it was not too long before other alliances were formed. Although this did not directly affect me I had to admire the way BA was carving out the market and to add to this the fact that in Europe I would say that pretty well every airline had some sort of alliance with BA. Finnair was, in fact, the first European airline to join the alliance shortly afterwards. It was also in the November when the first classic 747 was retired after nearly 30 years of service.

In the November things were brewing up again in the Middle East with President Clinton firing off some cruise missiles into Iraq and it seemed that once again another confrontation was in the making. Since I started flying way back in 1966 every year some sort of conflict in the Middle East happened with regular monotony. Also in the November the Russians launched the first sections of the joint 'International Space Station' that had been planned between the USA and Russia many years before. It eventually was planned that up to six crew could live on it in relative comfort for extended periods. Another major milestone was being achieved in space.

As for me I flew a new route for a change from Gatwick to Phoenix, Arizona with a shuttle flight to San Diego, California. To me Phoenix was on a par with Los Angeles in the eyes of an aircraft 'nutter' like me. Yes, after all these years I was still mad about aircraft of all shapes and sizes. So, with a couple of days clear off I go with a hire car exploring. South of the city after about two hours driving is the city of Tucson which boasts the huge US Air force base of Davis-Monthan which is the bone-yard of anything military that once flew. It boasts row upon row of aircraft just parked out in the sun that may be or maybe not used again. Alongside is a fantastic aircraft museum and so there I was, once again, in my element amongst these old machines.

What would my mother have said about my undying love of anything that went up into the air? I thought to myself while wandering around.

She would have probably said:

"There you are still with your head in the clouds."

The airport of San Diego was famous in the days of Charles Lindbergh and the airport was named after him. It was a tight fit for a -400 and seemed to sit right in the middle of the city with the wingtips overlapping the local highway. I felt that I could reach into the local '7-Eleven' and order a sandwich for the journey home. Anyway, the whole trip was about six days and made a pleasant change to the normal run of trips.

The usual domestic scene with the kid's birthdays in November came and went and it seemed that the domestic situation with Jo and the kids was ticking along OK as long as certain things were not mentioned. Paul was now 18 and still drifting in his adult world. He did get a job thanks to Moya with the reception area of the BA headquarters but I not sure how long that lasted. Jenny had done her state exams with reasonable passes and was looking at options. One of these was to go to the equestrian college in nearby Maidenhead since her love of horses seemed to be still very strong. We made enquiries as to the costs etc. and decided that maybe next year would be a good starting time. So the year drew to a close and yet another quite normal one was had by one and all.

So, in comes 1999 and so does the mighty Euro having been adopted by most of the EC country members with a few exceptions including the UK. No one will really know whether it was a good move or not but it would take a few years before it would actually come into circulation.

Jo and I had spent the New Year in Kuala Lumpur and got home early in January and so the cycle started all over again. The main topic of conversation was the fact that at the end of the year we were into a new century and our thoughts turned to where to spend it.

This time in the January we went to Goa for a two-week break and stayed in a beautiful hotel on the beach complete with swim-up bar. We did the complete package this time flying out on a Monarch A330 on a direct flight both ways from Gatwick. The other guests were mainly British so many friendships were made. It had a small 9-hole golf course within the grounds so the early mornings were taken care of. Being India and with both of us being a lover of India food it was like a gastronomic paradise. The sunsets were something to be seen complete with a cocktail or two.

In the February BA bought a small stake of Iberia, the Spanish national airline, together with American Airlines and the way was made clear for Iberia to join the oneworld alliance which had become effective 1st February.

In the news in February the US president Bill Clinton was acquitted by his government in impeachment proceedings following a fling he had with one of his staff, Monica Lewinsky. It was about this time that Osama Bin Laden was running amuck threatening the world and all the US judiciary were worried about were the morals of the president. I wager a bet that if all government officials who had had some sort of deviation of this sort resigned then there would be no world governments left to rule.

In the March I was sitting quietly at home with Jo working somewhere in Bracknell as a temp and the phone rang. I answered it and it was one of the scheduling staff asking me whether I was available for a draft trip to Caracas, Venezuela. On the 737 the draft, as I once explained, was very lucrative but to get it on the -400 was really lucrative but rare.

"No problem. When do you want me to come in?" I casually asked expecting that afternoon.

"Gwyn, the passengers are actually sitting on the aircraft now waiting for you," was the reply.

That woke me up and so I went into automatic mode dragging my suitcase and content into some sort of order, cleaning my teeth and brushing my hair all at the same time. I left a note for Jo since I could not get hold of her on her mobile. I fired away on all barrels and finally got to Heathrow within about one hour of the call. So, off I went flying and I rang Jo some hours later once in the hotel. A rather bemused Jo answered the phone.

"Oh, there you are then. When I got home the front door was wide open, the radio was belting away and the place looked like a bomb had hit it. Hopefully I'll see you later this evening."

When I explained that I was in Caracas and would not be home for a few days there was a stunned silence at the other end of the phone.

"That would explain the shambles here then," Jo said with a sound of resignation in her voice.

OK, the financial reward was good when I got it but it is not recommended if a partnership is struggling a bit. Anyway, I did get home after a few days and all was well except for the fact that the original roster had me off to Hong Kong the following day and would you believe it I had to go since they were short of crews. Not an easy life at my age I have to say!

In the March I don't know how I did it but I ended up in Lagos after a break of maybe 30 years or so. I found that nothing had changed. In fact, it was worse than before. While we waited for the transport to arrive outside the terminal I wandered outside for a cigarette and within seconds a security guard came up to me and told me to go inside since anyone outside could be mugged or at worse kidnapped at gunpoint. I did exactly as he said with no debate. Once in the transport we were what you might say, hermetically sealed in, under armed guard until within the heavily guarded grounds of the hotel. Hopefully this would be my last ever visit to Lagos. It was!

Also in the March we enrolled Jenny in the equestrian college previously mentioned and so we thought that all would be good from that point on for her education since she would leave after the three-year course with some sort of qualification. What a stupid thought!

It was in the April when the final DC-10 was retired from BA. These aircraft were inherited from BCAL and were sold off for conversion into freighters. Also in April two Libyans suspected of bringing down Panam 103 over Lockerbie back in 1988 were handed over to Scottish authorities for eventual trial in the Netherlands. Whether they did or didn't will always be a subject of debate. In the UK the TV presenter Jill Dando was shot dead outside her house in London. She was a lovely and well liked lady and there was a total mystery surrounding events with one Barry George being charged and then acquitted many years later. No culprit has been found to this day.

I did a flight to Entebbe, Uganda and Nairobi, Kenya in the April for another unknown reason. Like the Lagos trip I must have been in a 'memory lane' sort of phase since it was many years before when I had been there last. It was a bit nicer than going to Lagos and I did get a round of golf in Nairobi plus a nostalgic evening ride around the local game park. The 'Tusker' beer was still pretty good as well. By this time the airport boasted a brand new terminal which was a vast improvement on the old single storey one that I knew from the time before.

On 29th April Ian retired from the airline after just under 30 years of good service.

In the May BA again was in the spotlight with a new product for an improved Club World with flat beds similar to the First Class cabin. A new state-of-the-art entertainment system was to be installed with bigger screens and in-seat power for laptops available. Once again BA led the airline world in passenger comforts and the other lot, including Mr Branson, all followed suit like lambs. LanChile joined oneworld in the May. Another world alliance was cobbled together with Singapore Airlines taking the lead under the title of 'The Star Alliance'. I will always admire BA for the way it seems to tweak the market at just the right moment. BA also opened a brand new World Cargo Centre at Heathrow. It is a relatively unknown fact that BA was creating a cargo market that ranked high up the scale and the yields were such as to make an enterprise like this worthwhile.

In the computer world I was slowly getting my act together with

Microsoft Windows 95 and getting a modicum of success when along comes Windows 98 and the learning process starts all over again. I found the most useful button of the whole lot was 'spellcheck' which helped me to write something that is maybe partly understandable. Jo came to my aid as usual. Good girl! As for the mobile phone world I was just about keeping with the 'fanatics' but I actually found the phone a gross intrusion in my life and it spent most of the time 'off'.

I did do a trip to Houston, Texas at one point and made a trip down to the Johnson Space Centre which was where the astronauts did all their training. Considering my passion for space it was quite a trip. Outside the complex was a Saturn rocket displayed on its side. It was to be used for a final Apollo mission but was cancelled due to budget restraints and there it was for all to see. I never quite realised just how enormous these rockets were and I felt totally in awe as to how they managed to get them to work, let alone get them into space. The conducted tour was fascinating in its own right. While we stood in the viewing area overlooking the control room that would have been used for all the manned flights right back to John Glenn's Mercury to the present day space shuttle launches the guide remarked that there was more computing power in the modern personal computer that the whole of the Mercury, Gemini and Apollo programmes put together.

"That is what I call a statistic!" I muttered to myself.

It was quite ironic that in the July the Mercury capsule 'Liberty Bell 7' that was flown by the second astronaut into space, Virgil Grissom, was recovered from the Atlantic Ocean after 38 years on the sea bed. What had happened was that after Virgil 'splashed down' in the Atlantic an escape hatch blew out and the capsule sank. Virgil was blamed for the sinking but maintained his innocence and actually went on fly in the Gemini programme which vindicated him. He actually died in the Apollo 1 disaster years later.

By September it became obvious to Moya and me that Jenny was having trouble at the college. Moya got a letter confirming this fact and what had happened was that she had fallen in with bad company with a bunch of girls from Aylesbury and we had no choice but to take her out of the college with me picking up the tab for the wasted time she had spent there. I think on reflection I would say that my relationship with

Paul and Jenny was not always as I would have wanted it. Perhaps it was my fault or was it the fault of the divorce? Perhaps I was disappointed with both of them for not knowing what they wanted out of life. I will never know!

"I knew what I wanted to do so why not them?" I would say to Moya on many occasions.

BA decided in the September to start to dispose of the 757 fleet and those for the chop were earmarked to be converted into freighters for DHL. At the same time the new Airbus 320 ordered entered service. More airbuses were ordered. The BA fleet was getting bigger and bigger with maybe over 120 aircraft by now. The -400 fleet alone was now well over 50 aircraft.

In October there was yet another air crash involving an aircraft departing from JFK. On this occasion it was an EgyptAir 767 that mysteriously dived headlong into the Atlantic off the coast of Nantucket, Massachusetts and 217 people died. There were all sorts of speculations at the time as to the cause and in particular the mental state of the Co-pilot but in the end it remains one of the unexplained accidents.

Jo and I were still happy tucked away in Warfield with me disappearing on trips every now and again with maybe Jo along for company. Our health was good apart from my ever expanding girth and my ears whistling the odd tune every now and again. On one of our trips together we met a lovely couple who went by the name of Ed and Jan. Ed was a purser with BA and Jan had taken an early retirement package. It was one of those chance meetings where a friendship was sealed for life.

I did see Moya every now and then only to get up to date with the saga of the kids but each time it seemed like we were banging our heads against a brick wall. I loved my kids like any father would but it was hard work trying to understand them both.

In the December there was yet another air crash and this time it was a bit closer to home. A Korean Air Cargo 747 aircraft crashed shortly after departure from Stansted in Essex. It transpired that the fault lay with the pilots whereby they blindly followed an instrument that was misreading and they dived into the ground. All four pilots were killed and concluded a bad year in the air accident world. In Russia Boris Yeltsin resigned and in came Vladimir Putin.

As for the Millennium celebrations I did a trip to Singapore and on to Perth with Jo along for the ride and we spent the New Year at the Turi Beach resort which I mentioned before and it was quite an event with the year 2000 being ushered in whilst enjoying the cool evening air under the palm trees with a dip in the pool at midnight. And so my last full year in BA was looming.

It was shortly after we got home from Singapore when we flew to the island of Koh Samui in Thailand for a holiday. It was yet another beautiful unspoilt paradise by the sea. It had one of those airport terminals that was similar to an open air hut with the bags all carried by hand straight to the taxi from the aircraft.

I went to work in the February to find that, in my absence, BA had introduced a new cabin known as the 'World Traveller Plus' whereby passengers that had paid the full price for a ticket in World Traveller would have a bit more legroom and comforts than the people who had bought discounted tickets. I flew to New York with both the new all-sleeper Club World cabin and the new World Traveller Plus and once again BA had got it spot on with both cabins full. The reason for the trip to JFK was to do a sort of tour of all the places that I felt were important to me in my life with BA.

I was on a flight from Buenos Aires to Santiago, Chile and just as I closed the thrust levers, as they are called now, for the descent there was a large bang, like a backfire, from No. 3 engine and this was the first and thankfully last technical issue with the -400 and its Rolls Royce engines. What had happened was that one of the many air bleeds on the engine had failed to open and the engine had surged in protest. We were at a very light weight so to stop the engine as we did presented us with no problems on the landing but we did have an unscheduled night stop in Santiago. I had by this time done eight years or thereabouts on the -400 and this was the first bit of bother. Not bad when I remembered the old days when the classic was first introduced.

As the spring came along then so did my variety of trips that I elected to fly. I had covered Africa OK so off I went to India with Jo in tow and we arrived in Delhi. We had a few days off there so we planned a day trip to the Taj Mahal which brought many good memories back to me and it was wonderful to show Jo one of the wonders of the world. We travelled by train and arrived there in the searing heat in the late morning. At that particular time there was a heatwave across Northern India with the dial going up to over 40ºC so it was a bit of an endurance test. Anyway, after lunch in a local hotel the guide showed us over the fantastic monument and by about 4 pm we were totally burnt out by the heat and made our way to the railway station for the return journey to Delhi. There is something quite amazing about standing on the platform waiting for the train and seeing monkeys climbing all over the signal gantries and sitting on the rails as if they were waiting for the train to take them home after a day's work in the office. We finally got back to the hotel in the early evening and after a quick dinner we went off to the airline crew room for the usual 'hangar talk' for a few hours. The next night we were due to fly back to Heathrow but there I was totally laid out unable to move due to a bout of food poisoning. Not a pretty sight I have to say. Thank you very much, India, for leaving me with an everlasting memento. We eventually got home about two days later.

It was in the April that I took Jo on a day out and we went up the motorway to the famous aircraft museum at Duxford, Cambridgeshire to show her my lovely VC-10. G-ASGC, a super version, is there on display resplendent in the original BOAC colours complete with the famous 'Speedbird' emblem on the tail. I must admit the heartstrings tugged as we walked up to her. The steps were in place at the front right-hand door so up we went to look inside. As we entered the cabin I looked to the right into the flight deck and was shocked to see how black and dull it looked. The other thing that pulled me up short was the scenario where, maybe, up to five of us would cram into what seemed to be a telephone box. It was at that moment when a museum official rolled up to enquire as to whether we needed some help in explaining the working of the aircraft we were on. I mentioned to him my history and the fact that I had actually flown this aircraft in BOAC days. 'GC' was also the aircraft that I did my 'Atlantic dash' from New York to Prestwick shortly after I had become a Captain back in 1976. All changed at this point and he removed the barrier onto the flight deck and in we all went and I acquainted myself with the left-hand seat again.

My god, did I sit here for, maybe, eight hours in this dark and dingy place? I thought to myself.

Yes, I did and loved every minute of it! was my second thought.

Jo was fascinated with the cabin. It seemed that she was stepping back in time and looking at the days of real luxury air travel with none of the modern hype like:

"My IFE has packed up so what am I meant to do with myself for the next five hours?"

Or

"Please help me put the seat down flat so that I can sleep."

When you looked at the economy cabin the seats were quite spacious with loads of legroom. As for the first class ones they were really quite luxurious and if you consider back then, they only tilted back a certain amount but passengers used to sleep soundly. It was strange to imagine a Cabin Crew member mixing up a salad from the basic ingredients in one of the small galleys and then making up a meal tray from scratch. Thoughts of the famous 'steak and kidney pie' saga came flooding back together with the munching of caviar plus all the trimmings while pretending to be the Flight Navigator. I pointed out to the museum chap how we rigged up the sextant and he confessed that he never knew about that side of the Flight Deck scene. We must have sat there for, maybe, an hour exchanging notes. When Jo and I finally left for home my head was swimming with all things nostalgic. All it needed was Ian and Tony with us to crawl over the Trident aircraft that was parked next door and all three of us would have been crying in our beer.

In the May the Bob Ayling era came to a close when he left the airline and the Australian Rod Eddington joined BA as the Chief Executive. He hailed from managerial roles at Cathay Pacific and, prior to that, Ansett Airlines in Australia. The following month the last 737-200 left BA for pastures new. It was quite sad to see the aircraft go but it was the noise lobby that finally finished it off. Great aircraft in its day!

In the June I did a trip to Orlando, Florida and again Jo came along for the ride. The plan was that on the second day off there we would drive to Cape Canaveral to watch a shuttle launch. On the descent we passed just to the north of the launch pad and there was the shuttle sitting there being prepared for the lift-off. We were at about 8,000ft and so had a fantastic view of it all. The next day myself and the Co-pilot hired a car, leaving Jo to enjoy the shopping arcade, and off we went to the south and ended up at an airfield on the shores of Lake Kissimmee that boasted a small museum in one corner. As we looked around at the old classic machines there was the sound of a classic US military training aircraft known as the Harvard. It was like the American version of the Chipmunk that I learnt to fly on many years ago. There was a small office where the pilot disappeared into after he shut down the engine and I realised that he was offering pleasure flights around the lake. So off I go and end up in the front seat of the Harvard for a pleasure flight. As we taxied out the instructor casually asked what I did for a living as part of his routine and when I said that I flew the 747-400 all things changed.

"Right, Gwyn, you have control and prepare for take-off," he said calmly into the microphone.

It was like going back in time as I taxied along. All it needed was Mr Vickers in the back seat barking away at me. I even remembered the 'before take-off 'checklist.

As we drove down the runway I remembered to lift the tail and gently eased her into the air.

"There you are, Gwyn, climbing nicely at 90 knots as if you did it yesterday," he said.

We got to about two thousand feet and flew out over the lake when my enjoyment was interrupted.

"Right, Gwyn, when was the last time you did any aerobatics?" he said with a chuckle in his voice.

"About 35 years ago but I get the feeling that we are just about to do some more," I replied.

"You betcha!" he fired back at me.

We looked around to make sure we were alone and he then demonstrated a loop and a barrel role and then it was my turn. Right, it was a bit disjointed but I made it in one piece and so we spent the next ten minutes doing all sorts of gyrations in the sky and finished the flight with a low pass over the museum and then I even managed a landing of sorts. I quite amazed myself and felt pretty chuffed with it all. The only downside was that we got back to the hotel well into the evening with Jo not too happy with my timing.

"You should have married a bloody aeroplane, instead of a woman" was her comment as I strolled through the door. A large glass of wine was needed and quick.

The next day we made our way very early in the morning to Cape Canaveral and after a magnificent breakfast in McDonald's we arrived at a museum about five miles from the launch site and joined in with the general mood of waiting and watching. There were a couple of fun-fair type machines which we climbed aboard while waiting. We did regret the breakfast whilst we were suspended upside down hanging in our straps. Finally, we made our way onto the viewing balcony and could just make out the shuttle sitting on the launch pad. At the appointed hour a fiery mixture of smoke and flames belched out from the base of the space shuttle assembly and off she went into the Florida sky climbing majestically and accelerating like you could not believe it. After about ten seconds the ground shook and the noise reached us. It was pretty noisy out there. A bystander remarked:

"Pretty noisy you say! When the Saturn rockets took off for the moon a few years back you could not hear yourself speak."

It transpired that this guy has stood there on the same spot for every manned launch right back to the first one in 1961. Some achievement you might say!

Anyway, we watched the space shuttle as far as we could and could just make out the point when the booster rockets fell away. To actually witness a launch was, to me, like a boyhood dream come true, and there I was watching my dream. That trip had to be one of the most enjoyable ones I did if I considered my passion for aviation and space exclusively. It was nice to have Jo along as well.

The Concorde crash in Paris dominated the headlines in the July. BA was directly affected since apart from Air France they were the only operators of the aircraft. The immediate cause looked obvious from the various film footage shot that a fuel tank had ruptured and the left wing was on fire. The aircraft was doomed at that point and crashed into a hotel killing 113 people in all. There has been much speculation as to the cause of the fire with many theories being presented. The official line was that the aircraft hit a piece of metal on the runway during the take-off and that blew out one of the tyres with the remnants rupturing a fuel tank with disastrous consequences. Within days of the tragedy all Concorde aircraft were grounded and the flagship of BA was suddenly no longer. BA had had more success with the aircraft than did Air France and so took the bigger hit. It was very sad taxiing past the maintenance area and seeing the complete fleet all lined up neatly as if on parade.

I took Jo with me to Buenos Aires and showed her the sights including the famous 'Tango Show' at a local venue one evening and Jo fell in love with the place and gave me bit of a ribbing for not taking her before. It was quite an amusing start to the trip with me sitting in the flight deck and waiting for Jo to go through the rigours of Staff Travel. In Terminal 4 all staff passengers had to report to a small office in the reception area and await their fate. In the meantime I would do my business and sit patiently on the flight deck trying to get any information on Jo's progress with the aircraft dispatcher. On this occasion there was a total failure of the computerised departure control system and the dispatcher told me that no staff passengers would be accepted on any flights that night. Jo and I did have a plan B whereby she went home by taxi and that was that. I assumed that plan B was in operation and resigned myself to Jo not being around for my last flight to Buenos Aires. Suddenly the dispatcher called me to say that he did not know how she had done it but my wife was standing at the boarding gate.

"The boarding gate closes in two minutes. What shall I do, Captain?" he asked politely.

"Put her in seat 1A and then close the doors behind her would be my best solution," I replied with a smile.

This he did and off we went. I never did find out how Jo got to the boarding gate without a boarding card.

It was back in the April that I had taken Jo to Duxford to see the VC-10. And it made me think how nice it would be to take Jo for a flight in one. The RAF at the time were still flying quite a few out of RAF Brize

Norton, Oxfordshire so shortly after the museum visit I wrote to the Station Commander there and explained my situation and how I would love to go for a ride on one of their 'Shiny Tens'. I got a reply in late August inviting both of us to come along and enjoy a flight courtesy of the RAF.

So on a bright September morning we rolled up to the guard house at Brize Norton and after the short formalities we were directed to the departure hall. The funny thing was that the chap on the gate threw me a splendid salute as we drove away. The last time that I went into an RAF station it was me doing the saluting. Times had changed. I nearly saluted back though! The departure hall was like a miniature T4 and once registered we sat down near the window looking at the VC-10s all lined up. At this time the RAF had a total mix of aircraft. They still had the original aircraft as supplied in the mid-sixties but had been updated with air-to-air refuelling equipment. As the airlines finished with the Standard aircraft they were converted into dedicated air-to-air refuelling tankers. The same happened with the Super aircraft and so the RAF had maybe, 30 or so VC-10 aircraft of various origins flying with some able to carry passengers and some just fuel.

Anyway, Jo and I were sitting quietly when were joined by an RAF Officer who was, in fact, to be the Co-pilot with us that day for our flight. So off we went across the tarmac and climbed aboard XV109, our aircraft for the day. Jo was installed in a cabin seat and I was invited into the Flight Deck for the take-off. It was quite amazing to enter what used to be my domain and find a cheerful bunch of lads doing what pilots do best – reading the checks. All the sights and sounds came back to me as we started the engines and made our way out to the runway. I felt that I could recite the checklist as if it were yesterday. As we rolled down the runway the Flight Engineer pushed the engines all the way to full power. There was none of this fancy 'reduced power' in the RAF and that was that. I have to say that I felt a tingle in the spine as the sound of the engines hit the top notes with the familiar 'crackle' out the back end somewhere. As we climbed away after the take-off the VC-10 seemed to be hell-bent on going for the heavens and it was then that I realised the enormous power these aircraft had if compared to their weight. It is an interesting note that the original RAF VC-10 from way back was built with a fuselage of a standard aircraft but with engines that came with the super version. In other words if we ever thought we had pretty good performance then the RAF left us in the dirt. Anyway, once the flight settled down we found ourselves over the North Sea. I was chatting to the Flight Navigator (yes the RAF still amazingly enough still had Flight Navigators) and admiring his array of dials on his panel when my attention was drawn to a small CCTV display which showed a fighter jet of some sort which seemed to be about 20 metres away off the rear right-hand side.

"He is just popping in for some fuel out of our tanks," the Flight Navigator remarked.

At this point I wandered down the cabin and found Jo sitting in the last row and was surveying the contents of the standard RAF lunch-box. I once did the same many years ago and, believe me, the sandwiches were exactly the same, being about two inches thick and curled up at the edges. The other interesting item was the famous 'Pork Pie' which was totally alien to Jo. The Mars bar went down well though.

"Hi Jo, have a quick peep out of the window," I said.

Jo swung round to have a look out of the window and there was a Tornado fighter jet about 20 metres away guzzling fuel from us via a flexible hose. Jo nearly dropped her Pork Pie and was absolutely gobsmacked at the sight of this other aircraft being so near. The strange thing was that the pilot of the Tornado seemed to be looking straight at Jo.

"Perhaps he wants your Pork Pie or maybe your telephone number," I casually commented.

As the flight progressed then two more 'customers' turned up including the new Eurofighter. We finally landed back where we started from after about three hours. I have to say that the whole outing was fantastic and very nostalgic for me and to have Jo along was the icing on the cake. After we shut down the engines our guide for the day invited us to the mess for refreshments and we finally got home late in the afternoon. What a day!

In the October I was in Singapore when I heard the news that a Singapore Airlines -400 had crashed on take-off in Taiwan with a loss of 83 lives. At that time quite a few ex-BA pilots had retired from BA and were flying for Singapore Airlines so I made a few phone calls and breathed a sigh of relief that it was not one of my colleagues involved. The flight crew did survive the crash. What had happened was they had taken off on the wrong runway and had hit the construction equipment in place for ongoing runway repairs. The weather at the time of the accident was appalling. What can I say?

In the November George W Bush was elected to be the next president of the USA. Enough said!

As the winter approached Jo and I started to look at our plans as to where best to spend Xmas and opted for a longish trip out of Gatwick to Barbados. The Co-pilot was a wonderful chap called Simon Bedford who was an ex-RAF Red Arrows pilot and the three of us had a great few days together. For New Year's Eve we opted for a Hong Kong flight and I recall it was quite a night with most of the crew ending up invading our room until the early hours.

And so the final month for me in BA arrived in 2001.

On 17th January Tony retired from the airline just ten days ahead of me after over 34 years leaving just me to go last being the baby of the trio by ten days.

My final trip with BA was a simple Heathrow to Bangkok and on to Sydney and a return the same way. It was fortunate that we had a very nice Cabin Crew and on my final night in Bangkok we all gathered in our room since Jo was with me and they gave me a very nice retirement party together with a small presentation. It was really quite touching. The next evening we made our way to the airport and it all seemed a bit strange that I would be doing this for the last time. Jo got herself nicely tucked in and away we went back home. The landing at Heathrow wasn't too bad either. The CSD must have made a passenger announcement about this being my last flight since I heard a round of applause from down the back.

And so on 27th January 2001 I retired as a captain from British Airways after 34 years and six months' service. I had accumulated 25,200 hours' flying or just under three years continually in the air, 12 million miles done or nearly 25 times to the moon and back.

On reflection I have seen aviation go from Pilots, Flight Engineers and Flight Navigators to just Pilots running these big machines with comparative ease. Sometimes I have portrayed it as an easy life and maybe a bit too social but below the surface it was, and still is, a hard and exacting profession with many pitfalls.

I am proud to have succeeded in this profession without many problems in the job and a 'clean sheet' to the end. Amazingly enough I never failed a simulator check, route check or promotional checks although I must have brushed the edge some time on some occasions.

I started my flying on a simple Auster and then at Hamble came to grips with the Chipmunk and the mighty Apache. Once in the airline I got acquainted with the superb VC-10 followed by the classic 747-100. I then crossed the divide and flew the 737-200/300/400. Finally I finished my flying life on the 747-400.

I had some important stepping stones in my career such as surviving the rigours of the flying college at Hamble, attaining the coveted Flight Navigator's Licence and finally achieving the enviable rank of Captain at the tender age of 30.

"What was my most favourite aircraft?" you might ask.

"Well, the VC-10 of course without a shadow of a doubt" is my simple answer.

"What was my most favourite time in BA?" is another question.

"The short period on the VC-10 when I was a Captain" is my simple answer again.

The period operating the Internal German Services was a very, very close second though.

My only pitfalls were man-made and in my private life. Stupid boy!

As for retirement well, that is another story.

Maybe my head will go back in the clouds or maybe not, was my final thought for the day.

Part three of my life is in the making and a few surprises turn up since my retirement did not go exactly as planned.

1990 Charity Flight Berlin

1991 A view from the office surveying my domain

1993 BA 747-400 G-BNLB in Landor Colours Landing at Kai Tak, Hong Kong

1996 RMS Queen Mary, Long Beach

1996 Jo and me on the Queen Mary

1997 BA 747-400 G-BNLX in 'Chatham Historic Dockyard' colours

2000 Jenny and Paul

2000 "I'm thirsty, Mum and I need a drink"

THE FOLLOWING staff members are retiring or leaving after long periods of service:

Terry Allsopp, Equipment Support Manager, Equipment Services, Heathrow, after 30 years.

Dodie McQue, Duty Officer, Gatwick, after 35 years.

Susan Middleditch, Main Crew, Worldwide Fleet, Air Cabin Crew, Cabin Services, Gatwick, after two years.

Captain Jonathan Milward, 757/767 Fleet, Flight Crew, Flight Operations, Heathrow, after 33 years.

Keith Morgan, Purser, Air Cabin Crew, Cabin Services, Heathrow, after 16 years.

Captain Gwyn Mullett, 747/400 Fleet, Flight Crew, Flight Operations, Heathrow, after 34 years.

Graham Norris, Operations Duty Officer, Gatwick, after 34 years.

Darshna Pabari, Purser, Air Cabin Crew, Cabin Services, Heathrow, after 15 years.

Captain Anthony Partridge, 747/400 Fleet, Flight Crew, Flight Operations, Heathrow, after 34 years.

Captain John Penwill, 747/400 Fleet, Flight Crew, Flight Operations, Heathrow, after 33 years.

Allan Pilling, Ramp Agent, Distribution, Terminal 4, Heathrow, after 21 years.

Ian Pink, Senior Customer Service Agent, Gatwick, after 11 years.

Trish Randell, Flight Monitoring Agent, Gatwick, after 21 years.

Stephen Rankin, Aircraft Load Supervisor, Gatwick, after 23 years.

Captain Paul Richards, 747/400 Fleet, Flight Crew, Flight Operations, Heathrow, after 32 years.

Lindsey Roberts, Duty Officer, Gatwick, after 14 years.

Captain Denis Robinson, Concorde Fleet, Flight Crew, Flight Operations, Heathrow, after 33 years.

Christopher Rose, Flight Connections Agent, Gatwick, after 16 years.

Peter Russell, Technical Support Officer, Gatwick, after 20 years.

Patricia Scargill, Special Services Executive, Gatwick, after 22 years.

Michael Sealcoon, Station Maintenance Manager, Engineering, Egypt, after 32 years.

Andy Share, Senior Engineer Officer, 747C Fleet, Flight Crew, Flight Operations, Heathrow, after 38 years.

Captain David Shattock, 747/400 Fleet, Flight Crew, Flight Operations, Heathrow, after 30 years.

Gurmej Shina (known as Carol), Baggage Handler, Ground Transport Services, Heathrow, after 30 years.

Bhagwant Sidhu, Support Agent – Receipt Services, Accounting Operations, Odyssey Business Park, after 24 years.

John Sired, Equipment Support, Gatwick, after 17 years.

David Smith, Ramp Agent, Production, Terminal 1, Heathrow, after 14 years.

Michael Spencer, Aircraft Handler, Gatwick, after 16 years.

Adrian Spinner, Aircraft Handler, Gatwick, after 15 years.

Captain Peter Stanton, 747/400 Fleet, Flight Crew, Flight Operations, Heathrow, after 31 years.

Gillian Stemp, Senior Customer Service Agent, Gatwick, after 16 years.

Richard Stone, Loader Non Driver, Gatwick, after 23 years.

Peter Sullivan, Aircraft Load Supervisor, Gatwick, after 28 years.

Elizabeth Tame, Senior Customer Service Agent, Gatwick, after 22 years.

Paul Thomas, Operations Co-ordinat[or] ... years.

Michael ... Aircraft ... 28 year[s].

David ... Agent, ... David ... Engineer ... Engineer ... years.

Margar[et] ... omer S... after 31 ...

Clifford ... Loader/... 21 year[s].

Brian ... Distribu... row, aft[er] ...

Captain ... 757/76... Flight ... after 31 ...

Lloyd ... Officer, ... Flight ... after 31 ...

Peter W... Gatwick ... Terenc[e] ... Suppor[t] ... years. David ... Product ... row, aft[er] ...

2001 The Final Curtain, 27th January.

Lightning Source UK Ltd.
Milton Keynes UK
UKOW06f0106200515

251848UK00005B/15/P

9 781910 223352